Exploring Corporate Strategy

Fifth Edition

Instructors' Manual

Exploring Corporate Strategy

Fifth Edition

Instructors' Manual

Gerry Johnson
Cranfield School of Management

Kevan Scholes
Sheffield Business School

 PRENTICE HALL

London   New York   Toronto   Sydney   Tokyo
Singapore   Madrid   Mexico City   Munich   Paris

First published 1999 by
Prentice Hall Europe
Campus 400, Maylands Avenue
Hemel Hempstead
Hertfordshire, HP2 7EZ
A division of
Simon & Schuster International Group

0-13-525627-5

1 2 3 4 5   03 02 01 00 99

THANK YOU

to

Claire Parkin and Alison Southgate for their help with this manual; and

Case study authors for the work they have put into the teaching notes.

We know that teachers using *Exploring Corporate Strategy* will benefit considerably from all your hard work.

Contents

Introduction

1. INTRODUCTION

With the launch of this 5th edition, *Exploring Corporate Strategy* now represents one of the most comprehensive packages of material and support for teachers and students of strategy. The following materials and assistance are now available:

- The *text* with improved design and layout to assist readers – including section objectives and chapter learning outcomes, margin definitions, chapter summaries, additional reading, and much more.

- Eighty-one *illustrations,* each including questions to facilitate their use as mini-cases.

- Eleven chapter-end *case examples*. This is a new feature of the 5th edition and is designed to bridge the gap between the illustrations and the case studies (in the text and cases version). Each case example has questions relating to the major conceptual issues in the chapter.

- Chapter-end *work assignments,* which provide further opportunities for student assessment, additional work or self-assessment.

- Thirty-one case studies (text and cases version only), together with comprehensive teaching notes (in this manual). The case collection contains a rich mixture of material – including long and short cases from many different sectors and different countries.

- A *video,* which includes inputs from Gerry Johnson and Kevan Scholes together with additional in-depth material on four of the case studies (for de-briefing purposes).

- The *Exploring Corporate Strategy web site,* which is regularly updated and contains updates and new material. It also contains parts of this manual on the password protected 'tutor site'.

- 'Power Point' discs, which contain all the figures from the book, together with additional material. These can be incorporated directly into your teaching sessions.

- Tutors' workshops led by Gerry Johnson and Kevan Scholes are held annually in England and Scotland. These are practical days concerned with how teachers might gain most advantage from the book and associated materials. They also act as a forum to meet other strategy teachers.

Details on all of these items and extensive tutors' de-briefs around work assignments, illustrations, case examples and case studies are included in this manual.

2. USING THIS MANUAL

This manual is designed for teachers of strategy in planning how to gain maximum advantage from the text *Exploring Corporate Strategy* and the associated teaching and learning materials. It should provide help with:

- Planning a teaching approach to suit the type of participants, time available, etc.

- Deciding how to use the text, illustrations, case examples, readings and case studies in a teaching scheme.

- Choosing additional material to include in a course.

- Using the work assignments for each illustration, case examples from the end of each chapter.

- Preparing to teach the case studies.

- Using the video.

- Using the *Exploring Corporate Strategy* web site.

This manual has been written to assist a variety of teachers using *Exploring Corporate Strategy*. These opening sections are intended to be of particular use to teachers who are relatively new to teaching strategy or are designing new courses. Experienced teachers may wish to pass over sections 3 and 4.

3. PLANNING YOUR APPROACH

This section provides some general guidance on how the design of a strategy course can be varied to meet the requirements of the participants and the practicalities of the situation. The factors listed below will also influence the way in which the text, readings, work assignments, case examples, case studies and video can be used to best advantage.

3.1 Purpose of the course

Strategy courses can be designed to meet many different needs. At one extreme the course may mainly be concerned with raising *awareness* of why organisations need to change and develop over time and some of the ways in which this occurs. On the other hand, the course may be designed to improve the *skills* of participants in the formulation and implementation of strategy. Between these extremes are other purposes for strategy courses. For example, improving managers' understanding of how their job function *fits* the overall strategic development of the organisation; helping to break down the very narrow *operational outlook* of many managers; or *integrating* material from other parts of a business or management course. The following is some guidance on how the use of text and cases might be adapted to these various purposes.

- If *awareness* is the key purpose, it is advisable to use the text to provide a basic framework (say, through a lecture series) and devote as much time as possible to illustrative work. The illustrations and case examples in the text should prove valuable and teachers should try to supplement these with their own topical material (press cuttings, etc.). The *Exploring Corporate Strategy* web site is regularly updated with topical material on a chapter-by-chapter basis (see below). Where participants have access to live organisations use of issues from those organisations should be encouraged (e.g. by presentations). Guest speakers could also prove valuable – particularly if they have interesting success stories. The case studies and video can be used mainly to encourage discussion and illustrate particular aspects of strategy. Work assignments should be useful to consolidate some of the key concepts in strategic management.

- If *skills development* is most important, then the purpose of the text should be to give participants some concepts and analytical tools which they can apply and practise. Since the text does not aim to deal exhaustively with analytical methods, teachers may need to add readings concerned with specific techniques. Many of these are identified in our references and key readings (see particularly the book by Ambrosini with Johnson and Scholes (1998) in the key readings for several chapters), or may have been covered in other parts of their course of study (e.g. in finance or operational research). Most of the case examples and case studies lend themselves to an analytical approach, and participants should be set tasks that require them to produce detailed and practical solutions. Work assignments for the illustrations and at chapter ends should be useful to test skills development and the understanding of key concepts. With some groups it may be possible to require participants to try out their skills on real, company-based issues – say, through a project. For example, students can be asked to undertake a strategic analysis of a particular industry or company – largely from secondary data – to assess the strategic choices available and propose how issues of implementation would be managed. Many of the advanced-level work assignments are specifically designed to test readers' in-depth understanding of issues and/or ability to use them in a project situation.

- Where the *relationship* between strategy and the separate business functions is of primary importance group work (preferably with cross-functional teams) could be very helpful. This could be for work on the case studies, in-company work or business simulations.

3.2 Level of participant

The purpose of a strategy course is likely to differ with the level of participant (see Table 1). This could relate to their age, job function or type of course which they are studying (these may all be interrelated).

- For *younger* people with little full-time work experience teachers must take care how they use the text and cases. The text should prove useful in providing a systematic, analytical framework and illustrations of strategy in practice. It will probably be helpful to pay less detailed attention to chapters 9–11 than on courses for practising managers. It is also advised not to take chapter 2 in sequence but perhaps use it as a way of comparing theory and practice once students feel comfortable with some of the ideas/approaches (say after chapter 5 or chapter 8). The illustrations and case examples in the text (and associated work assignments) should be used to relate theory to practice. Case studies and the video should be used in fairly focused ways – in order to consolidate that stage in the learning – rather than in an all-embracing way until later in the course. Selected readings should also prove helpful. The standard work assignments will be the most appropriate for this group.

- Where participants have *some work experience* but are nevertheless fairly junior (e.g. final year sandwich students, many DMS classes, etc.) the same comments are relevant, except that there are more opportunities to encourage participants to relate to real-life situations through presentations, in-company projects, etc.

- For *more experienced managers* (e.g. in many part-time MBA programmes, in-company courses, etc.) it should be possible to take an entirely different approach. Teachers may wish to minimise their formal inputs of concepts and methods on the grounds that these are clearly laid out in the text and ought to be read prior to class sessions, or as a means of pulling together the issues discussed in class. It is then possible to devote the majority of time to applied work (the case studies, group projects, presentations, etc.). It could also prove useful to integrate the process issues raised in chapter 2 with the more rationalistic approach of chapter 1 as a basis for comparing different approaches to strategic management at the *start* of the course. It is also advised that teachers should devote considerable attention to chapters 9–11 (strategy implementation) as perhaps the critical issues confronting practising managers.

Table 1 Using the text and cases with different participants

	No work experience	Limited work experience	Experienced managers
1. Typical groups	Undergraduates	Sandwich degree students, younger DMS, full-time MBA	Part-time MBA, in-company courses
2. Sequencing of material from text	In chapter sequence except chapter 2 to follow chapter 5 or chapter 8	In chapter sequence	In chapter sequence (possibly highlighting of chapter 2 for senior managers)
3. Relative emphasis of issues	Main emphasis on chapters 1 and 3–8	More balanced emphasis	Highlight chapters 2 and 9–11
4. Text to read	After class sessions	After class sessions	Before or after class sessions
5. Applied work (case studies, etc.) used to:	Illustrate issues from the text in a carefully focused way	Practise analysis and conceptual understanding	As the core method of improving understanding and skills
6. Wider reading	Selected key readings	Selected key readings	Wider reading

3.3 Study mode

The mode of study should also influence course design.

- For *full-time* courses it is usually realistic to expect a good level of preparation of case study work and a chance for smaller groups to work together on tasks for significant periods of time (usually prior to a plenary discussion and/or presentation). A tightly organised package of student work (the case studies, group work, presentations) is, therefore, possible as an important way of consolidating the concepts/approaches from the text.

However, the chance of in-company work may be more limited – although projects based largely on secondary data can be very effective.

- In contrast, *part-time* students are usually more in touch with ongoing management issues but have less preparation time and find it more difficult to meet in groups. It may be that some group time needs to be built into the programme. It is also strongly advised that copies of selected readings are made available to part-time students (within copyright regulations). These readings may be used as a basis for student presentations – linking theory and practice. Both authors have used this approach very successfully.

- Increasingly, *distance learning* elements are being used in business and management programmes. The structured nature of the text together with the illustrations, case examples, readings, case studies, video, work assignments and web site material lends itself to form the backbone of learning modules. Section 4 below, which reviews work assignments, provides guidelines on how the issues and materials in the book can be used to provide a structured learning path for students.

3.4 Time available

The study hours available will also influence the course design and the use of text and cases.

- For *long* programmes (50 hours +) it should prove possible to use the text and cases extensively and to supplement the course with other materials and activities.

- For *shorter* programmes a more selective use of the materials is possible. For example, a course concerned largely with strategy formulation could confine the use of the text to chapters 1 and 3–8 and the associated illustrations, case examples, readings, case studies, video, work assignments and web site material. A course on strategic change and implementation would be centred on chapters 2 and 9–11. The other chapters would be recommended as follow-up or contextual reading.

- Where time is *very limited* – particularly with more experienced managers – sessions may consist of an introduction to some basic ideas through the frameworks from the text together with a case study (or similar activity). More extensive use of the text would be in the participants' own time either, pre- or post-course. Both of the authors regularly use such an approach on short courses for senior managers. The work assignments also provide a valuable checklist and/or self-study guide around these basic concepts.

One of the dangers which besets strategy teachers is that their course is reduced to remedial teaching on *functional* issues such as marketing, cash flow planning, etc. Clearly, the time available on the course, together with the extent to which the course is concerned with building skills, will determine whether or not participants will need to do pre-work on some of these issues. The readings in the text advise on good functional texts for this purpose (for example, reference 3 in chapter 4).

4. DESIGNING THE TEACHING SCHEME

4.1 Pre-course work

It should be clear from the above that there are many circumstances where pre-course work could be essential. The text and case book are designed to facilitate this. Where pre-course work is needed it is suggested that it is prescribed in the following way:

- The appropriate chapters of the book with a few suggested issues to bear in mind. For example, it might prove useful for participants to read chapters 1 and 2 and be expected to discuss what is meant by strategy and the different approaches that occur in practice.

- Preparation of *illustrations, case examples or case study* material. Here specific guidance can be found in the teaching notes in section 6 and in the work assignments.

- Any *company-specific data* that they might need. This could be very general. For example, after reading chapters 1 and 2 they may be asked to reflect on how strategic issues are managed in their own organisation. In contrast, if participants are to undertake project work they may need rather more detail (e.g. company reports or accounts). On some occasions it can prove helpful to ask participants to bring some topical data (e.g. articles or press cuttings) which might be used to develop a presentation on the course. You may choose to use the topical material from the *Exploring Corporate Strategy* web site as it is updated regularly.

4.2 Starting the course

The specific requirements of each course will vary, but here is some guidance on how courses in strategy might be started:

- A traditional approach would be to run through the issues in chapter 1 and relate them to the structure of the course. This is very successful if the course follows the text quite closely and in chapter sequence.

- With groups of experienced managers it is very stimulating to begin with a session on *different approaches* to strategy development – using the material from chapters 1 and 2. This does not preclude a follow-up that works through the chapters in sequence but helps put an analytical approach into context.

- An alternative approach is to begin the course with a *case study*, case example or *illustration*. *British Steel* (from the cases) and *Battle of the Browsers* and *IKEA* (in the text) are designed for this purpose. This starts participants talking about the strategic issues relevant to that company and industry, and gives many pointers to the issues that will be covered in the course.

- A similar opening can be achieved by asking one or more participants to talk about the key strategic issues in their *own* organisation or in an organisation which is well known to many participants (say, *Marks and Spencer*).

4.3 Planning the topics

The text lends itself to a wide range of different treatments and we would encourage teachers to use it in whatever way suits their own style and the needs of course participants. Approaches might include:

- The most straightforward teaching scheme is one that follows the topics from the text in the sequence outlined in section 3.2 above, using the basic frameworks provided in the text. For longer programmes this can provide an ideal backbone to a course. For example, on a final year undergraduate programme the text can be covered in twelve one-hour lectures leaving time for applied activities. It is strongly recommended that a lecture series of this type be used to *augment* the text and not just to churn it out verbatim. Selective use of the key readings should help in preparation. As mentioned in section 3.2 above, careful judgement needs to be made on when to introduce issues from chapter 2. With undergraduates these are often best delayed (say until after chapter 5 or chapter 8).

- On other courses the text can be used somewhat differently. For example, one of the authors teaches a part-time MBA course where the opening few weeks of the programme run parallel sessions following the analytical approach of chapters 1, 3 and 4, contrasted with more political/cultural views of strategic management (as in chapter 2 and 5). This is augmented by a readings programme and a group project running through the course.

4.4 Balance of the course

The teaching scheme will need to be properly balanced in relation to many of the needs identified in section 3 above in two different ways:

- The degree of *emphasis* given to different topics. This is particularly important in relation to the proportion of time devoted to strategy implementation (chapters 9–11) and to process issues (e.g. chapter 2) as against analytical approaches.

- The *mixture* and sequencing of lectures, seminars, case studies, group work, etc. These are largely determined by the circumstances for which the programme is designed as outline in section 3. It is useful to look at some typical ways in which this mix can be planned:

a) Case study/applied material-only courses where the text is used as pre-reading and/or follow-up. This approach is not very common on open access courses but can be very useful in an in-company workshop where a review of the organisation's own strategy forms the basis of the programme, and frameworks and techniques from the text are drawn upon as appropriate.

b) Case study/applied material-based programmes. Here the applied material is prepared before the class sessions and forms the basis of a discussion of key concepts and techniques during the session. This is the Harvard approach and the text could be used either as pre-reading or for follow-up. The case studies, case examples, illustrations, web site material and work assignments would form the basis of such a course.

c) Lecture and applied work. Here the formal lecture accounts for perhaps 20–30 per cent of the programme, the remainder being used for applied work – case studies, presentations, projects, etc. The text, case studies, case examples, illustration, web site materials and work assignments are ideal for providing the backbone of a course of this type. The dangers are that students do not read widely enough and teachers need to provide proper guidance on additional reading (including those identified at the end of each chapter).

d) Lecture and illustrative material. Here the lecture programme may amount to 50–70 per cent of the course with illustrations, case examples, case studies and web site material being used to provide practical examples of the issue in the text/lectures. This is only recommended for undergraduates.

4.5 Assessment

Many courses will require participants to be assessed. The text and case book (and the above advice on course design) provide opportunities for a wide variety of different assessments. For example:

- *Formal examinations* can be used to test understanding of the key concepts. There is the risk that students will give largely theoretical answers to questions. One way of avoiding this is to use short quotations from case studies, articles or illustrations as the basis of the issue that requires discussion in the examination question. This could include requiring answers that are directed at explaining concepts to managers.

- *Case study examinations* are a common assessment. The case is distributed before the examination and students prepare in groups. The examination is most often open book (with unseen questions), answered on an individual basis. The danger with this approach is that students overwhelm themselves with prior analysis and do not answer the questions on the paper.

- *Student presentations* are another method of assessment growing in popularity with strategy teachers. They can be used to assess student work on illustrations, case examples, case studies or in-company project work that they have undertaken. It is desirable to combine an assessment of the presentation with a write-up.

- *Executive reports* are used by one of the authors. These are an unannounced 30-minute write-up of the critical issues in a pre-seen case study or article in the form of an executive report.

- *Participant's topic* – where participants are required to present a write up and/or presentation on a strategic issue – often in the context of a topical situation or their own organisation.

- *Readings* – where a readings programme throughout the course is used as a basis of linking theory to practice and can be assessed through presentation and/or write-up.

- *Group projects* are an excellent form of learning and therefore lend themselves to be incorporated into the assessment package. Both authors have used group projects for assessment for several years. The group project provides an extra dimension from the individual project namely the *process* by which the group undertook the project and managed themselves. We would advise that the project write-up should include issues of process as well as content. Many teachers shy away from group projects because they feel that the assessment of individual contributions can be difficult (which it is!). However, the potential learning from group work is so great we would encourage teachers to experiment with assessing the project work. There are several ways in which worries about assessing individuals can be alleviated. First, the group project can be part of an assessment package and weighted accordingly (e.g. 30 per cent of the overall mark). Second, the formal requirement may be that the group project is assessed on a pass/fail basis only. The student's examination mark is that gained in other assessments. Third, the group can be given an overall group average mark and asked to advise the tutor on the individual marks of group members (in relation to their contribution). Where the authors have used this approach it has proved useful to provide *limits* within which individual marks can be varied (say, 10 marks) and to ensure that students are clear that the final decision rests with the tutor. Fourth, students can be asked to complete an individual write-up based on group work.

5. A GUIDE TO USING THE WORK ASSIGNMENTS

This section contains detailed guidance for using the work assignments which appear with each illustration, case example, web site material at the end of each chapter in *Exploring Corporate Strategy*. These notes are not intended to be prescriptive and teachers are encouraged to use these assignments in ways that best suit their learning situation.

The work assignments with each illustration are designed to consolidate one or two learning points from a part of the chapter. The work assignments with case examples and at the chapter end take the main issues from each chapter and suggest ways in which readers can consolidate their understanding by applying these concepts to appropriate case studies, illustrations and/or organisations of their own choice. The chapter-end work assignments are provided at two levels of difficulty in order to give maximum flexibility in their use:

Standard are straightforward applications of concepts or techniques to specific situations.

Advanced require a fuller analysis usually linking two or more concepts and/or situations and requiring reading round the issues.

The sections below provide chapter-by-chapter guidance on how tutors might use the work assignments to consolidate students' understanding of the concepts in *Exploring Corporate Strategy*. There are, however, a few general guidelines that you may wish to consider in deciding how to gain most benefit from incorporating these work assignments into the students' programme of study:

- Remember there are many different ways in which you can use these assignments. For example:

    1. as topics for student's to *pre-prepare* for a session where the concept or issue will be discussed in the light of their preparation.
    2. as the basis of a student's *presentation* in a class session.
    3. as a student *assessment*.
    4. as a *self-study package* which students use to test their own understanding.

- Although many of the chapter-end work assignments draw on illustrations and/or case studies in *Exploring Corporate Strategy* we have tried to write them in a way which does not make them entirely dependent on this specific source material. Most of these work assignments should be useable in a situation of the tutors'/students' choice.

- The reverse is also true; the use of illustrations, case examples and case studies should not be confined to the specific issues in the work assignments. With case studies you will find that the authors' teaching notes in section 6 below suggest many other issues and questions in *addition* to those cited in work assignments.

6. A GUIDE TO USING THE CASE STUDIES

Section 11 below contains comprehensive teaching notes for each of the 31 case studies that appear in the text and cases edition of *Exploring Corporate Strategy*. These notes have been prepared by the authors of each case study and edited by Kevan Scholes and Gerry Johnson. The facing page is a guide to the main focus of each case study and also appears in the book.

These case studies allow the reader to extend their linking of theory and practice by analysing the strategic issues of specific organisations in much greater depth – often providing solutions to some of the problems or difficulties identified in the cases. Cases are intended to serve as a basis for class discussion and not as an illustration of either good or bad management practice.

The case studies are not intended to be a comprehensive collection of material. They have been chosen (or specifically written) to provide readers with a core of cases which together cover most of the main issues in the text. As such they should provide a useful backbone to a programme of study, but could sensibly be supplemented by other material. In the 5th edition we have provided a mixture of longer and shorter cases to increase the flexibility for teachers. Additionally, there is a short case example at the end of each chapter (in both versions of the book). For example, when deciding on material for chapter 3 the case example, *Irish Ports*, tests a reader's understanding of the main issues influencing the competitive position of an organisation. Those wishing to test students' ability to undertake a comprehensive industry analysis would use *The European Brewing Industry*. However, if the purpose is more focused – illustrating the use of '5-Forces' analysis – the *Pharmaceuticals Industry* should be used. Some cases are written entirely from published sources, but most have been prepared in co-operation with and approval of the management of the organisation concerned. The video provides supplementary material for four of the case studies. Case studies can never fully capture the richness and complexity of real-life management scenarios and we would encourage readers and tutors to take every possible opportunity to explore the live strategic issues of organisations – both their own and others.

A GUIDE TO THE MAIN FOCUS OF CASES

Case	Introduction to strategy	Strategic management process	Business environment	Five forces	Resource and competence analysis	Stakeholder expectations/purposes	Culture	Overall strategic analysis	Corporate strategy/parenting	Competitive strategy	Strategic options	Diversification	Acquisitions	Strategy evaluation	Global management	Structure, organisation design	Resource planning and control	Managing change	Strategic leadership	Public sector management
British Steel, p. 551(U)	●●																			
New Town, p. 559		●●				●														●●
Castle Press, p. 567		●●																		
Pharmaceuticals, p. 574		●	●●																	
European Brewing, p. 582(U)		●●	●											●	●					
Kronenbourg, p. 607			●				●	●	●		●				●●					
Brewery Group Denmark, p. 622		●		●							●●				●	●●				
Stewart Grand Prix, p. 633(N)					●●												●			
Laura Ashley, p. 641					●●	●									●					
Iona, p. 656						●●	●													
Sheffield Theatres, p. 670					●	●●											●			
Fisons, p. 685						●●									●					
World Automobile Industry, p. 691			●●																	
Peugeot, p. 709(U)								●	●●	●					●	●				
Rover/Honda, p. 725									●	●●					●					
BMW, p. 738									●	●●			●●	●	●					
Barclaycard, p. 746(N)								●			●●			●						
Coopers Creek, p. 756					●											●●	●			
Dutch PTT Telecom, p. 768(N)											●●					●●				●
News Corporation, p. 779		●		●	●				●●				●●		●	●	●		●	
Nokia, p. 807					●					●		●●	●●		●					
Bord Gais Eireann (BGE), p. 827(N)																●●	●●			●
Doman, p. 838															●●		●●			
Royal Alexandra Hospital, p. 852(U)	●					●	●									●		●●	●	●
Burton Group A, p. 868(N)	●					●			●		●	●	●			●●		●	●●	
Burton Group B, p. 874(N)	●					●				●						●●		●●	●●	
Burton Group C, p. 882(N)	●					●				●						●			●●	
KPMG (B): Strategic Change, p. 891(U)						●	●									●	●	●●	●	
KPMG (C): Global Firm, p. 909(N)		●														●●	●			
UNHCR, p. 918(N)		●				●●	●											●●	●	●
Burmah Castrol, p. 935		●		●●					●●			●●				●	●			

Note: ●● = Major focus   U = Updated
       ● = Important subsidiary focus   N = New

7. A GUIDE TO USING THE VIDEO

A new feature accompanying the 4th and 5th editions is the video. This is a separately available item that can be purchased from Sheffield Hallam University Press. **An order form is enclosed.**

The video includes inputs from Kevan Scholes and Gerry Johnson on 'Strategy in Different Types of Organisations' and 'The Cultural Web' respectively. It also allows tutors to brief and de-brief four of the case studies as well as 'meet' key personalities from those organisations. The case studies included on the video are:

- **Brewery Group Denmark**, which explores the international strategy of a medium-sized company.

- **KPMG** the management of strategic change (in a professional service organisation).

- **Burmah Castrol Chemicals Group** examines corporate structure, portfolio management and corporate parenting.

- **The Iona Community** looks at mission and stakeholder analysis.

Each section of the video relating to a case study is structured for your convenient use – normally as follows:

- a brief (2–3 minutes) introduction to the organisation.

- a (10–12) minute brief or 'de-brief' by key personalities in the case covering their perspective on the issues in the case and future developments.

The teaching notes for the four cases indicate issues arising from the video as well as the case study itself.

The video has been prepared to allow for different uses:

- An input to a lecture (particularly the pieces by Kevan Scholes and Gerry Johnson).

- Briefing/de-briefing case sessions in class with students.

- Use by individual students in their library/learning centre.

EXPLORING CORPORATE STRATEGY

THE VIDEO

Gerry Johnson and Kevan Scholes

ORDER FORM

The video is available in VHS/PAL format and runs in total for 75 minutes. (The video is also available in other formats on request. A small supplement will be payable.)

Please supply the following:

Quantity @ £280.00 + VAT   ---------------

                              TOTAL (£)   --------------

Price includes postage and packing. All requests must include payment in full or an official order. Allow ten days for delivery.

Send to: **Sheffield Hallam University Press,**
           Adsetts Centre, City Campus, Sheffield, S1 1WB

           Tel: 0114 253 4702   Fax: 0114 253 4478

From: Name: _____ Position: _____

        Organisation:_____

        Address:_____

        _____

        Telephone: _____   Fax: _____

8. THE EXPLORING CORPORATE STRATEGY WEB SITE

Exploring Corporate Strategy was the first European text to be included in the Prentice Hall PHLIP (internet) site. The site is designed to provide assistance to readers and tutors and to supplement the text as follows:

- downloadable PowerPoint OHTs

- updates on the case study organisations

- additional illustrative material (chapter-by-chapter)

- parts of the contents of this instructor's manual.

The web site is divided into two parts. The student side has open access; the tutor access requires registration (on-line), verification of status and use of passwords.

The web site can be found at:

http://www.prenhall.com/phlip (click on 'strategy' on the subject list of the home page)

9. EXPLORING CORPORATE STRATEGY TEACHERS' WORKSHOPS

Each year since 1989 (in England) and 1995 (in Scotland) Gerry Johnson and Kevan Scholes have held one-day workshops for instructors who use *Exploring Corporate Strategy* or are considering doing so.

These have been practical days concerned with how teachers might gain most advantage from the book and the associated teaching/learning aids (illustrations, case studies, work assignments, video and web site materials).

Additionally, these annual workshops have provided a forum to meet the authors and other strategy teachers and share experiences of teaching problems and their solutions.

Further information about forthcoming workshops can be obtained from the publisher or from the authors:

Email: G.Johnson@cranfield.ac.uk
        KScholes@scholes.u-net.com

10. TEACHING NOTES FOR WORK ASSIGNMENTS, ILLUSTRATIONS AND CASE EXAMPLES

This section contains detailed guidance for using the work assignments that appear at the end of each chapter and with each illustration and chapter-end case example in *Exploring Corporate Strategy*. These notes are not intended to be prescriptive and teachers are encouraged to use these assignments in ways that best suit their learning situation.

You will find it helpful to read the brief guidelines for using working assignments in section 5 of this manual.

Chapter 1

ILLUSTRATION 1.1

Definitions and concepts

The purpose of these assignments is to encourage an early consolidation and testing of students' understanding of basic ideas of strategy.

Follow the advice in the tutors' brief for chapter-end work assignments 1.1 and 1.5.

ILLUSTRATION 1.2

Vocabulary

Follow the advice in the tutors' brief for chapter-end work assignment 1.2.

ILLUSTRATION 1.3

Strategy and Context

This allows students to test how the 'lead-edge' or 'emphasis' of strategic issues within our basic model may vary with circumstances. So, for example:

- Multinationals may be especially concerned with how to *structure* multiple products in multiple countries.

- An SBU within a conglomerate has to develop its strategy both in relation to the expectations of its *corporate parent* (a key stakeholder) but also, crucially, has to develop a *competitive strategy* for success in its markets.

- *Stakeholder influence and relationships* are also especially important in charities and public sector organisations.

- Achieving commitment and motivation around a common *mission* is also important in charities.

- Increasingly the notion of *competition* has been introduced in the public sector in order to improve efficiency and effectiveness of services.

You may also wish to show students the brief extract from the *Exploring Corporate Strategy video*, which deals with this issue.

Do not necessarily confine your discussion to the particular contexts we have shown in the text. Try additional ones such as 'the innovative context', 'the family business' or even sector-specific issues such as 'extractive industries' or 'healthcare'.

CASE EXAMPLE

Battle of the Browsers

This is an introductory case example to illustrate the various elements of strategy – as presented in Chapter 1. It shows how these apply to a particular industry and competitors within the industry. These are some of the issues to highlight:

Are These Issues Strategic?

Section 1.1 lists eight characteristics of strategic decisions. Students can 'apply' this list to the case example. They should conclude that from the viewpoint of both Microsoft and Netscape the issues are strategic by all these criteria. They do affect:

- Long-term direction
- Competitive advantage
- Scope of activities
- Exploitation of core competences
- Stakeholder expectations

Strategic Analysis

The main issues for Microsoft and Netscape are very similar – but the impact is different (often opposite) for each company:

Environment

- The dominant player (Microsoft)
- New entrant/new product
- Popularity of the internet (globally)
- Issues of competition policy (by governments)

Resources

For Microsoft:

- Vast resources (e.g. 2000 analysts used to 'catch up')
- Would win a price war
- A unique resource (Windows) could become a commodity.
- Core competence = large installed base ('network externalities')

For Netscape:

- Browser could 'commoditise' Windows
- Venture capital support
- Financial crisis
- Below threshold installed base?

Expectations

- The attitude/confidence of customers is critical. They do not want to be committed to a system that loses the battle of the browsers (cf. Betamax vs. VHS)
- The US Justice Department seem determined to stop monopoly
- Society will lose innovators if the likes of Netscape are not protected
- PC manufacturers appear indifferent to the debate

Strategic Choices

Encourage students to think about the various 'strands' that make up a strategic choice as outlined in section 1.2.2 (and, of course, more fully in chapters 6 and 7):

- The *basis* of Microsoft's advantage had been their ability to dominate the added-value activities in the value chain (the operating system). They reduce the earlier activities (hardware) to commodity status. Netscape presents the possibility that this history could be re-run with the PC+ operating system being the commodity and all the added value lying on the internet. The browser would then be the critical tool for the user. This is a vision that Bill Gates had described as the 'dumb computer terminal' and rich internet resources.

- There are several choices of development *direction* for each company. Critically they must decide on product development (the browser) and the extent to which it is integrated into the operating system (Microsoft) or free-standing (Netscape). Netscape must mitigate its risk through a mix of customer types. Both companies are playing in a global industry — the opportunities to specialise by geography are limited.

- The *method* of development is also important. Microsoft has the resources to go it alone. Netscape is running very close to the bone and may shortly need partners or may be the target for an acquisition.

The Strategic Context

The case example is from a highly globalised industry where the pace of innovation is rapid. Ask students to compare the specifics of the case example with the more general comments about such contexts in sections 1.3.2 and 1.3.4:

- These are 'global product' companies (as discussed in chapter 9). In principle Microsoft could be vulnerable to 'localisation' by competitors such as Netscape. In practice this is currently outweighed by the 'economics' of innovation in that industry.

- The ability to 'change the rules of the game' and develop new core competences is of critical importance. The 'dumb terminal' scenario mentioned above is an example of this.

ASSIGNMENT 1.1

Definitions

The purpose of this assignment is to check that students understand what is meant by strategy. It is unrealistic to expect a sophisticated understanding by the end of chapter 1, but it is useful to check if a basic level of understanding has been achieved. You might, therefore, expect a statement which addresses the ground covered in chapter 1 and the type of definition in the text; and critique the students' work in two ways:

- Are the students able to define a *long-term direction* being taken by an organisation which seeks to *position* it in such a way as to meet the *expectations of stakeholders* and employ *its resources* in such a way as to take advantages of *opportunities in its environment*?

- From the point of view of whether the chosen company has, in fact, got a clear strategy. For example, earlier in the 1990s the emphasis in British Steel was on rationalisation; is it clear what has emerged as the strategy for the company to achieve competitive advantage in world-wide markets? In this respect the question should be used to consider if the student can exercise a critical capacity towards assessing organisational strategy.

ASSIGNMENT 1.2

Vocabulary of Strategy

The purpose of this assignment is to generate a discussion about, and check understanding of, different expressions and terms relating to *strategy* – at least those covered in exhibit 1.1 and illustration 1.2.

The assignment should surface the fact that some terms are used more frequently and are more easily understandable than others. For example, students will probably find more examples of objectives or mission statements and the discussion of implementation of strategy than they will a clear statement of strategy itself.

You might encourage students to discuss the reasons for this. Clear statements of overall strategic direction are rather more difficult to construct than statements about where organisations want to go, or the operational detail of how they intend to get there. Asking students why they think this is will surface issues of the complexity of strategy development.

ASSIGNMENT 1.3

Strategic Development

Assignment 1.3 is an extension of the first two assignments. Given an understanding of concepts and terminology, it is useful to invite the students to explain the background to the development of strategy in an organisation. This raises important questions such as how the strategy has evolved; what factors did it appear to be responding to, which stakeholders have most influenced the strategy; what was the nature of the environment; and so on. Ensure the students address these issues.

This is also a useful exercise to ensure that students understand not just terminology, but broad influences on strategy development. It might also draw out distinctions between the strategy which is intended by an organisation; and what is actually happening (the realised strategy) and this usefully builds links to chapter 2.

ASSIGNMENT 1.4

Elements of Strategic Management

Assignment 1.4 requires students to use exhibit 1.4 as a guide to identifying the different influences on the strategy of an organisation. The British Steel case in the case section of the book is designed for this exercise and the teaching notes for that case study later in this manual provide a guide to its use. You might want to provide students with a 'blank' of exhibit 1.4 and ask them to complete it for British Steel.

British Steel is an interesting case to consider in relation to the influences on strategy, not least because of its history as a nationalised company. From the case study, it can be seen that the competitive pressures facing the business were exerting pressures demanding strategic choices to achieve a more competitive position. Students might, therefore, point to the importance of the business environment, the analysis of strategic capability and the problems of strategic choice as the main elements of strategy. However, it is worth posing the question as to how stakeholder expectations will have changed from the nationalised business of the past. In that period the key stakeholder influence of government would have been especially dominant, masking the impact of competitive forces and arguably leading to systems of control and management which were more bureaucratic.

The success of the company since 1989 has largely been through its ability to understand and manage the match between the three broad influences on strategy. As a privatised company the expectations of stakeholders changed to be more 'typically' commercial. This required a recognition of the trends for globalisation and the need to establish a clear positioning for British Steel. This, in turn, required drastic action in terms of the resources and competences of the organisation as described in the teaching notes (see below).

ASSIGNMENT 1.5

'Fit' and 'Stretch'

Ikea is a good illustration of how successful strategies can be accounted for both in terms of 'fit' and 'stretch'.

The success of Ikea could be put down to:

- The identification and exploitation of a substantial market segment concerned with price but wanting reasonable quality goods.

- The structure of the furniture industry traditionally which requires customers to wait weeks or months for deliveries; Ikea fulfils a need for immediate availability.

- Building on the increasing trend of out of town shopping as a leisure pursuit and the availability of transport for customers.

- Their international expansion has sought to build on market opportunities as they emerge throughout the world.

- However, the success can also be seen as the exploitation of the developing competences of Ikea:

- The early development of stores selling kit furniture has been refined over the decades to build an image of convenience and quality which itself has set standards and, in this way, created a market;

- Their buying and merchandising systems have also been developed to guarantee good design, good quality but at reasonable prices; and in turn these skills have been used to extend product ranges and develop the capabilities of suppliers;

- They have cleverly built the customer as an extension of their merchandising, reducing costs of distribution but making their products immediately accessible.

- By 1997 they were even extending the 'kit' approach to wholly new product fields such as housing.

Ikea can, then, be used to show that strategies do not develop successfully because of 'fit' *or* 'stretch'. Trying to decide which came first for Ikea – the market opportunity or the capabilities – is a futile exercise. It has taken advantage of both; the market has informed developing competences and developing competences yielded market opportunities.

ASSIGNMENT 1.6

Strategic Management by Context

The aim of assignment 1.6 is to make students understand that the elements of strategic management shown in exhibit 1.4 are likely to differ between different types of organisation. This is discussed in section 1.3 of the text. Students should be able to see differences in different contexts. Try to get them to consider this in terms of specific organisations they know, or from articles in the press on businesses and business problems; or from the case section of the book as suggested below. Some of the differences which should be identified might be:

- The complexity of a multinational business such as ISS or Burmah Castrol will mean that global logistics and structure and control are important. However, the students should also see that other elements of strategy are also there; both firms have portfolio strategic *choices* to make; have to integrate *acquisitions* and manage disposals; face differences of *culture* between countries; and determine ways to *control* their operations across the world.

- *Stakeholder values* are especially important in a partnership; and this might also be influenced by values associated with professions, as in an accountancy firm such as KPMG. *Strategic choice* processes have traditionally been more biased towards negotiation than top down edict and therefore, adaptive/incremental modes of strategy development have been more typical. However, increasingly the competitive nature of markets pose challenges of *strategic change* in both *structural* and *cultural* terms (see the KPMG teaching note).

- The influences on strategy in a public sector organisation require the student to recognise the nature of public control and influence. Determining and planning the *allocation of resources* in a context in which different *stakeholders* have significant influence is a major issue. In this respect, it might be interesting to ask students to compare the influences on the strategy of a charitable trust organisation such as the Sheffield Theatres or the Iona Community with its various *stakeholders* and substantial constraints on finance (see teacher's notes), with public sector organisations – for example, a nationalised company or a government agency. Increasingly issues of *strategic change* are also becoming very important in public sector organisations facing deregulation or forms of privatisation.

- A small business is typically heavily influenced by an individual (e.g. owner) or small group so understanding the values and views of such *stakeholders is* vital. However, typically small firms also face important *strategic choices* about the basis upon which they compete (e.g. should they seek particular market niches?), how they configure often scarce *resources* and maintain flexibility in strategic response. It can be useful to ask students to consider how these issues might change as businesses grow.

- For comments on the high-tech context see the notes on the chapter-end case example on Microsoft/Netscape.

Overall, students should understand that all the elements of strategic management are important in most organisations; but that the weighting between these elements may differ.

Chapter 2

ILLUSTRATION 2.1

Development Patterns

There could be different explanations of punctuated equilibrium. For example:

- Arguably strategies must change incrementally so strategic drift is inevitable. It is just a question of how long the drift goes on. So in relation to question 2, if this view is taken, the role of management is to spot when such drift is occurring and introduce the challenge required for strategic change earlier rather than later.

- Punctuated equilibrium could also be explained in terms of the cultural inertia of organisations. A key question then would become whether or not management are themselves captured by that culture. If so, perhaps only 'outsiders' from the culture can effect the sorts of changes required to prevent drift.

- There are those who would also argue that if strategic planning is done effectively, such drift, and therefore the phenomenon of punctuated equilibrium, will not take place. However students should be encouraged to read section 2.3.1 in chapter 2 before this is readily accepted.

- Others might argue that the pattern of punctuated equilibrium is inevitable; managers can do very little about it; it is the role of market forces to deal with underperforming organisations. Some will survive because change is forced upon them; others will go out of existence. It is the equivalent of a process of 'natural selection'.

The tutors' brief for chapter-end work assignment 2.6 might also be helpful with regard to these questions.

ILLUSTRATION 2.2

Planning

This question should be dealt with in conjunction with section 2.3.1 in the text. It is about the role of planning systems.

Students might argue that the main danger of the planning system in the NHS is that it becomes a bureaucratic 'ritual' more linked to a budgeting process to balance 'scarce' resources than to anything much to do with strategy. If so, students should be challenged to come up with changes that could be made. However, in line with Mintzberg's arguments, it should be debated as to whether it is the role of formal planning systems to develop the strategy itself – or to deal with the resource implications of the strategy once developed. If this were accepted, what approaches would be appropriate in the NHS for actually developing the strategy? This may lead to a discussion about the encouragement of strategic debate and challenge as well as data gathering and analysis.

The tutors' brief for illustration 2.6 might also be helpful here.

ILLUSTRATION 2.3

Incrementalism

The notes in the tutors' brief for chapter-end work assignment 2.4 deals with question 1 here.

As far as question 2 is concerned, again the tutors' brief for chapter-end work assignment 2.4 should be helpful as should the notes above with regard to the questions for illustration 2.1.

ILLUSTRATION 2.4

Culture – Both a Help and a Hindrance

These questions are designed to allow students to explain the idea of culture at the different levels shown in Exhibit 2.6. In particular that culture at any of these levels can be both a help and constraint.

In both the cultural contexts, managers used to these would find benefits of networking, ready understanding of business problems and, arguably, would be able readily to develop strategies in line with these ways of operating. Indeed, in the Scottish knitwear industry, the assumptions tend to define the market and what are and are not legitimate ways of operating. Students should be able to point out that these very benefits also lead to problems of myopia (e.g. in the case of the Scottish knitwear industry) and, quite likely, difficulties of operating with other nationals who are not part of the same culture (as the Chinese in East Asia might find).

The second question poses a particular problem. A new CEO of a Scottish knitwear firm seeking rapid growth would find it difficult to gain acceptance of the need to move into different markets; to develop new products not recognised as being 'legitimate'; or even to compete too aggressively with those other manufacturers within the same 'cultural network'.

ILLUSTRATION 2.5

Negotiation, Networking and Political Activity

Question 1 allows a discussion about the extent to which organisations, as groups of individuals with different interests, are inevitably political in their nature; and over time how cultures build up. The issue is to what extent this is problematic or beneficial. Many students will argue it is problematic because it gives rise to friction, conflict, bargaining and negotiation that result in 'satisficing' as opposed to optimal decisions. Others might argue for benefits. Organisational cultures provide for people 'guidelines of operating'. Although organisational politics can result in conflicts they can also surface differences and disagreements, which in themselves can be challenges contributing to strategy development. In any case is it realistic to conceive of organisations without such processes at work?

Question 2 requires students to see that different approaches to strategy development assume that bargaining, networking and political activity are dealt with differently. Planning tends to emphasise the idea that analysis and careful evaluation can overcome political activity and cultural inertia. Command assumes that given these forces, clear direction, vision or even edict from the top is required. Logical incrementalism assumes that bargaining and negotiation is inevitable but can be used proactively to surface issues and resolve them.

ILLUSTRATION 2.6

Configurations

The externally dependent strategy configuration is a useful one by which to explore several key themes in strategy development, notably the role of planning and the role of negotiation and bargaining (or the political dimension). Students should be able to understand that if strategic direction is substantially imposed externally, then internal competition for scarce resources may well be especially significant. There is also likely to be less personal ownership of strategy since it is more centrally directed. The two questions posed here allow this to be explored.

The first questions is about the role of planning. Students may see that in such circumstances planning may be less to do with deciding on a strategy than reporting on a strategy. The planning system may be to do with how the centre or external controller of strategy tries to ensure that they know about what is going on. It is more of a control mechanism than a decision-making mechanism. At its worst it can be the post-rationalisation and justification of the strategic direction that is being followed. This does, of course, raise the question about how strategists might have an influence in effecting the strategic direction of the organisation, which is the subject of question 2.

Students may see that if a strategist is to 'make a difference' in such circumstances they are likely to have to become proficient in negotiation and bargaining, both with their colleagues across internal departments; and also with the external agents that have a major influence on strategy development. This could be government in the case of public sector organisations; or parent companies in the case of a conglomerate. This does not, of course, mean that strategists should not be capable analysts, perhaps planners; it does mean that other skills of the strategist need to be recognised.

ILLUSTRATION 2.7

The Cultural Web

Although the cultural web is a very useful analytical tool students/managers can fall into several traps when undertaking an analysis:

- The web is mapped out but the detail hides 'the message'.

- The implications to the pursuit of particular strategies are not discussed.

These assignments address these two issues. Students should certainly understand different elements within the web (explained in section 2.8.1) but they should be pressed to extract the strong messages. For example, 'this is a culture of curing not caring!'. They should also be pressed to give specific examples of strategies which the culture would easily accommodate (e.g. more 'high-tech' surgery) and those which would struggle (health promotion schemes, increased home care, etc.).

ILLUSTRATION 2.8

Technological Change and Strategic Inertia

In addressing question 1 students may come to the conclusion that analytical, planning approaches to strategy will not have solved this problem; after all, the company knew the situation and knew of the need for change. Clearly cultural influences in terms of taken-for-granted assumptions and routine ways of behaving had resulted in incremental change and drift similar to the Icarus Paradox described in the chapter. Students may argue that the situation might have been avoided had there been more of a 'learning organisation' in place – a more open, challenging and questioning, experimentally based organisation. They may, however, also argue that given the major threat that the organisation faced in the absence of such a culture, there was need for a much more decisive leadership and intervention – more of a command approach to strategic change.

Students should also recognise, however, that effective processes in one organisation are not necessarily effective in others. The need here was for the assimilation of the need for innovation in a fast-changing, technological environment and at multiple points in the organisation. Other organisations may face more stable conditions where a more mechanistic approach to strategy development, and incremental change, may be more appropriate. Indeed in such organisations the characteristics of a learning organisation; or of directed change by a command type leader could be disruptive and harmful.

CASE EXAMPLE

KPMG (A): Strategy Development in a Partnership

The main purposes of this case are to allow students to consider:

- The way in which strategy development processes are likely to be linked to context (in this case a professional services partnership).

- How organisational culture affects strategy development.

The case study also provides a useful background to the other KPMG case studies provided in the case section of the book.

Some of the key points the case raises are:

- The nature of partnerships and the implications for strategic management. It is useful to get students to 'rehearse' what a partnership is like. It may be that members of the class have experience of this; and this can be drawn upon. If not some of the key points that need to be made are:

a) It is important to stress that partners are owners who are also working in the firm. Technically, at least, the senior partner is 'primus inter pares'.

b) In the past in KPMG people became partners by 'coat tailing' an influential partner. The consequence was that 'tribes' of partners and managers and staff built up who have confidence in each other and tend to work together. In this sense partnerships can work like 'clans' rather than hierarchies. There may be a formal structure but there is also an informal structure by which 'things get done'.

c) Partners may be very defensive and protective of their clients and fees generated from their work with clients. They may regard relationships with clients as 'their territory' rather a matter of corporate concern.

d) Partners are likely to be professionally trained and may see clients through a 'professional lens' such as that of an accountant rather than in the client's terms.

The case (and this culture) suggest that 'partner-centredness' may prevail over 'client-centredness'.

- As far as the influence on strategy development is concerned, students should be encouraged to consider what strategy development profile might be typical for a partnership such as KPMG. The evidence is that the 'muddling through' profile is likely to typify partnerships. Formal planning systems may or may not exist, but the real influence is likely to come from the negotiation and bargaining between partners within a strong professional culture. The result is likely to be gradual (incremental) development of strategy. There is unlikely to be a strong influence of an individual.

The case can also be used to carry out a cultural web exercise and consider the implications in terms of strategy development. The culture web (on page 28) is based on the case study. What does the web signify?

- The assumptions within the *paradigm* are about the standing and reputation of the firm, and the professionalism of individuals within that firm. The firm's perceived superiority is closely linked to individual (partner) capabilities, and their perceived closeness to the clients. Professionalism also relates to the conservative, uncontroversial, low-risk approach reflected in much of the routine behaviour and control systems concerned with quality control.

- Individual *partner power* was seen to be dominant. This might be in the form of named individuals, but as in most partnerships it was not a clear hierarchy of power. In many respects, indeed, power has to be seen within the context of a partnership as a network.

- As far as *organisation structure* is concerned, there is little in the case. Enough can be inferred for the students to see that the structure was complex. However, it might be questioned as to whether the formal structure is how the organisation actually operated; to what extent is the networking more influential? Students might point to disadvantages of such a system but there are also advantages since there could be a high degree of flexibility in the way the firm approaches clients and issues.

- Although *control systems* are not discussed extensively in the case study, as with many professional service and consultancy firms in which manpower is a key cost, controls over bookable time spent with clients and fee-earning was of central importance; and the quality control procedures were particularly concerned with, for example, the reports issued to clients. It also appears that they were somewhat cumbersome, time-consuming and historically based.

- The *routines and rituals* reflected partner centrality with the danger that looking after partners took precedence over looking after clients. Professionalism and quality were reflected in the practice of partners signing off anything which went to clients e.g. reports and most written correspondence. Internally there was a proliferation of committees and meetings: partners might take personal responsibility with regard to clients, but they wanted to have their say internally and collective decision-making (or sceptics might say lack of decision-making) was therefore the norm. As far as rituals were concerned the most significant were to do with the progress to partnership, reflected in appraisal systems assessing suitability of managers and the personal sponsorship by partners of managers.

- *Stories* were about individuals – heroes, villains and mavericks. Other stories reflected the network structure and the almost 'tribal' nature of the firm, with one 'tribe' telling stories about another. It was also recognised by the partners themselves that there were many stories told by the managers about the differences between partners (*them*) and everyone else (*us*). And, of course, a good deal of the *symbolism* was also to do with partnership, for example, in terms of the difference between partners and everyone else, shown in the access to dining rooms, etc.

The web also helps identify some of the blockages to change that might be highlighted in a forcefield analysis (useful as diagnosis for the KPMG (B) Managing Strategic Change case study in the text and cases).

- If clients are looking for services tailored to their needs, is this compatible with a *we can do anything* approach based around individual partner skills?

- Colin Sharman himself suggests that in the past there was a degree of *complacency*. Will the energy for change be achieved?

- What does *closeness to the client mean*? The risk is that it is to do with closeness to particular individuals – almost social relationships – rather than closeness to the problems that the client perceives as important.

- The *loose, and individually based, power structure* of the firm could be a problem if change is required. Resistance movements could occur and be difficult to overcome where power is fragmented.

- Many of the routines and control systems are about *quality*. But there is some evidence that quality is seen in relatively formalised terms – for example, the production of reports. Does this relate to client need if the clients are looking for the solution to problems?

- The routines of *individuality* in service delivery yet *collectivity* in internal decision-making might make refocusing on integration and co-ordination problematic.

- To what extent will the *dominant role of partners* linked to a them and us approach militate against the delivery of the new strategy?

There may also be features of the web which are potential facilitators of change. For example:

- There appears to be a strong *commitment to the future of the firm* by those who wish to become partners. They would not wish to see the firm stagnate.

- Clearly the firm is populated with intelligent and *able people*. On the face of it they should be able to see the need for change.

The Cultural Web of KPMG

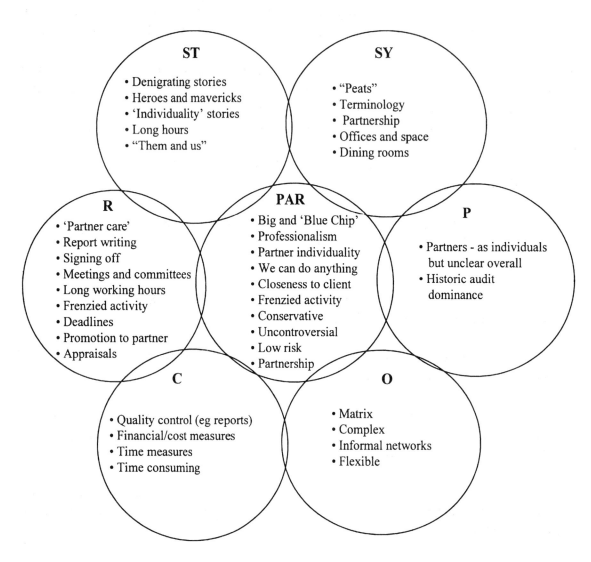

ASSIGNMENT 2.1

Tracing Strategy Development

The purpose of this assignment is to help the students understand the distinction between strategy as *intended* by the managers of an organisation and the *realised* strategy – that which is observably occurring in the market place and, for this assignment, as experienced by customers or users of the organisation. A good way of achieving this is to encourage students to consider organisations with long-standing strategic approaches to their market but which are trying to position themselves differently. The statements of intended strategy are likely to be views of where the managers would like the company to go, but there may be a legacy of the past which is difficult to change.

The exercise can be helped if students are directed towards annual reports, or statements of strategy or mission statements are provided from organisations with such long-standing strategy directions with which the students are familiar. The students should be encouraged to consider, for example:

- Whether the statement of overall strategic intent is demonstrated in practice.

- Whether statements of how competitive advantage is to be achieved are evident; for example, many service businesses make statements about excellence of customer service as a basis of competitive advantage; is this experienced in reality by the students?

- Annual reports often list steps which management intend to take which will have a major impact on strategy; are these evident in practice?

Students might also consider what, in their experience, are long-standing elements of strategy that they would experience as customers which are, or are not, in line with the intended strategy. Students may come to the conclusion that some of the elements of strategy which executives can directly control and influence (e.g. through decisions about product launches or capital investment) have more influence than where change in behaviour, attitude or culture especially matters, for example, in terms of how staff interface with customers.

ASSIGNMENT 2.2

Influences on Strategy Development

It is important for students to understand that there are many influences on how strategies develop in organisations (see sections 2.3–2.6 in chapter 2). However, students sometimes see these as mutually exclusive or contradictory accounts of how strategies develop. They need to understand that in most organisations there are multiple dimensions to how strategies develop. There are a number of cases in the case edition of the book which allow students to consider this, especially those on New Town and Castle Press. The teaching notes later in this volume show how students might approach an analysis of these cases.

If KPMG is considered then a contrast between strategy development in the KPMG (A) – cultural and political influences driving incrementalism – with KPMG (C) – more central "command" – might be useful.

The use of these cases is suggested because it is not usual to find published material which describes strategy development processes sufficiently. However, it could be that the class comprises of part-time students working in organisations. If this is so then they could be asked to profile strategy development processes as they experience them or observe them in their own organisations.

ASSIGNMENT 2.3

Planning Systems

This assignment requires students to consider the value of planning systems. Section 2.3.1 in chapter 2 sets out some of the benefits and problems that can occur with planning systems and the assignment encourages students to consider which of these apply in particular contexts. The tutor can therefore challenge the extent to which the students have thought through the practical benefits of planning.

The type of issues that might be surfaced include:

- Is planning actually to do with making strategic decisions? For example, in the NHS many of the decisions have been imposed by government; and the strategy of IKEA is strongly driven by the vision of the founder, as is the strategy of News Corporation by Rupert Murdoch.

- However, in both organisations strategic planning might give the sorts of benefits outlined in sections 2.3.1: the encouragement of analysis of strategic problems, questioning and challenging of the taken for granted, involvement and ownership in strategy making, co-ordination of resources, more effective communication of intended strategy and means of control of strategy implementation.

Students should also be encouraged to think about some of the dangers. For example:

- To what extent do plans result in intentions which are not delivered in the face of political and cultural dimensions of organisations. Managers in the NHS would argue that the planning systems introduced there, in themselves, did not address such dimensions. The plans may result in statements of strategy which are not owned within the organisation.

- The NHS might also be used as an example of the division between strategy making and operations. Staff within the NHS saw specialists being brought in to help draw up strategic plans or set up planning systems; whereas staff might argue they were busy caring for patients. Many saw strategic planning as removed from their day-to-day reality.

- There is also the danger that strategic planning can become ritualised: a procedure which managers go through, contributing to some overall plan which they do not see themselves part of. This may be the case in the NHS but is often the case in multinational corporations or large conglomerates in which the various parts of the organisation are distant from the centre.

- In turn this raises the important point that a plan is no substitution for a clarity of intent or vision. Students may recognise that in IKEA such a vision has driven the strategy development of the organisation. Plans here may be more to do with constructing a way of achieving this vision.

- Students might be encouraged to consider to what extent the benefits and dangers of planning systems vary by context. For example, is planning more likely to contribute to strategic decision-making in stable environments but, have more of co-ordinating and control role in complex organisations or those facing very dynamic environments.

ASSIGNMENT 2.4

Incremental Strategy Development

The quotations in illustration 2.3 are, on the whole, positive descriptions of incremental strategy development. Students may see that there are potential advantages in such an approach such as:

- The organisation building on what it knows and taking a cautious approach to strategy development.

- In this respect the organisation is learning from what it knows but also adjusting to new situations.

- Rather than taking risks or major changes in direction, small-scale 'experiments' might be possible; the organisation 'tests the water', advances further if the experiment works but can pull out if it does not.

- So incrementalism may be seen as a more flexible approach to strategy development rather than one off major decisions and commitment of investment.

- It could be that by strategy development in such ways there is more involvement in the strategy development process and hence a greater commitment to evolving strategy

- If the organisation is sensitive enough to its environment, through small-scale adjustments of incremental nature it may be capable of coping with change.

However, students should see that there are risks associated with such an approach:

- The organisation may see itself changing incrementally, when, in fact, it is stuck in its old way of doing things, interpreting changes in the environment according to such ways of doing things and therefore drifting (see section 2.8.2 in the text).

- Small-scale changes described as incremental strategy development may actually result from political and cultural processes which ensure that there is a continuity of strategy; that changes are not made which 'rock the boat' too much; again contributing to strategic drift.

- Can incremental change cope with major environmental changes or jolts? Is there a danger that when such processes become established that there is insufficient challenge or questioning of the strategy to adjust to such significant changes?

ASSIGNMENT 2.5

Logical Incrementalism, Muddling Through and Intuition

This is a conceptual assignment which requires students to consider both differences and overlap between these management processes. In summary:

- The overarching linkage is the notion that managers cannot entirely pre-plan and pre-ordain strategy.

- *Logical incrementalism* suggests that strategy is developed through *experimentation/trial and error,* and that managers do this in an essentially considered, logical way, taking into account both factors external to the organisation and internal resources and political realities.

- The notion of *muddling through* sees strategy more in terms of the *consequence* or *output* of managerial processes and emphasises rather less the idea that there is a logical search for strategic fit. In relation to some of the discussion in chapter 2 (e.g. see section 2.8.1) that the culture of the organisation and the collective experiences and organisational processes within it constrain significantly or guide strategic choice. The resulting pattern of strategy development tends to be incremental in nature. At its most beneficial this builds on what the organisation is familiar with and knows how to do; at its worst it is the product of compromise and muddling through.

- The idea of intuitive management suggests that individual managers' *experience and mental models* interpret their organisational environments and thus influence strategy. This raises the question of just what the nature of such influence is. There are different explanations here.

    a) One argument is that such individual's mental models do have an influence but the influences are moderated by the cultural and political processes of organisation and the collective paradigm or recipe which, in turn, can be said to account for incremental processes of strategy development. In effect individual differences are subordinated to organisational processes.

    b) A more extreme extension of this is that individuals who work in organisations actually come to adopt a mental model in line with the organisational paradigm. A frequent comment heard in organisations is that people do not use their 'initiative'; do not sufficiently draw on their personal experience and intuition.

- Another view is that organisations significantly undervalue and underestimate the importance of individuals' experience and their intuitive capabilities. Chaos theorists who write on management suggest that organisational environments are so difficult to predict that organisations should be more ready to rely on individuals' intuition. Another argument is the problems of strategic drift arising from the dominant influence of organisational culture would be overcome if there was more encouragement of challenge based on individuals' experience and intuition.

ASSIGNMENT 2.6

Strategic Drift

This is a complex assignment. It requires students to understand and discuss:

- The reasons for incremental/adaptive patterns of strategic change – in particular whether or not such adaptive patterns are the output of logical, incremental process or cultural/political processes.

- Therefore, the extent to which strategic drift is likely – even inevitable – in an organisation. (The key readings on incremental strategic change and drift by Quinn, Johnson and Miller might be useful here.)

- What can be done to prevent such drift if it is seen as a danger? Here the key question may be how challenges to the taken-for-granted of management in terms of organisational routines and the paradigm might occur. This relates to some of the issues discussed in Chapter 11 (see sections 11.4.2 and 11.4.3). It also raises the question, again, as to whether or not planning mechanisms are capable of achieving such challenge; or whether it is a matter of encouraging individuals to question and challenge strategies?

- It is strongly recommended that if this assignment is to be tackled tutors should follow up the references cited to build their own views on these issues.

Chapter 3

ILLUSTRATION 3.1

PEST Analysis

See tutors' brief for chapter-end work assignment 3.2

ILLUSTRATION 3.2

Globalisation

Students should employ the market convergence, cost advantage, government influence and global competition criteria for the industry of their choice. They should see, therefore, that there are different forces for globalisation in different industries. For example, if they choose brewing, they should see that historically there was little pressure for globalisation but that this is growing e.g. in terms of market convergence, arguably cost and more pronounced global competition.

ILLUSTRATION 3.3

Scenarios

See tutors' brief for chapter-end work assignment 3.5.

ILLUSTRATION 3.4

Barriers to Entry

Students should be able to apply their understanding of barriers to entry outlined to section 3.4.1 of the text to an industry of their choice.

The second question requires them to conceive of how these barriers might change. There are some obvious examples form illustration 3.4 itself. Government legislation might create changes. The growth in size of companies within an industry might build barriers in terms of economies of scale. Market share advantages can increase experience curve barriers. The building of heavyweight brands or marketing muscle can develop retaliatory capacity. The acquisition of brands, as has happened in the luxury car market, also changes traditional barriers.

ILLUSTRATION 3.5

5-Forces Analysis

This question is designed to encourage students to become 'comfortable' with 5-Forces analysis.

Also remind students of some of the *limitations* of 5-Forces analysis:

- It can 'compartmentalise' factors that are actually connected e.g. a new entrant may, in fact, gain entry by (partial) substitution of an incumbent's product/service. The new entrant may even be a supplier.

- It does not ask questions about underlying driving forces in the general environment which are changing the balance of power in the industry. For example, the plummeting cost of telecommunications are spawning vast numbers of 'direct-line' services for consumers. So the 5-Forces analysis needs to link through to the wider PEST analysis.

ILLUSTRATION 3.6

Collaborative Ventures in Pharmaceuticals

This illustration is useful in showing how the dimensions of the five forces can be used to shed light on the benefits of collaboration as well as on the nature of competitive environments. However, this needs to be considered in relation to potential risks as well as benefits.

The benefits of collaboration are clearly enough set out in the illustration. The risks may be less clear to students. It may be helpful to refer them to exhibit 7.13 in chapter 7 and the associated discussions concerning joint ventures. In this light there are apparent risks in each of the collaborative arrangements.

Astra has, no doubt, benefited from its association with Takeda; but Takeda is a powerful pharmaceuticals firm. The danger is that obtains market knowledge from the arrangement and uses this to break into the European gastrointestinal market. Arguably this is less of a risk with regard to the arrangement between Ashbourne and Eli Lilly. The latter is not so strong in gastrointestinal products and, arguably, more reliant on Ashbournes brand.

The arrangement between Roche and the health authorities and between Zeneca and Eli Lilly are similar in their risks; namely that the treatments are not as effective as the manufacturers expect, or have budgeted for, and that high costs and harmful relations between themselves and major buyers result.

ILLUSTRATION 3.7

Strategic Group Analysis

Strategic group analysis is an important idea, which students often find more difficult to undertake than they might expect.

Follow the general advice in the tutors' brief for chapter-end work assignment 3.6.

ILLUSTRATION 3.8

Competitor Analysis

Illustration 3.8 draws on only a few of the techniques listed in exhibit 3.13. There are others which can be used for competitive analysis depending on the purpose of the analysis. The question challenges the students to consider what circumstances other techniques might be sensible. For example:

- In considering possible future competitive moves, use of such techniques as follows might be appropriate:

  a) Strategic group analysis in order to establish the historic bases of competition and potential competitive gaps (section 3.5.1 and illustration 3.7)
  b) Market segmentation analysis to identify which markets and potential markets exist (3.5.2)
  c) Core competence analysis (4.3.2) and comparative SWOT analysis (4.6.1) together with an understanding of the bases of the current strategies of competitors (6.3) might provide an understanding likely competitive moves as might a review of the mission (5.6.1 and 6.2.2) and objectives (5.6.2/5.6.3) of competitors
  d) An analyses of the risks and acceptability to competitors of different possible strategies (8.3.2 and 8.3.3) might also be appropriate.

- It could, on the other hand, be that consideration is being given to the acquisition of a competitor. Here other techniques may be appropriate to use. For example:

  a) An analysis of the core assumptions (2.4.1) and organisational culture (2.8.1 and 5.5) of competitors in order to establish the compatibility of the firms;
  b) The differential impact of environmental forces (3.3.1) and competitive forces (3.4) on the firms;
  c) The similarity of value chain configurations (4.3.1) and core competences (4.3.2), together with an examination of the portfolios (4.5) of the different firms might also be useful in establishing the fit between them.

CASE EXAMPLES

Irish Ports

The case describes the changes that have occurred in port administration in Ireland, outlines the industry structure and the future development of the industry as Ireland becomes a member of EMU. The case study lends itself to an analysis of industry environment the use of Porter's Industry Analysis framework and scenario-building.

1. PEST Analysis of Irish Ports

Political/Legal Factors

- Establishment in 1991 of the Review Group to examine the port structures; Enactment of the Harbours Act 1996. Eight ports were vested as commercial harbour companies; EU decision to abolish duty free sales; deregulation in the Irish airline industry

Economic Factors

- Total co-financed investment of IR£163 million 1994–99; Strong GDP growth.
- Ireland becoming a member of the EMU, and the UK and Northern Ireland staying out; upgrading of Rosslare and Dun Laoghaire facilities to cope with the new high-speed RoRo ferries; the introduction by ferry companies of new ferries.

Sociocultural Factors

- Increased economic activity in Ireland this has increased the throughput through Irish ports; Due to lifestyle changes and increased levels disposable income people are taking more foreign holidays; therefore, there is an increased usage of ports and airports

Technological

- The competition between high-speed ferries (Stena) and traditional conventional ferries with added capacity and facilities on board (Irish Ferries); ferry companies have linked into computerisation travel reservation systems (Gaelio) and have developed to capability to take telephone bookings.

2. Students can use their PEST analysis as a basis to the decide which forces are the most significant drivers of change. This is were students gain insights into transforming the information generation through PEST analysis into identify the main environmental influences affecting Irish ports.

- *Changing Role of Government in Irish Port Management:* Stimulate competition, reduce costs and increase Ireland's competitiveness.
- *Abolition of Government Funding Post 1999:* Ports will examine means of increasing their revenues through improvement in port facilities.
- *Ireland's Entry Into EMU:* NI ports low cost base and tariff structure may become more attractive for Southern freight and sea passengers.
- *Strength of Sterling against the Euro.* This could result in traffic routing through NI ports purely based on cost.
- May attract foreign direct investment into NI away from ROI.
- *Increasing Competition from Airlines.*
- *Abolition of Duty Free Shopping* Subsidisation of unprofitable services will be no longer an option for ports, therefore the ports will have to examine other ways of increasing their revenue post abolition of duty free.

3. Applying the Porter framework may yield the following kind of analysis:

Potential Entrants
Low threat as barriers to entry are high. Theses barriers include available land, water depth, planning permission, sea and land access, etc.

Product Substitutes
The substitutes are airports and air freight. The threat is moderate. Ireland has three main airports, Dublin, Cork and Shannon, which have the capacity to handle large volumes of cargo and passengers. The switching cost can be high.

Power of Suppliers

Suppliers are construction and engineering companies who build and maintain port facilities, utilities and various government agencies. There power is low but if the definition of suppliers is broaden to include ferry companies (RoRo or LoLo) the power of the suppliers increases to being moderate.

Power of Buyers

Buyers are the ferry companies that operate from Irish ports. Depending on the size of the ferry operator (P&O, Stena, Irish Ferries) and the dependency of the port on a ferry company for business their power is high and is powerful catalysts for continuous port development. Stena is the sole ferry company operating from Dun Laoghaire, so their power is high. Dublin port has a number of ferry companies (Irish Ferries, P&O, Belfast Merchant Ferries, Seacat) operating from the port so their power is only moderate.

Industry Structure

There are twelve vested commercial ports in the ROI and three ports in NI, therefore there is intense competition, based primarily on price, service and location. The ports are also facing competition intense competition from the airports.

4. Uncertainties

The following 'uncertainties' could be used to build scenarios.

Abolition of Duty Free Sales

Implications:

- Increased prices due to loss of revenue from duty free sales.
- Increased competition within the industry.
- Ports with high cost base will become uncompetitive and may close down.

Decline in the Irish Economy

Implications:

- Decrease in the volume of throughput through Irish ports.
- People will have less disposable income hence will not be travelling frequently.
- Ferry companies will reduce their capacity, number of sailing and ships operating in the freight and sea passenger markets in line with the declining demand for their services.
- Increased competition among ports for a declining market.

Uncertainty Privatisation Post-1999

Implications:

- Privatisation likely to be triggered by the governments unwillingness to provide further funds for ports infrastructure investment.
- Stringent market performance standards being placed on individual ports.
- Ports that have not been performing will be closed down or sold to the highest bidder and this may result in a curtailment existing services.

- The closing down of unprofitable port services which will have a knock on effect on the Irish economy.

Building of a New Greenfield Port

Implications:

- Adds further capacity to the Irish ports sector.
- Increases the competitiveness and the attractiveness of sea transportation to both freight and sea passengers.
- Added services in RoRo, LoLo and bulk freight and intermodal connections to the port.
- Redistribution market share of individual ports in relation to freight and sea passengers.
- Lower cost base and prices.

Price competition in the short term between existing operators.

ASSIGNMENT 3.1

Stable, Dynamic and Complex Environments

The distinction between *stable* and *dynamic* environments is obviously to do with the rate and amount of change. The important point is that students should-understand that how strategies are managed in organisations may need to differ according to the nature of change. At one extreme students may argue that stable environments are those in which there is no change. There are, however, very few industry environments in which this is the case. Students may also recognise that there are different types and degrees of change. There are industries which are cyclical (e.g. construction or oil); there are those in which change can be rapid but common place (e.g. fashion), there are others in which change occurs but is unpredictable (at the time of writing, for example, the impact of biotechnology on pharmaceuticals).

In some respects the notion of *complexity* builds on this since it is environments which are difficult to comprehend or difficult to predict which are more complex. Arguably some of the hi-tech industries fall into this category. However, students should also identify that some industries also tend to be complex because organisations have made them more complex by their own corporate structures. Industries characterised by complex multinational corporations are an example of this.

The overall aim of this assignment is to sensitise students to the nature of different environments. In turn this might provide a good basis upon which to discuss the extent to which different approaches to managing strategy are appropriate to different environments: (see section 3.2 of chapter 3).

ASSIGNMENT 3.2

Auditing the Industry Environment

PEST analysis is a useful starting point for environmental analysis. Exhibit 3.3 provides a check list for this. Alternatively, a 'blank' of illustration 3.1 (included in the computer disc of exhibits from *Exploring Corporate Strategy*) can be provided to students who can then be asked to complete it for the forces at work in a particular industry.

The danger is that *long lists* of forces or influences can be generated by either device. So the second part of the assignment requires more consideration because it challenges students to assess which of the forces are likely to be of *most significance* in driving industry change. Here students should justify their views in terms of the evidence from the past and the likely impact in the future of any particular influence.

Taking the European brewing industry as an example, very long lists of environmental influences could be made by students. What matters is whether students can see the important influences on strategy of:

- Industry over-capacity;
- Mature markets in the North, yet potential for growth in the South;
- Changes in tastes for beer (and other drinks) by market sector;
- Growing Europeanisation.

They should recognise the resulting pressure for the development of brand led *pan-European strategies:* whilst more specific (sometimes country- based) consumer tastes and buying behaviour may exert a contrary pressure. Students can be asked to justify why they consider one influence to be more important than another.

ASSIGNMENT 3.3

Changes in Competitive Forces

For assignment 3.3 and 3.4 students should follow the 5 forces analysis guideline outlined in section 3.4 of the text. Assignment 3.3 requires them to identify and justify key forces (i.e. avoid just listing them); and also to identify likely changes in these forces which might prove to be important. The pharmaceutical industry provides a good basis for doing this and the teaching notes on the case study can be referred to here.

Students should, again, be expected to do more than simply list changes. Rather they should be expected to identify the implications of such changes. These are also discussed in the teaching note to the Pharmaceutical Industry case study in this manual.

ASSIGNMENT 3.4

Industry Comparisons of Environmental and Competitive Forces

This assignment requires students to apply both 5-Forces analysis and a more general audit of the industry environment (see assignment 3.2 above) to two industries in order to understand the differences in environmental and competitive forces at work.

Assignment 3.2 above emphasises the need not only to identify general influences but also key drivers of change in an industry. This assignment, therefore, should expect students to identify the differences in key drivers that might exist between industries. The case section of the book provides a number of industry cases which can be used for this purpose including The European Brewing Industry, World Automobile Industry and The Pharmaceutical Industry; and in each case extensive teaching notes are provided.

These cases can also be used for the purposes of comparing competitive forces; and again the teaching notes provide useful material here. However, in considering differences in competitive forces between industries, it is also useful to ask if such differences suggest that some industries are more or less attractive than others; and why this is the case. This could be achieved by analysing the factors affecting *competitive rivalry* in the different industries by choosing two industries which are fundamentally different in their competitive intensity; for example:

- An industry with little differentiation, substitutes (or ease of entry), powerful buyers, static demand, etc. (the coal industry or other commodity industries perhaps).

- A growth industry with opportunities for differentiation, high entry barriers and dependent buyers (some hi-tech industries perhaps).

If the industries in the case section of the book are used, students may consider that the automobile industry is more competitive than the European brewing industry. Both of these industries have forces which are leading to increased competition excess capacity, fairly static demand, and in the case of brewing, increased power of retailers. However, the entry of the Japanese into the European car market seems to be especially significant. Students might ask if such entry is possible in the brewing industry: would it be possible for the world's largest brewer Anheuser Busch to enter the world's largest beer consuming region?

Students should also understand that the fact that one industry appears to be more or less attractive than another is not necessarily a reason for neglecting the latter. If an organisation can develop a competitive advantage in an industry it can still be highly profitable.

ASSIGNMENT 3.5

Building Scenarios

Assignment 3.5 requires students to take their analysis further by focusing on change in industry characteristics and competitive forces through the construction of scenarios. Guidelines for the construction of scenarios are given in section 3.3.3 of the text and it is recommended that students follow these, building no more than three scenarios for a given industry. The work done in assignments 3.1–3.3 should provide the bases of identifying the key industry forces or influences which will enable them to do this. The teaching note on the pharmaceutical industry also discusses scenario-building exercise on that industry. Some of the problems of scenario building should be emphasised to students:

Students may try to build in *too many factors* and, therefore, not be able to limit the number of scenarios:

- They may find difficulty in generating scenarios with a *coherent* and compatible set of factors.

- Some may be wary of having to exercise *judgement;* and others will confuse judgement with hunch. Try to encourage a realistic debate which tests out assumptions and projections against known facts and trends.

A particularly useful exercise is to ask students to build scenarios for an industry for which there is a company case (or for their own industry/company if possible) and then to assess the company's strategic position in the light of the different scenarios (e.g. see the teaching notes on the World Automobile Industry and Peugeot).

One of the issues that might surface is the ease or difficulty with which scenarios can be constructed. It usually emerges that scenarios are much easier to construct where the number of key forces at work in an industry are relatively few. They are less easy to construct if the number of important forces is high because the number of variables the student is trying to handle becomes too great.

This, in turn, raises another issue. Scenarios are of particular use in uncertain environments as a means of helping managers to think through possible futures. However, uncertainty may arise for a number of reasons (see section 3.2 of the text). If uncertainty arises because of the unpredictability of a few forces, then arguably scenarios may be very helpful: but what if uncertainty arises primarily because there are a large number of forces at work, to what extent is scenario planning of use in such circumstances? There are a limited number of very important forces at work in the automobile industry: but what of fast-moving hi-tech industries where there are many different forces at work?

ASSIGNMENT 3.6

Strategic Groups

This assignment builds on the notion of strategic groups and strategic space outlined in section 3.5.1 in the text. Illustration 3.7 provides an example of how the exercise could be carried out. This could, for example, be applied to the European brewing industry, or the World Automobile industry:

- Exhibit 3.8 provides a useful checklist by which the different strategic characteristics of organisations can be considered. However, in addition, the checklist provided in section 3.5.5 (exhibit 3.13) on competitor analysis can also be used. The important point is to require students to identify the really important strategic characteristics that distinguish between companies. For example, in the European brewing industry this might be related to geographical coverage, strength of brands, diversification, size of firm, type of distribution, etc.

- Students can be encouraged to draw more than one strategic group map if they believe that a number of characteristics are important. However, if they do, it is useful to ask them to consider the extent to which different bases of such maps give rise to similar or different configurations. They might find, for example, that However, the maps are drawn up, some firms always tend to end up in the same groups. In other words some firms may have a very similar set of strategic characteristics.

- Assignment 3.6(b) requires the students to consider mobility barriers – the extent to which it is possible for firms to move between strategic groups; to change the type of strategies they are following. Some of the European brewers have tried to do this, for example, through acquisition strategies leading to much more diverse product portfolios and geographical coverage. What, if any, are the barriers to this? Could some firms achieve it more readily than others?

- The notion of *strategic space is* an interesting one and is raised in assignment 3 6(c). Are there strategies not being pursued currently but which are indicated as opportunities by such mapping? For example, Grolsch is a pan-European – indeed international – niche player. Is this a strategy which others could follow profitably in other niches? (see the Brewery Group Denmark case for a comparison). Students might uncover other spaces and argue for their attractiveness: if retailers are growing stronger, could there be an opportunity for an *own brand specialist* on a pan-European basis, for example? For any of the spaces so identified, students should be required to consider the types of strategic characteristics a firm would require if they were aiming to occupy such a space.

ASSIGNMENT 3.7

The Purpose of Scenario Planning

The purpose of assignment 3.7 is to ensure that students understand the purpose of scenario planning: specifically that students understand that:

- Scenarios are particularly important in changing industries, especially where some elements of change are uncertain but have a potentially high impact;

- Scenario planning is, therefore, useful where the future cannot be predicted; However, this does not mean that it is based on 'hunch' but rather on plausible views built on specifically identified variables which are both potential key drivers of industry change and uncertain;

- Scenarios provide the basis for asking 'what if?' questions rather than identifying most likely futures for specific decision-making purposes.

In the context of the pharmaceutical industry all of these points are relevant. There arc clear changes taking place in the industry which will have an impact on firms but some are more uncertain than others. These can be seen to result from key drivers of change (e.g. government action and scientific advance). And the scenarios which can be built pose important strategic questions to the firms in the industry. The teaching notes on the pharmaceutical industry case study discusses this more specifically.

ASSIGNMENTS 3.8 and 3.9

Integrating Tools for Environmental Analysis

The aim of these two assignments is to bring together the tools of analysis covered in the chapter. Exhibit 3.1 provides a useful framework for this purpose. In both cases the aims of the assignment are twofold:

1. To examine the extent to which students can *apply* the tools.

2. To require students to decide which are the most useful tools in *particular circumstances*. Specifically, assignment 3.8 requires students to consider the extent to which these techniques are important in *public sector organisations*. It might be useful to ask students to do a comparison between the value of these techniques in private versus public sector organisations.

Many public sector managers find the commercial approach and terminology of some of the concepts described in this chapter difficult to relate to. These are a number of ways in which you can counteract this:

- We have found little problem with section 3.2 concerned with the nature of the environment and environmental audits. Indeed, in one respect, the public sector tends to have been ahead of the private sector – in developing contingency plans for different scenarios.

- Forces analysis can be a problem. In dealing with this the first point to make is that competition is a reality for *all* organisations. However, in many public sector organisations, it is competition for resource rather than competition in the market place.

- Relationships with suppliers and buyers (many of whom may be internal) does matter. Many of the recent changes in public sector management have been attempts to improve performance through changing these relationships. (This is discussed more fully in chapter 4, section 4.3.4.)

- It is valuable to consider issues of new entrants and substitution too. First, because deregulation is happening in many public services. Second, even where monopolies are maintained, substitution is a real threat (for example, the use of fax instead of first class post).

- Competitive rivalry is also being explicitly encouraged – for example, through the publishing of comparative performance tables (e.g. examination success rates by schools in the UK).

- Having overcome these hurdles, our experience is that the importance of competitor analysis – section 3.5 is understood and students are well able to adapt and use techniques accordingly.

- Finally, concepts of 'market attractiveness' and 'market segmentation' are well understood in the public sector. Indeed, one of the outcomes of the last few years of financial pressures has been the need to be much clearer about the focus and positioning of a particular service.

ASSIGNMENT 3.10

Competitor Analysis

This is a demanding assignment requiring students to undertake a study of competitors within an industry. Exhibit 3.13 provides a checklist of the many tools explained in the book by which a competitor analysis might be undertaken. It should not be expected that students will employ all of these, but they should be able to draw on ones most useful for the purpose of their analysis. Students should be able to identify key issues relating to the strategy of competitors, for example, in terms of overall strategy intent, stated objectives, competitive strategy, etc. However, they should also be expected to see the importance of comparisons of various sorts between competitors. For example, in terms of:

- The extent to which environmental factors (PEST analysis) and forces in the competitive environment (5-Forces) have a differential impact on competitors.

- The similarity or differences of strategic characteristics (strategic group analysis);

- Which market segments are targeted by different competitors.

- The relative position of competitors in terms of customer needs (the customer matrix).

- The relative standing of competitors in terms of market attractiveness and market strength (attractiveness matrix);

These and other techniques allow, not only a description of the strategic standing of competitors, but a comparison between competitors.

Such a comparative exercise will require access to data for a number of firms within an industry. This can be obtained by reference to annual reports, for example, but it will require an extensive study by students, perhaps working in groups.

Chapter 4

ILLUSTRATION 4.1

Resources, Competences and Competitive Advantage

These assignments are designed to consolidate further students' understanding of these links.

Read the guidance in the tutors' brief for chapter-end work assignments 4.1 to 4.6.

ILLUSTRATION 4.2

Competences Analysis

The text makes the point that competences which provide competitive advantage (core competences) need to *both* provide customer value greater than competition and be difficult to imitate. In the illustration provided here service and delivery might be claimed by competitors to be their competences too. However, what is significant is *why* and *how* service and delivery are provided. The question is to what extent the way this company achieves it is sustainable and difficult to imitate. The basis of how service and delivery are provided, we see that it is not just to do with formal distribution and logistics systems but to do with a combination (linkages) of:

- Good relationships with buyers.
- Slack in plant utilisation (though contrary to company intent and policy).
- The use of local sub contractors.
- The bending of rules, probably by junior employees to take goods back from major suppliers when necessary.

The tutor might then add a point of information here: the major competitor of this firm is a major multinational which was much less flexible in its approach and required the supermarkets to conform to standardise policies.

The tutor might ask the students to put themselves in the position of the supermarket buyer and ask two questions:

- Who would you prefer to buy from?
- What would the multinational have to do to win back the business?

The second question refers to the nature of the learning organisation. A number of the characteristics are discerned in this organisation. It does appear that junior employees question and challenge the system to the point where they bend the rules. The evidence of organisational slack is apparent, at least on the production side. The network of relationships within the firm is likely to be based on informality, as indeed are the relationships with the buyers themselves. Students may detect, therefore, that the needs of the buyers and the market place are being "listened to" at multiple points in the organisation and this in turn is leading to flexible, perhaps experimental, solutions.

ILLUSTRATION 4.3

Cost Drivers

This is a neat example about how 'value analysis' can be so useful in improving value-for-money (in this case by cost reduction).

However, incumbent organisations usually do not have in place systems of analysis – or other avenues of challenge – which ask radical questions about business processes.

Incumbents are usually victims of the 'we've always done it this way' syndrome.

ILLUSTRATION 4.4

Managing Linkages

This is a straightforward illustration of the issues in exhibit 4.9 of the text, concerning the management of linkages for strategic advantage.

ILLUSTRATION 4.5

Knowledge Creation

Some students have real problems with 'soft' ideas like tacit knowledge. Indeed compared with the Japanese western managers have problems too. (You may say they are too rational for their own good?)

Try to ensure that the following points come out:

- The competitive advantage comes from the fact that the knowledge IS tacit. If you can't even explain it yourself it is very difficult to imitate.

- Therefore, it is not always incumbent on management to make the implicit explicit. Rather, let them cohabit in parallel.

- The danger of tacit knowledge is that it can prevent change to an organisation – which may be very problematic in the long run.

'Socialisation' may be a good place to start the spiral of knowledge creation for new product development. However, in other circumstances the spiral may start elsewhere. The General Electric example is now common practice on telephone help-lines (e.g. for IT products), where product improvement (e.g. software features) emerge from the collective experience of thousands of user queries through the processes described in the illustration.

ILLUSTRATION 4.6

Comparisons

When reviewing these questions try to pull out some of the following points:

- Since resource allocation is a political process don't expect to find a universally 'fair' basis of comparison. It doesn't exist.

- An 'overall' measure of comparison may be inappropriate for organisations (like local authorities) whose objectives are pluralistic.

- Expect those affected by the league tables to be highly political in the way they respond to and use the data (e.g. 'the data are inaccurate'; 'these measures are not relevant'; 'look how well we've done – so where are our rewards?'; 'when are you going to get tough with the poor performers?', etc.).

Refer to tutors' brief for chapter-end work assignment 4.8.

ILLUSTRATION 4.7

Benchmarking

The purpose of this illustration is to show the merits of benchmarking even in circumstances where it might be expected to be difficult. There are obvious dangers with the 'expert opinion' methodology described – in particular the problem of 'group-think' (they are all on the wrong track), or not seeking lessons from elsewhere (perhaps other strands of research).

However, the practical question is whether this benchmarking is helpful to individual laboratories. On the positive side is the reassurance (or otherwise) that the research priorities make sense and the information can help in making commercial judgements about potential partners. The danger for a company which is on the verge of the 'breakthrough' is that they speed up the learning curve of competitors at the very time that they would need to consolidate any lead. So the benefits and pitfalls of participating in peer-group benchmarking could be finely balanced.

ILLUSTRATION 4.8

SWOT Analysis

There are a number of potential pitfalls with 'scoring' methods of analysis (NOTE: Ranking in Chapter 8 (see illustration 8.3) is another scoring method – often built from a SWOT analysis). These assignments are designed to explore these points:

- Individual items in the SWOT analysis are not equally weighted. Indeed a single factor could dominate the whole analysis at a point in time (for example, a complete privatisation of the NHS; or a wonder new cure – say, for cancer).

- Would the *formal* assigning of weighting factors (not done here) make the analysis clearer/ more accurate. We feel that, on balance it leads to confusion or 'spurious accuracy'.

- It should be stressed to students that a SWOT (or subsequent ranking) analysis will not produce 'the answer'.

- The power of the analysis is to sharpen up the debate amongst the decision matters.

Refer to the general advice is the tutors' brief for chapter-end assignment 4.9

CASE EXAMPLE

Outsourcing

How outsourcing might improve strategic capability

The purpose of this question is to ensure that students understand that the strategic capability of an organisation is much more than simply an audit of the resources which the organisation owns. The outsourcing example shows how strategic capability is also related to:

- Resources of other organisations – accessed through an outsourcing agreement

- Improved competence in activities – by 'buying in' rather than 'in-house' delivery.

- Through managing linkages – with external providers (although this could be why out-sourcing fails).

- By preventing rigidities – or the 'not invented here syndrome'.

- By benchmarking – against best external standards.

Pros and Cons of Outsourcing/Co-sourcing

The following shows how three aspects of strategy could be affected by decisions on in-house provision, outsourcing or co-sourcing:

- Customer Service Standards: Outsourced provision is more likely to deliver 'best-in-class' customer service standards – but at a cost. The judgement is whether the benefits outweigh the costs.

- Closeness to the Customer: There are other dangers that outsourcing progressively isolates the company from its customers. This loss of 'sharp-end' market feedback may prove to be very problematic on issues like product development – co-sourcing would seek to mini-mise this risk whilst taking advantage of external expertise in customer care.

- Corporate/Product Image: There are clearly worries that out-sourcing customer care detracts from the corporate and/or product image. The companies cited in the case example seem to be aware of this but have judged it a risk worth taking. Co-sourcing would reduce this risk.

Checklist for Outsourcing

The following are some of the questions which should normally be asked prior to a decision on outsourcing:

- How would outsourcing improve value-for-money in the product/service. Would it:

    a) Maintain current standards at reduced cost?

    b) Improve standards at no additional cost?

    c) Both reduce cost and improve standards?

- Is the company capable of managing the 'external linkage' (represented by outsourcing) to ensure that value-for-money does increase?

- Will the company's competence decline by outsourcing? Does this matter?

How will key stakeholders (e.g. customers) react to the outsourcing arrangement? How will any negative issues be managed?

ASSIGNMENT 4.1

Resource Audit

The main danger with an audit approach to analysing strategic capability is that students can unwittingly assume that an impressive array of resources will necessarily lead to good competitive performance. A major theme of chapter 4 is that resources *per se* are of little competitive value unless the organisation is able to deploy and manage/control the resources effectively. Assignment 4.1 is the first step in this process and should be used to underline three main points:

- the difference between *necessary* resources and *unique* resources as shown in exhibit 4.2. In particular that uniqueness must satisfy *two* criteria; better than competitors and difficult to imitate.

- it is unusual for long-term competitive advantage to be sustained purely on the basis of unique resources unless they are exceptionally robust and difficult to initiate (e.g. tight patent protection).

- resources include those which can be *accessed* as well as owned – this leads to the importance of understanding the organisation's value-chain (assignments 4.2–4.5).

ASSIGNMENTS 4.2–4.6

Competences and Core Competences

These questions are designed to assist readers in progressively improving their understanding of the value chain concept and its use in resource analysis. Beginning with the initial *mapping* of the value chain and value system in assignment 4.2 the assignments require the reader to explain the *significance* of this to competitive advantage and how the management and control of *relationships* within the value system influence the competitive position of the company. Out of this should come an understanding of the nature of competences and the importance of identifying and exploiting core competences. Normally it would be useful to undertake this complete analysis on a single company such as Laura Ashley (from the case book) or the reader's own organisation. Section 4.3 in the text provides a step-by-step guide to such an analysis. It is important that students are able to identify the following:

- The analysis must identify the issues which are *critical* to the competitive advantage rather than simply a *necessary* part of the company's activities (see exhibit 4.2).

- *Linkages* in the value chain are an important aspect of sustaining competitive advantage and should be identified (see section 4.3.5 in the text). For example, in Laura Ashley the way in which the unique *design concept is* planned and managed through factors other than the products themselves, such as shop layout, advertising themes, etc. This makes the strategy more difficult to imitate. Assignment 4.4 is intended to remind readers of the importance of a *proactive* approach to managing linkages within the value system.

- Readers need to appreciate that the configuration of the value chain and the core competences will change depending on the competitive strategy of the organisation. Within any industry individual companies will *position* themselves differently. In reviewing assignment 4.5 it is helpful if readers are able to identify two or more *strategic groups* (see chapter 3) and compare and contrast the configuration of resources which are needed to sustain competitive advantage in each group. This should underline the fact that *repositioning* of an organisation is usually a major task. Students could also be reminded that core competences will need to change over time – even in the same industry (see exhibit 4.6).

ASSIGNMENT 4.7

Portfolio Analyses

This assignment is provided to assist students in using portfolio analyses appropriately. Our experience is that many students and managers have unrealistic expectations of portfolio analysis. They often believe it to be a *prescription* of what the organisation should look like and the type of activities it should develop. In *Exploring Corporate Strategy* we suggest a much less ambitious use – as a means of checking out the balance of an organisation's activities. Students are likely to encounter some of the difficulties explained in section 4.5 of the text and they should be encouraged to discuss them and how they can be overcome by using the guidelines provided in the text.

Portfolio analysis should also raise questions about an organisation's positioning vis-à-vis the competitors in its industry. In answering the question of how a portfolio should be strengthened this should be borne in mind. For example, would the *strategic* purpose of additions or deletions to the portfolio be one of underpinning a stronger competitive performance with a similar posture or about repositioning as a deliberate strategic move?

ASSIGNMENT 4.8

Benchmarking

Like many other analytical approaches benchmarking has often been over-sold and over-simplified as a universal answer to understanding an organisation's competitive position. The purpose of this question is to ensure that readers understand that being 'best-in-class' in every separate activity which an organisation under-takes will not, in itself, result in being a 'best-in-class' performer overall. We argue strongly in Chapter 4 that competitive advantage results from the combination of (some) unique resources, core competences in separate activities and the ability to manage both internal and external linkages between activities. So benchmarking must be done at all these three 'levels' (see exhibit 4.11).

ASSIGNMENT 4.9

SWOT Analysis

The text explains our view that SWOT is most valuable as a summary/pulling together of other analyses rather than an analysis in its own right. The critical issue is, therefore, the justification of the items which students have chosen to be on their shortlists. In particular student groups usually need pressing to:

- *Avoid long lists.* For example, the lists in illustration 4.8 of four main strengths and five main weaknesses were refined from a very much longer list through a process of debate and some redefinition and grouping. This *process* of debate is valuable in itself.

- Explain the relationship between these main areas of strengths or weaknesses and the key issues in the environment. There is a danger that these are two *separate* lists and the matrix shown in illustration 4.8 forces the connections to be made.

- Recognise that individual factors may be *either* a strength for a weakness depending on the choice of strategies. This is explained in section 4.6.1 of the text.

- State *priorities* and weightings to individual factors – again through the process of using the matrix.

In summarising answers to the question it can often be useful to ask students to explain verbally in two or three sentences their *overall* assessment of the organisation's position. This is a good test as to whether or not the points above have been addressed properly.

Chapter 5

ILLUSTRATION 5.1–5.3

Corporate Governance

Refer to the tutors' brief for chapter end work assignments 5.1–5.4.

ILLUSTRATION 5.4

Stakeholder Mapping

Refer to the tutors' brief for chapter end work assignment 5.5.

This further analysis of a different strategy for Tallman gmbh not only should provide a practical mapping exercise for students, but in doing so should underline the learning points from the text and previous tutor de-brief. Even at the simplest level it should remind students that *where* stakeholders line up on a map is entirely dependent on the strategy under consideration.

ILLUSTRATION 5.5

Business Ethics

As most students will be familiar with Body Shop it is a good illustration to use to debate the respective merits of ethical stances 2, 3 and 4 in section 5.4.1 of the text (see exhibit 5.7). Indeed, it is even useful for debating what *exactly* is meant by each of these categories. Most student groups are likely to conclude that Body Shop is somewhere between categories 3 and 4 – with a dose of category 2 too.

The cynics in the group may argue for 'enlightened self interest' – which is position 2 – and credit Anita Roddick with hitting on a brilliant source of differentiation from competitors, etc. The romantics in the group will see the power of personal zeal and how it has shaped, the priorities and direction of a whole business empire. They may argue that this might have proved impossible if this wasn't a privately owned company (too many cynics in the financial world!).

The students should then repeat the process for IKEA. The stance taken in the article is presented by the *Sunday Times* as close to position 1 ('The business of business is business'). IKEA would probably argue that it is really position 2 – that they do have a concern for social conditions but they are neither the government nor the employer. So their contribution is through business and technical assistance and providing orders.

ILLUSTRATION 5.6

Cross-cultural Strategies

The questions posed allow students to reflect back on cultural/legal differences between countries that can significantly affect the circumstances in which strategies are developed.

Students may at first feel that the high priority which UK banks enjoy is the root of all our problems. But make them think hard about this. If the risks of lending are raised won't some ventures which currently get funded (and subsequently succeed) never find funding?

The final question concerns the very special nature of Eurotunnel's 'problem'. They own a £10 billion hole in the ground that has no intrinsic value. If properly utilised this hole can provide highly competitive and profitable services. But who pays for the debt? Watch this space!!

ILLUSTRATION 5.7

Organisational Purposes

See tutors' brief for chapter-end work assignment 5.11.

CASE EXAMPLE

Manchester United

Corporate Governance

This question is designed to provoke a 'healthy debate' on whether profit-maximisation for shareholders is an appropriate purpose for a football club. Many will feel that it is not. However, Manchester United *is* a plc and has legal obligations to its shareholders. If this means 'trading-up' and disregarding the needs of many traditional supporters then *can* the Directors chose not to do this?

It is likely that many students will (therefore) come to the view that a plc is *not* an appropriate form of governance for a football club. Press them to see if they are happy to live with the consequences of traditional forms of ownership or other possibilities (e.g. a registered charity). The main stumbling block will be the issue of capital for ground and other improvements – this has been the big bonus of stockmarket flotation. The supporters of the plc would say that the last eight years of the Premier League illustrate this point perfectly.

Stakeholder Mapping

If students are asked to draw up stakeholder maps against one or more future strategies, be careful to avoid suggesting that there is one 'right' map for a particular strategy. The great virtue of stakeholder mapping as a technique is that it forces out into the open a debate and discussion about the 'stance' of different stakeholders. Encourage students to read section

5.3.2 of the text and illustration 5.4 for practical advice on how to undertake a stakeholder mapping.

A stakeholder map can be used to identify *political priorities*. These will clearly depend on the outcome that is favoured. Students are required to establish political priorities for both supporters and opponents of a strategy.

Ethical Stance

This should again produce much heated debate! Manchester United Directors (in 1998) probably are close to stereotype 2 in Figure 5.7 (longer-term shareholder interests). The problem should be clear from the case. Many stakeholders believe that their stance should be either 3 (multiple stakeholder obligations) or 4 (shaper of society).

Cultural Characteristics

Get students to identify the key changes in values, beliefs and assumptions between 1990 and 1997. Some of these should have emrged from the previous questions on ethical stance, but other issues should also be surfaced. For example:

- *Values* – have clearly shifted towards a more commercial agenda.

- *Beliefs* – Rogan Taylor's quotation says it all "It is more like a disciple going to a temple" – or rather it used to be.

- *Assumptions* – get students to list assumptions in 1990 and whether they still hold good. For example:

  - professional football is played for the benefit of supporters
  - profit is only a means to an end
  - television is not a substitute for the 'real-thing'
  - football should be owned and managed by those with football in their blood.

Mission Statement

Use this question to test whether students can encapsulate their own feelings about their answers/discussions around previous questions and then turn it into something (a mission statement) which clearly conveys what they feel about the purposes of Manchester United. Use Figure 5.13 to identify different kinds of mission statements. For example:

Secretive: "To provide a better than average return to shareholders"

Procedural: "To meet all our obligations to stakeholders"

Evangelical: "To be the best known club in the world"

Political: "To remain top of the Premier League whilst promoting the image of Manchester and providing a return to shareholders".

Expect more disagreements!

ASSIGNMENTS 5.1– 5.4

Corporate Governance

This series of assignments should allow students to reflect on the importance of corporate governance to strategic development and management of individual organisations. Together they are designed to provide a test of both the broad conceptual understanding of the student (assignments 5.1 and 5.2) and some of the more detailed aspects of governance (assignments 5.1, 5.3 and 5.4) The assignments can be used to underline the following specific points from section 5.3.2 in the text:

- Governance is only one of several factors which shapes and determines the organisational purposes (exhibit 5.1). So the *links* between governance and the other main issues also need to be understood.

- There are often *conflicts of interest* – particularly for directors and managers – as the different 'needs' of stakeholders are balanced (section 5.2.1). Managers can become very distant from the beneficiaries.

- This balance of power could be shifted – for example, through changing the requirements on information/reporting (exhibit 5.2 and section 5.2.6) or introducing new practices or codes of conduct (e.g. on executive pay – the subject of assignment 5.4).

- Assignment 5.3 (two-tier boards) should be used to widen the discussion of international comparisons, and whether it is either possible or desirable to 'transplant' one tradition to a new context (section 5.2.2 and exhibit 5.4).

ASSIGNMENT 5.5

Stakeholder Analysis

Many students find the concept of stakeholders very useful in understanding the *political* dimension of strategy. However, when they are asked to undertake an analysis of stakeholders they often find this to be much more difficult than they expected. Assignment 5.5 is designed to allow students to experience these practical difficulties and learn how to undertake a useful stakeholder analysis particularly using exhibit 5.5. For those teachers using the Sheffield Theatres case study there is more detailed guidance on this matter in the teaching notes later in this manual. The specific problems which students often encounter are as follows:

- First, despite the reference to this in the text, students often try to map out stakeholders in a position which would be accurate for *all circumstances* and strategies and over time. It is important that they appreciate that the positioning of stakeholders is strongly determined by specific events and strategies and is likely to vary over time.

- Second, they often describe stakeholders in ways which are too *generic*. For example, in the Sheffield Theatres analysis students may try to plot customers as a single stakeholder group but quickly realise that this is impractical. They may need to plot regular theatre-goers separately from occasional attendees from potential customers since the interests and power of these three sub-groups are substantially different.

- Third, in some cases it is important to distinguish between an *individual* and their *role*. This is particularly important if the current incumbent of a potentially powerful role has a low level of interest since a new individual filling that role could substantially redefine the stakeholder mapping.

- Following the mapping exercise the question is designed to encourage students to consider strategies for managing stakeholders both in terms of *maintenance* activity and *repositionings* which they feel would be crucial to the success of a strategy. (The Fisons case study in the book can be used to illustrate the catastrophic effect which poor stakeholder management can bring.)

- You may also wish to help students see the connections between the concept of the value chain (chapter 4) and stakeholder analysis. Both are concerned with understanding and *managing relationships*. So, if the rules concerning those relationships change (e.g. the idea of Target Investments and the use of service level agreements in the Sheffield Theatres case) this will change the stakeholder mapping – particularly in relation to power. If you are not using the Sheffield Theatres, Iona or Fisons case, you can deal with assignment 5.5 through your own examples. Service level agreements would be a more general example of a change in relationship as would the increased autonomy of divisions or subsidiaries within a group.

ASSIGNMENTS 5.6 AND 5.7

Business Ethics

These two assignments are best used together since assignment 5.6 is concerned with the overall stance and approach to business ethics and assignment 5.7 with the action agenda. As such it can be useful to see how different stances will be reflected in the emphasis given to different items on the agenda:

- Most observers would characterise Rupert Murdoch as position type '1' in exhibit 5.7, i.e. 'Short-term Shareholder Interests' are dominant. In the popular imagination he has often been held up as an archetypal *Defender of Free Enterprise*. Students should be asked to substantiate this claim. For example, the handling of the Wapping dispute, accounting practices, and marketing practices of the News Corporation will undoubtedly engender a lively discussion in your group!

- One interesting issue worth pursuing is whether the media are a special case which require additional regulation. This is an issue relevant to the satellite TV companies – particularly as ownership patterns globalise and the purchasing power (for example, for sporting events) vastly increase their power.

- One issue often lacking in a discussion of corporate social responsibility is its relationship to *competitive standing. You* might wish to present both sides of this argument. First, can the costs really be justified. Second, can social responsibility be presented as an added-value item (for example, in the way that Body Shop had built its business – illustration 5.5). This opens up the debate about positions 2, 3 and 4 in exhibit 5.7.

ASSIGNMENT 5.8

The Cultural Web

This assignment is designed to help students analyse organisational culture in a systematic way using the cultural web as a framework and exhibit 5.1 in the text as a checklist. You will need to bear in mind the following when reviewing student work:

- Exhibit 5.11 should assist in listing out factors under each element of the cultural web to produce a diagram rather like the one for the UK National Health Service in illustration 2.7 (chapter 2). However, students must list and justify *key factors* rather than endlessly long lists. For example, in illustration 2.7 'Clinical rituals and routines' have been identified as of major importance because they institutionalise both the internal power structures of the patient/doctor relationships in ways which almost certainly need to change if many of the future aspirations of stakeholders of the NHS are to be met.

- An assessment must be made of the ease or difficulty of changing any of the factors listed on the cultural web. This provides a connection to a later use of the cultural web in chapter 11, as a checklist for managing change.

ASSIGNMENTS 5.9 and 5.10

Characterising Culture

Whereas assignment 5.8 encouraged students to analyse culture item-by-item these two questions are designed to require a holistic view of organisation culture:

- Exhibit 5.12 relates the dominant culture of an organisation to the characteristics of strategy development. Students should be asked to *justify* the categorisation of organisations against these checklists.

- If time permits it would also prove useful to ask students two further questions about their analyses. First, is the organisational culture *suitable* for the circumstances the organisation is in? It may be that a previously stable environment has become turbulent and the *defender* culture will prove to be very problematic to company survival unless a secure niche can be identified and defended. Second, how they would effect a *shift* in culture.

- Cohesiveness of culture is usually found at a level below that of the whole corporate entity so the issue of the mix of sub-cultures also needs to addressed (see section 5.5.7 in the text).

- Assignment 5.10 will require further reading by students. The primary purpose is for students to question whether a *symptoms-based analysis* based on the cultural web is adequate. For example, Schein pays particular attention to the need to analyse the paradigm of an organisation in three layers (exhibit 5.10 of the text): values, beliefs and assumptions. Do the cultural web analyses of previous questions fully unearth this? Also divergent assumptions may be held together by the corporate glue of routines, systems, symbols, etc. and there is a danger that this diversity is missed or under-rated (as mentioned in section 5.5.7 of the text).

- Students are likely to feel that their cultural web analysis has only partly achieved this depth of understanding – and they should be encouraged to suggest ways in which it can be improved to overcome this shortcoming. For example, (referring to exhibit 5.11) it is important that students do more than simply *describe* the organisation through answers to these questions but use them to *infer* what the core values/beliefs/assumptions might be. So in the NHS (illustration 2.7) the issues about jargon and white coats are important as evidence of the rigid power structures and the parent/child attitude to patient relationships.

Chapter 6

ILLUSTRATION 6.1

Ownership Structures and Strategy

Trent Buses has been through a number of ownership changes. From being part of a major conglomerate, to state ownership and to private ownership as a result of a buyout. Moreover the buyout team have latterly considered floating the company on the stock exchange. It is, therefore, a good example for considering the impact of different ownership structures.

Question 1 is useful in getting the students to think about what a private owner (in this case by means of an MBO) would consider in thinking through a successful strategy for a business. King no doubt considered the market potential (chapter 3) and internal resource capabilities and competences (chapter 4) of a privatised Trent Buses. But no doubt he also considered the personal expectations of the different stakeholders in such a company (chapter 5) and the basis of an effective competitive strategy (chapter 6) in order to be successful in a highly competitive environment.

Question 2 requires students to think through the constraints of different ownership structures. For example:

- They may readily see that under public ownership, as suggested in the illustration, there would be major constraints on investment and localised decision-making, a bureaucratised management system and more attention, perhaps, to the requirements of the government than that of the local market.

- They should, however, be encouraged to think about the constraints that a company operating as a management buyout might face. Careful consideration had to be given in Trent, as in most MBOs, to cash flow, not least because of their reliance on venture capital investors. Moreover ensuring that the various stakeholders stick together through good and difficult times is important in a MBO.

- The students might also be encouraged to take a position on whether, in King's position they would have been attracted by the idea of flotation. No doubt potentially this could have made King and his colleagues very wealthy. Would they, like King, have been as concerned about the strategy of their organisation being heavily influenced by the expectation of city analysts. Might they, perhaps, have been concerned about the potential loss of control of 'their' business?

ILLUSTRATION 6.2

Strategic Intent

Repeatedly in *Exploring Corporate Strategy* we emphasise the importance of top managers 'steering' strategy through clear intent and direction as well as their more detailed plans and actions. The strong, simple, consistent message, which reminds people about corporate direction, is well illustrated by Komatsu.

Remind students that an organisation's greatest strength is often its greatest weakness too. The obsession with Caterpillar is all very well if the world is not changing in other ways. There was a need to pay more attention to the market and less to Caterpillar. The new rallying cry became 'the total technology enterprise'.

However, students should consider the extent to which this new intent has the power of the previous 'encircling Caterpillar'. Is it too generic? Does it have sufficient focus or motivating power?

ILLUSTRATION 6.3

Focused Global Strategies

Use exhibit 6.3 in the text to identify the global levers that the focused strategy of the Mittlelstands demonstrates. For example, a national niche would not have sufficient volume to cover the R&D costs – so globalisation is essential for reasons of economies of scale. Indeed many of the criteria of exhibit 6.3 are satisfied.

The dangers of focused differentiation in general (position 5 on the Strategy Clock) are well shown in the illustration. See section 6.3.4 of the text for a general checklist.

ILLUSTRATION 6.4

The Strategy Clock

The tutors' brief for chapter-end work 6.4 should help here but some particular points should be drawn out:

- Point 1 on the Strategy Clock has often been vacated by large players in the market who have tried to add value and not compete on price in commodity type markets. Further entrants may come from low cost producer nations who can therefore compete on price. In addition they may not have an established reputation upon which to base quality.

- Trading up through 2 and 3, as the Japanese did, is an interesting phenomenon. The question requires students to consider why market leaders did not respond. Was this a function of the Japanese cost structure? The speed of innovation in Japanese firms? The inertia of existing market leaders? A mixture of all of these?

- Entering through route 5 and moving elsewhere is discussed explicitly towards the end of section 6.3.4.

ILLUSTRATION 6.5

The 'No Frills' Strategy

easyJet is a good example of a no frills strategy. The questions require students to consider the basis of such a strategy and also the extent to which it is imitable.

Clearly easyJet strategy is not based on it being *lowest* cost in the market place if this is dependent on market share in the overall market for air travel. There are obviously other bigger players. The more relevant comparison, however, is by market segment. To what extent is the early entry of easyJet into the budget travel segment and its established of a substantial market share sufficient basis, in itself, to achieve lowest cost?

Students may arrive at the conclusion that market share *per se* is no defence. However, experience in managing the basis of low cost by driving out all aspects of cost within its value chain which does not deliver the core strategy may be more powerful. easyJet concentrates, simply, on providing low prices; there is no food on its flights, it is essentially paperless in terms of its office procedures and ticketing, there are no add on services such as connecting flights, they use Luton as cheap base and, linked to this are airborne longer than competitors operating from busier airports.

The question is the extent to which actual and potential competitors, seeing the success of easyJet could imitate and overtake them in delivering such services? Does easyJet's experience in all this and its undoubted entrepreneurial culture, provide lasting advantage; or is it possible, for example, the British Airways with its GO operation and its undoubted size and muscle could be in a position to overhaul easyJet's success?

ILLUSTRATION 6.6

Differentiation

Refer to tutors' brief for chapter-end work assignment 6.6.

In particular with regard to question 2 students might wish to consider trying to identify the core competences which British Airways have built (thus referring to section 4.3 in chapter 4). They could then consider how further differentiation could be based upon these competences as well as the need to meet increasingly sophisticated customer needs.

Clearly, the BA strategy can usefully be compared with easyJet's (illustration 6.5) as a basis for discussion of different bases of competitive strategy.

ILLUSTRATION 6.7

Questionable Bases of Differentiation

Students should ask themselves whether the British Airways illustration (6.6) meets the criteria set out in section 6.3.2 and overcomes the shortcomings shown in illustration 6.7.

These considerations can then be applied to the biscuit business. Students could consider bases of differentiation assuming the primary strategic customer is the retailer. What are the real needs of retailers dealing with fast moving consumer goods companies and are there any bases of meeting these that are likely to be difficult to imitate? Students may come to the realisation that this is much more likely to be about service to retailers than just products.

ILLUSTRATION 6.8

Stuck in the Middle

The illustration paints a picture of polarisation occurring in these industries with a few broad product line companies surviving whilst others need to find a niche of some kind.

If students have the text and case version of the book it would be interesting to look at European brewers ranked by market share (exhibit 1) and ask them where the 'cut off' comes before there are dangers of being 'stuck-in-the-middle'. For example, are Bass and Courage in that position? A comparison could then be made with other industries – or even the European Automobile Industry (see exhibit 7). Are Renault 'stuck in the middle'?

An interesting question to ask about banking is the likely future of the Halifax plc. Have they converted from being the dominant Building Society into a bank that is 'stuck in the middle'?

ILLUSTRATION 6.9

Corporate Parenting

In dealing with first question it might be appropriate to get students to work from a Unilever annual report to undertake a growth share matrix exercise. They may come to the conclusion that this would lead them to look for balance between cash cows (which might include food and detergents) and faster growing product sectors (which might include some personal products). They might also debate as to whether or not tea plantations and animal feeds are cash cows or dogs. However the emphasis here is on growth markets; and the need for the spread of investments between potential growth and businesses in mature markets yielding cash. On the other hand, the emphasis in the use of the parenting matrix is to do with the competences of the centre and the match between the competences of the centre and the businesses. The conclusion such an exercise comes to is that the businesses at the heart of the enterprise are those which can benefit most from the development of competences at the business level through value adding competences existing in the centre. This place is the food businesses at the heart of Unilever.

The second question can usefully be examined in relation to the chapter-end case for chapter 10 on Unilever. The starting point here is the recognition by Unilever that its central skills are to do with service elements such as research and development and marketing; but that its growth is likely to come from its ability to handle localised markets. The chapter-end case shows that Unilever has moved to (or reinforced) its commitments to 'growth at the periphery' by passing decision-making down to its fourteen consumer goods businesses organised by regions. It is recognised that the centre will play less of a role and act more as a skills resource with regard to these businesses. The three industrial goods companies, however, are organised globally with much more central influence; but these are recognised as not being at the heart of Unilever's business. This, of course, raise two questions. Where will Unilever go in terms of the development of its businesses in the future (will there be further disposals of the non heartland businesses for example); and what does this say for consumer-based businesses that they, themselves, recognise as actually or potentially global-ising (such as the detergents business?)

CASE EXAMPLE

The Virgin Group

This case allows students to consider issues raised in chapter 6. In particular:

- The relevance of the ownership structure of Virgin.

- The role of the corporate centre in relation to business units.

- The competitive positioning of businesses within the group.

In this sense it is a basis for considering some of the *bases* of strategy discussed in Chapter 6.

The main points the case can be used to consider include:

- The ownership structure of Virgin has changed from a private company to a publicly quoted company and back again to a private company over the years. Students might be encouraged to consider the advantages and disadvantages of these different ownership structures in two ways:

  a) The extent to which ownership structures influence strategies; but also
  b) The extent to which ownership is influenced by the strategies Branson wishes to follow.

For example, Branson found that institutional investors found it difficult to understand the nature of his company and the way he ran it. He elected to take it back into private ownership to give more latitude in this respect. However, other students might argue that there is little evidence from the data of a high degree of success from many of the businesses: they might argue that the discipline of public ownership would be beneficial (but to whom?).

- What is the role of the centre?

Different positions can be taken here:

a) Is the Virgin group just a holding company with a common brand? Clearly Virgin do not see it this way.

b) Is it, on the other hand, a traditional corporate group. Clearly not: it does not see its roles, for example, as balancing a portfolio, looking for related businesses in the conventional sense or striving for synergies.There is little attempt to transfer skills and expertise across businesses. So what is the role of the centre (e.g. in relation to exhibit 6.6 in the text).

c) Arguably it is a classic example of how the competences of the centre (not the businesses) are used to enhance the value of businesses − the ultimate parenting test (see section 6.4.3). The centre is slim (less than 20 people) it seeks out particular sorts of businesses: those in 'institutionalised markets' who have Virgin-type customers and can benefit from PR low cost based marketing. It brings particular parenting skills to bear: particularly the brand, PR skills, the Branson name and the ratcheting up of opportunities to break into markets by entrepreneurs.

d) Students might consider the extent to which there is evidence of success of this within the portfolio (clearly some businesses are more successful than others).

- The case also provides and opportunity to consider the basis of strategic positioning of some of the businesses. For example:

a) Virgin Atlantic, one of the most successful businesses within the group, can be compared the illustrations provided for British Airways and easyJet in Chapter 6. Such a comparison should show that Virgin is following a strategy of differentiation (as is BA) whereas easyJet is following a strategy of low price.

b) In turn comparisons with BA can be made (often with direct experience from those in the class) as to what the bases of differentiation are. The conclusion might be that they both provide service to customers but perhaps to different customer segments in different ways and with differing perceived success depending on the customer.

c) However students may consider that the strategies of the two are converging; and the evidence from the battles for dominance on transnational routes would suggest that the two companies see this too. So what should Virgin Atlantic do next?

ASSIGNMENT 6.1

Stakeholder Influence on Purpose and Strategy

The aim of this assignment is to require students to relate the influence of stakeholders (discussed in chapter 5) with issues of corporate governance (chapter 5) and strategy formulation (chapter 2). It is helpful in undertaking the assignment if students are asked to consider more than one organisation for this purpose, preferably organisations with different patterns of stakeholders.

Students might use exhibit 5.5 to map the influence of different stakeholders in the chosen organisations. They would see that an important stakeholder in IKEA is Ingvar Kamprad, although by 1996 he had no active part in strategic decision- making in the firm. His influence was more to do with the purpose of the organisation than specific strategic decisions. Other stakeholders, such as executives in IKEA, might have more direct power in terms of strategy formulation, but would be unlikely to take such decisions if they were not in line with overall purpose.

In some respects this situation approximates to that in the NHS. A major stakeholder is the UK government which has a strong influence on the purpose of the NHS, though it is executives who take particular strategic decisions. But what, here, of the aspirations and expectations of the community (actual or potential users)? And how much influence do they have?

The situation is evidently different in an organisation such as the Body Shop or News Corporation where Roddick and Murdoch are active in an executive capacity as well as being founders and a strong influence on purpose. However, certainly in the case of the Body Shop the expectation of shareholders and customers, would exercise a significant constraint on a change in the purpose of the organisation even in the unlikely event of the executives wishing to pursue strategies contrary to it.

In the case of the News Corporation, the aspirations of Murdoch to create an influential media network is well known internally and to external stakeholders (e.g. shareholders and banks). It might also be useful to ask students to compare such a situation with stakeholder patterns in organisations in which the stakeholder positions are less clear: a major multinational such as Shell, perhaps. Several questions arise: which stakeholders influence the purpose of the organisation? is there a clear purpose anyway? and what are the constraints on the executives' influence on strategy?

All these examples allow an exploration of the corporate governance question of who the executives of an organisation are answerable to and for what? Students might be asked to consider how they would answer such a question if they were a senior executive in any of the organisations considered in this assignment. They may well conclude that they would be much clearer about this in some organisations than others. For example, it might be easier in an organisation such the Body Shop or the News Corporation where there is a clarity of purpose associated with a dominant leader. In an organisation such as the NHS the situation may be more difficult. An executive might recognise the dominant stakeholder influence of the government but actually align more with a less dominant influence such as patients. Arguably in some other organisations, perhaps a multinational such as Shell, the question is even less clear, since it is more difficult to identify specific stakeholders with direct or dominant influence.

ASSIGNMENT 6.2

Privatisation of Public Services

These notes will not attempt to set out the arguments for or against the privatisation of public services. The assignment will, however, require students to consider this and perhaps undertake reading on this topic (see, for example, sections 1.3.5 and 6.2.1. See also relevant chapter references in these chapters).

The main purpose of the assignment is to require students to consider the question of privatisation of public services in the context of benefits to either users or taxpayers. This question raises, then, the issues of who the beneficiaries of such services are and what they value. In turn this raises:

• the importance of defining key beneficiaries (equivalent to key customers) in the public services;

• the trade-off of benefits between beneficiaries in the public services;

• the extent to which this is made more apparent because of privatisation; and the extent to which this is desirable.

Exhibit 6.4 could be used to require students to consider potential benefits of added value (e.g. in terms of choice, flexibility, speed of service, etc. to users) and lower cost to taxpayers or price (to users) according to perceived needs of users and taxpayers.

There are a number of issues that might be taken into account here:

- The extent to which different patterns of benefits to users or taxpayers emerge for different public services (e.g. health services compared with railways compared with water);

- The extent to which there is benefit to *both* the users and taxpayers for a given privatised service; or if the benefits to one conflict with the other;

- The extent to which differences emerge according to different types of users; for example, industrial buyers versus consumers for rail services; or well-off users of health services versus the unemployed.

ASSIGNMENT 6.3

Benefits and Drawbacks of Geographic Scope

For Burmah Castrol (Chemicals)

	Cost reduction	Quality	Customer requirements and leverage	Coordination costs
Global market participation	Probably few benefits given local sourcing and production	Quality service demanded by most sophisticated buyers could raise general quality	Building experience faster than competitors. Ability to service global customers	Difficulties of ensuring uniform quality of products and service
Global Products/ Services		Potential benefits of global standards of products and services; learning from best practice	Provides opportunities for entry into growth markets worldwide	Danger of growing diversity of products due to respons-iveness to local markets
Location of activities	Mainly localised servicing of customers + central control not an aid to cost reduction	Local nature of many SBUs could create problems in maintaining consistent service quality, potentially harming global reputation	Localised delivery means small-scale local competitors may be present with lower prices	Coordination problems and costs inevitably high given local location of activities

The purpose of this assignment is to require students to understand the benefits and problems of globalisation. The checklist in exhibit 6.3 can be applied to different organisations with different global strategies, and students will see that there are different benefits and drawbacks depending on those strategies. For example, if the benefits of globalisation for a corporation following an essentially global strategy (e.g. Ford) are examined in relation to one which is less global, then the reasons why a company like Ford is following a more global strategy become apparent. The suggestion in this assignment, however, is that an organisation with a more 'transnational' approach might be used so that the student might see how an organisation which is simultaneously trying to develop elements of global strategy but with local service provision experiences both benefits and drawbacks by so doing. The exhibit above relating to this assignment uses elements of exhibit 6.3 of the text as a model for showing the sort of benefits, problems and drawbacks the students might identify in this regard for Burmah Castrol (Chemicals), but also a similar approach could be applied to e.g. KMPG or even Brewery Group Denmark.

ASSIGNMENT 6.4

Understanding Competitive Strategies

The aim of assignments 6.4 and 6.5 is to develop students' understanding of competitive strategy concepts. Assignment 6.4 requires students to give examples of organisations according to the routes identified in exhibit 6.4 in the text and explain reasons for doing this. It allows the tutor to check if students understand the bases of the different routes. It may also raise the question as to whether the competitive strategy of a given organisation is clear — which is the subject of assignment 6.5.

- Route 1, the low-price, low-added value route is often overlooked. There are successful organisations following such a strategy. For example, the grocery retail outlet Netto is cited in the text. Also, as markets open up, new entrants may choose to follow this strategic route and easyJet is provided as an illustration of a no frills, low-price service.

- Route 2 is the low price strategy. It is often followed by small businesses competing against larger companies. They use their lower cost base to provide products or services which are very similar to the large organisations at a lower price. One danger here is the confusion between cost and price (see assignments 6.5 and 6.7).

- The Japanese in the car industry had used their cost advantages not only to deliver low price but also to re-invest in high quality and reliability. In many respects they were following route 3 for much of the 1980s and early 1990s. IKEA might be another example (see illustration 1.1) of an organisation successfully combining both low prices and perceived added value to the customer.

- Route 4 is a broad differentiation strategy; the sort of strategy followed, by a company such as Kellogg's in seeking to provide quality in terms of product, delivery, service, brand image, market support and product development superior to competitors.

- Other organisations claim to be following a differentiation strategy but the bases of differentiation in terms of added value to customer may not be clear. Firms may claim to be different but on a spurious basis (see illustration 6.6), for example.

- Route 5 is focused differentiation, examples of this might be a focus on clear demographic groups. For example, Saga specialise in insurance and holidays for the over-50s; fashion retailers and manufacturers seek to identify customers with particular tastes in fashion; industrial product companies may focus on particular industries or particular process needs.

ASSIGNMENT 6.5

Clarity of Competitive Strategy

Assignment 6.4 may raise questions about the clarity of competitive strategies. The sort of issues which may be surfaced are these:

- Peugeot raises the question of whether *cost reduction is* a viable competitive strategy. Many organisations claim to concentrate on cost reduction as a strategy. But how does this provide long term competitive advantage? Will it achieve the ability to price lower than competition in market terms? Peugeot's strategy of reducing costs substantially had led to improved performance, but it had not given them competitive advantage over comparable lower-priced Japanese cars.

In turn this raises the question of the extent to which Peugeot has, or can develop, a clear strategy which *does* provide a basis for competitive advantage. The teaching note on the case study discusses this.

- The teaching notes on Laura Ashley explore how the company experienced differing levels of success at different stages of its life. Arguably, its early success was because of the combination of skills and abilities of its founders also played a direct role in management; these created a set of *core competences* which clearly differentiated the company. Arguably as the company grew, its strategies became more ambitious and its geographic scope widened, these core competences were decreasingly evident.

- Similar questions and issues can be explored for other organisations. To what extent can the traces of their strategy be identified?

ASSIGNMENT 6.6

Differentiation

The purpose of this assignment is to establish if students are able to explain the concept of differentiation not only in terms of 'being different' or by citing the importance of route 4 in exhibit 6.4 in chapter 6, but rather in terms of, for example:

- That differentiation means both providing products or services valued by customers/users and doing this in ways which are difficult to imitate.

- This is likely to be achieved by building on core competences of the organisation which, themselves, are likely to be bundles of resources or capabilities rather than a particular resource, product or technology. Students should therefore be able to explain the links between the notion of differentiation and concepts such as core competences, linkages in the value chain, the importance of tacit knowledge and experience (arguably linked to the culture of organisations) and how all these may play a part in organisations achieving lasting bases of differentiation.

- However, the more perceptive students may point out that this is difficult to achieve and difficult to manage. That organisations may not be able to create bases of non-irritability readily. That for other organisations differentiation may be achieved by being flexible or faster to respond in markets than competitors, but that this, too, is a function of the culture of the organisation. Students should therefore be able to make linkages between the concepts and differentiation explained in chapter 6 and linkages in the value chain (chapter 4) and organisational culture (chapter 5).

- Overall, however, perhaps the most important basis of successful differentiation is the ability of an organisation to understand customer needs and what is valued by the customer better than competitors: And that there is a danger that differentiation is driven on technical grounds rather than by an awareness of customer needs.

ASSIGNMENT 6.7

Cost Leadership as a Strategy

If students undertake this assignment they should be expected to read *Competitive Strategy* (1980) by Michael Porter as well as the critique of his work cited in reference 13 in chapter 6.

In his book, Porter claimed that there were three fundamental ways in which firms can achieve sustainable competitive advantage. These include differentiation and focus but also include cost leadership. Since that time there have been a number of critiques of Porter's original arguments in this regard. These are not discussed in the text extensively but it is recognised that Porter's arguments have had a strong influence and it may therefore be useful to include some points here that students might raise or tutors might point out.

There are problems linked to the notion of *sustainable cost leadership*. Porter does not mean short-term cost advantage, or just low cost. Sustainable cost leadership means having the lowest cost compared with competitors over time. This is unlikely to be achieved simply by pruning costs: competitors can and will do that too. The question, then, is how competitive advantage can be achieved – if at all – through cost leadership.

It has been argued that cost leadership can be achieved by means of *substantial relative market share advantage* because this provides a firm with cost advantages through economies of scale, market power (for example, buying power) and experience curve effects (see chapter 4). However, it is not clear what 'substantial relative market share advantage' means: specifically what level of relative share advantages might be required.

In developing strategy, it is in any case dangerous to assume a direct link between relative market share advantage and sustainable advantage in the market because there is little evidence of sustainability. Dominant firms lose market share, and others overtake them.

Arguably market share itself is not what is important but rather the advantages that it can bestow. High relative share advantage can and should give cost advantages but if managers do not manage the business to achieve these advantages they will be lost and smaller-share businesses may overtake them.

Porter also describes the idea of cost leadership as if it is applicable across a whole industry as well as being applicable in market segments. This is a very important distinction. If the idea of cost leadership is to be taken seriously as an industry-wide strategy, it is problematic for all but a very few firms – indeed, arguably in a given industry, for all but one firm. It is therefore not a strategy which is generally applicable across an industry.

Porter has used the terms 'cost leadership' and 'low price' as though they are interchangeable. This cannot be: cost is an input measure to a firm, whereas price is an output measure. Because a firm is pursuing a cost leadership or cost reduction strategy, it does not necessarily mean that it will choose to price lower than competition. For example, it may choose to invest higher margins in R&D, or marketing – arguably what Kellogg's or Mars do.

The confusion between 'low cost' and 'low price' was shown in one illustration used in the 3rd edition of *Exploring Corporate Strategy* (reproduced as an additional teaching aid, see below). Porter argues that Sainsbury cannot be following a differentiation strategy because it advertises low prices. David Sainsbury finds this problematic, since his view is that Sainsbury is trying to keep down costs so that it can reinvest in unique benefits to the customer, as well as reducing price – and successfully so. Although Porter says that this is being 'stuck in the middle' and is dangerous, the evidence is that firms can do it successfully.

The generic strategy of Sainsbury

Michael Porter and David Sainsbury, chief executive of Sainsbury, discuss the generic strategy of the UK's largest grocery supermarket chain.

In a Thames Television programme in 1987 Michael Porter held a round table discussion of his principles of generic strategy with UK executives. In this conversation the following exchange too place between Michael Porter and David Sainsbury.

Sainsbury: I think Michael's ... discussion is enormously helpful in terms of how one looks for competitive advantage. The one bit I don't agree with is the idea that if you are stuck in the middle, that's some great disadvantage, because it seems to me that you do have customers who are only interested in price – in the food market it's quite a small bit, probably 10 per cent of the market. At the other end, you've got some people who are interested only in quality and will pay anything to get it. But the great majority of people are interested in both quality and price, which is summed up in the phrase 'really good value for money'. I think you can have a strategy which is focused, as we are, absolutely on that middle range. We're not ... interested in pure quality regardless of price, or just the price end of the market.

Porter: I think it's a very important point. David has shown me a model of a little truck which has the emblem of Sainsbury's on it. It say 'Good Food Costs Less at Sainsbury's'. I think that statement captures the positioning of Sainsbury's ... Now the question is, can you be low-cost and differentiated at the same time? If I read the slogan on the truck it says good food costs less. So I would say, your quality is good, but not unique. Your real strategy is low-cost, and that's your real source of advantage. You're not trying to both beat your competitors on having better quality food than theirs and be lower-cost in supplying it. Ultimately, if I read you correctly, you perceive your real advantage is going to be cost, but you're going to make sure your food is as good a quality as anybody else's ... If I went to Tesco and to Marks and Spencer and looked at their quality – I would find comparable quality. I wouldn't find better quality at Sainsbury's ... The ultimate test of differentiation, in my way of thinking, is do you command a premium price? How does Sainsbury's meet that test?

Sainsbury: I think you can make superior profits if at the same time you can keep costs down, and have prices which are competitive, and get tremendous turnover. Then you get cost advantages which enable you to actually make superior profits without commanding a premium price, because you can have the lower price.

Source: Used with permission from the *European Management Journal*, vol. 6, no. 1 (1987).

ASSIGNMENT 6.8

Competitive Strategies in the Public Sector

You may wish to refer back to some of the general comments about the concept of competition in the public services (assignment 3.8 in chapter 3).

Care then needs to be taken around the terminology – particularly because an overt price mechanism may not exist in some public services. So, referring to exhibit 6.4 in the text, in public services price may equate to *unit* cost since performance will be judged against the input of resources to supply the service. So the routes can then be described as follows:

- Route 1, low-cost/low-value: this is the outcome many claim is inevitable with public spending cuts leading to the unattractive positioning as a *service of last resort*. In the UK critics of the Conservative government of the 1990s argued this was the outcome of their policies towards the NHS.

- Route 2: this is the real challenge for many public services, the need to maintain quality whilst achieving progressive *efficiency gains*. It is what the Conservative government claimed it was trying to promote for the NHS.

- Routes 4 and 5 is an alternative for some parts of some public services and would be described as a *centre of excellence* strategy. It was this strategy adopted by parts of the NHS (e.g. some hospitals or units in hospitals) which sought to establish specialist reputations.

ASSIGNMENT 6.9

Parent Enhancement of SBU Strategies

This assignment requires students to assess how corporate parents add value, or could add value, to the strategies of their SBUs.

If the examples of the cases Burmah Castrol and the News Corporation are employed, then it is likely the students will recognise that Burmah Castrol has increasingly recognised the need for the centre to address this problem and is attempting to do so by building mechanisms whereby the centre can act in encouraging the transference of skills and, certainly in the case of Burmah Castrol Chemicals Group, in encouraging collaboration and co-operation between SBUs where appropriate. Students may also have recognised that in the case of Burmah Castrol Chemicals Group there have been elements of the Restructurer in their recent past.

Students may think that the News Corporation acts more in the role of a Restructurer, with the centre intervening more directly in SBUs where they deem it appropriate to transform business performance, direct strategy, and so on.

There are some additional points worth noting in this assignment:

- Section 9.4.1 in Chapter 9 provides a checklist of ways in which the centre can add value to SBUs in rather more detail. This is a useful checklist for students to draw upon in this exercise.

- Another way for students to undertake this assignment is for them to identify corporations for each role of corporate parent identified in exhibit 6.6. They can do this from the case studies and press commentaries with which they are familiar, for example. However, in each case they should be asked to justify why they have categorised them as they do and provide evidence from the checklist in Chapter 9 as to the activities undertaken by the parent.

- Another approach to this assignment is to ask students to consider the changing roles of corporate centres. For example, students might consider the changing role of Unilever centre (see notes on illustration 6.9 and the Chapter 10 case example) and compare this with other corporate centres. For example, they might consider the questions raised by Mike Dearden in the Burmah Castrol case, or the sorts of questions raised in a de-merger such as that of ICI, which resulted from the centre questioning how it could enhance SBU strategies more than it had done in the past.

Chapter 7

ILLUSTRATION 7.1

Development Directions

Refer to the tutors' brief for chapter-end work assignment 7.1.

The Marks and Spencer example is interesting as it shows an organisation planning to develop along several directions simultaneously:

- Consolidation (re-equipping stores)
- Market penetration (more space, Littlewoods stores)
- New segments (mega-stores, home-shopping, Brooks Brothers).
- New territories (Continental Europe, Hong Kong, Poland, Australia)
- Product Development (food)

Note that diversification is not included in their plans.

Ensure that students have a basis on which to 'evaluate' each of these options. Test the suitability against: market opportunity, organisation's competences and 'culture'.

The major concerns are that the organisation will be overstretched by pushing out on so many fronts simultaneously and that there are some inconsistencies – particularly in relation to the M&S image. For example, will the image be compromised by moving 'down-market' into mega-stores and a supermarket food portfolio?

ILLUSTRATION 7.2

Market Development

A straightforward illustration of market development including:

- continued geographical spread
- expansion into related segments (air-borne)
- reconsideration of development method (using acquisition to gain market share quickly in Italy).

ILLUSTRATIONS 7.3–7.6

Diversification

Refer to tutors' brief for chapter-end work assignments 7.4–7.6 and 7.8.

This is a collection of material that should allow students to become well versed on the advantages and disadvantages of diversification. In using this material try to refer students to the relevant discussion in the text. For example:

- They should use exhibit 7.9 to *classify* the various diversifications in the illustration.

- They can use exhibits 7.10 and 7.11 to *assess* the reasons why diversification might make sense (e.g. the insurance companies and the AA).

- They should be pressed to consider whether or not the companies in the illustration would have the necessary *competences* to support the strategy.

- Illustration 7.6 has been provided so that students can see that many diversifications have not worked out and companies are choosing to *specialise* by *de-merger*. Use exhibits 7.10 and 7.11 in *reverse* to assess the benefits of specialisation.

ILLUSTRATION 7.7

Mergers and Acquisitions

Refer to tutors' brief for chapter end work assignments 7.9.

ILLUSTRATION 7.8

Strategic Alliances

The purpose of these questions is to assess the extent to which public/private sector partnerships were simply designed with a cultural/political purpose in mind (to weaken the 'old guard' public sector management attitudes) or would stand up to a more 'commercial' appraisal of their worth.

The broad conclusion of the PFI example is as follows:

- The long-term benefits of PFI would be one of accessing private sector capital for public sector purposes.

- The immediate gain of improving management performance in the public sector by 'benchmarking' best practice was also useful but will quickly run its course. It is not a basis on which PFI would survive long-term since 'best-in-class' public sector managers would provide services at a level which then would make them unattractive 'targets' for the private sector (who would need also to make a profit margin).

Also refer to tutors' brief for chapter end work assignments 7.9 and 7.10.

CASE EXAMPLE

Lonely Planet

Directions of Development

As well as simply listing the 'pure' examples of development direction, ensure that students identify the fact that some developments are *by necessity* a combination of these pure types.

For example:

- Entry into France required a new (French language) product. This in turn required involvement in translation.

- Consolidation in the late 1990s requires new product development in response to multimedia development – for example, the need for the web site.

The pattern of developments is essentially incremental and cautious – which explains why other developments did not occur. In particular they have remained very focused in choice of market segment (back-packers). Nor have they been tempted to diversify to a whole range of associated products for back-packers.

The personal values of the Wheelers are quite central to this clear focus as seen in the quotations towards the end of the case example.

Methods of Development

Cautious, focused and incremental development of the type we see in Lonely Planet is usually characterised by a predominance of internal development and an aversion to acquisition. Joint ventures are used where they are necessary (e.g. franchising activities where the company does not have the resources or expertise). Lonely Planet's development is very typical of this approach. You might wish to ask students to identify opportunities that have been missing by this approach. Multi-media partnerships (e.g. with Microsoft) is the obvious example.

The Future

The closing comments from the Wheelers indicate that radical change is unlikely as long as they remain in control. So students need to take account of this in their analysis.

However, you might find it useful to ask students to identify development opportunities which they would support if the Wheelers were bought out. Again multi-media is an obvious choice. 'Trading up' into other segments of the travel guide market may be possible/sensible given their well-established name.

ASSIGNMENT 7.1

Strategic Options

The purpose of this assignment is to ensure that students are clear that a viable development strategy for an organisation will require a *consistent* package of three elements to the strategy. First, the broad basis of the strategy (as discussed in Chapter 6), second the development direction – covered in section 7.2 and third the development method covered in section 7.3. This is an issue where we have found that students are usually less than clear. There are many ways in which this point can .be emphasised with students and the question suggests several examples. In the case of Cooper's Creek – a small winemaker in New Zealand – they are clearly having to pursue a strategy *of focused differentiation* (point 5 on the strategy clock). Their cost base is too high for positionings 1, 2 or 3 and their resources are too limited for positioning 4. The students should then be asked to evaluate whether the development directions (market development into *selected* international markets) and their development method (internal development but with support from industry based association and concentration on a few large retail buyers, e.g. Tesco) are consistent. The teaching notes for the case study will help.

ASSIGNMENT 7.2

Evaluating Strategy Positions

In order to complete this assignment students need to relate both generalised strategic analysis of an industry and an analysis of the strategies being followed by individual companies in the context of Japanese incursions. For example, with regard to the entry of Japanese firms in the automobile industry, and the effects on Peugeot or Rover, the assignment requires students to examine the strategic position of these firms and the wisdom of the strategy being followed by the firms in the light of this. Given relatively static demand, over capacity, demands to reduce pollution, and the entry of other Far Eastern competitors, how well positioned are the firms? This requires the students to identify the strategies of the firms — not only in terms of their positioning but the implications to both development directions and methods.

- It appears that Rover was trying to focus its strategy more and build on the joint venture with the Japanese for the purpose of product development and realignment. Does this make sense and how does the BMW takeover affect this? (see the teaching notes).

- The Peugeot strategy is much more to do with keeping down costs, improving quality, but also arguing for *protection* against the Japanese. But are these effective defences against Japanese incursions? (again see the teaching note).

Peugeot and Rover are, therefore, good examples of different responses to the Japanese threat. This raises the question of whether one or the other was in a more advantageous position. If students believe one was indeed better positioned than the other; or that neither were well positioned, then it is worthwhile asking why they think this and what are the *implications* for strategies to combat Japanese incursions?

This discussion can be related back to the strategy clock concept to discuss possible strategic positioning against the Japanese. The really successful Japanese firms have based their strategies on low price and differentiation (the hybrid strategy), though they are increasingly enhancing quality and bases of differentiation — around, for example, service. If the students feel that the Peugeot or Rover strategies were unlikely to be successful, it might be useful to ask them what strategies would be successful.

Students may be critical of Calvet's approach in arguing for protectionist measures against the Japanese. However, he argued that the hybrid strategy followed by Japanese competitors in the automobile industry was only made possible because of what were effectively protectionist approaches in Japan. The debate can, therefore, usefully be broadened to more generalised industry-wide issues.

The automobile industry is used here as an example, but, of course, the same sort of debate could be undertaken for any of the industries in which Japanese incursion has taken place.

ASSIGNMENT 7.3

PIMS

Students find the PIMS research findings (for example, exhibits 7.3 to 7.7) very interesting but then fail to test their own organisation's strategies against the messages which emerge from PIMS. This assignment invites students to do just this. Two words of advice:

- Some students may try to use the PIMS findings as a *general prescription*. This is not the best use of the data base. Rather students should be asked to explain how the key findings might relate to specific strategies in specific companies.

- Depending on the time available, it could be useful for students to read the original PIMS newsletters rather than just the small selection we have included in the text of *Exploring Corporate Strategy.*

ASSIGNMENTS 7.4–7.6 and 7.8

Diversification

These assignments require students to consider the routes for diversification of an organisation. Exhibit 7.9 provides a basis for this. One way of undertaking assignments 7.4 and 7.5 is to ask students to map onto that exhibit the diversification undertaken by an organisation concerned. In many annual reports, students will be able to find lists of the interests of diversified firms. If the News Corporation case is used for assignment 7.5, appendix 2 in the case provides a listing of major acquisitions and disposals which could be used for this purpose. The students might identify the following:

The main product area for the News Corporation was newspapers and in this sense the students might see this as the *core* business and place it at the centre of the exhibit (i.e. in the box marked 'manufacturer'). Other interests can be mapped onto the rest of the exhibit.

- *Complementary products* include television stations, magazines and books.

- There has been *backward integration* into film and video production.

- There has also been very limited *forward integration* into encryption technology and telecommunications joint ventures. (which might also be regarded as backward integration for supply purposes).

- Some of the other diversified interests are less easy to position on exhibit 7.9; and this might usefully lead to a discussion of what is meant by *related and unrelated diversification.*

Students will, therefore, see that diversification has been achieved through a combination of horizontal, backward and forward integration. They might compare this with other organisations – for example, by answering assignment 7.8.

Assignment 7.6 has been added in this new edition of the book since the period from the mid-1990s was characterised by many high profile examples of de-mergers. The danger, of course, is more 'fashion and fad' behaviour amongst managers so students should be asked to consider how the examples in illustration 7.6 might stack up against the (reverse) checklist for unrelated diversification (exhibit 7.11). Again it is also likely to raise the question as to what exactly 'related' and 'unrelated' mean as discussed in section 7.2.4 of the text.

ASSIGNMENT 7.7

Synergy

This assignment is provided as a possible student assessment requiring further reading and linking diversification (a *direction* of development in section 7.2.4) with acquisition (a *method* of development in section 7.3.2). Students may also find exhibit 7.12 useful in asking the question as to whether the best conditions for synergy are likely to be created by internal development, acquisition or joint ventures/alliances. For example, an acquisition may provide the pressure to change but not the acceptance from the (new) SBUs.

ASSIGNMENT 7.9 and 7.10

Acquisitions, Mergers and Alliances

Section 7.3 and exhibit 7.13 in the text set out some reasons for different forms of alliance and acquisition. The purpose of this assignment is to ask students to consider reasons for such moves. The teaching note for Rover/Honda gives a good deal of background to the rationale for that joint venture; as do Illustrations 7.7 and 7.8 in the IT, and engineering industries and the public sector. However, you should also be looking to surface the reasons for mergers or acquisitions being followed rather than alliances (or vice versa). For example, exhibit 7.13 suggests that:

The main reason for the distinction between formal acquisitions and joint ventures are to do with the extent to which assets can be *separated* and the risk of assets being appropriated.

The implication is that joint ventures are more likely where assets can be separated and there is a low risk of appropriation of assets. It might be interesting to question the extent to which this logic applies to the examples given above:

1. It is at least arguable that there is a risk of appropriation of assets for the Rover/Honda joint venture.

2. The PFI initiative (illustration 7.8) might be viewed as having a significant political element – 'shaking up' the public sector.

Assignment 7.10 invites students to consider more fully one of the important findings of David Faulkner's research (see Recommended Key Readings, Chapter 7), and therefore, to read more fully around the issue of strategic alliances and company performance.

Chapter 8

ILLUSTRATION 8.1

Value Chain Analysis

Synergy is often the rationale suggested to justify particular strategy developments. In this illustration the extent of synergy is assessed for three different 're-configurations of the value chain'.

In all cases the strategies provide an opportunity to use the excess cash from current operations. Strategy 1 looks the most attractive – but note that a large part of the advantage is gained by exploiting his current name more widely and through increasing his purchasing power. He would need to be clear that both of these were likely to become real benefits.

Question 2 is concerned with issues of management control. With a string of shops he will need to hire managers and to shift his general effort to 'group work' issues such as purchasing and marketing (the two items which underpin the case for expansion). But is he competent to do this? The classic small business expansion dilemma.

ILLUSTRATION 8.2

Business Profiling (PIMS)

This illustration is designed to encourage students to consider the practical application of the PIMS database. The answers to the questions posed are:

- It is quite probable that a more qualitative assessment (perhaps as in illustration 8.1) might have put forward a plausible case for backward integration (at least when vertical integration was 'in fashion'). In that sense the PIMS profiling analysis would have been a surprise.

- The danger of all of these 'quasi-scientific' analyses (ranking and decision-trees share this danger) is that decision-makers expect a decision to emerge from the analysis. This is not how the data in illustration 8.2 should be used. Rather it should sharpen up the debate about the pros and cons of buying the supplier – and why it might run the risk of combining the weaknesses of the partners rather than their strengths.

ILLUSTRATION 8.3

Ranking

Refer also to tutors' brief for chapter-end work assignment 8.3.

The purpose of these questions is (again) to discourage students from believing that 'an answer' will emerge from the analysis. Students need to be able to argue for strategy 4 on a number of grounds. For example:

- It fits the circumstances well (most ticks), *but* in itself that should not justify its selection. Perhaps what is really needed is something that *transforms* this conservative family business (like opening retail outlets)?

- The family would support it (but again is this what 'the business' really needs). But if the family can't be persuaded the strategy will not be adopted.

ILLUSTRATION 8.4

Decision Trees

- The same eight options would be generated irrespective of sequence of criteria (remember, of course, that these are not the only eight options available to the firm).

- A fourth parameter (internal development or acquisition) will create a total of sixteen options. The current eight will each create two. For example, number 4 'gain market share' would divide into:

a) gain market share; hire legal assistants
b) gain market share; acquire competitors

- With four parameters it starts to become clear that these are not independent parameters. For example, it could be argued that all options requiring acquisition infer the need for high investment funds. So the acquisition of a direct local competitor should be excluded. In contrast the acquisition of a firm specialising in matrimonial law or geographical spread by acquisition should be kept in the tree. They both appear on the 'high investment' arm of the tree.

ILLUSTRATION 8.5

Cost-Benefit Analysis

Refer to tutors' brief for chapter-end work assignment 8.5.

ILLUSTRATION 8.6

Shareholder Value Analysis

This illustration is provided to exemplify the issues raised in the text discussion of shareholder-value analysis. The overall message is that crude, historically based accounting measures are not reliable when assessing the actual value created by major projects. Despite the difficulties of value-analysis, compounded by the uncertainties of forecasting considerable periods ahead, it is one way of assessing the 'value' of projects and the risks involved.

Some would argue that in situations of such great uncertainty good risk analysis is not enough. The company also needs to be good at those activities that could help reduce risk:

- monitoring of the environment and rapid feedback;

- contingency plans to cope with different emerging environments;

- a spread of risk in terms of the business portfolio;

- a strong balance sheet to ride out some failures.

ILLUSTRATION 8.7

Sensitivity Analysis

Refer to tutors' brief for chapter-end work assignment 8.6.

ILLUSTRATION 8.8

Funds Flow Analysis

- The major concern with this analysis is whether the capital investment has been accurately costed at £13.25 million. Other elements of the analysis are regarded as more accurate.

- This is not an uncommon situation and decision-makers are advised to give preliminary approval until firm quotations are obtained.

- Another concern might be the impact on the numbers during the period of commissioning the new stores. Disruption may dent sales a little and possibly push up short-term working capital requirements. Forecasting of *short-term funding requirements* would be a critical implementation issue.

ILLUSTRATION 8.9

Break-even Analysis

- The first question for decision-makers is whether entering a market at about 20 per cent market share is feasible without considerable backlash.

- It would be easiest to enter with strategy B (a common entry point for new entrants).

- But there are some real dangers. For example:

    a) corporate image may suffer (spill-over into other products?)
    b) has the company the expertise and infrastructure to service the retail trade directly?

ILLUSTRATION 8.10

Selection of Strategies

Refer to tutors' brief for chapter-end work assignment 8.7.

CASE EXAMPLE

Multi-Utilities

Suitability

Students need to recognise that not all 'tests' of suitability should/can be applied to a particular strategy or situation. They need to be selective in the use of analytical method. For example, in the case of a utility company developing (alone) into a multi-utility provider, the following questions would arise:

- Life cycle analyses — diversification of this type would be common in markets which are mature/saturated.
- Positioning — the critical issue here is whether the company would intend to 'convert' the majority of its current customer base to multi-utility *or* whether multi-utility is a small 'niche' within/beyond the current customer base. An alliance would have the advantage of bringing a wider customer base (although clearly with overlap).
- Value-Chain Analysis is central to the case for multi-utility. It is argued that both the infrastructure and expertise of a single utility provider can be exploited to advantage by the move to multi-utility.
- Portfolio Analyses — multi-utility can broaden the portfolio away from energy – particularly if telecommunic- ations and water are added.
- Business Profile — this should cause real concern. Is the case for multi-utility really so persuasive given what is happening in many other industries (e.g. back to basics as seen in illustration 7.6).

Screening

If possible use this exercise to allow students to learn the strengths and weaknesses of different screening methods as discussed in section 8.2.2.

Acceptability and Feasibility

Again, the purpose is to 'experience' the strengths and weaknesses of different analytical methods as outlined in exhibit 8.7 and section 8.4.

ASSIGNMENTS 8.1 and 8.2

Establishing the Rationale

The purpose of assignment 8.1 is to allow students to use a variety of 'tests' of suitability – represented by the five categories in exhibit 8.2 and explained in section 8.2.1 of the text. It should be remembered that the process of establishing the rationale may not require a detailed in-depth analysis but students should be able to answer the question 'why might this strategy work?'. For example, in the case of Peugeot one possible strategy is to consolidate their position in Western Europe and either ignore or try to frustrate the forces of globalisation in their industry. In looking at exhibit 8.2 students might reasonably conclude that in the short to medium-term this might be a good strategy for Peugeot – it fits their position of being a strong player in a mature market; it may give some cost advantages over more global players and it exploits current core competences. In the longer run there are clearly worries about such a parochial strategy – particularly in terms of loss of global market share; an over-commitment to one geographical segment and the inability to resource major technological and product developments.

Assignment 8.2 should be used to remind readers that detailed techniques such as a life cycle portfolio matrix (exhibit 8.3) should not be used in a prescriptive way. It cannot be used to determine exactly what the organisation *should* do. The value of the technique is two-fold.

1. It reduces the list of strategies which might work in any particular domain of the matrix – particularly in the 'corners'.

2. It is helpful as a reminder that strategies need to change and develop over time.

So the choice of strategy at any particular stage in the life cycle should be influenced by a view on where the organisation may wish to see itself later in the life cycle. For example, an organisation in *a favourable* position during growth may choose to *differentiate and focus its* activities of its longer-term expectations are to *harvest* good margins during maturity and then *withdraw*. In contrast if the organisation is planning to stay in for the long run – through maturity and decline it will probably focus its efforts on market share gain in maturity and therefore must, at a minimum, grow with the industry during growth. So life-cycle portfolio analysis should be used to sharpen up the debate on such choices rather than being regarded as a technique for choosing strategies.

ASSIGNMENT 8.3

Ranking

It is suggested that students use illustration 8.3 as a model against which they could undertake a ranking for Coopers Creek, Peugeot or an organisation of their choice. Issues to look for are:

- A recognition that the major benefit of such an exercise is to provide an initial screening of options against key strategic factors and not to produce a single preferred strategy. It helps cast light on the relative merits of the various strategies.

- The ranking in the right hand column of illustration 8.3 is not a simple addition of the scores in the previous column. There is some judgement on the weightings of these various factors. Some ranking techniques try to build this in more objectively by a more complex scoring process. Students can be asked their opinion on whether this added sophistication would improve the usefulness of the approach.

ASSIGNMENTS 8.4 and 8.5

Analysing Return

Assignments 8.4 and 8.5 together with the supporting case studies and/or illustration 8.5 are designed to encourage students to assess the strengths and weaknesses of the different techniques and measures of return. This is an area where many students are weak and either ignore financial analysis entirely or use financial data in a very mechanical and uncritical way.

The purpose of assignment 8.4 is to ensure that students can explain how financial performance measures relate to *strategic objectives*. We suggest that you take a number of specific examples and require students to explain this relationship. For example:

- The Coopers Creek case study ends with the statement: 'the key issue seemed to be how to balance sustaining and consolidating existing markets with developing new (international) ones'. Students can be asked which of the various financial measures would best suit each strand of this strategy. For example, it wouldn't necessarily be sensible to expect the same short term profitability for both existing and new business. In the latter case gain of market share would be a primary consideration – but at what financial cost?

- In the case of Peugeot the question could be applied comparatively to three different options; consolidation in Western Europe; extending into Eastern Europe and genuine globalisation.

Illustration 8.5 provides the basis for a critique of cost-benefit analysis both in terms of the factors chosen as benefits and the monetary value assigned to each factor. The following points should be borne in mind when reviewing the assignment:

- Some students may argue that cost benefit is too removed from hard facts. In these cases you could invite them to propose alternative methods for assessing projects of this type. The Rolls Royce Aero-Engines example (illustration 8.6) could be used for this purpose too – to dispel the myth that *woolliness* in evaluation is essentially a feature of the public sector (or previously public sector in the case of water companies).

- An interesting question which should always be asked about benefits is whether they are genuinely *additional* benefits or whether they have simply been *displaced* from elsewhere. For example, the multiplier effect on the local economy is likely to be a mixture of these in the sense that some of the spending by the imported workforce would otherwise have occurred elsewhere.

- An interesting debate may be engendered by the issue of assigning monetary value – particularly to items which are concerned with loss (or gain) of amenity or the changing quality of life. Illustration 8.5 explains how these were costed by the water company.

ASSIGNMENT 8.6

Sensitivity/Risk Analysis

Most students find sensitivity analysis a very *user friendly* technique and you may be using exercises with them (e.g. illustration 8.7) which allow them to undertake sensitivity analysis – hopefully using a spreadsheet package. Assignment 8.6 is designed to complement this practical work by testing students' conceptual understanding of evaluation. In reviewing the use of sensitivity analysis in strategy evaluation the following points should be stressed:

- Sensitivity analysis is perhaps most beneficial in unearthing the key factors/assumptions on which the evaluation hangs. It is useful for students to think through conceptually (rather than analytically) what these factors might be since this should improve their understanding of the *basis* of an organisation's competitive strategy.

- So for example, in the case of the Sheffield Theatres students can be asked how the technique could have helped the Director in November 1991 apparently heading for a £250,000 loss by the end of March, but in fact, turning this round to a small surplus. The key parameters in that case were *capacity fill* and *production variable costs* since other factors such as overhead and prices were more difficult to adjust over that period. Indeed the Director took the unprecedented step of cancelling previously announced productions and replacing them with popular shows.

- The key conclusion about sensitivity analysis – particularly when compared with more sophisticated techniques such as risk analysis is that it allows managers to *explore* the uncertainties and risks around decisions (see section 8.3.2 of the text)

ASSIGNMENT 8.7

Selection of Strategies

This assignment is designed to remind students that there is not just one way in which strategy selection either does, or should, occur. If you choose to use the Asda illustration (8.10) students can compare the old regime (largely 'command') with the new regime (which has large elements of 'learning from experience') and ask to what extent these two approaches fit the rapidly moving competitive world of grocery retailing. Also ask whether the 'elements of good practice' identified in exhibit 8.10 are in place and how the dangers are being avoided. For example:

- There are avenues of challenge in place – which at first were difficult to establish as they were very counter cultural.

- The communication devices – such as 'huddles', suggestions schemes and the physical layout were designed to promote both intra- and inter-group learning.

- The major danger is that big issues and changes are missed – such as new IT systems. There is nothing specifically about these in the illustration but you may wish to ask students who such decisions would get made.

ASSIGNMENT 8.8

Strategic Choice

This is an in-depth assignment for students. You should be looking for students to argue and justify the case that strategic choice should be a blend between the outcomes of *analytical techniques* and *management judgement. As* we indicate in the text perhaps the role of techniques should be to *raise the level of debate* when judgements are being made. More specifically you should expect the following points to be covered:

- Perhaps an important shortcoming of the strategic choice process in many organisations is that it is *ill-informed. So* analytical techniques, in general, should be helpful to the decision process.

- The danger is that techniques are allowed to *take over* the decision process and managers have unrealistic expectations of the techniques producing the 'right answer'.

- Another concern is that analytical techniques concentrate on those factors which lend themselves to analysis and ignore the 'softer' factors. This is the classic problem of allowing financial analyses (as illustrated in the chapter) to dominate the decision process. Students should be reminded that there are frameworks to assist with the softer factors – stakeholder mapping would be an example.

- Management judgement is likely to remain a key element of good strategic decision-making.

- Students should be reminded of the discussions in chapter 3 concerning the way in which the process of *strategic analysis* needs to take full account of the uncertainty facing the organisation – either through the pace of change or through complexity (see section 3.2). Some analytical techniques – such as scenarios – are also useful to the strategic choice process. They provide a framework within which management judgements can be made.

Chapter 9

ILLUSTRATIONS 9.1–9.3

Structure and Strategy

Refer to tutors' brief for chapter-end work assignments 9.1–9.3.

The purpose of these assignments is to ensure that students understand the strengths and weaknesses of different structural types. Also how structure will need to change with time as circumstances and priorities change. In reviewing these assignments try to make links back to the text as follows:

- Each of the text exhibits 9.1–9.5 has a list of advantages and disadvantages for the most common structural types. Use these as checklists to critique the specific companies in the illustration.

- ABB (illustration 9.2) is provided to illustrate section 9.2.7 in the text concerning network organisations.

- ABB also illustrates the later issues in section 9.4 of the text (centralisation and devolution) – so questions are also included on this theme.

- 3M (Illustration 9.3) is provided to illustrate section 9.2.8 of the text concerning global companies.

ILLUSTRATION 9.4 (Global Structures)

This illustration on Nestlé should be compared with the chapter-end case example (Unilever) since they are both major players in the same industry. The purpose of this illustration is to require students to consider the issues raised by exhibit 9.7 in the text (structural types in multinational companies).

The following points can be made:

- Global brand management is an important issue for both Nestlé and Unilever. So the need to organise marketing activities on a global basis is of major importance. There are clearly some concerns that the new approach to devolution in Unilever may weaken this central control. For Nestlé the issue is one of the hierarchy of brands – which also has a local/global dimension (largely historical as these brands were acquired).

- The issue of local production is interesting. At first sight both Nestlé and Unilever are operating a highly devolved approach to manufacture. This can be justified if each production unit operates above any 'economies of scale' threshold. Whether 489 factories meet this 'test' is doubtful.

- A more important consideration is the extent to which production standards, processes and product quality are dictated from the centre of the organisation. It is certain that they are – this is essential to the maintenance of consistency of the brands. So, apparently devolved organisations are, in fact, still highly centralised in relation to control of the key elements of product/market strategy.

ILLUSTRATION 9.5

Centralisation/Devolution

Refer to tutors' brief for chapter-end work assignments 9.4 and 9.5.

ILLUSTRATION 9.6

Organisational Configurations

This illustration is designed to allow students to 'explore' Mintzberg's configurations (see exhibit 9.14). The service factory in its present form is a machine bureaucracy. So the key question is whether or not this is an adequate configuration for the world of the late 1990s. The illustration itself hints at the fact that the answer is 'only in part'. The machine bureaucracy may cope well with the bulk of demand – when the environment is essentially 'simple/static'. It will not cope with the need for customisation around the standard product – as demanded by some customers.

The suggestion in the illustration is that the 'operating core' will be 'allowed' to use their professional judgement as to when a customised service can be offered – this variation is in line with the 'professional bureaucracy'.

In practice maintaining this combination of a standardised (no variations) service for the majority whilst allowing customisation for the minority is a difficult balance to strike. It requires high levels of control over where the 'boundary' should be. A machine bureaucracy would 'solve' this problem by defining several standard products and clear definitions of demarcation. A professional bureaucracy would train the operating core to ensure that the judgements made by separate employees are consistent.

CASE EXAMPLE

Unilever

Global Structures

Students may well find it difficult to categorise the Unilever structure into just one of the categories in exhibit 9.7. That in itself should be a learning point. The following points should be used in critiquing their approach:

- Historically there were *international subsidiaries* – but this quickly changed as the competitive advantage from global brands gained in significance.

- It could be argued that Unilever have, for the past 30 years, been attempting to become a transnational corporation – combining the benefits of global brands with the ability to tailor product portfolios (including local production) to the needs of separate markets. In this context the change of 1996 seems to be one of *emphasis* rather than fundamental philosophy. Local autonomy was to be increased. The possibility of damaging global brands is a clear risk.

Styles of Devolution/Portfolio Management

Unilever is clearly committed to a style of *strategic control* – the issue (again) is what particularly 'brand' of strategic control. Prior to 1996, the style was towards the *strategic planning* end of the spectrum. The changes move further away from this end.

The benefits and risks of these different styles are discussed in the text. The major worry for Unilever is that global brands become damaged by the actions of the heads of the 14 Business Groups. The role of Category Directors – and exactly what 'strategic oversight' of company products and brands means in practice is absolutely critical. This is a critically important *parenting* role – you should direct students to exhibit 6.7 and illustration 6.9 in Chapter 6 which gives some very useful background to this issue.

ASSIGNMENTS 9.1–9.3

Structural Types

These assignments are designed to encourage students to become familiar with the basic structural types as discussed in section 9.2 of the text. More importantly students need to understand the advantages and disadvantages of the different structures and the circumstances in which they are most likely to be appropriate. This is the way in which the discussion in the text is organised and students should be encouraged to 'test' their real organisation against these *pure* types of structure shown in exhibits 9.1–9.5. It is important not to miss the following key points:

- Most organisations will have their own *unique blend* between the pure types of structure – students need to be able to explain the reasons behind this mix. Some examples of commonly occurring hybrid structures are mentioned in section 9.2.6 of the text.

- Assignment 9.2 (ABB) concerns an organisation which operates as a transnational corporation where the role of the corporate centre is to ensure that added value does actually result from the process of making the network of semi-autonomous businesses work. Communication processes and systems are critically important to fulfilling this role. This assignment can be used to bridge two of the main issues in chapter 9 – structural types (section 9.2) and centralisation/devolution (the role of the corporate centre (section 9.4)).

- The link between the structure and the organisation's circumstances and strategies need to be explained and justified. This issue can be pursued in the multi-national context through assignment 9.3. For example, Illustration 9.3 (3M) traces the history of changing structures in adapting to increasing globalisation – from International Division through International Subsidiaries to a *de facto* matrix structure between subsidiaries (for sales/marketing) and global product divisions (whose status and role become progressively strengthened). Students could be asked whether 3M should move further towards a genuinely transnational corporation.

ASSIGNMENTS 9.4 and 9.5

Centralisation/Devolution

Assignment 9.4 is a comprehensive assignment which allows students to draw on a wide variety of sources from the illustrations, case studies and their own experience. The main purpose is for students to place their chosen organisation on the *Goold and Campbell* continuum as described in section 9.4 of the text. We have found this to be a most productive exercise – not only in terms of helping managers conceptualise where the organisation is currently placed but more importantly the extent to which this is appropriate given the strategies being pursued. For example:

- Students often assume that *financial control* is the way in which holding companies – such as the News Corporation – operate. In fact they operate somewhere between the pure stereotypes of strategic control and financial control. Students can be asked to identify the ways in which Rupert Murdoch fulfils the role of *Strategic Shaper* – e.g. through acquisitions and deletions.

- Burmah/Castrol describes the processes through which a corporate centre tries *to shape* the product/market strategies of separate divisions without reverting to a strategic planning role. Students can be asked whether they would tighten or loosen the corporate centre's control over these processes (i.e. move more towards *strategic planning or financial control* respectively).

- Peugeot has been included in this assignment to allow students to think through the issues of centralisation/devolution where a company is operating two subsidiaries in the same market. There is a difficult balancing act to be performed between some obvious economic benefits in centralisation in areas such as R&D, common components and production/management systems as against the need to keep the two marques (Peugeot and Citroen) distinctive in the market place. Hence the decision to allow each company to use its own distribution network. This underlines the need to avoid being over simplistic above the centralisation/devolution issue. (Readers can also be referred back to section 9.2.8 which discusses structural types in multi-national companies.)

- IBM (illustration 9.5) is about an organisation moving from a style of *strategic planning to* one of *strategic control*. Students need to justify this change (as being more than just a reaction to poor performance) and whether they would do things differently.

- Assignment 9.5 continues the process of justifying the extent of devolution which would fit particular circumstances and organisations. Section 9.4.1 provides a general 'checklist' as to how this best 'brand' of devolution might be determined. With practising managers press them hard to own up to issues which might be quite pragmatic and specific to their organisation (for example, that a particular manager really would not be able to cope with more devolved responsibility but in every other way is ideal for their job).

ASSIGNMENT 9.6

Organisational Configurations

Our experience of working with students on Mintzberg's organisational configurations has been mixed. Some students find it a most illuminating framework – particularly the idea of building blocks and co-ordinating mechanisms. Others find some of the terminology together with the large number of permutations rather off-putting and complex (compared say with simpler categorisations such as Goold and Campbell approach to the centralisation/ devolution). Students should benefit from undertaking a practical analysis/illustration of organisational configurations. This assignment is provided for this purpose and is designed to extract two key learning points:

- The configuration should relate to the internal and external circumstances of the organisation. For example, Illustration 9.5 explains IBM's reasons for moving to a divisionalised configuration and can be compared with the checklist in exhibit 9.14.

- Transitions from one configuration to another can be difficult and, perhaps, this is one reason why changes tend to be a result of crisis (or at least declining performance) as seen in the case of IBM.

- Students might ask the question as to how Rupert Murdoch has apparently managed to retain so much direct personal control of News Corporation. Two points need to be borne in mind. First, his main personal interventions are on the corporate level issues of acquisitions, disposals, major investment decisions, selecting senior managers and performance appraisal. Second, like many owners/managers, he has grown up with the company and has a depth of detailed knowledge and understanding which is rarely replaceable by a successor. In other words, he can cope with a configuration which theoretically the organisation should have outgrown.

ASSIGNMENT 9.7

Summary Assignment

This assignment is designed to draw together the three strands of organisational design namely: centralisation/devolution, organisational configuration and resource planning control (chapter 10). The assignment is repeated at the end of chapter 10 (assignment 10.10) as tutors may choose to use it at that stage. Students will probably find this most feasible by relating their answer to a single organisation, preferably their own. Perhaps the more able students will be capable of adding further, smaller examples too. This is a demanding assignment which would require significant additional reading (particularly Mintzberg and Quinn in the key readings). If the relationship between the strategy and organisation design is a central feature of a course this could form a terminal assignment.

- There are a number of ways in which this assignment can be approached but we have found the following to be successful:

- Structure your session(s) around one of the chapters 9–13 in Mintzberg and Quinn which deal with the *context* within which strategy is developed. (In some of our programmes we have this as a *series* of readings sessions interspersed throughout the course.)

- In each case the student can be required to critique the theory/practice match with examples of their own choice. So, for example, The News Corporation can be used to look at the diversified context (chapter 11), Sheffield Theatres and KPMG for the professional context (chapter 12), and so on.

- For each context students should be asked to identify the *key* features they would expect to see in place. For example, the diversified context usually pushes organisations towards the *divisionalised configuration* in exhibit 9.14 often accompanied by significant *devolution* and control systems highly geared to performance against simple (usually financial) targets. As discussed above Rupert Murdoch would appear to have more central control than might be typical – students need to discuss why this is so and whether company performance would improve if it changed.

Chapter 10

ILLUSTRATION 10.1

Competences for the Future

The Skandia illustration is an excellent example of how a detailed assessment of competences to underpin competitive advantage should be done. The critical element of the analysis – which the questions encourage students to critique – is the identification of the *value-creating processes*. These are the 'drivers' of the organisational requirements in the next column.

Also refer to the tutors' brief for chapter-end work assignment 10.1.

ILLUSTRATION 10.2

Business Process Re-engineering (BPR)

Refer to the tutors' brief for chapter-end work assignment 10.8.

You should also underline to students when answering question 3 that many organisations are too incremental with their exploitation of new technologies. They apply the technology to do the current tasks faster, cheaper or better. Not enough organisations ask the BPR question: 'If I were starting from scratch with this technology available how would I run this business (or this part of the business)?' Of course new entrants to an industry *do* start at that point and often steal a march of the incumbent companies.

The main danger of BPR is that of *sub-optimisation*. Improvements are made within the 'system' as defined, and problems (such as cost or quality control) are displaced to other parts of the wider value system. For example, cost reductions within a factory requiring increased stockholding downstream in warehouses or distributors.

ILLUSTRATION 10.3

Differentiation through Managing Linkages

One of these days we'll all start eating our words about M&S! In the meantime here are some guidelines for the questions. The company has several choices:

- *Imitation* – of supply chain management excellence. Many have tried this and failed.

- *Avoidance* – by choosing a positioning which avoids head-on competition with M&S. But many other competitors are doing this too.

- *Changing the rules of the game* – M&S's critical success factors relate to quality of production and service in the store. One option is to aggressively change consumer shopping patterns through exploiting IT with home-shopping, home delivery service. Someone will do this soon.

ILLUSTRATION 10.4

Critical Success Factors

Refer to tutors' brief for chapter-end work assignment 10.2.

ILLUSTRATION 10.5

Balanced Scorecard

Refer to tutors' brief for chapter-end work assignment 10.6.

ILLUSTRATION 10.6

Social Controls

This illustration relates to section 10.4.4 in the text. The key points behind the questions are as follows:

- Social controls are concerned with a pride/motivation to achieve high standards – this would be expected amongst craftsmen. So the `social network' helps spread best practice as each craftsman strives to achieve standards higher than their 'peers'.

- The danger is 'group think' – collectively they miss key issues or changes. The culture breeds rigidities. Benchmarking is too parochial. They fail to respond to key changes in their environment – in this case global marketing and IT.

- There are several key changes needed. First, as mentioned in the illustration, social controls through networking need to be 'shifted up a gear' through new global partnerships. Some firms are already doing this. Second, they may need to fall in with the controls and demands of major international companies if they are to find a route to international markets. This will be uncomfortable – but it may have to happen.

ILLUSTRATION 10.7

Entrepreneurship and innovation

The best way to review these questions is to refer to exhibit 10.10, which relates aspects of organisation design and control to 'circumstances'. Ask the students to compare the match between the 'vertical' and the 'horizontal' for two situations:

- Xerox as it was.
  Xerox as it wishes to be.

In principle the six 'action points' appear to move Xerox towards the kind of organisation needed to prosper in a highly dynamic environment and complex technologies:

- A strategy of differentiation;

- Devolution of strategic decision-making;

- A prospector culture;

- Move towards an 'adhocracy' (what they call the federation);

- The importance of social and self controls.

CASE EXAMPLE

Justice Sector Information Strategy in New Zealand

Improving Value-for-Money

Value-for-money is likely to be increased by the information strategy as follows:

1. Value improvement

    a) fewer miscarriages of justice (from improved completeness of data)
    b) access to other agencies' data
    c) accuracy/speed of data collection/analysis/dissemination
    d) improved resource allocation (from better management information)

2. Cost reduction

    a) data sharing
    b) reduced duplication

Management Control

The case example nicely illustrates the tension which often exists between the two 'sides' of the value-for-money equation when trying to improve performance. If cost reduction were the only important parameter this could undoubtedly be best achieved by the more directive methods of centralised planning and direct supervision by the Ministry of Justice. However, this would cut across the desire to 'separate power' between agencies as a key safeguard to maintain the integrity (value) of the justice system. Historically this has meant little co-ordination and social and self controls being dominant – which have not delivered an integrated information strategy. Nor would 'market mechanisms' achieve the outcome without some significant 'constraint' from the centre – on the very issues outlined in the case example (data protocols, communications, etc.).

The use of centrally imposed performance targets *is* of particular importance here – since it fits the 'middle ground' and is in line with the devolved philosophy.

Resource Allocations

The information strategy – if implemented successfully – should allow the Ministry of Justice to advise the government on changes in the resource allocations between agencies. However, it is not at all clear whether this would, in fact, result in re-allocation of resources between agencies. This is a highly political issue and would require significant changes in the decision-making processes and behaviours of politicians. For example, zero-based budgeting could be attempted with better information – but could politicians change their habits of a lifetime (fighting for 'their' department)?

Other Methods

This final question extends this discussion about other elements of any improvement process. For example:

- The possibility of changing attitudes and behaviours to become more 'corporate' rather than parochially based around single agencies. This would require both managers and politicians to change behaviours quite markedly as mentioned above. This would require a sophisticated change process as discussed in chapter 11 (section 11.4).

- Some students might argue that the problem is essentially structural. If all these agencies were more clearly subordinate to (or even part of) the Ministry of Justice, *then* more corporate purpose could be achieved. There are two concerns with this argument:

1. There is no evidence that 'super-ministries' or any other monolithic empire actually delivers value-for-money in the long run. They get bogged down in their own self-importance.

2. Remember the principle of 'separation of power' to maintain justice and avoid political domination. This should not be taken lightly – it is a key aspect of what 'value' means from a justice system.

ASSIGNMENT 10.1

Resource Configurations

This assignment relates to section 10.2 and exhibit 10.2. It is useful to take two quite different development directions for an organisation – say new product launch or geographic expansion – and ask students to list out the *specific* ways in which the resource configuration might need to be changed to support each strategy. For example, new product development would require the *protection* of new products from competitor imitation and the competences to manage the complex set of *internal linkages* illustrated in exhibit 10.3. In contrast geographical expansion may be particularly challenging for the organisation due to its *lack of experience* in new markets which it may choose to solve by the use of local agents. This will require the creation and management of new *external linkages* in the value chain. This analysis should also remind students of two important issues about resourcing new strategies:

- Although the evaluation criterion *of feasibility* is essentially concerned with the issue of resource capability to undertake a strategy it is often the case that strategies which look feasible during evaluation may not do so when the much more *detailed* assessment of resource configuration is undertaken. So evaluation and resource planning should be seen as iterative and not sequential tasks. Resource planning may require a re-evaluation of feasibility to be undertaken.

- The analysis should remind us that resources which lie outside the organisation need to be considered too and that linkages between resources are often as important as the resources *per se.* For example, supplier vetting or the training of distributors may be critical to the success of a strategy.

ASSIGNMENT 10.2

Critical Success Factors

Students will commonly finish their analysis of resource configuration short of a satisfactory identification of the *critical success factors* and the *underlying competences* needed to underpin these factors. This question is designed to allow students to push their analysis to this further step. The worked example shown in illustration 10.4 should be a useful guide to students in ensuring that their analysis achieves:

- *A relevant* list of critical success factors. A common mistake is to list too many factors and/or to list those factors which are necessary to run the business rather than *critical to* competitive advantage.

- A list of underlying competences which students can *justify.* Again the temptation tends to be to list too many and to be unclear as to how they underpin the critical success factors. An interesting example in illustration 10.4 is the approach to royalty payments to freelance software writers. This is clearly an activity to get right – but what choices has the company got and how would students rate the various approaches (e.g. one-off fees, percentage of sales, risk-sharing, long-term contracts)?

- The need to identify specific *performance* targets as shown in illustration 10.4, e.g. in responding to customer enquiries.

ASSIGNMENT 10.3

Configuration and Generic Strategies

- The competences needed to support different types of strategy will differ (as shown in exhibit 10.4). Students often overlook this critical issue and assume that there is a single best resource configuration. The major difficulties which organisations experience in this respect are when they are attempting to shift the basis of their generic strategy and fail to analyse and implement the significant changes which are needed (as discussed in 10.2.5 of the text). This assignment is designed for students to think through the detailed difficulties of such changes.

Difficulties are also encountered because many organisations will be positioning different SBUs in different ways. So questions arise as to whether the same resource configuration can support all SBUs as against the cost of configuring different parts of the organisations in different ways. Added to this are the jealousies and tensions which arise between SBUs as a result of different approaches to resourcing.

ASSIGNMENT 10.4

Network Analysis

It can be useful for students to draw up a network for a project (possibly concerned with some of their own activities within the university for undergraduates) and to ask four questions:

- How could the time to completion be shortened?

- What might the costs of this shortening be?

- What benefits would the shortening bring to the customer and, hence, to the competitive advantage of the organisation?

- Do these benefits outweigh the costs?

The purpose of these questions is to ensure that students understand at specific resource planning decisions need to be justified within this broad strategic framework.

ASSIGNMENT 10.5

Resource Allocation

This assignment is designed to explore the issues in section 10.4 of the text. It is our experience that students/managers are often unfamiliar with the basic *philosophy* underlying the approach to resource allocation mechanisms used in their own organisations. They can usually describe, blow by blow, the *mechanics* of resource allocation (how budgets are set etc.) but when asked *why* it is done that way or whether it is appropriate they have no frame of reference to critique their organisation's approach. Exhibit 10.6 in the text is designed to provide this reference point and the assignment should use it as a broad framework within which to explore the various approaches being used by organisations. The following issues might be emphasised:

- The link between resource allocation methodology (exhibit 10.6) and the *competitive strategy* of the organisation needs to be emphasised. So, in assessing whether the current approach is appropriate students need to explain how it relates to the situation the company is in. It can be common to find a mismatch. For example, organisations which have an approach designed in a time of higher stability in the environment find real difficulties with reallocating resources to new priorities because of the constraints of a formula approach. Or the reverse may be the case. A fast moving entrepreneurial organisation may have grown to a position where its future survival is (at least partly) dependent on a system for more careful and considered allocation of resources against priorities – either through the development of a *project appraisal system* or the use of formula driven budgets in some areas of the business.

- In large organisations a methodology for resource allocation needs to be developed at several levels. For example, for many public sector organisations a key question becomes whether an organisation which is being subjected to a new methodology externally (i.e. the receipt of income) should reflect this in the way they allocate resources internally –

between departments and divisions. The arguments used by individual organisations in practice are interesting in this respect. For example, some organisations take the view that the budgets of internal departments or divisions should be directly related to the success/ failure of bidding externally – this is the extreme *market-driven* view in exhibit 10.6. In contrast others specifically disconnect these processes regarding the external bidding as a *tactical* process of attempting to maximise the organisation's income and then the *strategic* allocation can be made internally. This raises the question as to whether external funding bodies have any real control over their sector's strategy. A different approach of *imposed priorities* could, arguably, improve this control. (For teachers particularly interested in this issue, a full-length case study is lodged in the European Case Clearing House at Cranfield UK entitled: *Higher Education in the UK: Funding New Strategies for the 1990's* by Bernard Jones and Kevan Scholes.)

ASSIGNMENT 10.6

Balanced Scorecards

The major learning points of this assignment are in section 10.4.3 of the text. The conceptual advantages of balanced scorecards as an approach to performance assessment are:

- It acknowledges plural rather than single measures.

- It allows a mixture of quantitative and qualitative performance indicators (PIs).

- It uses PIs which are relevant to a particular strategy.

However, the practical problems should not be underrated. In particular where should be the 'centre of gravity' of this balance i.e. the relative weightings of various measures. Some may need to dominate others – for example, cash flow for the small company illustrated in exhibit 10.8.

ASSIGNMENT 10.7

Responsibility Centres

Practising managers should find that this assignment provides a useful opportunity to review the way in which performance is controlled in their own organisation. In doing so they should improve their understanding of the pros and cons of different approaches. For example:

- Sales forces are often controlled as a revenue centre with the obvious potential pitfall that they will chase sales volume at the expense of sales margin. BUT if they are to be more targeted towards profit they will need to be allowed more control over the cost base?

- Cost centres may make sense for 'production' departments in a machine bureaucracy – particularly if the organisation's competitive advantage is cost leadership reflected in low prices. BUT this is likely to disconnect the thinking within production departments from the broad strategy of the organisation which could be very problematic if the organisation plans to reposition in its markets (or introduce new products which will be competing through added-value).

ASSIGNMENT 10.8

Business Process Re-engineering and the Impact of IT

Business Process Re-engineering (BPR) was, for many organisations, the fad of the mid-1990s which they ignored at their peril – but from which many failed to gain real advantage. The assignment is designed to require students to move away from this 'mechanical', technique-driven view of the impact of IT on organisation strategy to a broader conceptual understanding of the issues within which specific approaches such as BPR – will have a sensible place. In other words, it is designed for students to expand the issues and thoughts in section 10.5 of the text. Information and IT impacts on strategy implementation in many ways as discussed in that section.

ASSIGNMENTS 10.9 and 10.10

Summary Assignments

Assignment 10.9 requires students to see the links between approaches to resource allocation and control and other aspects of strategy implementation and how these need to reflect the circumstances in which the organisation is operating. For example:

- The use of particular methodologies of resource allocation (such as competitive bidding) may be more appropriate and achievable when the organisational design has separate divisions with a significant degree of devolved responsibilities for strategies and control and reward systems closely related to this structure. This broad 'package' is likely to be appropriate for organisations facing a dynamic environment and/or where there is complexity as a result of diversity (of products and/or markets).

- Students need to be reminded that one of the real practical problems of coping with changed circumstances is that managers choose single dimension solutions – such as changing the structure – which may well make the situation worse if the other elements of the 'package' are not reviewed and changed. This is the key message behind exhibit 10.10 and the Xerox illustration (10.7).

Assignment 10.10 is a repeat of assignment 9.7 (in chapter 9) in case a summary type assignment is chosen at the end of either chapter. It is reviewed in chapter 9 of this manual.

Chapter 11

ILLUSTRATION 11.1

Planned Strategic Change

The first point that should be emphasised here is that exhibit 11.3 is built on a model of change which may not necessarily be accepted by Gemini. Students should therefore understand that exhibit 11.3 does not describe the only model of change. However, it does raise important questions.

Question 1, for example, might lead students to the conclusion that the Gemini approach tends to emphasise rather more continual movement and learning than does the staged model of exhibit 11.3. There is not as much evidence within the Gemini approach of challenges and triggers for unfreezing, or of a re-freezing process. A discussion could take place as to whether these stages are, in fact, necessarily required.

Question 2 asks the students to consider the extent to which the Gemini approach is more or less suited to different types of change (as in exhibit 11.2). Do they see it as more suited to incremental type change or transformational change? If the latter, is more emphasis on unfreezing mechanisms required? Is the heavy emphasis on carrying groups of people with the change process more or less suited to any of the types of change set out in exhibit 11.2? The approach seems to emphasise the need to win 'hearts and minds'. Is this more or less suited to any of the types of change?

ILLUSTRATION 11.2

Diagnosing Strategic Change Needs

The tutors' brief for chapter-end work assignment 11.2 and the case study notes on KPMG will be of help with these questions. The following needs to be drawn out:

- Clearly, Hay will not want to lose the forces likely to prevent change that they already have, but add to these whilst countering some of the forces acting against change.

- The problem they might find is that some of the forces against change are very much to do with the reasons people work in an organisation such as Hay: individualism, for example. In addition, there is a risk that trying to co-ordinate information would lead to even more complicated structures and bureaucracy.

The KPMG (A) case study provides a good opportunity for students to map similar webs. They could also consider how similar these are to Hay, by implication questioning the extent to which 'an audit firm that operates in consultancy' is similar to other consultancy firms.

ILLUSTRATION 11.3

Styles of Managing Change

Refer to tutors' brief for chapter-end work assignment 11.3.

ILLUSTRATION 11.4

Organisational Routines/Symbols

These illustrations are designed to remind students that a powerful influence on people's attitude to change and the adoption of new strategies is in the work routines which are the everyday 'reality' of most employees.

So in changing work routines the change agent would have different purposes (as illustrated by the examples):

- The practical need to change the patterns of work to support a new strategy. For example, for reasons of cost reduction, quality of product/service or speed to market.

- The symbolic impact of changing routines – signalling a break with the past. The first example of telephone response times illustrates this well. Customers would probably be happy to wait for six rings - but two rings symbolises *internally* a dramatic change in attitude to the importance of customers.

- The possibility that a change in routines leads to a change in belief or assumptions about what matters and, therefore, can help lead a change in strategy or approach to strategy development.

ILLUSTRATION 11.5

Symbolic Action

These questions build on those for illustration 11.4 in so far as they emphasise the importance of changes in everyday organisational reality as bases of achieving strategic change. Here, however, students are required to find further examples of symbolic aspects of change. Some important points need to be drawn out:

- Do the symbols suggested actually signal elements of the new strategy, or are they just about making changes for changes sake? It is worth encouraging students to explore this.

- Arguably such changes are ignored because symbols are taken for granted in organisations. You might want to challenge students about the symbols of their personal lives (dress, etc.). Such symbols are often taken for granted at one level but they should know of situations in which changes may have powerful effects (e.g. job interviews).

ILLUSTRATION 11.6

Political Processes

It is interesting to present the students with the task of considering how these three principles relate to different stakeholders. This is the point of question 1.

Exhibit 11.8 details many different political mechanisms. The role of elites, sub-systems and symbolic mechanisms all relate to the principles set out in illustration 11.6. You may wish to choose an organisation in which the students could map out the power/interest matrix and then consider these different mechanisms in relation to the principles, as applied to that matrix.

ILLUSTRATION 11.7

Middle Management Contribution to Competitive Success

A frequent question asked by students is how they might influence strategy given that they are unlikely to be appointed to a senior executive position in a company. What influence can middle management have? Illustration 11.7 provides a basis for discussing this.

In this illustration it is evident that the middle manager concerned indulged in what is sometimes known as 'skunk works'. He saw a problem as an opportunity to make a change and developed a solution to it with which he experimented. He chose not to refer this to senior management but to develop it on his own initiative. This later happened to coincide with top management turning their attention to automated assembly procedures. Students may wish to debate the extent to which the latitude for such experimentation and 'skunk works' is a possibility in organisations; the extent to which middle management is in fact so far constrained that it cannot experiment and try out new ideas. Floyd and Wooldridge in the book referred to in the illustration argue that the latitude is often much more available than middle managers recognise and also that the role of middle management in strategy development is often insufficiently recognised by senior management.

It is then useful to consider other ways in which middle management may have an influence. In fact this might be considerable for example:

- They do contribute to *planning systems* where they exist and can build their insight and analysis into such systems.

- *Networks of influence* are important and in this respect the informal links up, down and across the organisation can provide an important basis to make a difference.

- *Lobbying* does take place formally and informally.

- *Rule bending* does occur; middle managers may not always follow prescribed rules.

- Middle managers can be influential *role models* of new approaches (e.g. in customer care).

- *Patience and persistence* is important. Managers often expect to have 'instant wins'. Influence can take time.

CASE EXAMPLE

South African Fabrication (SAF)

This case study is useful to consider a number of the main points emphasised in chapter 11, notably:

- The importance of understanding the context for change in an organisation.

- The nature and role of the change agent.

- The importance of different mechanisms/levers for change available to the change agent.

The case can also be used to compare with other change contexts (such as the KPMG, UNHCR or Royal Alexandra cases).

The case study can be used to address the following:

- The importance of identifying whether or not the *context for change* is such as to allow the management of strategic change. A number of points are raised about this in the case study for example:

    1. Is there a clear strategy? Is more customer focus really a strategy? What does this mean? Might it be differently interpreted throughout the organisation?
    2. Is there a trigger for change? Is the opening up of markets itself a sufficient trigger?
    3. To what extent are barriers or blockages to change identified? In particular to what extent are they identified and accepted by those who are likely to have an influence on change (including the CEO)?
    4. Is there sufficient challenge and questioning of the status quo in the organisation?

- The role of the *change agent* is problematic in this case study. It seems that the consultant might be regarded as the change agent by the CEO. Is this realistic? The students should be encouraged to consider the role of the CEO both as potential change agent and also as potential blocker of change. Comparisons might be made with other change agents in other cases (e.g. Colin Sharman in KPMG, Martin Hill at the Royal Alexandra or Lynn Wallis in UNHCR).

- What are the *levers for change* available which are likely to have a major influence? This can usefully be looked at from different perspectives: For example:

    a) From the point of view of the consultant it may be that the most important lever is to get the chief executive to take responsibility for the change programme personally; and to address some of his behavioural/attitudinal problems. The students may, on the other hand, not see this a feasible. If so, what can the consultant do? On the other hand the students may point out that the new parent company may intervene to remove the CEO.
    b) Students might also be asked to consider what they would do if they were appointed as a new chief executive. They may see the need to get some 'ownership' of a change of strategy. What does 'customer focus' mean to those who work in the firm; and how might this take form in everyday terms? This raises the importance of changing everyday aspects of strategy in terms of changes in, e.g., routines and symbols.

- The final question posed in the case study encourages students to think about changes to such *routines* and *symbols*. What could be done specifically in this regard. Students may suggest:

a) Changes in rituals (such as the way meetings are conducted).
b) Changes in the layout and refurbishing of offices to make them more customer-friendly or emphasise the importance of customers, e.g., by what is on the walls.
c) The everyday behaviour of sales people, telephonists, and so on.

- It is also worthwhile challenging the students as to what the corresponding behavioural changes would need to be for top management. Presumably the CEO would become more listening, more participative with a great deal more informality and less stress on hierarchy.

ASSIGNMENT 11.1

Blockages to Change

There are several examples in the text of cultural webs (e.g. NHS in chapter 2, Hay in chapter 11 and the Royal Alexandra case study). Also the teaching notes for KPMG (A) case study show an example of the use of the cultural web to identify the blockages to strategic change. It should be possible to undertake this type of analysis and interpretation from any reasonably full cultural web – including those which students may have produced if they have undertaken assignment 5.8 in chapter 5.

It is worth noting:

- In the strategic change literature impediments to change are often conceived as the results of a lack of fit between strategy and structure or systems. It is often these issues on which consultants also concentrate their attention and recommendations. The cultural web helps to show that blockages may often be as much to do with more everyday aspects of an organisation such as the *routines, rituals, symbols, language* and even *stories* in the organisation. For example, there is evidence that, if change is seen as threatening, people in an organisation will refer back to stories and rituals which reinforce the past The way in which the symbols and rituals of a partnership might act to block change is discussed with regard to Hay in chapter 11 and in the notes to the KPMG case (also see 11.2 below). The point that needs to be emphasised is that if the everyday characteristics of an organisation remain then, for most people in that organisation, there is no change in their day-to-day reality.

- It is useful to look for linkages within webs which might account for blockages. For example, power bases in the organisation often lead to the building of organisation structures which in turn reinforce power bases. In addition, powerful individuals or groups may control information through systems, control rituals of training and assessment; and they in turn may become symbols of the organisation as it was.

ASSIGNMENT 11.2

Redrawing the Cultural Web

Section 11.3.2 in chapter 11 uses illustration 11.2 to show how the drawing up of a cultural web, its re-drawing and the use of force field analysis can help identify blockages for change in an organisation. Students undertaking this assignment might therefore refer to that section of the book and follow the procedures described there for the exercise.

Students will therefore require either to draw on a suitable case study such as KPMG (see teaching note) for this purpose or an organisation with which they are familiar.

The challenge for students having redrawn the cultural web is not only to identify blockages to change (see 11.1 above) but to ask the question 'what can be managed to achieve the required change'. Students may see that changing organisational structures and control systems may be easier than changing some of the more symbolic and everyday aspects of everyday life. It is useful to challenge students by asking them how routines, symbols and stories can be changed and what the impact of such changes might be. Sections 11.4.3–11.4.5 in chapter 11 and the references and key readings provided can help students think about this.

They may see, for example, that:

- Many organisational rituals are capable of being managed, changed, removed on added (see assignment 11.4).

- So too, on the face of it, are routines. Arguably this is what techniques such as BPR and TQM try to address. However, there may be routines which are, so embedded in organisational culture that they are very difficult to influence.

- Managers consciously or unconsciously manage symbols. Indeed arguably they are, themselves, symbols. The difficulty, however, is to be able to predict the effect of manipulating such symbols since their influence is dependent on how they are perceived and understood.

- Arguably stories are the most difficult to manage. Managers try to do this by, e.g., newsletters but often find that more informal rumour and gossip are more powerful but more difficult to influence.

ASSIGNMENT 11.3

Styles of Managing Change

The aim of this assignment is to require students to distinguish between different styles of managing strategic change. For example:

- With regard to Burton, students might regard Ladislas Rice's style as analytically based persuasion, whereas they might see Ralph Halpen's style as one of intervention (even manipulation) and directive. They might see Hoerner as directive too.

- Ask students to discuss the benefits and problems of each style. In either case it is useful to ask students to discuss the extent to which different styles are appropriate in different contexts. Exhibit 11.6 should help them to do this.

- An interesting focus of debate is the extent to which styles may be more suited to adaptive or transformational change. If students do not like the idea of a strongly directive (or even coercive) style, and find the idea of intervention somewhat manipulative, ask them how they believe transformational change might be achieved.

- A directive style might appeal to them, but what if there is resistance to such direction? They may well argue in favour of the power of logical persuasion. This leads once again into debates on the strength of the paradigm, organisational culture, and so on.

It is also useful to ask student to identify change agents (e.g. from newspaper articles) who fit one of each of the different styles described in exhibit 11.6. In so doing you should require students to provide evidence to support their assertions about the styles of management-and you could also ask them to discuss the benefits and problems each style. In either case it is useful to ask students to discuss the extent to which different styles are appropriate in different contexts. Exhibit 11.6 should help them this.

A useful way of developing the assignment is to begin by reference to case studies, but also ask students to look at their own organisations, or examples of interventions written up in the press, in order to evaluate the likely effectiveness of such styles of change agency.

(The Burton and KPMG teaching notes are useful in relation to this assignment.)

ASSIGNMENT 11.4

Rituals as a Means of Change

Exhibit 11.7 is a useful starting point to get students to think about the power of ritual organisations. The exhibit provides definitions and illustrations which can be built upon

Rather than using a case study it is helpful if an organisation with which the students familiar is used. An obvious one is the student's university or department; or perhaps students union. Ask the students to propose some significant strategic change as a point for discussion. They will probably suggest something in their own interest perhaps that the department should become much more customer – that is student focused. The assignment can then be built around such a strategic change by asking student to pinpoint changes and rituals which could foster such a strategy.

Taking the example above, the students might identify the need for more rituals which focus staff attention on the students. They might identify:

- *Rights of enhancement* for staff who emphasise better teaching; and corresponding rights of degradation for poorer teachers.

- In traditional universities which emphasise research extensively, they may even argue that *rights of passage* in terms of promotion should be more oriented around teacher quality than research!

- *Rites of integration* might include much more open staff/student consult committees

- And *rites of conflict reduction* more social interaction between staff and students; no doubt paid for by the department!

ASSIGNMENT 11.5

Change Processes

This assignment is probably best suited to students who are in a work situation (e.g. part-time MBA students). And who can track a change programme in their organisation either as it happens or historically.

We have used a similar approach for tracking the effects of both *organisational rituals* and means of *communication*.

Chapter 11 provides a framework for both rituals (see exhibit 11.7) and communication (see section 11.4.6) which can provide the basis for students to undertake their own research For example, they might use exhibit 11.7 on rituals as suggested in assignment 11.4 as a checklist but go further as follows:

- First map out the events, as they recall them, to do with a change programme in their organisation. This could be done in terms of a historical chronology of events. However, it is helpful if they then check this chronology with two other people in their organisation.

- Using exhibit 11.7 as a checklist the student can then identify which rituals were: a) introduced and b) done away with at the various stages in the change programme. Again it is useful if this is checked with colleagues. It my be, for example, that colleagues recall different rituals being introduced or being done away with.

- Students should then consider and ask colleagues about their views on the impact of the addition or deletion of rituals. For example, a pattern which emerged in a study carried out at Cranfield was the prevalence of rituals of challenge and questioning in the unfreezing stages of a change programme. It also emerged from a variety of MBA student projects on this topic that the doing away of existing rituals tended to be a more powerful signal of change than the introduction of new rituals.

A similar exercise can be undertaken for means of communication during change programmes, again exploring the question of which means of communication appear to have more or less impact in what circumstances and why.

ASSIGNMENT 11.6

Pascale's Maxim

Pascale's argument is closely related to that made by Beer and his colleagues at Harvard and the references for both are given in chapter 11. The argument is that, traditionally writers and managers have conceived a change programme in terms of the primary need of convincing people of the need to change their beliefs and values so that their behaviour will change (a 'programmatic' view). Both Pascale and Beer argue that there is evidence to suggest that attitudes and beliefs are more likely to change after and because of behaviour change (a 'task alignment' view). These differences are summarised below.

Contrasting Assumptions About Managing Change

Programmatic	Task alignment
Problems in behaviour are a function of individual knowledge, attitudes and beliefs	Individual knowledge, attitudes and beliefs are shaped by day-to-day patterns of behavioural interactions (routines)
The primary target of renewal should be the content of attitudes and ideas; actual behaviour should be secondary	The primary target of renewal should be behaviour; attitudes and ideas should be secondary
Behaviour can be isolated and changed individually	Problems in behaviour come from a circular pattern, but the effects of the organisational system are greater than those of the individual on the system
The target for renewal should be at the individual level	The target for renewal should be at the level of roles, responsibilities, relationships and routines

(Adapted from Beer *et al.*, 'Why Change Programs Don't Produce Change', HBR, Nov.–Dec., 1990).

This assignment provides students with a basis for exploring these different approaches on the basis of their own experience, what they have read, and also on the basis of their own views.

The students should be encouraged to read the references pertinent to these arguments provided in the text, in particular the article by Michael Beer and his colleagues from Harvard. They might then be encouraged to undertake one of the following exercises:

1. If they are part-time students it might be possible for them to consider a change event in their experience and identify a) whether the orientation was one of programmatic or task alignment change and b) how successful this was. Assignment 11.5 might be usefully employed in relation to this.

2. Alternatively students could consider one or more proposed change events and map out what would be involved in attempting change by programmatic means versus a task alignment approach. This could be done for example, by considering the NHS (perhaps using the Royal Alexandra case), UNHCR and KPMG.

Students may come to the conclusion that the two approaches are not necessarily alternatives but are mutually reinforcing. However, they may also conclude that programmatic change by itself is unlikely to be effective unless behaviour is changed.

ASSIGNMENT 11.7

Stakeholders and Strategic Change

The purpose of this assignment is to require students to understand that different approaches to strategic change may be necessary with different stakeholders.

It is suggested that as a first stage in this assignment a stakeholder power/interest matrix based on exhibit 5.5 in chapter 5 is drawn up for the situation or case study used.

Students should recognise that in change situations the power to block changes should also be taken into account, which could mean that, for example, that field staff in UNHCR or staff and junior management in KPMG could exert significant powers in this respect.

Having identified the different stakeholder power configurations, students should consider appropriate approaches to strategic change by a change agent drawing on the frameworks in Chapter 11. In particular they should consider the styles of change and the means of communication appropriate according to stakeholder groups. In the latter case (communication) it might also be useful to encourage students to look at the role of symbolic aspects of communication as well as more formal communication. In discussions of this sort in previous classes patterns have emerged similar to that below.

STAKEHOLDERS AND MANAGEMENT STYLES

LEVEL OF INTEREST

		Low	High
POWER	**Low**	● Direction/edict style ● Regular general communication ● Symbolic signalling	● Direction/education style ● Regular general communication ● Symbolic signalling
	High	● Education/intervention style ● Personal memoing ● Face to face IF blockages	● Participation/intervention style ● Face to face communication

Students should also consider how change agents would overcome political blockages to change and exhibits 11.8 and 11.9 can provide useful checklists for considering this. In addition section 5.3.3 in chapter 5 identifies bases of power and methods of assessing power, so students should be encourage to refer to this in considering appropriate political approaches.

Drawing on the discussion on political strategies in chapter 11 students might consider some of the following issues:

- An early requirement might be to identify an overall political strategy. For example, this might be for the change agent to ensure he or she keeps or develops facilitating power whilst removing, or dividing, blocking power. Exhibit 11.9 can help with this.

- If resistance does occur, are there ways of breaking it down, or the political weight of those leading that resistance? Would actual or symbolic rewards for supporters or those accelerating change be helpful? Would association within eminent outside support be useful symbolically? Can political elites be divided?

- In achieving change might the involvement of waverers in the partial implementation of such change help? In achieving compliance to change there may be a need for symbolic activity to diminish the power of those seen to be resistant, whilst boosting that for the supporters of power.

One way of undertaking this exercise is to play it out in the class by asking students (or groups of students) to play the role of different stakeholder groups interacting with someone playing the role of the change agent.

ASSIGNMENT 11.8

Change Agency

The purpose of this assignment is to assist students in linking concepts about strategic change to the practice of management by considering the activities of change agents.

A number of points need emphasising:

- Encourage students to distinguish between *what* the executives decide to do and *how* they set about doing it. Get the students to focus more on the latter for this exercise. Encourage them to read between the lines to interpret what the executives actually did.

- Also try to ensure that they systematically and explicitly use concepts and frameworks related to managing change to examine and critique practice, rather than just give a catalogue of executive actions.

- Therefore, encourage students to draw on the range of topics covered in chapter 11 (also chapters 2, 5, 9 and 10).

- Also encourage students to use the practical experience of the executives as a basis for critique of the relevance of the concepts and frameworks.

- It might be possible to draw together the work of individual students to consider the key lessons on successful change agency learned from their work. Students could compare what emerges with exhibit 11.11 from the Buchanan and Boddy book.

- The final section of the book also provides an overview of how the various aspects of managing strategy and strategic change interrelate. Have the students taken this inter-relatedness into account in their critique of change agency?

Teaching Notes For Case Studies

This section contains comprehensive teaching notes for each of the twenty-six case studies which appear in the text and cases edition of *Exploring Corporate Strategy*. These notes have been prepared by the authors of each case study and edited by Kevan Scholes and Gerry Johnson.

The following page shows a guide to the main focus of each case study and also appears in a similar form in the book.

Nine cases new to the fifth edition are marked (N); cases revised from the fourth edition are marked (U)

You will probably find it helpful to read the brief guidelines for using case studies in section 5 at the beginning of this manual.

A GUIDE TO THE MAIN FOCUS OF CASES

Case	Introduction to strategy	Strategic management process	Business environment	Five forces	Resource and competence analysis	Stakeholder expectations/purposes	Culture	Overall strategic analysis	Corporate strategy/parenting	Competitive strategy	Strategic options	Diversification	Acquisitions	Strategy evaluation	Global management	Structure, organisation design	Resource planning and control	Managing change	Strategic leadership	Public sector management
British Steel, p. 551(U)	●●																			
New Town, p. 559		●●				●														●●
Castle Press, p. 567		●●																		
Pharmaceuticals, p. 574			●	●●																
European Brewing, p. 582(U)		●●	●												●	●				
Kronenbourg, p. 607				●		●	●	●		●			●●							
Brewery Group Denmark, p. 622	●				●						●●			●	●●					
Stewart Grand Prix, p. 633(N)					●●												●			
Laura Ashley, p. 641					●●	●										●				
Iona, p. 656						●●	●													
Sheffield Theatres, p. 670					●	●●											●			
Fisons, p. 685						●●								●						
World Automobile Industry, p. 691			●●																	
Peugeot, p. 709(U)								●		●●	●			●	●					
Rover/Honda, p. 725										●	●●				●					
BMW, p. 738										●	●●		●●	●	●					
Barclaycard, p. 746(N)								●			●●			●						
Coopers Creek, p. 756					●									●●	●					
Dutch PTT Telecom, p. 768(N)											●●			●●						●
News Corporation, p. 779	●				●	●			●●			●●		●	●	●			●	
Nokia, p. 807					●					●		●●	●●		●					
Bord Gais Eireann (BGE), p. 827(N)																●●	●●			●
Doman, p. 838														●●			●●			
Royal Alexandra Hospital, p. 852(U)	●				●		●									●		●●	●	●
Burton Group A, p. 868(N)	●					●		●		●	●	●				●●		●	●●	
Burton Group B, p. 874(N)	●					●				●								●●	●●	
Burton Group C, p. 882(N)	●					●				●						●			●●	
KPMG (B): Strategic Change, p. 891(U)						●	●									●	●	●●	●	
KPMG (C): Global Firm, p. 909(N)		●													●●	●				
UNHCR, p. 918(N)	●					●●	●											●●	●	●
Burmah Castrol, p. 935	●				●●				●●		●●				●	●				

Note: ●● = Major focus U = Updated

    ● = Important subsidiary focus N = New

TEACHING NOTES

British Steel
Kevan Scholes

1. INTRODUCTION

This case study concerns one of the UK's largest and best-known manufacturing companies – British Steel. It covers the period before and after privatisation in 1989 and through to 1997. In reviewing the history of the company during its period of nationalisation (1967 to 1989) it seeks to highlight many of the reasons for good or poor performance. The period from 1989 to 1992 was the time when British Steel became an internationally competitive company. Indeed in 1990/91 it was the world's most profitable steel company. The case follows the company through the next recession (1991/93) underlining the importance of a strong balance sheet in a cyclical industry. The main issues for the company by 1997 are its plans to become a truly global steel company in the face of difficult issues in its business environment – particularly the dramatic rise in the value of the sterling against the DM during 1997. There is also the possibility that mergers between competitors within Europe will weaken the company's position.

2. POSITION OF THE CASE

The case study has been written for use as an introductory case to allow students to identify the reasons why and how organisations change over time. The case will be particularly useful to illustrate the need to develop an international strategy – even in such traditional industries as steel. It is a core case study for chapter 1 of *Exploring Corporate Strategy*.

3. LEARNING OBJECTIVES

The case is primarily designed to help students understand key concepts and frameworks in chapter 1 rather than any in-depth analysis. In addition it should flag up issues which will be discussed more fully in later chapters. In particular it can be used to illustrate the following issues from the text:

a) Aspects of *strategic analysis* (section 1.2.1). There are many examples of environmental, resource and stakeholder issues in the case.

b) *Strategic choice* (section 1.2.2). How should British Steel decide which strategies to following in the face of tough international competition?

c) *Strategy implementation* (section 1.2.3) issues are also prominent in the case study. Issues relating to organisational structure, centralisation versus devolution, reward systems/

incentives, ownership and control. The need to switch from being a UK-based company (50 per cent/60 per cent market share) with exports to a different form of international company.

4. TEACHING SCHEME

As an introductory case, *British Steel* lends itself to many different treatments. It is most likely to be used as a basis for plenary discussion rather than small group work.

5. QUESTIONS FOR DISCUSSION

The following questions should prove useful in unearthing some of the issues outlined in section 3 above:

(i)   What were the most important issues in British Steel's environment which shaped its development both prior to privatisation (1989) and subsequently.

(ii)   How has the strategic capability of British Steel changed over the last ten years)? To what extent are the international comparisons in the case study useful in understanding past performance and guiding future choices of strategy?

(iii) On what basis should British Steel compete in the future if it is to survive in an increasingly intentional world?

(iv)   Which aspects of strategy implementation were handled particularly well or badly during the period of the case study? How might these need to change in order to fulfil the vision of being a genuinely global steel company?

6. CASE ANALYSIS

6.1 Environmental issues

In addition to listing the various environmental issues (e.g. exchange rates, international-isation of steel market, cyclical demand, etc.) students should be pressed to say how these impacted *differently* on British Steel compared with other steel producers world-wide. For example, the current trends in exchange rates were particularly favourable to British Steel for a considerable period of time – but turned dramatically against the company in 1997. A 5-Forces analysis (see chapter 3 of *Exploring Corporate Strategy*) would show important issues in the immediate competitive environment such as substitution, poorly performing customers and the advent of Japanese transplants in the UK. Students may also be encouraged to ask whether the early privatisation of British Steel (compared with European counterparts) was a threat or an opportunity.

By 1997 it should be clear that the short-term difficulties (e.g. subsidised competitors) are likely to turn into longer-term advantages for British Steel as the 'playing field is levelled'.

However, the movement in exchange rates and the advent of the Labour government (probably heralding an increase in the social costs of employment) have accelerated the need for some radical thinking about cost structure and where costs might be reduced without harming product or service quality. Three areas have been identified: (1) further productivity gains (delayering of management and the creation of the multi-skilled technician shopfloor worker); (2) tougher supply chain management; and (3) crucial to the first two, the investment in, and exploitation of, IT.

6.2 Strategic capability

The case study should be useful to debate the importance of the various measures of resource *utilisation,* which are almost exclusively concerned with *efficiency.* By 1997 this was a particularly pressing issue as a result of the adverse exchange rate movements and the likelihood of increased social costs (more in line with France and Germany; see appendix 3). Students should be asked to critique the three-pronged attack on costs. It is an excellent example of analysing and implementing changes through the value chain. The point should also be made that reducing cost is not in itself a strategy. It is how this improved cost position is exploited which is crucial. Indeed, it would be useful to press the class to identify the different ways in which an international cost advantage could be exploited strategically. For example, in ensuring that profits are ploughed back into product development and strategic investments to support further international expansion.

The company's extensive involvement in steel stockholding (distribution) can also be discussed – does it give them competitive advantage? This will be a useful introduction to the discussion of *Generic Strategies* in chapter 6.

6.3 Basis of competitive advantage

This question is designed to encourage brief discussion of *generic competitive strategies* as mentioned above. It is particularly important to review this in the light of British Steel's stated objective of becoming a genuinely international company. Historically, the political case for a home based bulk supplier of steel had been strong (and was, at least partly, behind the nationalisation in 1967). However, in a commercial international world could British Steel maintain this 60 per cent share of the UK as the market's bulk supplier? Or did inter-nationalisation infer a specialist (differentiated) role for British Steel – not just in overseas markets but in the UK too? This should be a very useful discussion for the class – they can be asked to critique the formula for international development spelt out in the case and, in particular, why different approaches have been chosen for different geographical regions. These issues of international development will be dealt with in later chapters of *Exploring Corporate Strategy* (e.g. chapter 9).

6.4 Implementation issues

One of the stated reasons for improved performance immediately prior to and following privatisation in 1989 was an increase in the *devolved* powers of divisional managers. This can be used as an introductory discussion of the advantages and disadvantages of *centralisation* and *devolution* (discussed more fully in chapter 9).

Given the intentions of British Steel to become a truly international company the class can be asked to outline how this would be implemented. This should help highlight the implementation issues as discussed in chapter 9–11. For example:

- What *structural* changes would be required? (see exhibit 9.7)?

- How far should the philosophy *of devolution* be extended internationally – won't they lose the ability to co-ordinate activities centrally?

- Should they develop new markets themselves or through acquisitions or by strategic alliances? (see chapter 7).

- What could be the *cultural* barriers to becoming a multinational company and how could they be overcome? (See exhibits 2.10 [the *cultural web*] and exhibit 5.9).

- How will they manage the process of creating the multi-skilled technician shopfloor worker in an industry steeped in a history of hard manual labour?

TEACHING NOTES

Strategy Development at New Town Council and Castle Press
Andy Baily and Julie Verity

1. INTRODUCTION

The two cases, New Town Council and Castle Press, illustrate the process of strategy development within different organisational contexts. Both cases are based on the views of the strategy development process as seen by members of the respective management teams. The New Town case describes how four members of the management team view their strategy process while the Castle Press case describe how five members of the top management team view the process.

Both cases are constructed around two general themes. The process of strategy, development and the general organisational context Links between the process and context are made. The case notes below deal with both cases.

2. POSITION

The two cases are suitable for examining the process of strategy development and demonstrating that this process is likely to be multifaceted in nature and vary b! organisational context. They are appropriate for introducing students to the complexity of the strategy development process and understanding this process through a multidimensional framework.

These issues are examined in *Exploring Corporate Strategy,* chapter 2.

3. LEARNING OBJECTIVES

If the strategic direction of an organisation is to be managed this must take into account organisation's process of strategy development. The six dimensional framework provides a basis for understanding the strategy development process. I provides a structure to illustrate that:

- strategy development is unlikely to be a unidimensional process;

- the strategy development process is likely to be characterised by an interrelationship between multiple dimensions;

- strategy is not necessarily developed in a rational planning manner;

- social, political and cultural aspects of an organisation can impact on the strategy development process;

- the strategy development process is likely to be related to the context of an organisation,

- to manage an organisation's strategy and its strategic direction means managing the actual strategy development process of an organisation not an archetypal process.

The two cases illustrate differences in the strategy development process. They demonstrate that the process of managing strategy development in one organisation may not be the same as, or appropriate, to managing strategy development in another organisation.

4. TEACHING PROCESS

The two cases can be used either jointly or separately. Individual students could prepare one or both of the cases for classroom discussion. If students are working in groups, some could prepare an analysis of New Town whilst the remainder do the same for Castle Press. As part of their case analysis, students could 'plot' the strategy development process on a blank 'Strategy Development Profile' (figure 1) using the characteristics in figure 2 as a guideline. These 'profiles' could be used to explore differences in perceptions of the process and also aid the cross case comparison. Strategy Development Profiles for both New Town Council and Castle Press as seen by the executives themselves are attached for tutor use both as profiles (figures 3 and 4) and as text (figures 5 and 6).

Group presentations can be made in plenary session, from which comparisons and similarities could be drawn between the two organisations. For students with management experience, the debate should include their own experiences of organisational life and strategy development.

Questions appropriate for students to prepare prior to the session include:

- *How is strategy formulated at New Town Council/Castle Press?*

- *Why is strategy developed in the manner it is at New Town Council/Castle Press?*

Direct students to chapter 2 and ask that they use the framework to answer the first of these two questions. In addressing the first questions students might also 'plot' their view of the strategy development process as characterised by the six dimensional framework to produce a *Strategy Development Profile* for each organisation.

The classroom preamble and introduction to the session could be conducted along the following lines:

Present the idea of a linear, structured, rational process of strategy development to the class. Past management research has been very influential in persuading practitioners that the 'correct' strategy process is a rational, systematic process, often guided by the application of planning frameworks. This view has gained prominence, in part, because it is simple, straight-forward and appealing. It is also easy to explain – there is a beginning – *analysis of the external and internal environment,* a middle – *selection of the optimum solution,* and an end – *production of a plan to guide successful implementation.* The result has been acceptance that, a rational, planned approach to strategy development is 'good practice'.

Research has demonstrated that many organisations do not pursue this planned path to a strategic direction. Organisations are open to an array of internal and external influences in the process of formulating a strategy. Consequently, the strategy development process of an organisation is likely to reflect the mix of influences which come together to direct how strategy emerges.

Ask students for feedback from their analyses of the case(s). Guide the group to discuss issues such as formal and informal processes: how many processes are at play and what are the relative power of these? Try and separate issues of process and causal factors asking – *why was it like this?* Reinforce the issue that there is no 'overarching best way' to develop strategy, the process which exists within an organisation must be managed to deliver the desired strategy and changes to the strategy development process must be undertaken from an organisation's present process.

Ask the group to compare and contrast the strategy development process in New Town with that of Castle Press, both in terms of what the processes are and why they are as they are.

5. QUESTIONS FOR DISCUSSION

The cases provide material which will enable discussion of questions such as:

- How do strategies come about in organisations?

a) What is the strategy process at New Town Council?
b) What is the strategy process at Castle Press?

- What influences the process of strategy development?

c) Why is the strategy development process at New Town as it is?
d) Why is the strategy development process at Castle Press as it is?

- What are the main differences/similarities in the strategy development process between the two cases?

- Why do these differences exist?

  For example, the Chief Executive at New Town is not entirely happy with the process of strategy development in his organisation, he would like to change it. What options are attractive to him and his team? Why? Is a different process feasible and if so, how could he manage such a change?

6. CASE ANALYSIS/COMMENTARY

6.1 New Town Council

The strategy development process

The dominant strategy development processes in operation at New Town Council are Political and Enforced Choice, each giving similar weighting from the analysis.

The Political process is extensively illustrated. The key characteristics relate to power, need for networking, influence through politicking.

Political examples from the case:

- individuals and groups determine the nature of the organisation and its strategy;

- *'No one individual has dominated NTC and there are up to eight major influences fighting for their livelihood right now.' – Chief Executive;*

- power lies in directorates according to: size, budget, focus of service, and especially the strength of personality of the head individual;

- powerful directors gain more resources and gain more support from Members;

- while there maybe competition between directorates compromise also exists;

- networking is required to get things done;

- the acceptability of strategic options are sounded out through informal contacts;

- Members can block implementation so there is a need to get them on side.

Why political?

- structure of isolated directorates – little cross-directorate communication;

- lack of consistent direction from Members; conflicting objectives;

- the political situation of a hung council creates a lack of direction;

- New Town Council/ Castle Press;

- the top management team have differing views of how to deliver objectives;

- reduction in resources/reduced budgets;

- where the focus is on common cross-organisational issues (e.g. Local Government Review) political processes are reduced.

Examples of Enforced Choice are also evident. The existence and nature of a local government authority are determined to a large extent by central government. For example, at the time of writing this case the whole existence of New Town Council was under review.

Enforced choice – examples from the case:

- strategy does not emerge solely from inside the organisation, but from outside;

- government mandates to provide services;

- there are attempts to manage the external environment in terms of: seeking what the community wants, organising the community to support the council; understanding central government's thrust, but also getting what the Council want; there is also a sense of being something other than what central government dictates.

Why enforced choice?

- context of operation – public sector;

- unstable and unpredictable environment due to macro level changes;

- primary purpose is service to the external community;

- resources are supplied from outside. Previously resources were abundant and the budget prioritisation processes were ad hoc, but resources are now constrained;

- hangover influence from the Development Corporation (DC) – previously the DC was the driving influence, now it is no longer in existence. NTC have lived under this influence, and have to change to a more leading role.

The political and the enforced choice processes are intrinsically linked.

- *'There is no doubt that we have to accommodate ourselves to deliver what central government want, but there are ways and means of getting what you want as well.'* – Chief Executive

- the government mandate to provide service links into the political activity with the reduction in resources – 'struggle *with the budget whereby the money that we get from Government has been held at current level or reduced, year-on-year, whilst they have mandated we provide extra'* – Commercial Director

- Incrementalism and Cultural dimensions are also characteristic, but less so compared with the dominant dimensions described above.

Incrementalism – Examples from the case:

- strategy develops in fits and starts;

- fire-fighting is common;

- localised achievements unrelated to overall purpose (small steps);

- reactive rather than proactive;

- strategy developing from the interaction of long term community aspirations and the short-term objectives of the council.

Why incrementalism?

- due to party political situation; because of the hung council;

- year-on-year funding/government funding cuts whilst mandated to provide more services;

- difficulty of perceiving the future.

Cultural – examples from the Case

- employees have long memories and preconceived ideas about what works and what doesn't;

- culture is about trying new things, not being restricted by constraints (links with incrementalism);

- culture is about being the follower, second in line, to the DC;

- historically not budget-constrained;

- anti-policy line (in terms of anti-planning and anti-Central Government).

Cultural influences due to:

- expectations of public service institutionalised into the purpose and values of organisation;

- people employed by the Council – long service, or employed from other councils.

The two remaining dimensions – Command and Planning – are not especially characteristic of this organisation's strategy development process.

Command – examples from the Case:

- The Chief Executive (CE) is a moderating influence on power groups;

- CE is not the most powerful person in the organisation;

- CE is democratic and a facilitator – achieves desires without force – operating to moderate the power of other individuals;

From the case it is unclear whether this is a role borne from necessity or from the CE's own preferred style of working. It would be useful to speculate – or ask the group for their own experiences – on the outcome of a different style of management in this position. Would a change of personality change the strategy process significantly, given the influences already playing on this organisation? Is this style of leadership successful – one interviewee suggested that, in retrospect, a lot had been achieved with this man at the helm.

Planning – examples from Case

- community consultation and strategic plan, yearly reviews by small policy team – *'As a result of this review process, this year, there are some fairly significant changes to the strategy document.' – Central Services Director.*

An issue to raise here concerns strategy as action or espoused action – a plan is not an organisations strategy.

- planning in directorates – aggregated to be organisational strategy;

- don't do formal strategic planning;

- lack of strategic planning tradition;

Reasons for a lack of planning:

- instability and unpredictability of operating environment;

- blown off-course by inflation; staff turnover – creating internal focus.

Planning was seen by interviewees as the notionally preferred approach and as a means of improving the present process – which was difficult to work with. However, the environment they were operating within rarely supported a more formal approach. Does the current structure and operating environment mitigate against planning? One Officer commented:

In a way it [current process] *works. It is very flexible and we may be doing exactly the wrong thing in trying to fit a rigid framework onto something that is inherently unstable. In which case we need to try and get this message over to staff, who see the process as it currently is – as a mess and difficult to work in.*

Despite a realisation that planning, in this sort of environment, did not appear very practicable, the over-riding desire of the team was to have more focus, more guidance and more of a sense of strategy in a very formal sense. Why? Maybe the CE got it right when he explained that people were more comfortable with a process based on rational thinking and predictable futures. Even if this was not possible, maybe putting effort into achieving it would make organisational life more acceptable to those playing in the team.

6.2 Castle Press

The strategy development process

The dominant process drivers in Castle Press are planning and cultural, but the strategy development process appears to be in transition.

Planning

- long tradition of planning; established part of yearly routine;

- planning formats; monitoring and review systems;

planning is not seen to be everything, it is recognised that it is part of a broader intentional approach, for example, in combination with incremental moves and also:

'I don't think planning should be the starting point. I think it should be the knowledge of the market, the vision and flare which start the process, which are then supported by planning. The worry is that if we're not careful and we do what is required, we might think we've done it all and that doesn't leave us much scope for very rapid reactive responses and any sort of vision. I would rather see a sort of visionary responsiveness coming in rather than going too far down the planning line.' – Publishing Director

- planning as means of gaining consensus; need consensus for implementation.

The nature of the planning activity can be questioned.

Is planning really driving the process or is it a routine and a cultural activity?

- *'In my view, the information for strategy development tends to be more informal than formal We are not very good at collating centrally what is key information about the external environment. It tends to be much more in people's heads rather than having a resource that can be consulted and information taken from there.' Publishing Director*

Why planning?

- imposed by parent – but accepted by Castle TMT;

- historic activity;

- stable markets; the markets are only just starting to change;

- internal stability of past – being the market leader;

- growing demand within the market;

- smaller TMT allows planning as it is described here to work (but is this the planning which is described in texts?);

- move from internal to external focus has increased the need for planning;

- need to commission books five years ahead of peak sales

- planning to ensure widespread involvement and development of consensus

Cultural

- common way of doing things – *'There is a strong feeling here and within the Group of "we have always done things this way". It is an even stronger culture in Castle Press*

where, in its specialist area of publishing it is very much in a world of its own.' –
Production Director

- strong common shared values; of Castle and/or profession

- strategy is historic – 'We *were locked-in to the past and into the way we did things before.*
  If an area had a certain level of resources one year, it would get more of the same next
  year. That was the business approach, more of the same and building on what we already
  had.' – Publishing Director (this also relates to incremental activity)

- Accepted industry ways of doing things

Why cultural?

- long tenure of TMT in Castle Press or group; new people from similar areas – 'In *the TMT*
  and more generally, we are limited (in terms of experience) to Castle and then to a slightly
  wider level of publishing. We have deliberately recruited people who don't have any
  experience in either, but there aren't that many of them at the moment.' – Publishing
  Director

- strong professional ethos

- niche market

- stable markets; only just starting to change

- internal stability of past – being market leader

- aspects of old culture are likely to diminish with the re-focus in the organisation and the
  desire for growth and planning

- strategy needs to fit with culture to take senior managers along and ensure implementation

- employees proud of publishing specialist books

- there are common shared values.

Incremental

- Incrementalism linked in with planning to be 'logical incremental'

- *The strategy process is mainly planning But, because we are dealing with global markets*
  and there are always things happening, like economic changes in various parts of the
  world, we have to react to these rather than plan for them! We might be able to plan that
  something could happen but to predict when and where is not so easy – we have to react to
  these external influences.' – Publishing Director

- planning is revised and modified as the organisation progresses

- starting to develop – 'This *incremental approach, that's what we're getting more of now and its because the environment is changing New opportunities are arising. Before, we never really took them. Over the last couple of years we have started to take more risks in the hope that they will work. We try to set things up in a way where we can keep it low key and we can withdraw if it doesn't work but if it looks as if it's a success we can build on it.* – Publishing Director

- more experimentation developing

- becoming more risk taking through experimentation and incrementalism.

Why incremental?

- more changeable nature of the environment

- need to react to new opportunities

- globalisation and need to respond to local markets rapidly; can plan for some issues but the 'ferocious competition' at local level means a need for rapid incremental change.

It may be worth emphasising these changes in the strategy development processes at Castle Press. There has always been a strong emphasis on formal planning. However, given the increasingly competitive nature of their environment, the business was trying to become more flexible in its response to such forces.

Command – is not seen

> *'I am not a commanding manager. I seek consensus, I am methodological, I'm a planning type of manager.'* – Managing Director.

Enforced Choice – some enforced choice is seen from the parent but this is limited.

- Drive for strategic change due to drop in market position – supported by strong message from corporate centre – *go for growth* – with the stated objective of doubling turnover by the year 2000.

- *The Group do constrain us in the level of profit they demand. They have the power to tell us to make 5 per cent or 15 per cent profit this year; this limits what we can do. The divisional structure does mean we operate in a fairly well-defined area of operation When we have suggested operating outside these areas we have been told it is not our responsibility.'* – Marketing Director

Political – there is not a great deal of political activity

Power is associated with departments core to the business and not those which service the business – though it is not about individuals – for example, the Production Director with little power sees political activity, the Publishing Direction with power sees little political activity.

- drive for consensus reduces political activity

- consensus leads to lack of politics – '*I don't think there is really any conflict. I think there are differences, we all know where we're trying to get, but the difference is about how we should get there.*' – *Publishing Director*

- there are disagreements but these are resolved through consensus development and planning activity

- in TMT there is not one dominant player

A Note on Executive Agreement in Process in the Cases

Students may well observe that the patterns described above are not seen uniformly by all the executives. Two points are worth noting:

1. It is rare for all executives in an organisation to perceive the same processes at work. It would be surprising if they did given different backgrounds, different responsibilities and different involvement in the strategy process. However, general tendencies can be observed.

2. There was a good deal more uniformity in the views of the Castle executives than in New Town. This is not surprising. First, because there were more dimensions of the strategy development process perceived to be at work in New Town. It was a more complex process than at Castle. Second, because the planning dimension dominant at Castle is more readily recognised by executives as a 'legitimate' influence on strategy.

Figure 1 STRATEGY DEVELOPMENT PROFILE

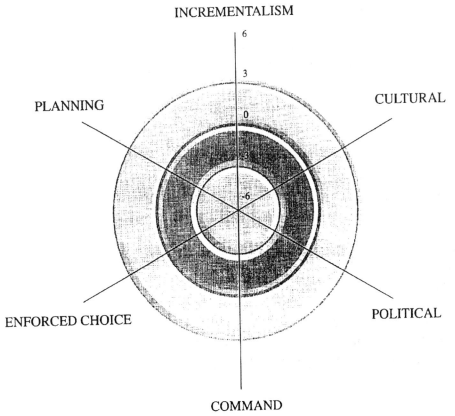

Figure 2 CHARACTERISTICS OF THE SIX DIMENSIONS

Planning

Strategies are the outcome of rational, sequential planned and methodical procedures.

Strategic goals are set by sen ior organisational flg ures .

The organisation and environment are analysed.

Definite and precise objectives are set.

Precise plans for implementation are developed.

The strategy is made explicit in the form of detailed plans.

Incrementalism

Strategy is continually adjusted to match changes in the operating environment.

Strategy options are continually assessed for fit.

Early commitment to a strategy is tentative and subject to review.

Strategy develops through experimentation and gradual implementation.

Successful options gain additional resources.

Strategy develops through small scale changes.

Cultural

A 'way of doing things' in the organisation impacts on strategic direction.

Strategies are evolved in accordance with a set of shared assumptions that exist in the organisation.

A core set of shared assumptions based on past experience and history guide strategic actions.

Political

Strategies are developed by negotiation and bargaining between groups.

The interest groups seek to realise their own desired objectives.

Influence in strategy formulation increases with power.

Power comes from the ability to create or control the flow of scarce resources.

Interest groups form coalitions to further their desired strategy.

The control and provision of information is also a source of power.

A strategy acceptable to the most powerful interest groups is developed.

Command

An individual is the driving force behind the organisation's strategy.

Strategy is primarily associated with the institutional power of an individual or small group.

The strategy represents the aspirations for the organisation's future of this individual.

The individual becomes the representation of the strategy for the organisation.

An individual has a high degree of control over strategy.

Enforced Choice

Strategies are prescribed by the operating environment.

Strategic choice is limited by external forces which the organisation is unable to control.

Strategic change is instigated from outside the organisation.

Organisations are not able to influence their operating environments.

Barriers in the environment severely restrict strategic mobility.

Figure 3 GROUP PROFILE – NEW TOWN COUNCIL

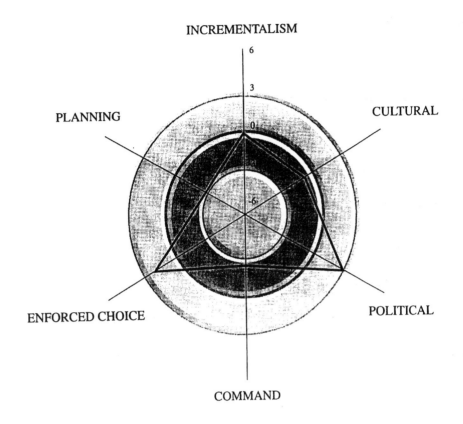

Figure 4 GROUP PROFILE – CASTLE PRESS

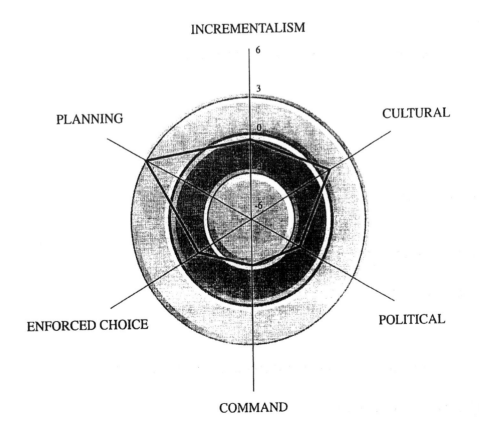

Figure 5 (a) How strategy is developed in . . .

New Town Borough Council

Political

- power (directorates; individuals; members)

- need for networking

- informal process of 'sounding out'

- influence through politicking

Enforced Choice

- nature of New Town as an organisation – a local authority

- operates under central government edict; government mandates to provide services

- strategy does not emerge solely from inside New Town, but from outside

- responds to need of local community

Incrementalism

- strategy develops in fits and starts

- fire-fighting is common

- localised achievements unrelated to overall purpose (small steps)

Planning

- little tradition of planning

Command

- Chief executive is moderating influence not commanding influence

Figure 5 (b) Why the process is as it is in . . .

New Town Borough Council

Political

- structure of isolated directorates – little cross directorate communication

- conflicting objectives / hung council

- differing views of TMT over how to deliver objectives

- resource constraints

Enforced Choice

- context of operation – public sector

- unstable and unpredictable environment due to macro level changes

- primary purpose is to service the external community

- resources externally derived

Incrementalism

- due to party political situation – hung council

- year on year funding

- difficulty of perceiving the future

Figure 6 (a) How strategy is developed in . ..

Castle Press

Planning

- long tradition of planning

- established part of yearly routine

- planning formats; monitoring and review systems

Cultural

- common way of doing things at Castle

- accepted industry recipes

- strong shared values – both at Castle and professionally

- strategy is historic

Incrementalism

- revision and modification as organisation progresses

- a more incremental / experimentation approach is developing

Enforced Choice

- group influences strategy development process

Political

- limited

- drive for consensus reduce political activity

Figure 6 (b) Why the process is as it is in . . .

Castle Press

Planning

- imposed by parent – but accepted by Castle TMT

- historic activity

- stable markets – markets only just starting to change

- growing demand within markets

- time horizons of products

- planning to ensure widespread involvement and development of consensus

Cultural

- long tenure of TMT

- similarity of TMT and organisational members

- strong professional ethos

- stable markets

- cultural supported by conservatism within Castle and unwillingness to change

Incrementalism

- changing nature of environment

- need to react to new opportunities

TEACHING NOTES

The Pharmaceutical Industry
Gerry Johnson and Tony Jacobs

1. INTRODUCTION

The case describes how the pharmaceutical industry has changed since its modern beginnings in the early 1950s. The various forces affecting the competitive environment of the industry are discussed in terms of the past and the immediate future, principal of which has been the move from competition based around brand names and 'muscle marketing' to providing low-cost drugs to large institutional buyers who are increasingly price-sensitive and no longer brand-loyal.

2. POSITION OF THE CASE

The Pharmaceutical Industry case study lends itself to:

- The examination of an organisation's competitive environment, in particular at the level of the SBU, using Porter's (1980) 5-Forces analysis framework.

- How scenario planning techniques can be used to consider the environmental influences which may effect an industry.

- Considering the impact of change in the environment on pharmaceutical firms.

3. LEARNING OBJECTIVES

The Pharmaceutical case study allows students to gain a greater understanding of how to assess the competitive environment of an industry at the level of a SBU. It provides an opportunity for students to conduct Five Forces analysis. Comparison between the past forces with those of the immediate future will lead to an appreciation of the fact that forces change over time and can pose serious threats or perhaps open up opportunities for individual companies to develop competitive advantages. This case also allows students to develop their understanding of the purpose of scenario planning and apply scenario planning techniques to an industry.

4. TEACHING PROCESS

The topic of Environmental Analysis is discussed in chapter 3 of *Exploring Corporate Strategy,* in particular sections 3.3.3 The Use of Scenarios and 3.4 The Competitive Environment: 5-Forces Analysis are relevant. This chapter should be viewed as essential reading for students prior to using this case.

Students, individually or in groups, should draw up five forces maps. The tutor can then lead a class discussion drawing together the five forces maps for the past and the future. Comparing the two maps the tutor can then facilitate a discussion on the importance of understanding how to conduct such analysis, the fact that this can help identify possible bases of advantage and the fact that the forces acting on an industry can change over time. Section 3.4.6 Key Questions Arising from 5-Forces Analysis may be used to help focus the discussion.

The students may then be split into sub-groups to use Scenario Planning techniques to construct views of the future of the Pharmaceutical industry.

5. QUESTIONS FOR DISCUSSION

1. Using the 5-Forces framework map out the environmental forces affecting the Pharmaceutical industry for both the past and the immediate future.

2. Use Scenario Planning Techniques to consider the various environmental influences which may affect the Pharmaceutical industry.

3. What are the likely implications of the changing business environment in harmaceutical firms?

6. CASE ANALYSIS

Since its origins, primarily postwar, the Pharmaceutical industry has operated within a relatively stable environment. Profitability was far in excess of other industries and competition was centred on brand reputation and marketing skills.

However, by the mid-1980s the environment had changed and was viewed as being far from stable. Governments around the world had begun to realise that the cost of healthcare provision had increased far beyond their ability to pay for it. Their efforts to control these costs have dramatically reduced the industry's profitability and changed the balance of the competitive forces of the industry substantially.

6.1 5-Forces analysis

Using the 5-Forces framework map out the environmental forces affecting the Pharmaceutical industry for both the past and the immediate future.

When considering the environmental factors that affected the Pharmaceutical industry in the past, students are likely to mention the points shown in figure 1.

When considering the environmental factors that are currently affecting this industry and will continue to do so in the near future students are likely to mention the points shown in figure 2.

The tutor may then facilitate a class discussion on what can be learned from a five forces analysis, specifically:

- The importance of identifying the *key forces* in the competitive environment rather than just listing all the forces at work. In the case of the pharmaceutical industry students may identify these as the growing influence of government on the cost of the health services; the resulting growth in power of buyers; and the likelihood of substitution.

- Whether there are *underlying forces* behind these; in the case of the pharmaceutical industry, clearly the cost of health services and government concern about this is a key underlying force.

- The identification of *changes* in industry forces and the implication of these; in the case of the pharmaceutical industry the implication being that it has moved from a situation of relatively low competitive rivalry to one of intense rivalry in a relatively short period of time.

6.2 Scenario planning

Use Scenario Planning Techniques to consider the various environmental influences which may affect the Pharmaceutical industry.

Tutors should ensure that students understand the purpose of scenario planning. The topic is covered in chapter 3 of *Exploring Corporate Strategy* (section 3.3.3 The Use of Scenarios**).**

Students should be expected to identify the key and underlying forces which act upon an industry, focusing in particular on those that will have high potential impact and are uncertain in nature.

In the case of the pharmaceutical industry students should identify what the key forces are at work in the industry and the extent to which these have high impact and are uncertain (see illustration 3.3(a)). Students may identify the following forces which are likely to have a high impact on the industry.

Key Forces:

a) Increasing concentration of buyers.
b) Increasing power of distributors.
c) Generic substitutes.
d) Scientific Advances leading to big-technological substitutes.
e) Government pressure on costs and intervention.
f) Harmonisation of government approaches to healthcare.
g) The globalisation of Japanese firms and resulting entry into Europe.
h) The growth in pharmaceutical sales in developing markets.
i) Continued mergers and acquisitions leading to more rapid concentration in the industry.

Tutors might ask students to map the extent to which they believe these are certain or uncertain. The scale below represents the views of Graham Leask on this.

Certain	Uncertain
a.e.f.c.b.	i.g.h.d

It is the factors with high impact and greatest uncertainty that would be used to develop scenarios, i.e.:

- Continued mergers and acquisitions activity leading to further concentration in the industry.

- Scientific advances leading to biotechnological substitutes.

- Growth in the pharmaceutical sales in developing markets.

- The entry of Japanese pharmaceutical firms.

Next, students should be encouraged to identify different possible futures by factor:

d)	I) significant substitution	II) little substitution
g)	I) entry of Japanese	II) no (or limited) entry
h)	I) no significant development	II) significant development
i)	I) increase in mergers and acquisitions activity	II) decrease in mergers and acquisitions activity

On the basis of these factors three scenarios can be built.

Scenario 1: Benign
Increased opportunities for pharmaceutical sales in developing countries (h II); with little substitution from biotech (d II); no (or limited) entry by the Japanese (g II); and a decrease in mergers and acquisitions activity (i II).

Scenario 2: Hostile
Significant substitution from biotech (d I, entry of Japanese pharmaceutical firms into Europe (g I; and increase in mergers and acquisition activity leading to pressures on profit performance (i I; and no significant opportunities for pharmaceutical sales in developing countries (h I).

Scenario 3: 'Industry Wisdom'
Relatively little substitution by biotechnology products in the foreseeable future (d II); However, substantial entry by Japanese firms into Europe (g I; continued mergers and acquisition activity leading to increasing concentration in the industry (i I); However, increasing opportunities for pharmaceutical sales in developing countries (h II).

6.3 Implications

What are the likely implications of the changing business environment in pharmaceutical firms ?

Students should be able to recognise that industry environmental analysis does not end with the construction of a five forces map and the building of various scenarios. If the industry's environment is changing, analysis of the impact of these changes is necessary.

Questioned on the implications of these changes in the pharmaceutical industry, students should identify that:

- Access to customers is crucial, especially the big purchasers such as Health Trusts.

- Risk/Return Equation has changed. This could mean that there are fewer 'blockbuster' drugs in the future, significant as the traditional route to success had been through new drugs.

- Sales force – Large and expensive and increasingly important to maintain sales, However, will this method of reaching the customers continue with the pressure on costs increasing.

- Substitution by generic drugs leading to:

j) Price competition.
k) Drug companies looking for niche markets.
l) Alliances, joint ventures and other forms of collaboration in the industry.

- Increased merger, acquisition and divestment activity.

- Restructuring cost containment programmes.

REFERENCES

G. Johnson and K. Scholes (1997) *Exploring Corporate Strategy,* 4th edition. Prentice Hall.

Figure 1 FIVE FORCES ANALYSIS OF THE PHARMACEUTICAL INDUSTRY: PAST FACTORS

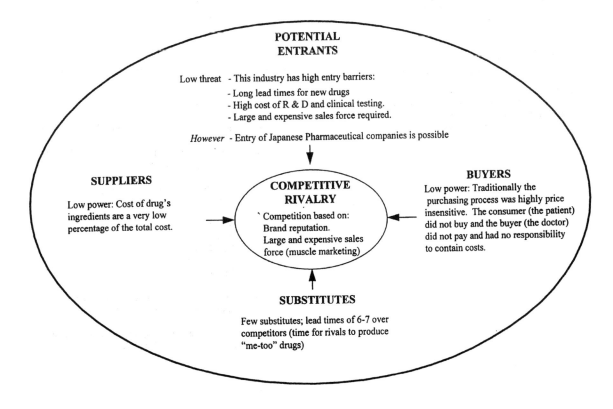

Figure 2 FIVE FORCES ANALYSIS OF THE PHARMACEUTICAL INDUSTRY: FUTURE FACTORS

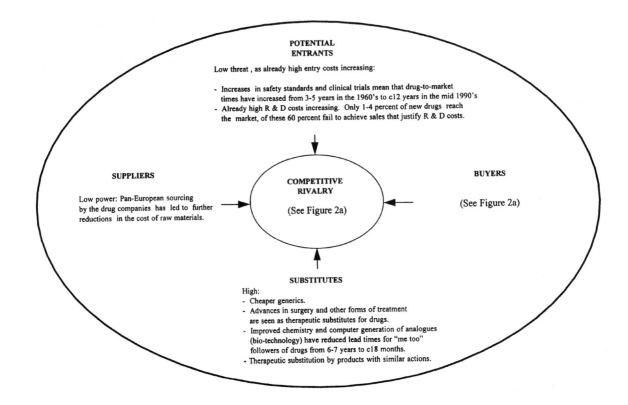

Figure 2a FIVE FORCES ANALYSIS OF THE PHARMACEUTICAL INDUSTRY: FUTURE FACTORS

COMPETITIVE RIVALRY
(see main Figure 2)

High:
- High cost of R & D expenditure is effectively an exit barrier.

- Very profitable industry, however declining margins.

- Mergers and acquisitions in the industry have been driven by a need to improve efficiency and broaden the base of innovation and have led to economies of scale, better sales and marketing and more efficient R & D efforts.

BUYERS
(see main Figure 2)

High and increasing power:
- Loss of brand loyalty as GP's are forced to become cost conscious through the use of Prescribing Budgets and Fund Holding GP status.

- Patients expectations rising.

- Government policy to increase competition (the "internal market".)

- Regional Health Authorities given control over both GP's and hospitals' cost of drugs and service budgets.

- Governments imposing price controls eg through:
  - Black Lists
  - Positive Lists
  - Negative Lists
  - Price Freezes
  - Price Reductions
  - Price Banding
  - Patient Co-payments

- Growth of distributors of drugs who, acting as middlemen, buy drugs in bulk to achieve cost reductions.

- The harmonisation of government approaches to health care, potentially leading to a more global market.

TEACHING NOTES

The European Brewing Industry
Tony Jacobs and Murray Steele

1. INTRODUCTION

The European Brewing Industry case study presents a review of one of Europe's most interesting industries. It is also an industry of which most students have some personal experience, and this adds to its richness.

Information is presented at the total European industry level; individual country level; and major competitor level. When used with the Kronenbourg and Brewery Group Denmark (BGD) cases, or other brewing companies, it offers students the opportunity to analyse an industry and some of the competitors in depth.

2. POSITION OF THE CASE

The case study should be used as part of a strategy course dealing with industry analysis and international strategy formulation. It lends itself to the use of the Porter Industry analysis framework and forces students to consider the effectiveness of the Porter framework, when used to analyse an industry which crosses national boundaries. Consequently, students should have been introduced to the issues of competitive analysis, including the Porter framework, in chapter 3 of *Exploring Corporate Strategy,* prior to studying the case.

When students have analysed the industry they can then consider the international strategies of Kronenbourg and BGD, as well as the companies in the case study.

3. LEARNING OBJECTIVES

The principal learning objective is for students to practise the analysis of the industry dynamics and understand the key forces in the industry of which competitors must be aware. Another objective which the cases offers is to help students understand that blindly applying analytical frameworks can be unproductive. The Porter framework when applied at the total industry level does not provide much meaningful information. When applied to each national industry it does. This is due to the significant differences which exist in the European brewing industry from country to country.

4. QUESTIONS FOR DISCUSSION

The following assignment questions can be used to stimulate students thinking:

1. Identify the principal trends in the European brewing industry.

2. How relevant do you think the Porter framework is to an industry like the European brewing industry ?

3. Choose any one national brewing industry and analyse it using the Porter framework.

4. How do you feel the industry will develop during the latter half of the 1990s?

5. Choose one of the companies in section II of the case study and analyse its prospects relative to the industry.

5. CASE ANALYSIS

When starting the case, with question 1, it is suggested that the teacher facilitates the discussion by making overhead projector transparencies of exhibits 1–4 and 6–11. It is worth pointing out to students, prior to their preparation, that half the case study is, in fact, tables and not to be put off by the length. Alternatively, if you have a whole day they need only prepare section I, as there will be time to read the other sections during the day.

5.1 Identify the principal trends in the European brewing industry

From the various tables the following trends can be identified:

- The industry as a whole is not especially concentrated. The top five brewers have a combined market share of 35.2 per cent (see exhibit 1).

- There is a wide *variation* of industry structures across Europe. Denmark, Holland, Italy, Belgium and France are in a monopoly situation. Spain and the United Kingdom are becoming increasingly concentrated and Germany is fragmented (see exhibit 2).

- There has already been much *cross-border* business development, principally by acquisition. There has been little acquisition in the UK and Germany, and virtually no acquisitions by UK or German brewers in the rest of Europe (see exhibit 3).

- The general consumption trend is slow decline in the northern European countries and slow growth in the southern European or sunbelt countries (see exhibit 4).

- Having well-known brands is a critical success factor in the European brewing industry (exhibit 5).

- As sales growth rates mature, segments are beginning to appear in the marketplace (exhibit 6).

- There is a wide diversity, not only in duty *rates,* but also in systems of duty collection, across Europe. Harmonising these is going to be a major problem for the industry. Personal imports (e.g. from France to the UK) will continue whilst the difference in duty rates is so great.

- There is a wide diversity of patterns of *consumption,* and types of *containers* used across Europe (exhibits 7 and 8).

- There are two different types of *distribution systems* — one for the UK and Germany, where the brewers own significant numbers of outlets, and another for the other European countries where the brewers do not own as many/or no outlets.

- *Imports* as a percentage of consumption vary from country to country. This can be explained by a variety of factors, e.g. the growth of imports in the sunbelt countries matches the rise in consumption; in the UK the rise in imports is caused by more consumers taking foreign holidays; the static rate of imports in Germany, Denmark and Belgium reflects the consumers preference for home produced beers (exhibit 10).

- Those countries with substantial exports of beer — Denmark, Belgium, Ireland and Holland — do so because their domestic markets are too small to allow significant expansion (exhibit 11).

- From this list of trends the students can be asked to define a series of critical success factors which companies need to have to be effective competitors. The list might include strong brands; a strong home market position, cross border operations, either by acquisition or licence; products in the major segments, etc. The research findings about the brewing industry from the MODEM study can also be introduced here. The general findings of the MODEM study were published in The Business of Europe: Managing Change (reference 1).

At this point in the teaching of the case, it is interesting to ask students what environmental factors are likely to affect the industry's development. More perceptive students may comment on the changing *demographics* in Europe. Exhibit 1 shows the number of people aged between 20 and 29 for the major European countries. This exhibit is very important for the brewing industry. The 20–29 age group are the major consumers of beer. A 20–29 year old male consumes 70 per cent more beer than a 40–49 year old male.

Other factors to consider are EC legislation, drink driving legislation, the move to healthier living

5.2 How relevant do you think the Porter framework is to an industry like the European brewing industry?

This question can be dealt with in a plenary session.

Using the Porter framework for the brewing industry does raise the question as to what the appropriate *level* of analysis is. Is the industry to be regarded as European- or country-based? The students should see that a European dimension for the analyses could be problematic. It may be that the Porter framework has to be applied on a more restricted geographic basis, thought there are certain forces at work — which are European-wide.

Applying the Porter framework normally yields the following kind of analysis:

- *Potential Entrants* — the obvious ones are the Japanese and the Americans. Their products are distributed in Europe, but they have never acquired or built a brewery. Anheuser Busch have been rumoured to be studying the European industry for some years prior to making a full-scale acquisition, but have not done so yet. Students may conclude that while Europe, particularly with the Single European Act 1992, may appear to Americans and Japanese as moving towards a single, homogeneous market, the truth is quite different. Europe is a series of very different markets with very different characteristics. Consequently, major entries may be unlikely.

- *Product Substitutes* – these are interesting. Students will mention soft drinks, e.g. Coca-Cola, wine and beverages such as tea and coffee. In the sunbelt countries, beer is being substituted for wine; and in northern Europe, wine is being substituted for beer, soft drinks and tea and coffee are general substitutes across Europe. Consequently, substitutes are a major threat to the beer industry.

- *Power of Suppliers* – suppliers have little power. The raw materials are readily available and easy to switch from one supplier to another, In some case the brewers may own the sources of supply.

- *Power of Customers* – customer preferences vary significantly across Europe. German consumers have great loyalty to their local regional beers. The Danes and the Dutch principally drink their nationally brewed favourites. The British drink from probably the widest selection of brands in Europe. Not only are many continental European brands available in the UK, but also many other international brands. The British beer drinker has become quite cosmopolitan. There is then a diversity of customer tastes. In this sense, buying power may be weak. However, in some countries, particularly France, Denmark and to some extent the UK, buying power of retailers is of major importance. In France, for example, the increasing concentration of supermarkets is becoming a major concern of brewers, given the high percentage of beer sold through that channel.

- *Industry Structure* – over the last decade the European brewing competitors, with the exception of the British and the German brewers, have spread across Europe. Heineken is a good example of this. Their main brand, Heineken, is available in every European country and they have operations in France, Spain, Italy Ireland and Greece. However, competition still varies from country to country.

This raises the interesting question as to which forces are likely to dominate in the future: to what extent, for example, will indigenous, country-based forces predominate over the growing European-wide forces in this country?

5.3 Choose any one national brewing industry and analyse it using the Porter framework

Question 3 can be used to really reinforce the students' understanding of the effective use of the Porter framework. Groups of students could choose one of the national industries and prepare a presentation which assesses the dynamics of the industry. It would be too lengthy an exercise to cover in any detail every industry in this teaching note. Again this exercise should highlight the diversity in industry dynamics which exists in national industries across Europe.

The three most interesting industries are probably Germany, the UK, and Spain. Analysis of these three industries shows that the Porter framework is very useful for analysing the attractiveness and dynamics of a national industry. However, its inadequacy for analysing an industry which traverses national boundaries is highlighted. The buying power and consumer preferences and the influences which affect them vary significantly over the three industries:

German consumers traditionally are very loyal to their local brewery, hence national brands and concentration in the brewing industry have been slow to develop. Imports are also negligible despite the European Court of Justice's ruling on the *Reinheitsgebot* or purity laws.

British beer drinkers have switched from their traditional ale beers to continental lagers as a result of foreign European holidays and heavy advertising, consequently the proportion of imports has been rising.

Although distribution in Spain is currently split 25 per cent through supermarkets and 75 per cent through cafés, bars, hotels and restaurants, the changing Spanish lifestyles have led to a definite increase in the buying of beer from supermarkets to drink at home.

5.4 How do you feel the industry will develop during the latter half of the 1990s?

This question could be addressed in plenary by asking the students to define how they see the industry taking shape. They may suggest the following:

- *Greater consolidation,* by further acquisition, across Europe. Students should be prompted to discuss the conundrum of Germany. Will it concentrate, and if so, at what rate, and what will the influences be? Some German supermarket chains have recently centralised their buying of beer. This has led to certain beer brands being sold nationally in Germany and will probably lead to more concentration of breweries. However, the low profitability of German brewers will ensure that the pace of this consolidation is not as fast as it has been in other European countries.

- The issue of *bipolarisation* should also be raised – which brewers will become competitors across a wide range, and which will focus on niches? Students should be asked to identify which brewers fall into which category. The issue of bipolarisation has some serious implications for British brewers, as by 1996 only Bass and Scottish Courage appear to have the necessary resources to compete effectively on a European scale.

- Continued *decline* in sales growth. This will happen more prominently in northern European countries where drink driving legislation is more rigorously enforced and health concourses is greater. Also wine, soft drinks and warm beverages such as tea and coffee are substituting for beer.

- Further *segmentation* of the market. As sales growth rates slow, brewing executives will seek to develop segments to generate growth of their businesses.

- *Brands* becoming more important. A critical success factor for competitors in the industry will be to have pan-European brands which, in a marketing sense, are appropriately implemented country by country and region by region. Substantial media advertising and sponsorship expenditure will be made to capture and retain loyal consumers.

- *Supermarket chains* taking an increasing share of distribution. Across Europe, sales of beer from supermarkets are either already at high levels, e.g. Denmark 95 per cent, or increasing significantly. Supermarkets will offer wide ranges of popular brands at competitive prices and become the most competitive force in the marketplace. Brewers will be unable to afford the risk of not doing business with the major European supermarket chains.

The final pages of the European brewing industry chapter from *The Business of Europe: Managing Change* also offers some further thoughts on the future development of the European brewing industry.

Another way of dealing with the future of the industry is to ask students, working in groups to build scenarios. (See section 3.3.3 in *Exploring Corporate Strategy*.)

Students might do this from the point of view of one of the brewing firms. It would involve:

- The identification of key forces such as the ones identified above.

- The building of two or three scenarios around 'optimistic', 'pessimistic' and 'dominant theme' scenarios using the key forces (see section 3.3.3 in the text).

- An examination of the strategic positions of their companies and competitors in the light of the scenarios (e.g. using the type of impact analysis discussed in section 3.3.1 in the text).

5.5 Choose one of the companies from section 3 of the case and analyse its prospects relative to the industry

This can also be extended to include the Kronenbourg and BGD case studies where a comparison between the international strategies of these two brewers can be compared, in particular their different entry strategies into the various European markets. There are separate teaching notes for Kronenbourg and BGD. The prospects for the individual companies can be assessed from a number of considerations. First, their position relative to the current industry critical success factors and secondly their merits relative to how the students predict the industry will develop.

REFERENCE

R. Calori and P. Lawrence, 1991. *The Business of Europe: Managing Change*, Sage.

Exhibit 1 Number of people aged between 20 and 29 years (000s)

Country	1995	2020	%Change
Belgium	1,368	1,273	− 6.9
France	8,592	7,780	− 9.5
Holland	2,452	2,212	− 9.8
Spain	6,538	3,739	− 42.8
United Kingdom	8,578	7,837	− 8.6
Germany	12,660	9,440	− 25.4
Denmark	782	727	− 7.0

Source: Eurostat

TEACHING NOTES

Brasseries Kronenbourg
Roland Calori and Philippe Monin

1. INTRODUCTION

This case study describes the strategy of Brasseries Kronenbourg, the main company in the Beer Division of the French Group Danone, the third biggest food marketer in Europe, challenging Nestlé and Unilever.

Brasseries Kronenbourg and the other breweries where Danone had dominant stakes were the second largest in Europe, behind Heineken, and produced about 26 million hectolitres in 1994.

First, the case describes the positions of Kronenbourg and the Beer Division of Danone. Second, it provides some background information on the Danone Group (history, portfolio of businesses and strategic decision process). Then the case is focused on the international strategy and the international organisation of Kronenbourg and of the Beer Division of Danone. Finally, it presents the future challenges as perceived by the top management of Kronenbourg.

2. POSITION OF THE CASE

We recommend the class should discuss the Kronenbourg case study after analysing the brewing industry (cf. *The European Brewing Industry* case study, in this volume).

The Kronenbourg case study fits a session on international strategy and organisation. It might follow a lecture on strategy formulation, a lecture on the transnational organisation, or a lecture on the transition from a multi-domestic competitive system to a mixed industry (cf. Prahalad and Doz, 1987; Bartlett and Ghoshal, 1989). Comparisons with competitors such as Heineken, Interbrew or Brewery Group Denmark (BGD) would be useful in order to understand the specific strategic recipe of Kronenbourg and Danone in the beer industry.

3. LEARNING OBJECTIVES

The first learning objective is to develop the students' ability in strategy evaluation and reformulation in an international, especially European, context. The second learning objective is to understand the battle for international acquisitions and expansion in the context of a fragmented multi-domestic industry which becomes mixed. This learning objective will be aided if The European Brewing Industry case, the Kronenbourg case and other international beer businesses (e.g. BGD) are used together in order to compare international strategies and organisational designs. Third, more specific to Kronenbourg, the case study can be used to give an illustration of a complex structure of international operations, balancing integration and differentiation, and allow a useful debate on this issue. In this respect it fits Bartlett and Ghoshal's concepts of the transnational organisation (see Bartlett and Ghoshal, 1989, as an additional reading).

4. TEACHING PROCESS

Students should have worked *before* the class on the analysis of the European brewing industry. Otherwise the tutor should start with a discussion of the characteristics of the context (particularly, forces driving global integration and forces driving local responsiveness). Concerning the Kronenbourg case itself, the students could follow four steps.

1. Assess the strengths and weaknesses of the Beer Division of Danone, including Kronenbourg, in the light of the evolution of competitive forces in the brewing industry.

2. Make clear the strategy of in particular its international strategy. A comparison with the main competitors presented in the *European Brewing Industry* case would be useful (Heineken and Carlsberg). This phase should also reveal the paradigm of Danone, the paradigm of the Beer Division and the paradigm of Kronenbourg.

3. Make clear the organisation of international operations at the Beer Division of Danone and evaluate the fit between the organisational design, the international strategy and the type of industry. This analysis could be based on the integration/differentiation framework suggested by Lawrence and Lorsch (1969).

4. Finally, the class might propose a reformulation of, including Kronenbourg, the international strategy of the Beer Division at Danone, and also some organisational changes in line with the new strategy and the changing competitive forces.

Sub-groups of students might prepare recommendations on these issues. The tutor may select two contrasted propositions and start a discussion about these alternatives. The extreme solutions could be: the status quo vs. a high growth world-wide strategy with a tighter coordination of activities (*à la* Heineken or Carlsberg).

In a more complex all-embracing teaching scheme where the Kronenbourg and BGD case studies would be used in parallel, the European brewing industry could be a common starting point. Then the class could be divided into sub-groups representing different international strategies: The Beer Division at Danone BGD and Heineken (etc.). Each sub-group would present the strategy for their company, discuss the logic of the different strategies and examine, where appropriate, the extent to which the companies compete with each other.

5. QUESTIONS FOR DISCUSSION

When the Brasseries Kronenbourg case is studied after the dynamics of the industry (cf. The European Brewing Industry) several issues have been already addressed by the students:

- the forces that drive global integration (at the industry level and for each market segment),

- the forces that drive local responsiveness (at the industry level and for each market segment),

- strategic groups of competitors, types of international strategies in the beer industry.

More specifically with regard to Kronenbourg/Danone, five questions can guide the preparation of the case and discussion.

1. What, including Kronenbourg, are the strengths and weaknesses of the Beer Division of Danone, considering the evolution of the industry and compared with the major competitors in Europe, e.g. Heineken and Carlsberg.

2. Analyse, including Kronenbourg, the international strategy of the Beer Division of Danone. Compare and evaluate the international strategy of Danone's Beer Division with the international strategies of other companies in the industry.

3. Analyse the organisational design of the international operations of the Beer Division of Danone, evaluate the integration and differentiation mechanisms. Is this organisation consistent with the international strategy of the Beer Division?

4. Which specific opportunities and constraints may arise in the Beer Division from belonging to a diversified corporation such as Danone?

5. Should the Beer Division of Danone (including Kronenbourg) reformulate its international strategy? In which directions? Should organisational changes be made in order to improve the effectiveness of the Beer Division on the international scene? If so, what changes?

6. CASE ANALYSIS

Before getting to Kronenbourg-Danone itself, the tutor should make sure that students have a good understanding of the dynamics of the brewing industry (cf. The European Brewing Industry) particularly concerning the following characteristics:

- The market was becoming more and more segmented, with new niche products.

- Upmarket premium beers had increasing success.

- Consumers cared more and more about health and pleasure.

- Demand had stagnated (with slow growth in Southern Europe and slow decline in Northern Europe).

- The bargaining power of retail chains was increasing,

- Economies of scale (particularly in marketing) and brand image were key success factors.

- The industry underwent high concentration since the 1980s, except in Germany where the market was much more fragmented.

- There was overcapacity in Europe.

- There were important differences between European countries, (differences in consumer preferences, in distribution channels, in packaging, etc.), in particular the UK and Germany were very specific markets, hence the industry was multi-domestic. But under the pressure of integration forces (economies of scale in production and marketing, international strategies of some competitors) the industry was becoming mixed (in the terms used by Prahalad and Doz, 1987).

- The Single European Market did not eradicate the differences, However, it seemed to have an impact on the harmonisation of taxes and prices (downwards) and on more strict regulations to limit the consumption of alcohol (health) and to protect the environment.

- The brewing industry had become dual, on the one hand some segments were international: a few upmarket beer brands (Heineken, Carlsberg, Stella Artois), non-alcoholic beer, and some foreign specialities (offering more diversity to consumers), on the other hand, the mass market remained multi-domestic (due to basic local preferences and high transportation costs relative to added value).

The analysis of the Beer Division at Danone should be made considering these characteristics of the industry.

6.1   Strengths and weaknesses of the Beer Division of Danone, including Brasseries Kronenbourg

The company had particular strengths in the following domains:

- The financial power of the Danone Group,

- High productivity, competitive costs and relatively high operating income (compared to the average of the industry),

- Product and packaging innovation (compared to Heineken, for instance),

- A strong position in the segment of non alcoholic beer (Tourtel, Silver),

- Strong positions in France, in Spain, in Italy (Southern Europe) and Belgium.

But the Beer Division of Danone (including Kronenbourg) also had weaknesses:

- No strong international brand (compared to Heineken and Carlsberg for example),

- Not enough speciality upmarket beers in its portfolio (in spite of the variety of brands at Alken Maes),

- Relatively weak international positions outside Southern Europe and Belgium (compared to Heineken, Carlsberg or Interbrew).

Danone armed to be among the world leaders in the businesses in which it was involved, but it had not yet reached this position in the beer industry; the group was surprisingly prudent as far as the international development of the Beer Division was concerned. Indeed the sales growth was moderate during the period 1990–94.

6.2 The strategy of the Beer Division of Danone (including Kronenbourg)

The top managers of Kronenbourg and the Beer Division of Danone viewed brewing as a heavy industry, with high capital intensity. The strategy was based on productivity gains and product innovation. Danone also relied upon its participative style of management. Basically, Kronenbourg tried to 'de-banalise' the beer market, particularly in France, with new products and new packaging (cf. 'K', 'Kronenbourg British Tradition', 'Kronenbourg German Tradition'). The double brand and parallel product ranges in France (Kronenbourg and Kanterbrau) resulted from the history of the Beer Division and were seen as a way to maintain brand diversity in the home market, However, industrial and logistical synergies were implemented in order to improve competitiveness.

- The international strategy of Kronenbourg was determined by the international strategy of the Beer Division of Danone. The guiding principle came from the Group and had been expressed by Antoine Riboud: to become the number one or the number two. In the Beer division the criteria for selecting international targets were clear: permeability of the market, growing demand and opportunities of concentration. However, in the mid-1990s, such criteria restricted the range of possible targets for the Group in the beer industry.

- The dichotomy between upmarket beers which could be exported (due to high added value) and the mass market which required local presence and a broad access to distribution channels was in line with market trends.

- Acquisitions and joint ventures were the preferred modes of development in foreign proprietary markets. Given the overcapacity in Europe, acquisitions were the best way to achieve market presence quickly (before other international competitors) and to gain access to distribution channels (which were more or less held by local brewers). Such a strategy was particularly effective when the target firm had a strong position.

- As the beer industry became mixed, the decision to keep the local brands (hence developing the portfolio of brands) and to add the international brands of the Group to the portfolio of the acquired firm, seemed to be the best strategy. The result was a *dual* international strategy in the case of Danone: some brands were international and required an international brand strategy, some others brands were local and responded to the specificities of local markets.

To some extent there were similarities between the international strategy of the Beer Division of Danone and the international strategy of Heineken in Europe: acquisitions, dual brand strategies. But there was a difference in the sense that Heineken relied more on its core product, the Heineken beer in the green bottle, and aimed at making it a pure global product (such as Coca-Cola). Moreover, Heineken had much stronger positions in other continents. Carlsberg also defended its core brands (Carlsberg and Tuborg) on a worldwide basis. Interbrew also showed worldwide ambitions with the acquisition of Labatt in 1995.

At the beginning of the 1990s several other international competitors became more active, Fosters' Brewing Group became number four with acquisitions and JVs in several continents, Guinness broadened its beer portfolio with the acquisition of Cruz del Campo, Miller showed some interest in Heineken, Heineken launched operations in Hungary and in Vietnam (etc.). In this context the Beer Division of Danone did not seem to be very proactive.

Thus two key questions should be raised:

1. Should the Beer Division of Danone have a more global strategy?

2. Was the Kronenbourg brand strong enough to compete outside its traditional markets?

It seemed that Danone had the financial resources to set up a more ambitious worldwide strategy, but was beer a priority business for Danone?

6.3 The organisation of the Beer Division

According to Porter's model of international strategies, the strategy of the Beer Division appeared to be *country-centred*. The configuration of activities was dispersed, the dispersion had been increased at the beginning of the 1990s with new productions sites for Tourtel and Kronenbourg in Italy and in Spain. The coordination of activities remained very low in spite of recent marketing coordination by international brand managers (for Kronenbourg and Tourtel).

The logic of differentiation between countries dominated the organisation of the Beer Division. Departments within the Beer Division corresponded to the companies acquired or in joint ventures in the different countries.

Four factors may have explained this organisational design:

1. the specificities of each local market, each country called for a specific market strategy (high local responsiveness);

2. the development by acquisitions and joint ventures may have allowed less consolidation in order to reduce the risk of cultural clashes;

3. the fact that, for several years, Danone had had minority stakes in several foreign units;

4. the combination of local brands and international brands in the product portfolio of each country subsidiary.

At the beginning of the 1990s, the Beer Division was organised as a loose federation of companies, in order to preserve high local responsiveness. However, some integration mechanisms balanced international differentiation.

- All departments followed the planning procedure of Danone. In this process the strategies of departments (country subsidiaries and JVs) were debated with the Top Executive Committee of Danone (premier rond), and Antoine Riboud himself gave his opinion. Put differently, strategic decisions were centralised and operational decisions were de-centralised.

- In order to coordinate the international strategy for the three international brands (Kronenbourg, 1664, and Tourtel) European brand managers had been put in place. Moreover, Kronenbourg had direct control over its own sales subsidiaries in other foreign countries

This subtle combination of differentiation and integration seemed to fit the industry context at the beginning of the 1990s. However, this organisational formula might not be adequate in case of quick international development in other zones and for pushing global brands.

As a comparison, Heineken operations were more strongly coordinated, with functional departments acting as consultants, and stronger marketing and technical synergies across borders.

6.4 Belonging to Danone

At this stage of the case study it may be useful to reflect on the opportunities and constraints of being part of the Danone Group. The major opportunities had to do with the access to financial resources. One may also mention the access to skills and supply in packaging, and more generally to skilled labour. There were no significant marketing synergies between the divisions of Danone, However, the access to far foreign markets could be facilitated by the presence of another division.

On the other hand, the fact of belonging to Danone restrained the strategic freedom of the companies in the Beer Division. As cash was managed and distributed by the corporate level, any department or division might be treated as a cash cow, financing other (more attractive) businesses. There was no straight answer to the question: 'Was beer a priority business for Danone?' Indeed, there were some worrying ambiguities in the situation of the Beer Division in 1995: on the one hand, everyone knew that Danone aimed to be the number one or the number two in its business, on the other hand, the group was not very active in the rush for worldwide acquisitions in the beer industry. And brewing accounted for less than 10 per cent of Danone's turnover. Students might speculate on the possibility for Danone to sell off its beer business.

6.5 New strategy, new organisation

As suggested earlier, this part of the class discussion could be prepared by sub-groups of students, and the more contrasted propositions could be discussed by the whole class. Some groups may recommend a status quo, but others will recommend strategic and organisational adaptations at the level of the Beer Division.

For example, a more aggressive international strategy might be proposed, e.g.:

- Danone should consolidate its positions in Italy, in Spain, and in Belgium.

- A leader in the brewing industry should not neglect the British and the German markets, which, together, represent about two-thirds of the European market. Danone should enter the German market by acquisition or through an alliance. Indeed, some German breweries had already reached a significant size (e.g. Oetker, Brau und Brunnen). Danone should also be more active in the UK and seize opportunities in the restructuring of the British brewing industry.

- The Beer Division should look for growth opportunities in Eastern Europe and in the Far East, first select one target country in the area and start with a joint venture. The Beer Division should exploit the opportunity to develop the San Miguel brand in South-East Asia. Depending on the success of these ventures more ambitious goals could be set in the long term.

- Canadian, US and Mexican market were already dominated by very strong competitors and offered little opportunities for a new entrant.

- The development of premium beers called for particular efforts to promote the '1664' internationally and for a diversification of the portfolio of specialities sold across borders. The Beer Division should start to sell more of the upmarket Belgium beers of its subsidiary, Alken Maes, across Europe, the best Italian beer from Peroni and the best Spanish, San Miguel, should also be promoted in the other European countries. This is not to say that they should become global brands, they could be added to the international product portfolio in order to increase its diversity and attractiveness.

In order to catch up with the global strategies of Heineken and Carlsberg, marketing budgets supporting the image of Danone's international brands (1664, Kronenbourg and Tourtel) should be increased dramatically.

With this new strategy, students might propose that the federal organisation of 1994 should be modified. For example:

For the international brands, European production and logistics had already been reorganised (except in the UK and Germany). Starting from 1995, European marketing should be strengthened in order to manage product and packaging homogenisation, European pricing policy, European advertising and distribution (sales and adaptations of advertising campaigns would remain local). More power should be given to international brand managers within this European marketing department. Strategic decisions should be taken at the level of the Beer Division and involve country managers within a European council.

In order to achieve technical synergies across borders, a technical department could be created at the level of the Beer Division (it could include technical specialists coming from Kronenbourg).

Given the specifics of each national market, each national subsidiary could remain a department within the Beer Division.

A New Venture department could be created in order to launch new foreign operations. As soon as a foreign operation was established and reached a significant size, it could become a department. The rest of the international activities, exportations in other geographic zones, could be coordinated by an export department.

In such a reorganisation Kronenbourg might lose some power, and the Beer Division might gain some power, with its increasing coordination role.

The challenge for Danone was to increase integration while maintaining differentiation. This was a condition to become one of the world leaders in the brewing industry, in transition from multi-domestic to transnational.

REFERENCES

Bartlett, C.A. and Ghoshal, S. 1989. *Managing Across Borders, the Transnational Solution,* Boston: Harvard Business School Press.

Lawrence, P.R and Lorsch, J.W. 1969. *Developing Organizations: Diagnosis and Action,* Reading, MA: Addison-Wesley.

Porter, M.E. (ed.) 1986. *Competition in Global Industries,* Boston, MA: Harvard Business School Press.

Prahalad, C.K. and Doz, Y. 1987. *The Multinational Mission, Balancing Local Demands and Global Vision,* New York: The Free Press.

TEACHING NOTES

The Brewery Group Denmark
Flemming Agersnap

1. INTRODUCTION

The case study recounts the strategic moves of Brewery Group Denmark (BGD); a small Danish brewery fighting for a position in a world market.

BGD is an example of a firm finding its market position by distinctive choices vis-à-vis very big international competitors. By an exclusive focus on marketing imported beer and a selective appointment of distributors, BGD has carved out a distinctive market niche.

BGD has also been successful in entering a wide number of markets through local alliances. It can be argued that, in so doing it spreads the risks and means of expansion, but on the other hand, that it makes the group very vulnerable as long as the new relationships are dependent on one person, the international sales director.

2. POSITION OF THE CASE

The case can be used to explore aspects of *international strategy* as it relates to smaller firms. Within this theme, other sub-themes are interesting.

The case may be used as a basis for discussing *a company's competitive position* or the identification of *market segment*. It may also serve well in sessions dealing with *strategic choice*, as an example of focused differentiation – establishing a position in markets dominated by big producers. It may also be the basis of a discussion of the means of *implementation* of the chosen strategy.

3. LEARNING OBJECTIVES

There are three key learning objectives. The first objective is to show the potentials for small companies coexisting with giant competitors in an international context.

The second objective is to illustrate how a coherent international strategy can be built allowing for different local marketing strategies.

The third is to show how different international strategies are viable in different circumstances by comparing BGD's strategies with the international strategies of other brewers or firms in related industries.

4. QUESTIONS FOR DISCUSSION

1. Identify the common elements in the strategies pursued by BGD in Brazil, Russia, China, Italy and the Baltic States.

2. How do the differences in approach in these countries relate to local market characteristics?

3. Compare the international strategy of BGD with that of another major international brewer (e.g. Kronenbourg) and/or smaller companies following international strategies in brewing (e.g. Grolsch) or related industries (e.g. Coopers Creek in the wine industry).

4. Critically assess BGD's capability to continue its international expansion.

5. Would you propose any changes to BGD's strategy?

5. TEACHING SCHEME

We recommend the use of the BGD case study together with the note on the European brewing industry and other case studies of brewer (e.g. Kronenbourg) and/or of a case such as Coopers Creek which shows how another small company in a related industry (win) has achieved an international position.

The tutor might follow the following steps:

- The class could begin with an assessment of the strategic position of BGD. This should be discussed in relation to its external environment and its internal strengths and weaknesses.

- Students might then discuss the *strategy* of BGD, especially its international strategy. (The domestic strategy is not described sufficiently in the case for close analysis; the favourable development on the domestic market is mainly due to developments in the market of soft drinks). The students may focus on the differences in strategy between the major brewers (those following national strategies and those following international strategies) and this small brewery.

- Students may then discuss the *implementation of strategy* which will include choice of partners, channels of distribution, investment in advertising, etc. It may also involve the internal organisation (separation of brewing and marketing, staffing with 'not-brewing professional' in the sales organisation, present vulnerability and plans for future staffing, etc.).

- This discussion might be developed into a question such as 'What is the *winning formula* for a small player on the international scene?' This will naturally combine a discussion of their overall strategy with the approaches taken to implementing it.

- This discussion could move on to the *sustainability* of a strategy of international expansion.

- Finally, the students might discuss whether *changes in strategy* might be proposed. Possible subjects may be introduction of more brands (maybe some locally produced), concentration around fewer markets, how to handle the upcoming need for more production capacity (maybe solved by acquiring other small Danish breweries).

- There is a *video de-brief* of BGD available. This comprises an interview with Claus Nielsen which covers:

   a) his views on the reasons for success of the strategy;

   b) insights into problems in implementing it;

   c) an update on developments in BGD.

The video can be used to round off the class session and to compare student views with those of Claus Nielsen.

6. CASE ANALYSIS/COMMENTARY

6.1 The strategic position of BGD

The strengths of BGD include:

- a distinctive position in its markets and the know-how of how to maintain such a position;

- a strong position in relation to exported Danish beer (building on the reputation of Danish beer) and to 'ethnic' beer (especially malt beer);

- a small, flexible sales organisation;

- its partnership relationship with agents, with BGD as sole supplier of beers, thus absence of internal brand competition in the distribution channel;

- a division of work 'between 'professional' brewers in production and 'professional internationalists; in sales with an emphasis on maintaining high quality in both arenas.

The weaknesses might be:

- small production capacity;

- modest financial capital;

- vulnerability due to rapid expansion (e.g. can the sales organisation keep pace with growth?).

The strengths and weaknesses might be related to market trends like growing income levels, growing interest of beer consumption (in some markets, declining in others), growing emphasis on premium and strong beers, emphasis on brand image, international over-capacity in production. It might also be interesting to question whether the dominant position of Carlsberg in Denmark provides a spur to the success international strategy of BGD; arguably it has forced the company to take an international dimension to its strategy.

6.2 The BGD strategy

BGD is a good example of differentiation on an international scale. Management has recognised that is cannot hope to compete locally with Carlsberg; nor can it compete on an global scale with major beer producers. It has therefore opted for a strategy which requires the careful identification of geographical segments in the beer market particularly suited to its own offering (i.e. high quality branded Danish beer). The important point to note, however, is that none of these markets is identical. The market in Russia is different from China which in turn is different from Brazil and the Baltic's States and soon. Focused differentiation does not mean offering the same product or service to each segment; but rather ensuring that the product or service offering is tailored to the particular needs of that segment. In this sense the core competences underpinning the BGD strategy are much more to do with the know-how and experience which have been built up in delivering this strategy that it is in product or technology. A useful question to ask students is the extent to which they believe other brewing companies could have readily followed the same path (i.e. imitated) BGD.

The BGD case therefore also relates to the issue of *market segmentation.* In assessing a market segments the crucial question is not only how big the segment is, but also how distinctively it may be exploited so that is differentiated from other segments, and how interesting the segment may be to other breweries.

Imported Danish beer is also an important component of the strategy instead of just offering one more taste in the beer market the emphasis on imported beer opens up developments parallel those within the wine market. There the prices range from the lowest level to prices 10 times as high which requires a guarantee of 'origine controlle' and a selective system for distribution. BGD is attempting to obtain a price premium but beer is subject to fiercer local competition than is the case of wine and, so far, the differences in beer taste are not recognised as much as differences in wine taste. Furthermore local production enjoys considerable savings on transportation. On the other hand, the high prices on imported beer and the modest demand are exactly the major elements that make such market segments uninteresting to the multinational breweries and manageable to BGD. The big breweries want volume and will embark on local production and mass advertising. To preserve the distinction BGD emphasises sales and promotion in better bars and restaurants.

6.3 Strategy implementation and the winning formula

Evidently BGD has achieved a good deal of success with its strategy. A useful approach in considering why is to ask students to relate the content of the strategy to the way in which they are implementing it. Focused differentiation, arguably, requires a quite different approach to managing the business than would, for example, broader-based differentiation. The winning formula seems to be built on:

- the focused differentiation approach discussed above;
- a concentration on the segments at the top end of most markets (though note malt beer may be an exception);

- considerable attention given to the identification of such market segments both by Claus Nielsen at the centre but also in partnership with local agents and management;

- the careful choice of partners so that BGD's products are dominant in their portfolio and not competing with other beers;

- the use of indigenous agents as channels of distribution;

- the insistence on branding and point of sale advertising to underpin the brand;

- sales organisation such that local managers are held responsible for local operations; but Claus Nielsen and the head office sales organisation retain an overarching brief for the international strategy;

- the considerable personal dedication and time of Claus Nielsen to co-ordinating this strategy;

- the separation of the technical aspects of brewing from the sales and marketing activity internationally;

- the determination and persistence to find ways of effecting an approach to succeeding in given markets (e.g. Russia and China).

6.4 Changes in strategy

The class might end by raising questions concerned with possible changes required in the strategy. For example:

- The question as to whether the choice of 'top end' segments is always most appropriate, for example, whether there needs to be any connection between the market position taken in countries as wide apart as Italy and China It might also be discussed whether a market position established in one market may be used as spearhead to sell another beer brand (e.g. the THOR brand possibly- adapted to local tastes) produced locally or licensed by a BGD-owned brewery.

- Whether the sales and management organisation of BGD can sustain the growth that is being followed? The sales organisation has been developed so that each major market has a person responsible for export to that market. Yet it may take some time before these employees really can relieve the international sales director of the major responsibility. Is it possible to continue to open up new segments with the same reliance on Claus Nielsen to co-ordinate this: or is the organisation likely to suffer from an increasing reliance on localised management. How soon will the organisation become victim to the transnational problem that faces other organisations? And what would happen if Claus Nielsen left BGD?

- Will demand created by the successful international strategy eventually outstrip production in Denmark? Is it therefore sensible to curtail international expansion; develop local production facilities further in Denmark; or move towards local production in local markets?

TEACHING NOTES

Stewart Grand Prix
Mark Jenkins

1. INTRODUCTION

This teaching note provides guidance for using the Stewart Grand Prix case study. The case is written to illustrate the role of resources and competences in achieving a given strategy. In particular the case illustrates the different resources and competences which are required to enter into a new, although related area of activity. The case also suggests that the management task is not just a question of acquiring the needed resources and competences but also ensuring that these integrate to create a coherent organisation. The case can also be used in conjunction with a series of Formula One case studies by the author: *The Formula One Constructors; Scuderia Ferrari 1975–1977; McLaren International 1988–1991; Williams Grand Prix Engineering 1992–1994.*

2. POSITION OF THE CASE

The case is concerned with resource, competences and strategic capability, which is covered in chapter 4 of exploring *Corporate Strategy.*

3. LEARNING OBJECTIVES

The case provides an overview of the creation of Formula One team Stewart Grand Prix (SGP) from the existing operation of Paul Stewart Racing (PSR). The case is presented in a chronological form and focuses on the period between 1995 and 1997. It allows the tutor to address the following learning objectives:

- How resources and competences combine to create strategic capability.

- How entering new areas of activity, however apparently similar, often requires the development of new resources and competences.

- To explore where the core competences of an organisation may reside and the potential they create.

- That no single resource or competence provides the basis of performance, this is created by the integration of many factors to create strategic capability.

4. QUESTIONS FOR DISCUSSION

What are the necessary resources and threshold levels of competence needed to compete in Formula One?

This question is concerned with identifying industry factors which are needed to operate at this level. Addressing this question will also enable the students to explore how resources and competences may be defined in practice and how the two areas are interdependent in the way they create strategic capability.

What is the fit between the strategic capability of Paul Stewart Racing (PSR) and the competitive environment of F1?

This question moves the discussion into the strategy of PSR and the challenges raised in entering the environment of F1. It requires the students to bring together their assessment of the industry (external) with their assessment of PSR (internal).

How did SGP gain the strategic capability to compete in F1?

We now move from analysis of the situation to review what they actually did. This question raises issues around how organisations may go about creating new areas of capability.

What are the potential core competences of SGP?

Core competences are defined as the ways in which SGP could, in the future, out-perform the competition. Here the students are being asked to look ahead in terms of the future sources of sustainable competitive advantage.

Do you think that Paul Stewart has made the right decision in entering F1? What would your recommendations be to him?

This final questions asks the students to think more critically about their analysis and to formulate some coherent recommendations from it.

5. TEACHING SCHEME

The Stewart Grand Prix case can be used in isolation as a basis for exploring organisational resources and competences. It can also be used in conjunction with the other Formula One cases to consider how sustainable competitive advantage is created and sustained. This outline considers how the case can be used to illustrate and explore the issues raised in chapter 4 of *Exploring Corporate Strategy*.

A possible outline for the session is provided as follows:

- The class could begin with a discussion on the Formula One industry. This could usefully draw from the experiences and perspectives of the students. It is also helpful to focus on what the differences and similarities between F1 and other industries may be. For example, differences would be concerned with the clear industry definition and the idea that F1 is itself an entertainment product competing with other forms of entertainment. The similarities would be in terms of the highly competitive nature of the industry with an increasingly fast rate of innovation and change, particularly in terms of the application of technology.

- The discussion (or short presentations from syndicate groups) could now begin to focus down to Stewart Grand Prix. This is usefully started through a review of Paul Stewart Racing (PSR). It is important to consider how this organisation has developed and how the strategy of the organisation may be described. It is also worthwhile raising the question here as to whether there were other directions in which PSR could have gone i.e. were there other strategic options or was the move into F1 the only possible direction?

- Students may then discuss the implementation of the strategy. In this context they need to examine how particular resources and competences were applied, acquired or stretched. A useful point to ask during this discussion would be whether any team could have done the same things which SGP managed to do.

- The discussion now moves to the future of SGP. The students should be able to identify the future sources of advantage and also what some of the threats and opportunities may be in the future.

6. CASE ANALYSIS

6.1 What are the necessary resources and threshold levels of competence needed to compete in Formula One?

The case suggests a number of factors some of which may be common to the lower formula and some which are unique to F1. The important point to emphasise is that the students should be clear about the distinction and interdependency between the resources and competences needed to compete.

The students will probably identify some of the following:

Resources:

Factory facilities for construction of cars (there may be some discussion as to whether the team needs certain resources such as wind-tunnels, or engines because these can be acquired from outside suppliers)

Computer-based design systems

People: key individuals such as management and drivers and also those with particular technical and commercial expertise

Transporters

Finance through sponsors

Race-cars (it may be useful to enter into the discussion as to whether the cars are a resource or the output of the competences – in fact it is both, but it is important to emphasise the inter-dependence between resources and competences).

Competences:

The ability to prepare and set up cars

Defining the strategy and tactics of a race

Identifying and recruiting talented drivers

Marketing and PR skills

Raising finance through relationships with sponsors

Global logistics (moving equipment and people around the world)

Design and construction of racing cars

Some other competences which are implicit in the case:

Creating alliances with suppliers e.g. in the case of SGP with Cosworth on engines and Bridgestone on tyres.

Financial control: whilst this is by no-means a low-cost operation it still has to operate within a budget and therefore financial skills are important, particularly when we are dealing with such vast sums of money.

Business planning

6.2   What is the fit between the strategic capability of Paul Stewart Racing (PSR) and the competitive environment of F1?

In order to define strategic capability the students will need to undertake two separate levels of analysis: the resource audit (section 4.2) and identification of competences.

Resource Audit of PSR:

Physical resources

Modern factory in north Milton Keynes

State of the art transporters

Human resources

These included mechanics and technicians and key individuals such as David Stubbs, team manager, Nigel Newton, finance director, Rob Armstrong, commercial director, drivers such as Rubens Barrichello and of course Paul and Jackie Stewart both of whom have experience as managers and drivers.

Financial resources

We are told that PSR have a track record of excellence in managing sponsors which we can assume means that they are relatively solvent, however the case also makes the point that this is an efficient business, it is therefore unlikely to have huge reserves of cash hanging around.

Intangibles

This will generate some debate around the Stewart brand, i.e. the name and reputation of Jackie Stewart. Whilst Stewart has not taken a proactive role in PSR his association with it through Paul Stewart is possibly the most significant resource which PSR have. Other intangibles could relate to relationships with sponsors and the image of PSR separate from Jackie Stewart.

Competences

The case identifies that PSR have many of the basic competences needed for F1 such as managing the race team, selecting and recruiting drivers, managing sponsors, etc. There is an issue of how sensitive these competences are to scale. Are the competences the same for achieving a £25,000 sponsorship deal to a £25 million sponsorship deal? Is managing a F3 team the same as a F1 team? This would begin to suggest that whilst on the surface the competence is the same the kinds of resources needed may actually be significantly different (different calibre people, new systems, new facilities). This again, emphasises the linkage between resources and competences.

Using the frameworks outline in section 4.3.3 further assessment of PSR's position can be made:

Cost efficiency:

Whilst PSRs activities are significant in terms of the lower formula in F1 terms they are a small operation who are likely to be around a twentieth the size of an F1 team. It is unlikely that they have any advantages in terms of economies of scale or supply costs. They have no product/process design skills and no experience in terms of the design and construction of race cars.

Value added:

Here the position looks more positive. Whilst there is a worthwhile discussion here around who are the customers, e.g. is it sponsors, the enthusiast, or the media. PSR have shown themselves to be very good at creating customer value through managing corporate clients, when this is coupled with the Stewart 'brand' then there is some level of competence here, even when compared with established F1 teams.

Linkages:

It can be assumed in terms of PSR that the racing experience of Paul Stewart has put him in good position to provide bridges between the different areas of PSR.

Assuming the students have already considered the threshold competences for competing in F1, it is worth focusing on two aspects of the 'gap' between PSR's strategic capability and the threshold competences of F1. These are concerned with two areas: the competence of designing and constructing the race car and the level of financing required taking the fund raising activity into a whole new level of activity.

6.3 How did SGP gain the strategic capability to compete in F1?

This question focuses on how they actually went about creating the capability needed to compete in F1. Capability was generated in three ways: First by acquiring new resources to generate capability – in particular, this involved the recruitment of Alan Jenkins and the design team and the acquisition of computer systems to aid the design process. Second, capability came from the stretching of existing resources and competences – this relates to the fund raising activities. Whilst Jackie Stewart had played a relatively low-key role in PSR for SGP he came to the fore as chief fund-raiser using his name and contacts to help generate the finance needed. The third route was through alliances or partnerships, in particular the relationship with Cosworth and Ford provided SGP with the engine development capability they needed (currently only Ferrari build their own engines in F1).

This discussion should raise some of the issues around how organisations should approach competing in new areas of activity – the pros and cons between acquiring capability from outside, through alliances or developing it from inside.

The balance of the elements is also referred to in the case. This is related to Paul Stewart's comments about the role of the driver. SGP could have put everything into getting the best driver and this could have had a positive effect on other aspects of the business eg sponsorship, car development. However one of the problems with drivers is that they tend to move around a lot – and are therefore highly mobile resources which are relatively easy for the competition to acquire. Stewart is trying to keep a balance between the different parts of the business in order to build the 'solid platform' which he refers to at Williams. It is this solid platform which provides the potential for a sustained advantage.

6.4 What are the potential core competences of SGP?

These relate to the future sources of competitive advantage – what are the resources/ capabilities that may be unique to SGP and difficult for competitors to acquire of copy. Potential core competences include:

Relationship with non-tobacco sponsors

Relationship with Ford and with Cosworth

Jackie Stewart's wider contacts

Staircase of talent through PSR – future sources of talented drivers

Totally computerised design process

The Stewart management team

It is worthwhile challenging these in terms of how easy it would be for other teams to do these things: For example, all the F1 teams are moving toward a fully computerised design and manufacturing process, most of them have some involvement with other levels of motorsport to identify talented drivers. This will probably distil the whole thing down to Jackie Stewart and his contacts.

6.5   Do you think that Paul Stewart has made the right decision in entering F1? What would your recommendations be to him?

Use this discussion to explore some of the other potential options which PSR could have taken. For example both, Indycar and saloon car racing involve the racing of cars rather than their design and construction. It could be argued that these areas of activity were more closely aligned to PSRs strategic capability and that it would have been easier for them to develop successful activites in these areas rather than F1.

The recommendations would need to relate to how the core competences identified would be developed and used to create a sustained advantage. However it is also important to stress the how the technical side of the operation is absorbed into SGP as a whole. The PSR culture has been about racing, not building cars. A key issue is for them to create the linkages where the technical competence which they have acquired becomes a fundamental part of the SGP operation.

7. CASE UPDATE

The period on which the case focuses ends with the 1997 F1 season. The 1998 season produced some interesting issues concerning the viability of the SGP strategy and the nature of resources and competences in a highly competitive environment. The following overview picks up on some of the key issues to date, this may be useful as a closing discussion with the students.

The start of 1998 was nothing short of disastrous for SGP. Both cars retired within 8 laps in two of the early races – this included Magnussen crashing into Barrichello at the San Marino Grand Prix in Italy. Up to May 1998 highest position was tenth. Some of the possible reasons for this are summarised below.

1998 introduced a new set of regulations which meant that the cars were narrower and used thinner tyres. This meant major redesigns on all F1 cars, SGP had therefore to redesign their car all over again whilst at the same time racing in their first season of F1. This combined with relatively little testing over the winter meant that SGP had an even greater challenge in their second year than the first.

The team had also introduced a new carbon-fibre gearbox (also used by Arrows). Whilst this should provide a weight advantage, it was shown to be unreliable.

Bridgestone tyres have been shown to give an advantage, however in 1998 larger and more powerful teams (such as McLaren) switched to Bridgestone, this meant that SGP had less of an advantage, and were also less influential on the tyre development which Bridgestone were undertaking. Bridgestone therefore became a less restricted resource and also one which SGP had less influence over.

Whilst he was very successful in Formula Three, Jan Magnussen failed to translate this promise into F1. One of the assumptions of the staircase of talent, is that a good driver in F3 will make a good driver in F1 where the pressure is significantly higher. Whilst there are many examples of those who have succeeded at both levels, there are also many who have not. The rumour is currently that SGP are looking to replace Magnussen with a driver who has more experience in F1. Again this relates to how transferable a particular resource is from one context to another.

Of greatest concern to SGP is that they have been outperformed by teams such as Tyrrell who are using an inferior version of the Ford engine. Ford are clearly looking for rapid progress with SGP and it has been rumoured that they have been talking to Benetton (third in the 1997 constructors championship) about future engine supply in order to make a more accurate comparison with SGP. Whilst Ford are contractually tied to provide SGP with the most advanced engine until the end of 2000, this will come under increasing pressure if SGP are not able to demonstrate winning potential.

TEACHING NOTES

Laura Ashley Holdings plc
J. L. Heath[1]

1. INTRODUCTION

The case describes the growth and development of a leading clothing, home furnishings and related products group from its origins in the early 1950s until 1995. Over this period the business grew from a home-based husband and wife concern to an international group whose brand name Laura Ashley was recognised around the world and regarded by many as the group's major asset.

The case is in three parts.

Part 1 outlines the development of the company to 1985 when it became a quoted UK public company, and describes the group's continued growth through further store openings, acquisitions and the broadening of its product range.

Part 2 describes the difficulties faced by the Group as its over-ambitious expansion plans coincided with the onset of the economic downturns of the late 1980s and early 1990s. The Group narrowly survived a cash crisis in 1990 and was forced to make significant cutbacks involving the closure of established facilities and the divestment of some recent acquisitions. A new CEO, Dr Jim Maxmin, was appointed in September 1991 and the case summarises his assessment of the group's situation and the actions he set in train in an attempt to improve the Group's performance and potential. Despite the changes Dr Maxmin implemented the Group continued to struggle and he resigned in April 1994.

Part 3 describes the Group's change of emphasis following Dr Maxmin's departure, from investment in the Laura Ashley brand to a concerted attack on costs. On her appointment in June 1995 as Laura Ashley's new CEO, Ann Iverson announced her intention of re-establishing a 'retail culture' and a strong unified look across the Group's product range. The case concludes with a summary of Miss Iverson's assessment of the business and her proposals for returning the Group to a satisfactory level of performance within three years.

2. POSITION OF THE CASE

The case is a suitable vehicle with which to explore a range of corporate strategy and strategic management issues. It lends itself to examination of an organisation's *strategic capability,* and how this is related to the resources available to the organisation and the way in which these have been deployed to create competences in specific activities and through linking activities together. In particular it is a useful case to identify how competitive advantage can accrue from exploiting unique resources and core competences but how these need to change

---

[1] ©J.L.Heath, 1996, 1999.

with time as the company's competitive position and dominant strategies change. These issues are examined in *Exploring Corporate Strategy,* chapters 4 and 10.

3. LEARNING OBJECTIVES

An understanding of an organisation's strategic capability is essential in assessing the appropriateness of present or proposed strategies. This understanding can be developed in part through a detailed analysis of the organisation's resources, how these resources are, or may be deployed, and crucially, the nature of the linkages between and among these resources.

Value chain analysis provides an appropriate framework for such an examination. It provides a useful structure for:

- Identifying organisational and intra-organisational activities and assessing their present and potential contribution to added value.

- Identifying core competences through examination of cost efficiency, value creation and linkages between elements in the chain.

- Assessing the robustness of core competences to imitation and/or competitive threat.

The case illustrates how competitive advantage may be eroded as the management problems of coping with organic and acquisitive growth, expanding international operations, and environmental change of various kinds, all increase in complexity. As a result mismatches arise between the organisation's strategic capability and its competitive environment that are difficult to correct.

4. TEACHING PROCESS

The case can be used in several ways. Typically, the tutor may lead a class discussion involving all course members whose analyses are probed and/or elaborated by the tutor and course members. An alternative approach is to invite sub-groups to prepare reports on a particular issue for presentation at plenary session. In this way, each group focuses on a specific issue in detail, but also shares in the overall analysis of the case. Some groups may be given, or asked to obtain information on Laura Ashley's competitors and requested to present comparative analyses.

This case supports a range of strategic management issues beyond those of resource analysis, competence and strategic capability, and has been used both for class discussion and examination purposes on a variety of management programmes, in particular BABS, DMS and MBA.

5. QUESTIONS FOR DISCUSSION

These can be varied depending on the time available and the learning/assessment objectives involved. As a basis for opening a class discussion, a broad introductory question such as the following is generally satisfactory:

I. How do you account for the success of the Laura Ashley group to 1985? What were the key factors contributing to its success?

Once these introductory questions have been discussed more specific questions can be introduced at appropriate points to focus discussion on particular issues, or move the discussion on to successive stages in Laura Ashley's development. Some suggestions are given below.

2. To what extent do you think that Laura Ashley had the capability to embark on a strategy of international expansion?

3. What advantages and disadvantages did Laura Ashley draw from its vertically integrated structure during the different stages of the Group's development?

4. How do you account for the problems Laura Ashley faced during the 1990s? What weaknesses did these expose? How did the company respond to these problems? What other options were open to it in coping with the difficulties it faced?

6. CASE ANALYSIS

Some of the issues that may be explored in discussing the above questions are outlined below. Whilst the following comments relate mainly to broad issues of resources, competence, strategic capability and control, the case also allows some issues to be given particular emphasis if tutors wish (leadership style, for example).

References to relevant sections in *Exploring Corporate Strategy* are shown in brackets.

6.1 Key factors contributing to the successes of Laura Ashley to 1985

The early successes of the company were undoubtedly rooted in the combination of skills, interests and personalities of its founders. Laura Ashley's flair as a designer, and Bernard Ashley's interest in production, coupled with his business ability and tenacity were important in establishing the business. The Ashleys also had vision and from the start they strove to build a truly international company.

Laura's designs were rooted in traditional English country values and very much in tune with an emerging mood of nostalgia within society. She had an intuitive feel for her customers' mood, and during her lifetime this was reflected in the subtle development of her designs. (4.7)

Her untimely death was an undoubted loss to the company, even though by this time her design philosophy had been absorbed within the group. The influence she may have continued to exert within the company had she lived can be a matter only of speculation. Laura Ashley brought to the Group not only her design skills but a personality that complemented and balanced that of her husband. With her death the group lost not only her design flair but also her stabilising influence on Group development. (10.4)

The direct involvement of the founders in design, manufacturing and retail operations contributed significantly to shaping the organisation's culture as the business developed. It also provided direct supervision which seems to have worked well while the Group's activities were confined mainly to a limited range of fabrics and dresses within the UK. (10.4.2)

As Laura Ashley's international potential became apparent however, Bernard Ashley spent more time abroad and devoted less attention to UK operations. As the driving force behind Laura Ashley's growth Bernard Ashley took the major strategic decisions whilst others dutifully maintained the course their 'captain' had set.

The Laura Ashley group had considerable strengths in *design, manufacturing* (before comparable overseas sources emerged) and *retailing* Its early, and considerable investment in IT suggests that the problems of integrating these functions were understood and were, initially, actively addressed. (4.7)

6.2 The capability of Laura Ashley to pursue a strategy of international expansion

Successful overseas expansion depends on an effective combination of a number of factors. It is clearly important for the marketing mix to match the requirements of overseas target groups. The 4 Ps of Product, Promotion, Price and Place must be appropriate for the intended markets. Laura Ashley's designs and image proved appealing to significant market segments in the US, continental Europe and the more affluent areas of the Pacific Basin. Bernard Ashley's frequent and prolonged trips abroad were successful in attracting substantial overseas business. Product, price and promotion appear to have been effectively matched to overseas markets, but distribution proved to be the weak link within the 'mix'. Adherence to a vertically integrated business in which overseas markets were supplied from the UK proved a severe handicap to cost effective and timely distribution. As the volume of business grew it appears that investment in additional manufacturing capacity was adequate to support it, but the *scheduling* of this capacity had serious shortcomings. This was due not only to the complexities inherent in an ever widening product range, but from inadequate information and control systems with which to manage this growing complexity. (10.5)

At a relatively early stage in its development Laura Ashley made much of its investment in IT and the importance of what it termed its 'informatics' capability. However, this appears not to have been adequately updated to keep pace with the company's growth in overseas markets, especially within the US, the most important of these. The recognition of this weakness by Jim Maxmin and his significant but belated attempt to remedy this with significant investments in new technology is discussed in the second half of the case. His decision to spend £3 million on 'upgrading and unifying computer systems' suggests that these 'resources' had been neglected in previous years. This view is further supported by the revelation that there were no standard shop operating procedures in operation in the US. (Informal industry sources refer to the widespread practice among US shop managers of phoning around the country to locate out-of-stock items for which they had customers. If these were located store managers made their own informal arrangements for getting these items to their own shop). (10.4 and 10.5)

The management problems of an international business differ according to the way in which its overseas business is conducted. Sales through a single intermediary within a foreign country is relatively straightforward in management terms compared with the ownership and active management of one's own retail and/or manufacturing facilities within overseas markets. It can be useful to discuss with students ways in which the export activities of a business typically evolve, and the advantages and disadvantages of different forms of overseas business. Laura Ashley seems to have encountered few problems in its sales through overseas partners, or even in its shops-within-shops approach common in continental Europe. The problems of actively managing its own, rapidly growing retail chain in the US was by comparison a continuing headache for the Group. (9.2.8)

Laura Ashley seems not to have had the depth of management necessary to support its ambitious expansion plans. It is clear too from the case that the Group had not been able to ensure the appointment of managers of a suitable standard in its US operations. There is evidence later in the case, that until the introduction of staff training and management development programmes by Jim Maxmin in 1992, formal staff development had not been regarded as a priority. (10.4)

6.3 Advantages and disadvantages of vertical integration

The theoretical advantages of vertical integration, principally the control and integration of different parts of the value chain, are extremely difficult to realise in practice. (4.3) This becomes increasingly so as product range and geographical locations become more diverse. So although the Group's vertically integrated structure provided potential for closer control of quality and cost in the early years, as the company grew and expanded overseas the difficulties of realising actual benefits from vertical integration became more evident. Rapid growth added to the difficulties of effectively integrating the various elements in the value chain. At times manufacturing capacity was reported to be lying idle and at others late delivery to its shops resulted in lost sales. High UK manufacturing, distribution and stock-holding costs, and the increasing ability of lower cost producers to achieve high quality standards made UK manufacturing less and less viable for the group. However, the Ashleys had a strong commitment to the group's manufacturing centre in Wales and Sir Bernard's reluctance to take the harsh decision to withdraw from UK manufacturing was criticised in some quarters.

'Too great an attachment, However, well meant, to an under-managed Welsh-based manufacturing operation has proved to be a liability, particularly in supplying remote US markets when the dollar has been in long-term decline' (The Independent, 25 August 1990)

6.4 How do you account for the problems Laura Ashley faced during the 1990s? What weaknesses did these expose? How did the company respond to these problems it faced? What other options were open to it in coping with the difficulties it faced?

(a) Inbound and outbound logistics

In terms of the value chain Laura Ashley had considerable shortcomings in relation to inbound and outbound logistics. (10.3) These were eventually addressed by Jim Maxmin, and in dramatic fashion, through his strategic alliance with Federal Express from March 1992 (see below).

There is evidence that the company's growth overstretched its management resources and insufficient control was maintained over its affairs. The replacement of departing senior staff was sometimes unduly delayed with existing managers taking on yet greater burdens as a result.

The Ashley family's dominant stake in the business and Sir Bernard's reluctance to take certain decisions were also matters that attracted press comment. (10.6.3)

> *'Sir Bernard Ashley has not been interested in new suggestions. John James needed to have more fire in his belly to cope with this' (Sunday Times, 4 July 1990)*

> *'Only when the company makes a decisive break from the family tradition will it change its luck for the better' (Investors Chronicle, 27 April 1990)*

> *'A lack of consistent management and a finger in every pie philosophy' (Daily Telegraph, 28 September 1990)*

Jim Maxmin recognised, and began to address these and other HRM shortcomings, with the recruitment of Denise Lincoln as Global Human Resources Director, and her symbolic appointment to the main board.

(b) Acquisitions

The strategic rationale for these may have been sound but the company's ability to manage and integrate 'their acquisitions was extremely questionable. (The effective management of acquisition is well demonstrated by Electrolux's acquisition of Zanussi.)[2]

Although some of the acquired companies were relatively small concerns and unlikely to have significant effect on the group as a whole, they undoubtedly absorbed a considerable proportion of an already stretched management's energies. (7.3.2)

(c) Strategic alliance with Federal Express

Laura Ashley's alliance with Federal Express provides a useful example of the mutual benefits that may be available through the merging of complementary competences. It was through this new partnership that Jim Maxmin sought, in part, to reconfigure Laura Ashley's existing resources. (10.2) (7.3.3)

The service cultures of the Laura Ashley and Federal Express were complementary. Jim Maxmin considered Laura Ashley's core strengths to be brand management and the handling of customers, not distribution and systems. However, the latter were the key resources of Federal Express, in which they were world leaders and in which they invested $300 million a year to maintain that position. For Laura Ashley the alliance provided direct access to new systems for which no alternatives were available within so short a time frame.

No competitive bids for distribution were sought by Laura Ashley. Instead, Jim Maxmin wished to forge a win-win partnership with Federal Express based on mutual trust. The two

---

[2] See case study, Electrolux - The Acquisition and Integration of Zanussi, by S. Ghoshal and P. Haspeslagh, INSEAD-CEPED, 1990.

companies agreed on a 'transparent, co-operative venture' with the business of each party open to inspection by the other. It was a loose alliance based on trust in which both parties would work together to develop each other's business. (10.4.4) (7.3.3)

Although the potential benefits of the alliance were clear, there were also associated risks. Since the partnership was highly visible, failure would be very embarrassing for both parties. Laura Ashley would be faced once more with an ineffective distribution system and for Federal Express there would be a significant setback to its strategy of global partnerships. (7.3.3)

(d) Networks and relationships

As a result of failure to meet post-flotation expectation of profit performance, press comment has sometimes been less than helpful to the group. The need for the company's relations with the press and City of London to be addressed were recognised in the 1991 annual report. The breakdown of relations with Lazard's over the appointment of Ann Iverson in 1995 is further evidence of the difficulty Laura Ashley's 'old guard' sometimes had in maintaining good relationships with its various stakeholders.

The importance of networks as a strategic resource is explored by Kay[3] and may usefully be discussed in relation to the case. The importance of both internal and external networks, and the maintenance of sound relationships with stakeholders, can be a fruitful general area of discussion and one for which the Laura Ashley case provides a number of insights. (9.2.7)

Dealing with the often conflicting expectations and priorities of stakeholders is a major challenge of strategic management. The ability of a manager to pursue a well considered strategy over the medium to longer term may be significantly constrained by the insistence of some powerful stakeholders for higher short-term returns.

It would appear that this was a major factor in Jim Maxmin's departure from Laura Ashley. His failure to turn Laura Ashley's US operations around within the period he had originally forecast damaged his credibility. This reduced his ability to retain sufficient support from key stakeholders to continue with his chosen turnaround strategy. Also, Maxmin's management style had not been wholeheartedly endorsed by some of his most senior colleagues. Whilst his enabling style had been well received by staff at lower levels, his expectation that top managers should all spend some time working in the group's shops had not gone down well with all of them!

(e) Brand management

Jim Maxmin's view that:

> *'Laura Ashley is a brand. It is not a retailing company. It is not a fashion company. It is not a production or manufacturing company'*

provides a useful basis for a concluding phase of the case discussion. Students can be asked whether they agree or disagree with this view. The discussion may then move on to examine

---

[3] J. Kay, *Foundations of Corporate Success*, Oxford University Press, 1993.

the strategic challenges associated with international brand management and what might be done in order to *'unleash the intrinsic strength of that fantastic brand'*. (10.2)

By 1998 the optimism of 1995 had proven to be ill-founded. Iverson was dismissed in November 1997 after a series of events reported in the press, including:

- issuing three profit warnings within a year;

- extremely high stock levels, resulting in huge discounts on surplus stock;

- halting the US expansion programme after too many shops were opened in wrong locations, and concentrating too heavily on home furnishings;

- giving shareholders unrealistic recovery expectations;

- the unsuccessful re-launch of the Laura Ashley brand.

The company was left with a weak financial position, resulting in the closure of the Welsh factories. In May 1998, Laura Ashley was saved from bankruptcy by a £44 million cash injection from a Malaysian tycoon who obtained a 40 percent share of the business. The departure of Sir Bernard Ashley as a director followed the Malaysian backing. In August 1998 David Hoare, who had taken over as Chief Executive when Iverson left, was also replaced.

TEACHING NOTES

The Iona Community
Peter Jones

1. INTRODUCTION

The case organisation is a voluntary group (albeit legally a limited company), centred in Scotland but having a widespread reputation. Its founder was made a Lord for his pioneering work in and through the Iona Community. The organisation must adapt to changed and changing needs from those which pertained when the organisation was set up. However, members expectations of how the organisation should adapt to the 1990s differ. This raises many of the issues of chapter 5 of *Exploring Corporate Strategy.*

2. POSITION OF THE CASE

The case illustrates the *role of values and history* in the management and decisions of an organisation. It shows how, as time moves on an organisation needs to *redefine its role,* but the difficulties of doing this when:

• there are strong values underpinning the organisation,

• there is a need to take organisation members along with any changes,

• when members adherence to the organisation is largely emotional rather than monetary.

It also shows that there may well be *conflicts between the espoused aims and the practicality of implementing these aims.*

3. LEARNING OBJECTIVES

The case is designed to give practise at teasing out the softer issues of strategy formation (and students should make reference to Chapter 5 of the text in their analysis). Key aspects are:

• the role of culture

• can 'commercial' needs sit alongside the Community's religious and social values?

Some of the issues are heightened in a voluntary organisation where organisational members can leave much more easily than in a commercial organisation because there are no financial aspects tying the member to the organisation (indeed the reverse!)

4. TEACHING SCHEME

There is a possibility that some students may be 'turned off' by the setting of the case. It is essential that the lecturer set the scene that all organisations need to consider issues of values in strategy. Just because the setting is a religious community makes it no more and no less appropriate.

The case is essentially one where discussion is needed. The video (available separately) is best used at the start of the session as it clarifies and amplifies issues arising in the case, rather than bringing them to a conclusion. There has, to date (1997), been little resolution of the issues facing the Community.

In considering the issue of the lease renewal, it would be possible to set up an intergroup discussion between three groups representing:

1. Iona Abbey Ltd (Crichton Lang), wanting a realistic and probably much higher rent.

2. Community members opposed to a renewal if a higher rent means putting the weekly charges up much.

3. Community members prepared to 'run a commercial hotel' (and use profits to subsidise other activities).

For discussion purposes you could suggest a rent such that at the Abbey the weekly fees to break even doubled.

5. QUESTIONS FOR DISCUSSION

1. What *values* pervade the organisation? How do they a) help, b) hinder and c) limit what the organisation wishes to do?

2. Who are your *key stakeholders?* What do they want out of the Community? What does the Community need from them? In what ways do they impinge upon and/or limit freedom of action?

3. Is the organisation doing a good job? What *measures of success* does it use? What measures would you use?

4. What is the *cohesion (if any) behind the main activities* undertaken by the Community? How are they held together? Do they need to be? Can cross-subsidy be made to work? Is there any overarching strategy behind the organisation?

5. *Who does or should define strategy* in the organisation? How do different views get resolved?

6. CASE ANALYSIS

6.1 Values

The organisation is clearly an *ideological* stereotype in terms of section 5.4.1.

The Community is a Christian group who wish to further a particular set of ideals, particularly around issues of peace and justice in society. These ideals are likely to exist in members before they join the Community but are reinforced by the 2-year initiation period and the regular meetings in Family groups and at Plenaries. The founder's early mission (of trying to train Church of Scotland church ministers to relate to poor urban communities on the mainland of Scotland) seems to be taking a back-seat, though there are echoes of this in their 'bias to the poor', and the wish to use the Island centres for groups from poorer communities.

These values bind members together despite difficulties of distance.

The values could set them at odds with trustees of the Abbey who may not be so 'radical' in their outlook. This could rear its head on the new lease issue. For the Community the issues posed are:

'Do we want to run the centres as a commercial venture? What would we do if the lease went up to such an extent that we had to charge fees which only well-off people could afford? Are we in the hotel business?'

Currently these have not been forced upon them, and so they can be (and in the case writer's view have been) ducked.

The values are those of a 'movement' and may get in the way of some 'efficiency' issues; e.g. the willingness to charge a premium at the Abbey, where demand is considerably in excess of bed spaces. Yet there is not unanimity on all issues. Having similar values does not guarantee identical answers to all issues from all members.

The value of 'Bias to the Poor' is fairly universal but students could discuss the extent to which it can be (easily) operationalised in the context of the subsidies, and whether it conflicts with other values (e.g. fairness). This could lead to the danger of having values which are too simplistic, i.e. ones to which lip-service can be paid but which are difficult to enforce.

6.2 Stakeholders

One way to analyse stakeholders is to use a Power-Interest matrix (section 5.3.2). In isolation from specific strategies this may be of little help, as power/influence can change with strategy. However, it might be legitimate to say that for most likely strategies the following general positions hold:

High power/ high interest –
    Members, especially committed ones.

High power/ low interest –
    Abbey trustees (historically) – interest changing under new Chief
Executive of Iona Abbey Ltd?

Low power/ high interest –
   Full-time staff; Associates & Friends

Low power/ low interest –
   Church of Scotland and other denominations. Guests to Centres

A key feature for the Community is the relationship with Iona Abbey Limited. After decades of low interest the new Chief Executive of Iona Abbey Limited (a Mr Crichton Lang) is potentially challenging the Community's position as the 'public face/perception' of Iona His demands and vision for Iona could conflict with the Community's. The Community have not had to deal with (such) an entrepreneur before!

Will he face them with uncomfortable questions about the role of the Centres? EG about costs and thus prices; about whether they will need to employ more staff to maintain the fabric if he pulls out? about whether they are set up to 'run a building'?

Another key issue is the extent to which all members should be allowed to 'use/hijack the Community' to 'peddle their own concerns'. What central control is there to be on what the Community lends its name to? And how are members to be made accountable for their actions in the Community's name? This relates to the wider question of 'How does a voluntary organisation maintain discipline/standards among its members?' (See also discussion in section 6.4 on Cohesion.)

6.3 Success

The definitions of success are loose and anecdotal for the Community as a whole. (See the two statements by the Community Leader). This is *not to be confused with having no objectives*. The Community has a two paragraph statement of its Purpose and six stated goals. Whilst not quoted in the case they are of similar ilk to the statements in the Case by the Leader, Norman Shanks.

However, they appear to have no quantitative measures besides financial ones. Numerical growth of membership has been explicitly ruled out as an objective and thus a measure of success, at least by Norman Shanks.

This poses students (and lecturers!) with the question of whether every organisation needs to or should have quantifiable measures. The case writer is not here prepared to enter that particular fray, at least not in this teaching note!

As far as one can tell (final section of case) the financial measure seems to be 'Are we solvent?'/'can we keep going?'. For three of the last four years they have needed to dip into reserves (see case appendix 2). The question of whether the main financial assets (the Island centres) are operating at a profit is a difficult question to answer definitively, confused as it is by two factors:

a) the rent issue – they pay no rent for use of the Abbey.

b) the accounts – where an expenditure of £99,000 for 'Islands Administration' needs to be off set against the surpluses on The Abbey, the Mac centre and the shops. Thus which part is making a profit is not clear (see case appendix 2).

There is a case for trying to apportion these expenses out, particularly as the 'Lease question' becomes higher profile. The debate about what level to charge for a week at the Centres will need to be informed by a more accurate understanding of their costs. This should be worked on now to prepare for the debate. (Case writer's note: there was no sign this was appreciated, or was being done.)

6.4 Internal cohesion of activities

The links between the three main strands of activity (Islands Centres, Mainland Work, and Publishing) are not strong. They exist but it is easier to see three strands rather than one dominant theme. Whether there should be more links is an open question. This begs the question of whether strategy is a matter of consistency of activity or cohesive values or what? Students should realise there is no definitive answer to this issue, but is one all organisations will wrestle with.

Part of the difficulty of reviewing strategy (see next section) is that some 'pet projects' could be questioned? Individual members hold different aspects dear in the package of activities of the organisation. Questioning/ curtailing/discontinuing these could well lead to such members leaving the organisation. Thus deleting activities is much more difficult than adding new activities. This is a feature of voluntary organisations and explains seemingly unrelated activities continuing side by side. The question of coherence poses threatening questions for members, and is thus likely to be ducked.

6.5 Who defines strategy?

It is not clear who defines strategy. Formally it is the role of the Plenary meeting but in practice this is too cumbersome a body, and in any case it never involves all members (see attendance details in the Case.) It is a vehicle for expressing opinions on direction; but these take concrete shape within a committee structure. The role of 'volunteer' versus 'paid employee' is here an issue. In the case there appears to be a 'conflict of expectations' between the roles (section 5.2.7), particularly on the extent to which committees decide operational matters vis-à-vis policy matters. Students might well discuss whether such a simple distinction is possible?

In evaluating strategy it seems that the criteria of 'suitable' and 'acceptable' have taken more precedence over 'feasible'; particularly on the issue of 'bias to the poor'. But the outcome is not proving acceptable, so a continuing dialogue takes place. Is this a problem when all 3 criteria are not explicitly considered?

An as yet unresolved issue is, who will head up strategy on the 'renewal of the lease' issue? How will potential conflicts with Iona Abbey Ltd be handled? The issue could provoke considerable debate and conflict within the Community and the decision structures seem cumbersome to deal with such. This is a not untypical feature of voluntary organisations, they are often slow at taking difficult polarising decisions, because of the need to carry members along. The pressures of real-time decision-making conflict with the demands of corporate-wide consensus.

TEACHING NOTES

Sheffield Theatres Trust
Gareth Morgan and Kevan Scholes

1. INTRODUCTION

The case study concerns a charitable trust which is responsible for two of the UK's leading provincial theatres – the Crucible and Lyceum Theatres in Sheffield (plus a third stage – the Studio). It covers the period from 1971 (when the Crucible theatre opened) to 1996 by which time it had become part of *Sheffield Theatres Trust* together with its refurbished sister theatre – the *Lyceum* – and under the management of a single Chief Executive, Stephen Barry. During the 25-year period, the theatre saw many new developments and significant changes in its environment – particularly regarding its funding.

There were a number of financial crises during the period, leading each time to changes in the organisation and management of the theatres. The period from 1992 saw the Crucible having to adjust to some new challenges brought about by the popularity of the Lyceum, a major financial fraud, further declines in public sector grants, and two years of poor sales at the box office.

The case study incorporates information from the previous *Crucible Theatre* case studies (1976, 1988, and 1992).

2. POSITION OF THE CASE

Sheffield Theatres Trust is a core case study for the issues raised in chapter 5 of *Exploring Corporate Strategy*.

The case study should be used to show the importance of identifying *stakeholder groups,* analysing their *expectations* regarding the performance of the theatres (section 5.3), and formulating strategies which take account of these conflicting expectations (chapter 8, section 8.3.3).

This new version of the case study is presented in a more concise form than previously, and it has been rewritten to reflect the new Trust structure adopted in 1995 which gives parity between the production and touring sides, as represented by the Crucible and Lyceum respectively. This case can also be used to cover relationships within the *value chain* and how they can be managed (see for example the discussions in chapter 4 section 4.3.1), particularly in relation to the use of *contracts and performance indicators* in the public sector.

3. LEARNING OBJECTIVES

It is very common for students of Corporate Strategy to have a naive view of the *political* dimension of strategy formulation. All too often they regard organisations as having pre-ordained objectives inferring that strategy formulation is simply a logical process of defining how these objectives will be pursued.

The *Sheffield Theatres* case illustrates quite clearly that strategy formulation is not such a simple process and, therefore, it is crucial to analyse the *political* context within which strategies are formulated. *Stakeholder analysis* (section 5.3 in the text) is a useful method of analysing this political dimension.

The fact that the theatre has both commercial and public service objectives to pursue simultaneously should make it clear that strategy formulation usually proceeds through a process of balancing and compromise and not through optimisation.

Specifically the case can be used to illustrate the following issues from the text:

a) The factors which influence the *expectations* and objectives of individuals and groups (exhibit 5.9).

b) Identifying and the analysing *conflicts* of expectations (exhibit 5.3).

c) *Stakeholder mapping* (section 5.3.2).

d) Organisational *purposes* and the nature of objectives (section 5.6)

e) Linkages within the *value chain* (chapter 4, section 4.3.5)

4. TEACHING SCHEME

The teaching approach clearly depends upon the nature and size of the group and the time available. However, the session will normally open by identifying stakeholders (using question 1 below).

One very successful approach, if circumstances permit, is to divide into sub-groups representing the interests of different stakeholders. These could include:

- the external funders: Yorkshire and Humberside Arts; Sheffield City Council (together or separately);

- the chairs of the Boards: the main Board of Sheffield Theatres Trust; also the chair of the Lyceum Trust, and the chair of the Advisory Council;

- the different roles within theatres management: Chief Executive; Artistic Director; Marketing Director; Financial Director (and their respective departments);

- customers and potential customers.

Those groups playing stakeholders (other than management) will answer question 2 below (*Is the theatre successful?*). The theatre management will answer question 3 (*stakeholder mapping*).

These smaller groups will then be asked to discuss and present recommendations on the *strategy* the theatre should be pursuing, how they could *influence* the Board of Directors to follow this strategy, and how they would assess *performance*. Then the group role playing the theatre management report their analysis and respond to the points made by stakeholder groups.

A similar approach can be used when considering the issue *of funding mechanisms* (Question 6). The case may then be used as a basis for discussion of strategy in relation to *marketing in a not-for-profit organisation*: for example there is a balance, reflected in the interests of different stakeholders, between the need to maximise revenue and the desire for high artistic standards. It is also possible to share views on the pros and cons of introducing a *contractual* relationship between the theatre and its funding bodies. This discussion should be generalised to draw some conclusions about the benefits (or otherwise) of such approaches in the management of public services.

5. QUESTIONS FOR DISCUSSION

Experience in using the case study on many occasions leads us to suggest very simple/broad questions which-allow the groups to find their way around the data in the case study and relate it to some of the conceptual frameworks in the text. Question 6 has been added to cover the 'new funding issues. The most successful questions have been:

Question No.	**Relates to**:
1. Who and what influences the Director in formulating theatre policy?	3(a) and (b)
2. Is the theatre successful?	3(b), (c) and (d)
3. Map out the major stakeholders (for example by using the *Power/Interest matrix* (exhibit 5.5), as a basis of describing your strategy for managing stakeholder expectations.	3(c)
4. If you wished to influence a change in theatre policy how would you achieve it? Particularly when using sub-groups as in 4 above).	3(c)
5. How would your stakeholder mapping in Question 3 change if the theatres were considering adopting either of the following strategies:	3(c)

(i) Becoming a *commercial* theatre (no public funding)

(ii) Becoming a *civic* theatre (part of Sheffield City Council with no Arts Council funding).

6. Explain and justify your attitude towards the increased emphasis on marketing which is likely to arise from the appointment of a new marketing director and the requirement from Sheffield City Council for the theatres to produce a three year business plan. How will this alter the relationships between the Trust and its funding bodies? (See section 6.4 below.)

3(d) and (e)

6. CASE ANALYSIS

6.1 Who/what influences policy?

Exhibit 5.9 in chapter 5 should provide a useful framework for identifying the key individuals/groups/factors. A typical analysis is shown in appendix 1.

6.2 Is the theatre successful?

This question allows a full discussion of the expectations of stakeholders and the criteria by which they judge success or failure. Some useful pointers for guiding discussion are included in appendix 2.

If students are divided into sub-groups representing stakeholders it is usually very interesting to explore the various perceptions of *quality* for a service organisation like a theatre.

The students should be pushed to use the data in the case study to support their arguments.

6.3 Stakeholder mapping

Students should be pressed to assess the *interest* and *power* of the various stakeholders (for example, by using exhibit 5.5 in the text). Appendix 3 shows a typical stakeholder mapping – as seen by a student group role-playing the theatre management. Note student groups may map this differently – the key issue is that they are asked to *explain* and *justify* their mapping and how it influences their approach to managing relationships with stakeholders. It is also important to re-emphasise that stakeholder maps are difficult to draw *in general* they tend to be most useful in assessing how stakeholders lie in relation to *specific* events or strategies.

There are several issues which are unique to the *Sheffield Theatres* which should not be missed:

- the providers of revenue grants (Arts Council and Local Authority) also provided capital for the building or renovation of the theatres. Legally they cannot recover this investment if the theatres closed nor are the buildings very useful for any other purpose. So, they are likely to continue supporting the theatre since the political flack from pulling out is likely to be high. However, they do not need to support any particular group of managers – and during a crisis (e.g. 1982) a change of management is the price to pay for their continued support.

- the Crucible and Lyceum are crucial assets to the City of Sheffield in its attempts to regenerate the economy of the region. Persuading companies to relocate to Sheffield is helped by the presence of theatres of national standing.

- as usual the management are the crucial power holders and the way in which the other stakeholders are managed strongly influences the extent to which they are likely to use their power in an obstructive way.

- in an organisation providing a highly professional service the personal reputation and credibility of the artistic director and chief executive in the national arena is a crucial source of power.

6.4 New funding methods

The case includes examples of virtually all the main kinds of funding that apply in the non-profit sector, and students should be asked to assess the merits and conflicting stakeholder expectations in relation to these different forms of income:

a) *grants* – the traditional means of public sector support for non-profit organisations.

b) *service level agreements* – a grant tied to specific conditions on required results this is essentially what was being proposed in terms of the 'target investments' suggestion by the City Council.

c) *contractual funding* – where a non-profit organisation agrees contractually to provide a service in return for payment by the public sector – this situation implied in relation to the Lyceum building, and it was possible that the main Arts Council and/or City Council funding might at some point switch to a contractual arrangement.

d) *primary purpose trading* – in this case, selling seats for performances (charities are not prevented from trading if it relates to their primary purpose)

e) *trading for fund-raising purposes* – commercial sponsorship and sales via the bar, restaurant and shop (via Offstage Ltd)

f) *donated income from individuals* – e.g. the Programme Development Fund.

Appendix 4 shows a possible analysis on this issue.

Appendix 1 Influences on Strategy

A. Frame of Reference	Individual/Group/Factor
1. Values of Society	Significant changes over the later period – public sector becoming more commercial/accountable Public sector scrutiny of performance
2. Organised Groups	The acting profession. The national arts network.
3. Organisational Culture	*The show must go on* Lead by example – not bureaucracy The *season* as a time horizon Anti-commercial? Professional
B. Stakeholders	The Chief Executive Other Directors Theatre Board Local Authority Arts Council Directors of Plays Writers Actors Other Employees Touring Companies Customers Potential Customers Donors Competitors Critics Unions Local Community

Appendix 2   Stakeholder Expectations

Stakeholder	Criteria for Success
1. Arts Council	'Quality' Numbers Financial
2. Local Authority	Type of Plays/Events Numbers Financial Breadth of Appeal
3. Directors of Plays	'Quality' Variety New Plays
4. Actors/Writers	New Productions Employment 'Quality'
5. Touring Companies	Good Venue Financial
6. Customers	Content of Play 'Quality' Value for Money

Appendix 3
Sheffield Theatres – Stakeholder Mapping (for current strategy)

A) Key Stakeholder Relationships:

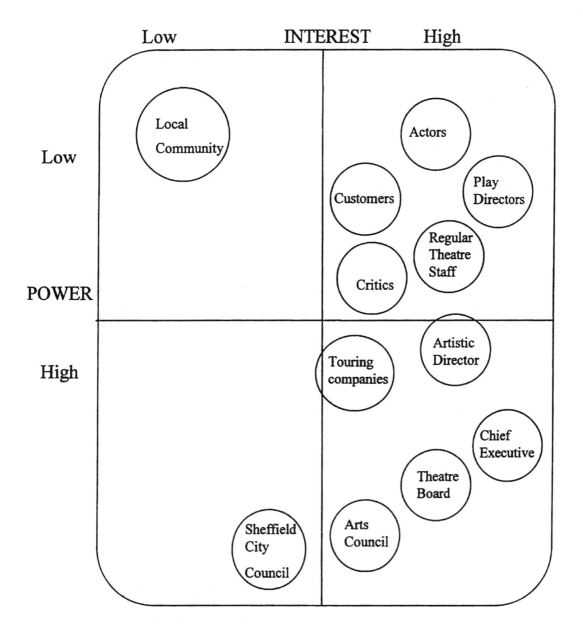

B) Students should also be asked to consider how this mapping might change in relation to specific strategy changes as in Question 5. They can then follow the process described in section 5.3.3 of the text to identify how they would establish the political priorities for each of the new strategies in the question.

Appendix 4   Advantages/Disadvantages of Differing Funding Sources

Advantages	Disadvantages
Grants	
Income can be used in a flexible way to cover core costs.	Very susceptible to being withdrawn or reduced in changing political climate.
Service Level Agreements	
A grant tied to a service level agreement helps clarify what the theatres are expected to achieve - hence the theatre can demonstrate tangible results to justify the funding.	Can lead to a loss of flexibility - if the service-level agreement is very specific, all effort goes into meeting the performance indicators in the agreement, possibly at the expense of other aims.
Contractual Funding	
Emphasises role of non-profit organisations as service providers in partnership with the public sector. Any surplus made on contract work can be used as desired, unlike restricted grants.	Tendering for contracts can be expensive and time-consuming, with services having to be costed as cheaply as possible if competing for funds. Can be difficult to cover overheads fully.
Primary Purpose Trading	
Prime means of generating income in an organisation like a theatre. Depends only on the theatre's own marketing success - not on outside funders with their own agendas.	In a non-commercial theatre this can never be sufficient on its own. Revenue is very variable with changes in people's disposable income and according to competition for leisure spending.
Trading for Fundraising Purposes	
A very attractive source of additional revenue.	Catering sales vary with theatre attendances, and excessive prices would discourage ticket sales. Income such as sponsorship is limited by competition from other forms of promotion.
Donated Income from Individuals	
This is a very important area of income for many charities. Can be used with few restrictions.	Theatres not often seen as 'worthy cause' - unlikely to attract money from those seriously interested in arts/theatre.

TEACHING NOTES

Fisons – the Fall from Grace
Helen Peck[1]

1. INTRODUCTION

The case study covers the period from 1990 to 1995, which saw the spectacular decline of Fisons through a series of events apparently triggered by difficulties in the environmental effects of the Company's smallest division – Horticultural – and its peat-digging activities. From a position of great strength in the late 1980s – when Fisons was generally regarded as a superbly managed company – the company in 1995 was reduced to a cash-rich pharmaceutical division turning in losses, the other two divisions having been sold. Rumours of takeover persisted.

2. POSITION OF THE CASE

Fisons is a short case which can be used to illustrate the importance of managing *stakeholder expectations* and relationships and, as such, links particularly to section 5.3 of chapter 5 in *Exploring Corporate Strategy*.

3. LEARNING OBJECTIVES

The case can be used to illustrate the following main issues from the text:

1. The need to identify stakeholders (5.3.1)

2. Stakeholder mapping (5.3.2)

3. Assessing the power of stakeholders (5.3.3)

4. Styles of managing change (exhibit 11.3)

In addition it raises two other issues which students may find of interest:

1. The ethical issue regarding the environmental impact of the peat digging activities (5.4.2).

2. The dangers of a 'domino effect' (reverse synergy) through divisions or subsidiaries in a diversified group when they trade under the same name (7.2.4).

---

[1] These teaching notes have been written by Kevan Scholes with Helen Peck's approval.

4. TEACHING SCHEME

The case is nicely focused on the issues of managing stakeholder relationships. As such it lends itself to a straightforward process of asking students to use analytical tools (in particular *stakeholder mapping)* as a way of analysing the case. This analysis could either be done prior to a class session or in student groups within a session.

5. QUESTIONS FOR DISCUSSION

3. Map out the key stakeholders of Fison on the Power/Interest Matrix seen by management in early 1990.

4. Describe the style of management adopted towards each stakeholder and how these stakeholders reacted to that style.

5. By describing the actions of stakeholders between 1990 and 1995 explain how the map had changed from that of 1990.

6. If the company could re-live this period what advice would you give them regarding the management of relationships with stakeholders?

6. CASE ANALYSIS

6.1 Stakeholder mapping (1990)

Appendix 1 is the kind of stakeholder map which the management of Fisons may well have produced at the beginning of 1990. (Note that students may produce different maps – which may be OK if they can justify their reasons.) This would be a fairly typical 'view of the world' taken by an organisation which had performed well in a reasonably favourable business environment. At this state students should remember two things:

- Stakeholders in Box C have many other business interests other than Fisons and often 'manage by exception'. So, provided all was well they will let management get on with driving strategy in the company.

- Stakeholders in Box B may appear to have little power BUT it is dangerous to ignore them (as subsequent events clearly show).

6.2 Styles for managing stakeholders

Often students forget that when discussing styles for managing change (for example as in exhibit 11.3 of the text) that a *single style is* unlikely to be appropriate). Different styles may be more or less appropriate for different stakeholders. One factor which might determine the adopted style would be the 'positioning' of stakeholders in the power/interest matrix. Appendix 2 is a (tentative) suggestions as to how this might look (as a generalisation or at least a starting point for discussion). This would raise some important questions when compared with Fison's approach:

1. Their communication with outside stakeholders and/or their involvement with aspects of the company's developing strategies were very low compared to other companies in their sectors.

2. This secretive style must have appeared very much like 'edict' to city analysts, institutional shareholders and environmental groups.

3. This was not a problem until they got into difficulties – firstly over the environmental issues and then (separately) with the FDA. Those stakeholders who might have been expected to be helpful in overcoming difficulties – or at least in riding them out – were ill-informed and disinclined to help because of this secretive style.

6.3 Changes to the stakeholder map by 1995

Students could either construct a new map (see appendix 3) or make additions and show movements on/from their 1990 map. The analysis should illustrate the following point:

- A company cannot really survive a political situation as portrayed in the map of appendix 3. Indeed Fisons eventually chose to sell their Horticultural Division to alleviate these pressures and the Scientific Equipment business to survive the financial decline.

- The move from the 1990 map to the 1995 situation did not occur in one step but through a series of interconnected changes – each change triggering yet more problems for the Company.

- The initiative trigger was the Thorne Moor incident and the way it was handled. This incited environmental groups to increase their power in a number of ways. The first of these was *collaboration* between ten groups.

Secondly, this campaigning group's *lobbying* brought on board The Prince of Wales.

- The *lobbying* was then directed at organisations in Box C – crucially 50 investment managers controlling 42 per cent of Fisons shares. In the absence of better communication from the company they were encouraged to oppose peat cutting activities.

- The company's refusal to listen to institutional-shareholders resulted in adverse lobbying in Parliament, with 34 local authorities (who otherwise were entirely indifferent to Fisons) and with major distributors of the company's goods.

- Perhaps the company could have ridden out all this adverse political activity against the strategies of its smallest division (Horticulture) if everything had been going well in the main division (Pharmaceuticals). The real disaster for the company was the adverse publicity from the firm's activities split over into the difficulties the company started to experience with the FDA. City analysts and institutional shareholders – who might have been expected to assist/support the management against a media witch hunt' were themselves disheartened with the company. This stated the downward spiral of share price and the ultimate break-up of the group.

6.4 How could things have been managed better

Having worked through the previous questions students should have some useful thoughts on how things could have been managed better. For example:

If you look again at appendix 2 these would appear to be a case for a less secretive and more proactive communication strategy to stakeholders in both boxes C and B. Certainty major competitors were doing so.

An earlier and clearer recognition that they may be unable to contain any damage to the Horticultural division should have alerted managers to the potential magnitude of the impact on the company as a whole.

One major danger with a secretive style is that stakeholders may draw the conclusion that things are always likely to be worse than the management line' – even if they are not. This was a major problem for Fisons once they started to communicate the difficulties they were having with the FDA. So a secretive style may be fine when credibility is high but will not work once this credibility is damaged.

APPENDIX 1

Fisons Stakeholder Mapping – Current Strategy in 1990

LEVEL OF INTEREST

	Low	High
Low	A	Environental groups (-) B Competitor (-)
High	C City Analysts Institutional Shareholders FDA	D Management (+)

POWER (on left side, between Low and High)

APPENDIX 2

Styles and Stakeholders?

LEVEL OF INTEREST

		Low	**High**
POWER	**Low**	A Minimal effort *EDICT*	B Keep informed *COMMUNICATION*
	High	C Keep satisfied *INTERVENTION*	D Key players **PARTICIPATION**

APPENDIX 3

Fisons Stakeholder Mapping – 1995

LEVEL OF INTEREST

	Low	High
Low		Environmental Groups (-)
High		Management (+) Competitors (-) City Analysts (-) Prince Charles (-) Institutional Shareholders (-) Distributors (B&Q) (-) 34 Local Authorities (-) Media (-) FDA (-)

POWER

TEACHING NOTES

Note on the World Automobile Industry (1996)
Ranjit Das

1. INTRODUCTION

This note briefly highlights the market trends facing the automobile industry in the different geographic regions of the world. This note can be used separately as a basis for industry analysis. However, it will be more powerful when used as a first stage before working on the *PSA Peugeot Citroën, Rover/Honda alliance* or BMW *acquisition of Rover* case studies.

The automobile industry is of particular interest because it was undergoing rapid changes not least because of competition from the producers based in the Asia-Pacific region. It also represented a very important part of European economies in terms of GNP and employment and illustrates the process of globalisation of an industry; key issues for the 1990s. It is also likely to be familiar to most student groups.

2. POSITION OF THE CASE

The note can be used for teaching industry analysis, in particular to illustrate the globalisation of industries. The case therefore complements chapter 3 of the text. It also provides a useful basis for applying models of the international dynamics of industries such as the ones proposed by Prahlad and Doz (1987) or by Bartlett and Ghoshal (1989). As such it fits with courses in international strategic management. In addition, as noted above, it can be particularly helpful when used as a first stage industry background to the company specific cases: *PSA Peugeot Citroën, Rover/Honda alliance* and *BMW acquisition of Rover.*

The case discusses five main geographic regions: the traditional trading regions of Western Europe, NAFTA and Japan respectively and the progress in the developing regions of Eastern Europe and Asia-Pacific. Within each of the five major markets discussed in the note students can consider the degree of uncertainty and complexity of the industry's environment and the different environmental influences affecting the development of firms in the industry.

3. LEARNING OBJECTIVES

An understanding of the key environmental influences in this industry is essential. The case, together with topical media information available on this popular subject, allows readers to undertake a PEST analysis of the industry.

Strategies and strategic groups, a key concept in chapter 3 can also be explored. The issue of a global vs. multi-domestic strategy can be discussed and future scenarios for the industry can be drawn.

4. TEACHING PROCESS

As part of their background preparation, before the note is used in class, tutors could ask students to supplement the information in the note. Students can collate up-to-date information on the strategies of the major manufacturers like General Motors, Ford, Chrysler, Toyota, Nissan, Volkswagen, etc. from data sources such as quality newspapers.

The teaching scheme could start with considering the key environmental influences on this industry. The data in the case could then be analysed. Different study groups could be given different regions of the world and asked to present a summary of the data. The case will provide maximum learning benefit only if time is taken by the student to comprehend the trends in demand and production shown in the various tables.

Analysing the data at the world level will probably lead to the conclusion that European car manufacturers had significant positions only in Europe; Americans had significant market share in North America and western European and that the Japanese were the only global players in the industry. A fuller analysis of the European market should lead to the conclusion that European car manufacturers had strong positions in their respective national markets and weaker positions abroad.

As a second stage the *strategies* of the main competitors at the beginning of the 1990's could be analysed and summarised according to key strategic dimensions (preferably prepared before the session). During the session the class could also try to define and map out the possible strategic groups of competitors and reach an agreement on the most relevant strategic groupings.

As a third stage the students could evaluate the forces for *global integration* and the forces for *local responsiveness* in order to understand the globalisation process in the industry. A complementary reading of Prahalad and Doz's model (1987) would be a useful guide to the analysis. Alternatively the case study could be used before a more general lecture or the reading. In both cases, the class discussion should follow two steps: first *evaluation* of the forces in the 1990s: second, possible *evolution* of the forces in the late 1990s.

The fourth stage of the discussion could be the formulation of *scenarios* for the late 1990s. A fruitful discussion on such issues may require additional readings: for example the *PSA Peugeot Citroën, Rover/Honda alliance* and BMW *acquisition of Rover* case studies in *Exploring Corporate Strategy:* or press reports giving prospects for the industry. The class discussion should start with listing of events and trends which may have an impact on the dynamics of the industry. These events can then be grouped into contrasting scenarios for the 1990s.

5. QUESTIONS FOR DISCUSSION

The five questions below correspond to the main issues presented in the teaching scheme above:

1. Discuss the major environmental developments within the industry which could affect a company's ability to build and sustain its competitive advantage.

2. Evaluate the respective market positions of the competitors in the automobile industry from the Triad (the US, the European and the Japanese car manufacturers), first at the world level, second at the European market level.

3. Define the strategic profiles of each of the main competitors along key strategic dimensions with the purpose of identifying strategic groups of competitors.

4. a) Review and evaluate the main forces for global integration and the main forces for local responsiveness in the automobile industry.
    b) According to the balance of these forces in 1996, how could the automobile industry be positioned in terms of Prahalad and Doz's model of international dynamics of industries?
    c) In which direction could these forces of global integration and local responsiveness evolve during the late 1990s?
    d) Bearing in mind international dynamics of the industry assess the potential of each of the main competitors in the late 1990s.

5. a) Considering the possible key trends and events in the automobile industry and the levels of uncertainty, propose scenarios for a 10 year horizon from 1996.
    b) Assess the potential of each of the main European competitors in the case of any two scenarios.

6. CASE ANALYSIS

This section builds on the teaching scheme outlined above.

6.1 Environmental developments

There were several major environmental developments which could alter the nature of competition in this industry since these developments could redefine the way products were designed and/or built, or the way markets were served. The developments could be discussed under the traditional PEST headings and a few such issues are discussed below. Some of the issues raised by the students may not fall neatly under any of the PEST headings but should still be discussed. It must be stressed that the list below is not meant to be definitive; simply indicative of the kind of issues that could be raised in class. The students should identify the fact that the environmental influences vary from region to region and so it is difficult to draw too many generalisations for the global industry.

*   Technological developments redefined the way vehicles were designed and manufactured. Leading edge companies used Computer Aided Design and Computer Aided Manufacturing (CADCAM) techniques and new materials were used in cars (e.g. Audi's aluminium car). Thus, the industry had sharply reduced costs and cut the production times.

*   The economic barrier of restricting Japanese imports into Western Europe and North America acted as a trigger for many Japanese manufacturers to establish production operations in North America and Europe.

*   The changing currency exchange rates, specifically the appreciating yen, made import entry of US and European manufacturers into Japan viable and further triggered the push by Japanese companies to build operations abroad.

- Government regulations have affected the industry. In China, India and Vietnam the different government policies have opened up the market for foreign direct investment to varying degrees.

- Economic downturns in the industry should be discussed. A good example was the adverse affect Mexico's currency devaluation had on the whole of NAFTA. At the end of 1994 manufacturers in North America had not foreseen the economic downturn that cooled the economy.

- Lower than expected sales in the US in the mid-1990s was also caused by the industry producing better quality cars and extensive use of discounting.

- Societal changes that affected the industry include the idea that cars may not be the status symbols they once were and the fact that more women were making decisions to buy cars and the industry had not focused on this shift.

- Societal changes in favour of customised as opposed to mass produced cars may account for the growth in niches in the market, e.g. people carriers, off-road vehicles, two-seater sports cars, etc.

- There has also been an increase in both the number of competitors in the industry and in their geographic spread. There are European, Japanese, American, Korean, Malaysian, Indian and Eastern European companies all competing both nationally and internationally (although this is not strictly a PEST issue, students may raise this as a point)

- National car manufacturers had strong positions in their home country but much weaker positions abroad – see tables 1 to 5, appendix one. Please note that the information in the tables are supplementary to the case to aid the tutor in developing country-specific discussions.

- EU policies could open up the quasi-protected markets of Spain and France.

- The market shares of the Japanese in Europe could alter as the European production operations came on line.

6.2 Competitor market positions

The analysis of market positions is a key issue because market positions reflect the level of competitive strength of the firms involved and are an important aspect of the strategies of the competitors (question 2 above). Such an analysis also helps define the characteristics of the industry in the 1990s (question 3).

The case provides information on the respective positions of the US, the European and the Japanese car manufacturers. Three of the Japanese manufacturers (Toyota, Nissan and Honda) were the only ones who had significant positions in the three traditional vehicle markets of North America, Western Europe and Japan. The Japanese manufacturers had also established a strong position in the Asian markets. Americans had significant positions in North America and Western Europe and had a patchy presence in Asia (slow to develop operations in China, but quick to develop ventures in India) and the Europeans had significant positions only in Europe.

The following explanations could emerge from the discussion:

- The Japanese companies had significant competitive advantages which allowed them to penetrate other continents (superior quality, quick renewal of models etc.) and which limited the penetration of foreigners in the Japanese market;

- The liberal policy of the North Americans towards imports and local manufacture had allowed the Japanese to take a high share of the US market;

- The liberal policy of some of the European countries had allowed the Japanese to take significant positions (in the Benelux and in Scandinavia for instance); the semi liberal positions (limitation agreements) of some other countries (the UK and Germany) had led to significant Japanese shares. The protectionist policies of some other European countries (Italy, France and Spain) had limited the Japanese to a very low share;

- The significant share of the Americans in Europe had been built since the 1950s mainly through local production and management. As a result Ford Europe, Opel and Vauxhall (GM) were considered as European competitors.

The evaluation of the markets and positions in Europe shows that:

- Europe was becoming the main battle ground for the car manufacturers.

- Germany was the biggest market in Europe.

- Volkswagen Group had a slightly dominant position in the region (16%) but six other manufacturers held between 6 and 13% of the market each.

- National car manufacturers had strong positions in their home country but much weaker positions abroad – see tables 1 to 5, appendix one. Please note that the information in the tables are supplementary to the case to aid the tutor in developing country-specific discussions.

- EU policies could open up the quasi-protected markets of Spain and France.

- The market shares of Japanese in Europe could alter as the European production operations came on line.

6.3 Strategies and strategic groups

Strategic groups refer to the distribution of firms that pursue similar types of strategies within an industry in response to environment forces. The class discussion could start with listing the key strategic variables by which to describe the firm's strategies in the industry. These may include:

- The dominant *objectives* of the company (market share, profitability/long-term, short-term).

- The geographic *market* targeted.

- The *range* of products or market segments in the portfolio (e.g. luxury vs. mass market vs. niches).

- The main source of *competitive advantage:* whether in terms of differentiation/low cost/both or in terms of a combination of specific attributes (such as quality, performance, comfort, security).

- The *development method* (internal vs. acquisitions vs. strategic alliances).

- The pricing policies used by different firms.

- The degree of *technological/design leadership(leaders or* followers?).

- The choice of *distribution channels* (use of third party dealers or a company-owned dealership).

The strategic profile of each of the main competitors could then be drawn from this list of variables. The students should select those variables which differentiate the competitors most and hence define clear strategic groups.

The *geographic market* targeted and the *range of products* in the portfolio are the two useful dimensions for identifying strategic groups (figure 1). Students may come up with other variables and other maps (there is no one best map).

Rivals within the same strategic group are more likely to compete directly with each other than with members of firms in other strategic groups because firms in the same group are likely to pursue the same type of competitive strategies and thus view each other as the 'immediate enemies' rather than firms located in other strategic groups.

It may also be argued that significant strategic differences exist between competitors classified into the same group (for instance Peugeot and Fiat or Peugeot and Renault). The view that each company has a unique competitive strategy should also be considered. Both views can complement each other in order to understand competition. What really matters is that a debate is generated about:

- *Characteristics* of competitive strategies.

- The extent of *similarities* and *differences* of competitive strategy in the industry.

- The existence of *mobility barriers* for firms.

The relative strength of the five forces will vary across strategic groups as well. Therefore, firms in different strategic groups will tend to adopt different competitive strategies.

6.4 Global integration vs. local responsiveness

Prahalad and Doz suggest that it is useful to analyse international competition according to a mix of pressures for global integration and pressures for local responsiveness, and to summarise the analysis on the 'Integration Responsiveness Grid' – see figure 2 (Prahalad and Doz, 1987, pp. 13–37). In the class discussion the pressures for a Global Strategy vs. a Multi-domestic Strategy in the Automobile Industry could be reviewed and evaluated.

For a company following a global strategy the firm's competitive position in one country is influenced by its position in other countries. A global strategy is one in which the firm seeks to operate with worldwide consistency and a highly standardised approach across different markets. A global strategy requires the firm to integrate its activities on a world-wide scale to capture the linkages among countries. A global strategy involves standardisation of product ranges, maximising global economies of scale by building plants and facilities that serve regional as opposed to national markets, leveraging technologies across many markets, co-ordinating marketing and sales worldwide, and competing against global competitors through cross-subsidisation.

The following forces of global integration seemed to characterise the industry in the mid-1990s:

- The emergence of global competitors (Toyota, Honda and Nissan).

- The high technological intensity both for product development (clean cars, electronics) and processes (automation) which results in high investment intensity.

- The pressure for cost reduction.

- The universal nature of customers' needs.

For a company following a multi-domestic strategy the firm adjusts its products and operations according to each country or market it serves. Thus the competitive strategy followed by the firm in one country is independent of the strategy followed in other countries. Competition occurs on a country by country basis because firms treat each market as being unique and distinctive from other markets. A multi-domestic strategy involves adaptation of products to national tastes, conducting operations in each market separately, and co-ordinating marketing and sales within individual markets.

Although forces for local responsiveness were still present in the mid-1990s indications were that such barriers to a global strategy were being removed:

- Exclusive distribution channels had been a barrier to entry in several European markets and in Japan (a new competitor had to create their own distribution network). However, new EU legislation and pressures on the Japanese government raised hopes for a more open market by 2000.

- Some local customer preferences (Germans for instance had the reputation of preferring German cars) existed but the fact that manufacturers were developing 'world cars' seemed to indicate that they thought that there was a convergence in customer tastes and preferences.

- There were signs of erosion of the policy of limiting imports from Japan and of Japanese transplants imposed by some governments in Europe in order to protect their national champions.

As a second stage the class discussion might focus on the possible evolution of the forces which promoted the shift from national to international sales and manufacturing:

- Homogeneous product requirements. Customers, no matter where they were located, wanted similar types of products and services. Companies like Ford and Toyota began to develop a template 'world car' which was then adapted for regional customer preferences, e.g. Ford Mondeo, Toyota Corolla.

- Rising costs of R&D meant that firms had sell to more people in more markets to recoup the heavy investment costs that accompanied new product and process development.

- Rising economies of scale and cost pressures meant that firms had to build plants and other facilities that required it to meet a significant percentage of world demand before it broke even financially.

- Government policies influenced companies to build local operations, particularly if these policies are designed to help firms receive subsidies for product development and market expansion. Such policies were seen in China, India, and Vietnam but were implemented to varying degrees. The Chinese government were quite strict in allowing foreign companies to develop operations in China. The European manufacturers like Volkswagen and Mercedes seemed to have.

- The Reduction in factor costs (particularly capital and labour) made it attractive for numerous American, European, and Japanese firms to build new factories and facilities elsewhere around the world. In turn, these investments helped local economies develop faster and to become important consumers of other countries' products. Examples include Toyota and Nissan developing plants in the UK due to the cheaper cost of manufacturing in the UK compared to Japan. Another example is BMW's acquisition of Rover in the UK again due to the cheaper production costs enjoyed by Rover.

- One could argue that the main pressures for global integration would remain strong. The technological intensity could even increase dramatically under the ecological pressures and the increasing need for comfort and security. The universality of customers' needs could also increase with the world homogenisation of life styles.

- At this stage of the discussion the tutor may wish to stimulate a discussion on the arguments for liberalism (UK being an example) and the arguments for protectionism (France being an example) towards Japanese imports and transplants in Europe. Alternatively the tutor could ask students to assess the readiness of each competitor to face globalisation of the industry. The ones who will survive could be the ones with strong international positions, high market share, and financial resources and with a strong network of alliances in order to succeed in technological developments (products and processes).

The resulting position of the car industry on the integration-responsiveness grid is presented in figure 2. In 1995 the car industry was not purely global, even if strong pressures for global integration were at work. All the vehicle manufacturers realised the value in following a global strategy as opposed to a multi-domestic strategy but a lack of financial resources prevented all but the largest firms (General Motors, Ford, Chrysler, Toyota, Nissan, Honda) from developing a truly global strategy. Only Toyota, Nissan and Honda had achieved a global strategy

6.5 Scenarios for the 1990s

The 1990s bring significant uncertainties for the automobile industry. Some key events and trends, could be considered in order to develop scenarios. The first stage of the discussion could consist of *listing* the key issues that affect or could affect the industry. This has been discussed already in considering the PEST analysis. In a second stage, the *major events* could be selected and classified according to their expected impact on the European market:

- The *attitude of the EU* towards Japanese competition in Europe is the major variable. The Peugeot SA case study gives the position of the EU at the end of 1995.

- The uncertain development of markets in China, India and Eastern Europe is the second major variable for which estimates varied greatly between experts.

- The *overcapacity in Europe* which could lead to price wars should also be considered.

Combining these variables leads to different scenarios, for example:

- A possible scenario is that the greatest growth in demand would be seen in Asia but the region suffers from having a relatively small market on a global scale. Thus, the traditional markets of Japan, the NAFTA region, and Western Europe would still have a great influence on this industry in the years leading up to the new century. Overcapacity in these traditional markets will only intensify competition for sales leading to more joint ventures to squeeze out the 'also ran's' and gain market share and spread the cost of new product development. Niche markets may also be formed and serviced, e.g. off-road, people carriers.

- An alternative scenario is that Mexico's poor economic performance stops the regeneration of the American economy leading to a collapse of the fragile South American economy. Civil wars may occur in both Russia and China as their leaders fall from grace or die of old age. Thus the eastern European region and Asia, the 'star' regions of the next decade, may be thrown into turmoil.

As one cannot predict such events and trends, the ultimate recommendation for managers involved in the industry could be to *scan* these variables which are the source of major uncertainties. The second recommendation in order to be less sensitive to price wars would be to improve *productivity* and *differentiate* models, such a strategy would require high skills and financial resources to start with.

Since developments in the automobile industry are widely publicised by the press, it is recommended that tutors gather additional information on the decisions of the EU and on the strategic moves of the main competitors as they are published.

REFERENCES

Prahalad, C. K. and Doz Y.; *The Multinational Mission: Balancing Local Demands and Global Vision;* The Free Press; 1987.

Bartlett, C. A. and Ghoshal S.; *Managing Across Borders: The Transnational Solution;* Hutchinson Business Books; 1989.

Porter, M. E.; *Competitive Advantage*; The Free Press; 1985.

Calori R. and Lawrence P. (eds); *The Business of Europe: Managing Change*; Sage Publications, 1991.

APPENDIX 1

Table 1: 1995 Passenger car market shares in France

MANUFACTURER	MARKET SHARE
PSA (Peugeot-Citroën) *	30.6
Renault	30.5
Volkswagen Group (VW, Audi, Seat, Skoda) **	8.1
Ford	7.4
Opel/GM	6.8
Fiat	5.1
BMW/Rover	3.0
Others	8.5
Total	100

Source: Trade Journals.
* Market share broken down to 17.8 per cent Peugeot, 12.8 per cent Citroën
** Market share broken down to 5.6 per cent VW, 1.6 per cent SEAT, 0.9 per cent Audi

Table 2: 1995 Passenger car market shares in Germany

MANUFACTURER	MARKET SHARE
Volkswagen Group (VW, Audi, Seat, Skoda) *	27.6
Opel/GM	16.8
Ford	11.7
Mercedes-Benz	7.3
BMW	6.6
Renault	5.1
PSA (Peugeot-Citroën)	4.5
Fiat	4.2
Nissan	2.0
Toyota	2.3
Mazda	2.4
Others	9.5
Total	100

Source: Trade Journals
* Market share broken down to 19.5 per cent VW, 6.5 per cent Audi, 1.6 per cent SEAT
** Market share broken down to 2.7 per cent Peugeot, 1.8 per cent Citroën

Table 3: 1995 Passenger car market shares in Italy

MANUFACTURER	MARKET SHARE
Fiat Group	
(Fiat, Lancia, Alfa Romeo, Maserati)*	46.1
Volkswagen Group	
(VW, Audi, Seat, Skoda) **	10.7
Ford	8.8
Opel/GM	8.1
PSA (Peugeot-Citroën) * * *	6.6
Renault	6.5
BMW/Rover	3.4
Nissan	2.1
Others	7.7
Total	100

Source: Trade Journals.
* Market shares broken down to 35.6 per cent Fiat, 6.9 per cent Lancia, 3.6 per cent Alfa Romeo.
** Market shares broken down to 7.3 per cent VW, 1.9 per cent SEAT, 1.5 per cent Audi.
*** Market shares broken down to 3.5 per cent Peugeot, 3.1 per cent Citroën.

Table 4: 1995 Passenger car market shares in Spain

MANUFACTURER	MARKET SHARE
PSA (Peugeot-Citroën) *	20.7
Volkswagen Group	
(VW, Audi, Seat, Skoda) **	19.1
Renault	14.1
Ford	13.8
Opel/GM	11.1
Fiat Group	
(Fiat, Lancia, Alfa Romeo, Maserati)	7.5
BMW/Rover	3.4
Others	10.3
Total	100

Source: Trade Journals.
* Market shares broken down to 11.4 per cent Peugeot, 9.3 per cent Citroen.
** Market shares broken down to 10.5 per cent SEAT, 6.2 per cent VW, 2.4 per cent Audi .

Table 5: 1995 Passenger car market shares in UK

MANUFACTURER	MARKET SHARE
Ford	21.5
GM/Vauxhall	15.7
BMW/Rover*	14.4
PSA (Peugeot-Citroën) **	12.2
Renault	6.6
Nissan	4.6
Volkswagen	3 9
Fiat	3 5
Toyota	2.7
Honda	2.3
Volvo	2.2
Others	10.4
Total	100

Source: Trade Journals.
* Market shares broken down to 11.3 per cent Rover, 3.1 per cent BMW.
** Market shares broken down to 7.8 per cent Peugeot, 4.4 per cent Citroën.

Figure 1 A POSSIBLE STRATEGIC GROUP MAP IN 1996

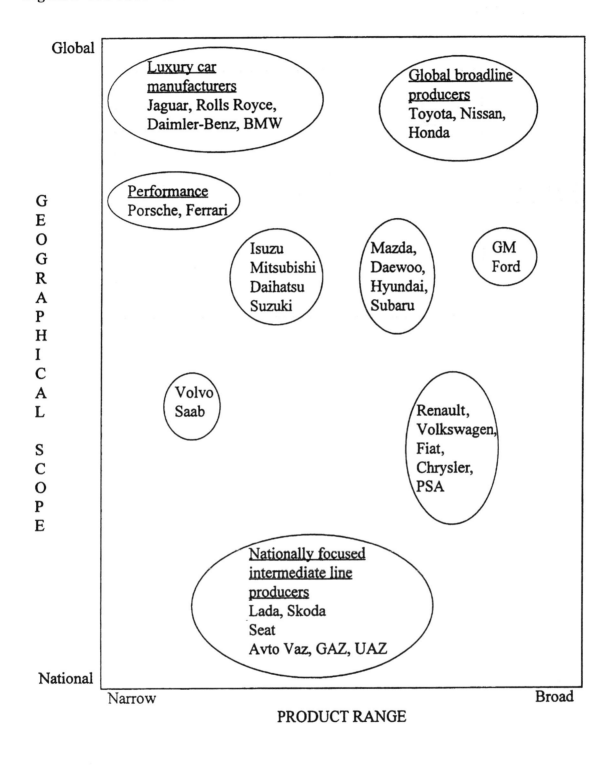

Figure 2   THE DYNAMICS OF INTERNATIONAL COMPETITION IN THE CAR
INDUSTRY

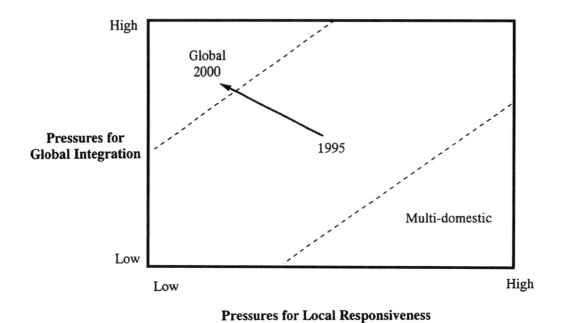

TEACHING NOTES

PSA – Peugeot-Citroën
Roland Calori, Philippe Very and Michael Berthelier

1. INTRODUCTION

The case describes the strategy of PSA Peugeot-Citroën in the automobile industry. The group includes two generalist car manufacturing companies: Automobiles Peugeot and Automobiles Citroen. In 1995 it was the third largest car manufacturer in Europe with a 12 per cent market share, and the largest French exporter.

The case first outlines the development of the company to 1995, and the role of Jacques Calvet who became President du Directoire of the holding company in 1984. Then the case describes the current strategy of Peugeot-Citroën, with a particular emphasis on the internationalisation of the Group. The case concludes with the future challenges perceived by the top management for the year 2000 and beyond: the prospect of free competition starting from the year 2000 in Europe, the overcapacity and price competition in the industry, and the opportunity of a come back of Peugeot-Citroën in the North American market.

2. POSITION OF THE CASE

The Peugeot-Citroën case study may be discussed after the study of the world car industry (industry analysis based on the *Note on the world automobile industry,* in this volume). The Peugeot-Citroën case study can usefully fit in a session on strategy evaluation and formulation and/or a session on international strategy. As far as international strategy is concerned, the case illustrates strategic moves within an industry that is becoming global. It also gives an opportunity to discuss the political aspects of strategies at the EEC level, more precisely the attitude toward foreign competition. These issues are examined *in Exploring Corporate Strategy,* chapters 6–8.

3. LEARNING OBJECTIVES

We recommend the use of the *Note on the world automobile industry* before working on the Peugeot-Citroën case study. From the industry analysis, students should understand the process of globalisation, the market trends and the positions of the main competitors.

The Peugeot-Citroën case allows students to examine the strategy of a company facing intense rivalry in the context of industry globalisation.

More precisely, three complimentary learning objectives could be reached with this case:

- Evaluating the current strategy of a company within a global industry, particularly its international strategy,

- Formulating international strategy in a major European company facing high market uncertainties and increasing worldwide competition,

- Understanding the political aspects of international corporate strategies, the role of governments, the EC (protectionism vs. liberalism).

4. TEACHING PROCESS

We assume that students have worked *before* on the analysis of the world automobile industry: trends in demand, international positions of competitors, discussion on the forces that drive global integration vs. local responsiveness, scenario planning at a 10-year horizon.

Otherwise, the tutor should start with a discussion of these elements of the context. Then, concerning the Peugeot-Citroën case itself, the tutor could follow four steps.

- Evaluate the performance and the resources, strengths and weaknesses, of Peugeot-Citroën, compared to other competitors, first in 1994, second in the light of the possible future evolutions of the industry,

- Define the paradigm and the strategy of Peugeot-Citroën and then evaluate the current strategy in the light of the possible future evolutions of the industry (markets, competitors...),

- Discuss the protectionist position of Jacques Calvet vis-à-vis Japanese competition in Europe. This could be done by role playing forming two camps: the *liberals* and the *protectionists,*

- Re-formulate the strategy of Peugeot-Citroën, in particular its international strategy in the light of the possible industry scenarios for the year 2000 and beyond. The class could be divided into several small groups, each preparing recommendations to Jacques Calvet, then the most contrasted strategies could be discussed in class.

A more extensive and all-embracing teaching scheme using:

- the note on the world automobile industry,

- the Peugeot-Citroën case study,

- the BMW-Rover case study,

could allow a stimulating role playing between students: one sub-group playing the role of the consultants (working on the three documents); another sub-group representing the top management team of Peugeot-Citroën working on the *Note on the world automobile industry* and on the Peugeot-Citroën case; and a third one playing the role of the top management team of BMW-Rover working on the *Note on the world automobile industry* and on the BMW-Rover case. The two top management teams could successively present their diagnosis and their respective strategies. Then both could react to each other strategies, and discuss their positions towards Japanese competition (in the way European car manufacturers do in the European association ACEA). Finally the consultants could propose a reformulation of the strategies of the two companies and their arbitrage on the position vis-à-vis the Japanese.

5. QUESTIONS FOR DISCUSSION

When the Peugeot-Citroën case study is used together with the note on the world automobile industry, the questions concerning the dynamics of the industry should be addressed first (see the corresponding teaching note on the automobile industry).

More specifically with regard to Peugeot-Citroën, six broad questions could guide the preparation of the case and the discussion:

1. What were the strengths and weaknesses of Peugeot-Citroën in 1995 compared to its competitors?

2. Define the paradigm and the strategy of Peugeot-Citroën, in particular its international strategy, and evaluate it in the light of possible future evolutions of the industry (markets, competitors...).

3. Was the protectionist position held by Jacques Calvet against Japanese competition 'defendable'?

4. In the light of possible future developments of the car industry, should the 'strategy of Peugeot-Citroën be re-formulated, in particular its international – strategy? In which ways?

5. Could Peugeot-Citroën re-enter the North American market?

6. Jacques Calvet might leave Peugeot-Citroën in the late 1990s, what consequences might his departure have on the group? How should the succession be managed?

6. CASE ANALYSIS

The issues that may be explored in discussing the above questions are outlined below.

Before getting to Peugeot-Citroën itself, the tutor should make sure that students have a good understanding of the context (cf. *Note on the world automobile industry)*, particularly concerning the following characteristics:

• Slow demand growth, except in 'other Asian countries',

• The main Japanese competitors were involved in the three zones of the Triad, North American competitors had strong positions in North America and Europe, whereas most European competitors only had significant positions in Europe,

- The increase in R&D investments and shorter cycle times were key forces driving the global integration of the industry,

- The difficult access to distribution channels in Europe and in Japan drove local responsiveness in these zones, the North American market was more competitive, particularly under the pressure of mega-dealers,

- New competitors emerged, particularly the Koreans,

- The protectionist measures taken by the EC were expected to be abolished by the year 2000,

- Car manufacturers were involved into multiple strategic alliances in order to face intense rivalry.

6.1 What were the strengths and weaknesses of Peugeot-Citroën in 1994?

Among the strengths of Peugeot-Citroën several characteristics should be pointed out:

- The virtuous circle in which high profits were re-invested in order to improve productivity which in turn generated high profits. Jacques Calvet emphasised rigorous management, productivity gains and relatively high prices. As a result, the profitability of Peugeot-Citroën was high compared to other competitors (1993 was an exception, when demand fell on the key markets for the Group). High positive cash flows were necessary to finance important investments both for improving manufacturing processes and for speeding up new product development.

- Peugeot-Citroën demonstrated their ability to catch up with the Japanese and improved the new product development cycle.

- They had some very successful! models such as the Peugeot 205, and the Peugeot 405 in the late 1980s, the Peugeot 306 and the Citroen Xantia at the beginning of the 1990s.

- They were present in new high growth markets: China, India, South East Asia, Argentina however, these did not represent a high volume of sales in 1994).

- They had high market shares in France, in the UK, in Spain and in Africa.

- They had distinctive skills in Diesel engines and electric cars.

- The two brands had good image in several European countries and in Africa (cf. the successes in rallies).

- Their manufacturing operations were located in countries (France, Spain, Portugal) with relatively competitive manpower costs, as compared to Northern European competitors.

On the other hand, Peugeot-Citroën had several weaknesses in the mid-1990s.

- Peugeot-Citroën still had some weaknesses as compared to the best Japanese competitors such as Toyota: lower profitability, lower quality (in terms of defects), longer cycle time in new product development. However, Peugeot-Citroën had continuously narrowed the gap with the best practice in these domains.

Compared to other European car manufacturers, in particular to the market leader, the Volkswagen Group (VW, Audi, Seat and Skoda):

- Peugeot-Citroën had a relatively weak position and image in Germany, which was the largest and the most competitive market in Europe,

- Peugeot-Citroën had a relatively weak position in Eastern Europe, in Japan and was not present in North America, it remained very much focused on Western Europe,

- The company had weak positions in the up market segment ('executive') and was not involved in the luxury car segment which was the most global business within the industry,

- Its network of alliances seemed to be less developed than the networks of the other competitors, particularly Peugeot-Citroën had no inter-continental alliance.

These weaknesses would become more problematic in a scenario of quick globalisation of the car industry, in which the Japanese would double their market share in Europe. Also, some strengths might become liabilities, for instance diesel cars were questioned by environmentalists in 1995.

The evaluation can be organised as a review of the points emerging from the whole class, but the tutor should ask students to be selective in their assessment and identify the key factors of success and failure.

6.2 The paradigm and the strategy of Peugeot-Citroën

In 1990 Jacques Calvet announced that the strategic intent of the group was to become the leader in the European market. The goal had changed by 1995, market leadership was no more paramount. There were several reasons for this change:

- The successful growth strategy of the market leader, the Volkswagen Group with four complementary brands – Audi, Volkswagen, Seat and Skoda – backed up by the reunification of Germany and the development of market economies in Eastern Europe.

- The monetary fluctuations which were favourable to the Fiat Group in Italy (the Italian lira depreciated by 25 per cent in the mid-1990s).

Peugeot-Citroën was still looking for growth and trying to increase its market share in neighbouring markets – Germany, the United Kingdom – and in the high growth potential markets of Asia. However, profitability had become the main goal of the group. More than ever, the 'virtuous circle' described by Jacques Calvet: 'profits-investments-productivity gains', was at the core of the paradigm of Peugeot-Citroën. The second element of the paradigm was the preference for 'doing it yourself' or 'fighting alone against the enemy'. This bias may have originated in the difficulties that Peugeot underwent when trying to consolidate its operations with those of Chrysler Europe and then Citroën, and from the financial difficulties of the mid-1980s which were solved without the help of the French State. Related to this attitude was the definite 'no' to any cooperation with the Japanese and the efforts to maintain protectionistic barriers around the European market, which was viewed as the territory of European-based car manufacturers. Indeed Peugeot-Citroën was managed with a strong paradigm, personified by Jacques Calvet, who had led the recovery of the Group in the late 1980s.

These basic principles certainly influenced the strategies of Peugeot-Citroën. A comparison with the Volkswagen Group is striking on each of these point: the VW Group favoured gains in market share (some said at any price when it took over Skoda) and growth by acquisitions and alliances (including alliances with the Japanese).

The *strategy* of Peugeot-Citroën was based on four pillars:

1. Peugeot-Citroën tried to compete simultaneously on costs (productivity), quality (catching up with the Japanese) and quick renewal of models (in the two parallel product lines). Such a strategy seemed to be a condition of long term survival in the automobile industry.

2. Synergies between the two product lines, Peugeot and Citroen, were viewed as crucial in order to keep R&D, purchasing and manufacturing costs as low as possible.

3. The company tried to strengthen its leadership in the areas where it had some distinctive competences: diesel engines and electric cars, this strategy relied on a very active lobbying at the EC and French government levels.

4. Peugeot-Citroën considered Western Europe as its priority market area, and targeted a few high growth potential markets in Asia, in South America and in the Mediterranean Basin.

The international strategy of the group can be defined in terms of geographical scope, attitude towards foreign competition, configuration and coordination of activities (cf. Porter, 1986).

The geographic scope was between a 'global strategy' and a 'country-centred strategy/ protected markets' (Porter, 1986, p. 46). Western Europe was viewed as the priority protected market but Peugeot-Citroën also targeted some high growth potential markets in other continents (China, India, Malaysia, Argentina) and some neighbouring countries of the Mediterranean Basin (Morocco, Tunisia, Egypt, Turkey).

Peugeot-Citroën preferred to remain independent in its international development, alliances with foreigners were limited to countries where host governments pushed firms towards cooperation (China, India, Malaysia). The group was actively lobbying at the EC level in order to maintain barriers to Japanese competition in Europe.

The configuration of activities was relatively dispersed as far as manufacturing (assembly) was concerned and relatively concentrated as far as marketing, R&D, and procurement were concerned. The coordination of activities was high (cf. Porter, 1986, p. 28). As a whole, the activities of Peugeot-Citroën seemed to be more concentrated and coordinated than the activities of the Volkswagen Group.

Considering possible future evolutions of the industry, such a strategy might raise problems. In case of a price war in Europe, Peugeot-Citroën would be obliged to sacrifice its profitability or lose market share. In a scenario of increased technological intensity, and quick globalisation of the market, the Group could suffer from an insufficient network of alliances. In a scenario of quick development in Eastern Europe the Group might lose opportunities compared to Fiat and Volkswagen. Indeed in 1995, Peugeot-Citroën was still too dependent on a few Western European markets.

6.3 The attitude against Japanese competition

The protectionist position held by Jacques Calvet against Japanese competition was built on sound arguments: the whole Japanese system was the source of competitive advantage. But on the other hand his position went against free trade and against any form of cooperation; This may sound out of date when considering Porter's argument (*The Competitive Advantage of Nations*, 1990): competitive pressure is a key source of progress. Jacques Calvet argued that in the case of the European car industry, too much competitive pressure, too early, might lead to an economic and social disaster and that the Japanese played the game with different societal and competitive rules.

A stimulating discussion could be launched with the students formulating arguments for and against protectionism. As suggested earlier, this could even take the form of role playing, dividing the class in two camps: the 'liberals' and the 'protectionists'. Reading from Porter's *Competitive Advantage of Nations* may provide useful insights on this issue (pp. 131–75 and pp. 384–421).

Actually the European Commission had changed its position in 1991 from liberal (according to the White Book on the Single European Market) to some protectionism, under the pressure of the majority of the European car manufacturers (including GM and Ford Europe); Jacques Calvet could argue that his vision was right. One could also argue that such an extremist view and position was a way to mobilise the company against a common 'enemy': the Japanese.

6.4 Should Peugeot-Citroën change strategy?

The answer to this question should be given in the light of possible evolutions of the car industry at a 10-year horizon. First the class should review the major possible events and trends which may affect the industry, and estimate subjective probabilities.

- The major factor in the dynamics of the industry appeared to be the attitude of the EU towards Japanese importations and transplants in Europe after 1 January 2000. Starting from this date free competition was expected, in this scenario the Japanese might take about 25 per cent of the European market (on average), that is to say they would double their market share, at the expense of the other competitors. Considering the relatively low expected growth rate of European markets and the overcapacity (already in 1995), competition would become very intense after the year 2000 and the weakest European manufacturers would be in great difficulty.

Was the survival of Peugeot-Citroën threatened in this scenario? Students could discuss this issue which can be put another way: who are the two weakest European car manufacturers in the mid 1990s? Peugeot-Citroën should catch up with the Japanese before the year 2000, improvements in the quality of vehicles and the development of new models should become priority objectives for the Group. Peugeot-Citroën should also become less dependent on their core markets (France, Spain, Italy, still protected from Japanese imports in 1995) and improve their penetration of the European territory (including Germany, the rest of Northern Europe and Central Europe).

- Several factors pushed the industry towards a price war in the mid-1990s: overcapacity, monetary fluctuations, and parallel distribution (since the 1993 Single European Market). Peugeot-Citroën should be prepared for a price war, and keep on improving productivity year after year. However, they could hardly compete for the lowest cost/lowest price position.

- All these arguments also confirmed the necessity to give priority to *quality* and to *differentiation* in order to be less constrained by price wars. The content of a differentiation strategy remained to be defined, based on a more careful market analysis. One component of this strategy appeared to be crucial: improving the position of Peugeot-Citroën in the up market segment ('executive') that allowed higher added value.

- Peugeot-Citroën should gain market share in Germany, by far the largest and richest market in Europe. The question was how? Probably with better upmarket models, top quality vehicles and good customer service. Market evolutions in Eastern Europe were uncertain but market growth was expected to be higher than in the West. Peugeot-Citroën could be more active in some of these proximate emerging markets.

- Outside Europe the priority given to large countries with high potential growth (Chine India) and a few other countries in Asia, in South America and in the Mediterranean Basin, seemed to be relevant. But the sales turnover of the group in these areas was still very low in 1995. The demand take off might take a long time, and building market share would probably require high commercial and industrial investments at the turn of the century. It might become necessary to share the investments and risks with another car manufacturer.

- The arguments developed in the text of the case to preserve two marques, Peugeot and Citroën, were relevant. The alternative of focusing on one marque should only be considered in a scenario of financial difficulties and steep decrease of the market share of the Group.

- Peugeot-Citroën had to compete with two full ranges of models (mini, super mini, lower medium, upper medium, executive). Concerning market niches (four wheeldrive, cabriolets, etc.) in which demand was growing, the solution of co-development appeared to be the best one, in order to share investments and risks (cf. the Peugeot-Citroën-Fiat joint venture).

- Indeed several arguments suggested to reconsider the cooperative strategies of Peugeot-Citroën and strengthen cooperative agreements for the development of new models and the geographical extension. The option of a merger with another car manufacturer (e.g. the Fiat Group or Chrysler) could also be discussed. Subgroups of students could prepare and present arguments for and against a merger. For instance several arguments could be put forward *against* the idea of a merger between Peugeot-Citroën and the Fiat group: more flexible alliances (such as agreements on joint R&D) put off the need for a merger, the geographical positions of the two groups were not complementary at the world level, the product ranges were not complementary, the paradigm of PSA might exclude this solution.

Several arguments could be put forward for a merger: the group would become the European leader in terms of market share with a broad range of marques, bargaining power would be increased, economies of scale could be achieved in R&D, the position of the Fiat Group in Eastern Europe could be a basis for an ambitious strategy in this zone. The comparison to other mergers in the automobile industry would be interesting, e.g. the failed merger between Renault and Volvo, and the acquisition of Rover by BMW.

6.5 Should Peugeot-Citroën re-enter the North American market?

In a global car manufacturing industry in the 21st century, Peugeot-Citroën could not ignore a market expected to represent 25 per cent of world sales. However, the North American market was so competitive that it might discourage European car manufacturers, at least the ones who were not involved in upmarket and luxury cars (such as Mercedes, BMW and Volvo).

There is no easy answer to this question, and the pros and cons could usefully exchange arguments within the class.

The presence of Peugeot-Citroën in the US market could bring additional sales in order to amortise R&D investments, the group could also learn from the market and technological evolutions in this zone, and create the possibility of retaliation strategies across continents. On the other hand, profitability might be low for a new comer trying to build market share. The past experience of European manufacturers showed that they only succeeded with high added value luxury cars. Several conditions should be fulfilled before Peugeot-Citroën could re-enter the US market: wait for the growth of the next market cycle (1998), have at least three new competitive models (including one in the executive segment) develop a national distribution network, share the risk and the investment with a partner: for instance the Fiat Group.

6.6 What consequences could arise from the departure of Jacques Calvet?

Jacques Calvet personified the paradigm of Peugeot-Citroën. The challenge was to retain the positive aspects: rigorous management, high investments, and to modify some other aspects of the paradigm. A more proactive attitude towards Japanese competition and international strategic alliances could help the group in the context of global competition. There was also the risk of political struggles at the top, particularly between Peugeot and Citroen. Arguably the early actions of Jean-Martin Folz contributed, then, not only to an improved cost base and greater efficiency, but also to avoiding portential political problems.

The improved product ranges of later 1990s also helped performance. However, the overall positioning of PSA as an essentially European-based car producer remained an issue, highlighted by the acquisition of Chrysler by Mercedes.

REFERENCES

Porter, M.E. (ed.) *(1986). Competition in Global Industries* (chapter 1), Boston: Harvard Business School Press.

Porter, M.E. (1990). *The Competitive Advantage of Nations,* New York: The Free Press.

TEACHING NOTES

Rover/Honda Alliance
David Faulkner

1. INTRODUCTION

This note refers to the Rover/Honda strategic alliance case study. It suggests how the case might be used, identifies some learning objectives in relation to it, and lists some of the issues likely *to* arise in case discussion. The case can be used in conjunction *with A Note on the World Automobile Industry by* R. Das and *The BMW acquisition of the Rover Group* by N. Potter. The case is specifically written to demonstrate some of the key characteristics found in international strategic alliances, but also raises questions about the overall strategy of Rover and Honda.

2. POSITION OF THE CASE

This case is concerned with strategic choice and is particularly relevant to chapters 6–8 of *Exploring Corporate Strategy* and especially the issue of strategic alliances discussed in chapter 7.

3. LEARNING OBJECTIVES

This case can be used *with* the Peugeot-Citroën case to consider and compare different strategies in the automobile industry. Since a key element of Rover's strategy during the period covered in the case was its alliance with Honda the case can also be used to consider *strategic alliances*. Here the aim of the case is to require the students to consider:

- The *benefits* of strategic alliances to competitors with limited resources in industries facing globalisation of markets.

- The *conditions,* both external and internal, likely to lead to such alliances.

- The *key factors* involved in making alliances successful.

- The importance of organisational learning to the *evolution* of alliances.

- The *role* alliances can play in helping companies to implement their chosen competitive strategy.

4. TEACHING SCHEME

Prior to the session students would benefit from reading the relevant sections of chapter 7 in *Exploring Corporate Strategy* (particularly section 7.3.3) together with the following articles:

- *The Global Logic of Strategic Alliances* by Kenichi Ohrnae (Harvard Business Review, March-April 1989), and

- *Collaborate with Your Competitors and Win* by G. Hamel, Y. L. Doz and C. K. Prahalad (Harvard Business Review, January–February 1989).

They should also read the case, the industry note and, if emphasis is to be placed on Strategic Alliances, *The BMW acquisition of the Rover Group* case. Students should prepare case analyses on the questions below. The case study, student presentations and plenary discussions should take approximately 3 hours.

5. QUESTIONS FOR DISCUSSION

1. What circumstances had brought Honda and Rover together?

2. What factors kept them together until 1993?

6. CASE ANALYSIS

The class might commence with a discussion of Rover and Honda's strategic positions, and options at the time that the alliance was set up.

6.1 Strategic positions of the partners

This should reveal Rover's feelings of resource inadequacy in relation to developing their product range and their concern for their growing reputation for variable quality. It might also highlight Honda's feelings of difficulty in entering the European market effectively.

The students could be asked to consider what was the situation in the global automobile industry; in what stage of development did it seem to be in life-cycle terms, and what were the forces impacting it and constraining its profitability? Furthermore, what did the future look like for the industry? Here emphasis is likely to be placed on the maturity of the industry, its uncertain short-term growth prospects, and the technological scale and scope economies that made it very difficult for a medium-sized car producer to survive in such an industry, primarily because the cost structures of the large players could not be matched.

In these circumstances it will become clear that two major strategic options were:

- Become a clearly differentiated *niche* player where costs are not key.

- Form an *alliance to* become a big player through the joint enterprise.

Students may of course come up with other possible options, and these could then be analysed and evaluated in terms of their *suitability, feasibility and acceptability.*

Rover's and Honda's competitive positions and their overall objectives and resource and skill limitations could then be assessed. What were their respective strategies for development, or in Rover's case recovery? Industry statistics clearly show both companies to be sub-optimal in size terms, at least at the outset of the alliance, and Honda's felt need to get into Europe, and develop European styling skills, may be set alongside Rover's even more pressing need to develop total quality management skills. Their resource needs, and possible seeds of future problems may be assessed at this stage. It may be useful to identify their *complementarities*:

ROVER	HONDA
+	+
Good styling for European tastes	Dynamic reputation in USA and Japan
Established European presence	State of the art production processes
Wide supplier network	Total quality approach
Wide distributor network	Solid financial position
−	−
Inadequate range, particularly in middle segment	No European presence
Reputation for poor quality	Poor styling for European tastes
Excess manufacturing capacity	Too small to compete successfully with the global majors
Loss making	
Poor manufacturing work practices	

6.2 Alliance formation

A discussion might then follow on what strategic alliances are in contrast, for example, to licensing agreements, projects or franchises. And what types of alliance exist, e.g. joint ventures, flexible collaborations, and consortia involving several partners, and when each is appropriate. Students should be referred to section 7.3.3 in *Exploring Corporate Strategy.*

The class might consider:

- What are some of the basic *reasons* for the development of alliances? Here such factors as globalisation, resource and skill shortages, the need for speed and to spread risk, local knowledge, or the threat of predators may well be surfaced. These points should be noted for more detailed discussion later in the session.

- When is one type of alliance more *appropriate* than another? Here the issues of whether the alliance is a separate business (in which case a joint venture might be best) or whether the proposed relationship is at the outset of indeterminate nature and scope (in which case a flexible collaboration is probably best) might be discussed.

- If the class consider the alliance to have been a positive move, the question has to be addressed of what form of alliance would best meet the needs of the prospective partners.

The two basic issues here are: Why did they not chose to form a joint venture and was a two company alliance likely to be powerful enough over time to become a global winner, or would a *consortium* have been preferable? Here are some of the reasons for adopting one form rather than another:

a) Joint venture companies are used when distinct businesses *circumscribe* the boundaries of the alliance activity. Joint ventures reduce the risk of culture conflict, since the JV can develop its own culture distinct from either parent.

b) Two company collaborations are very flexible, and are easier to unwind than are separate company joint ventures, with their own assets, and potential income streams to divide up. Collaborations are entered into when the nature of the task is uncertain, and the response needs to be flexible.

c) Consortia are formed in large projects which are too big for two companies. They are difficult to manage because of the number of separate agendas that have to be allowed for in strategic decision-making. But they provide large resources, and skills which, if well managed, can make the new enterprise a world competitor in a very short time-scale.

The case sets out clearly what actually happened. The students should consider and evaluate the pros and cons of alternative courses of action that were open to the prospective partners at the time of the alliance negotiation, and subsequently. What would be the major arguments for and against the alternative alliance forms in the Rover/Honda case? At this stage the tutor might make a short presentation on the nature of alliances, their varied forms and the arguments for and against the adoption of each form.

6.3 Alliance management

The class might then move on to a discussion of the best way to run an alliance. In addressing this issue the class might consider why so many alliances fail. Here issues of conflicting culture, lack of trust or commitment by one or more of the partners, clashing objectives, or the lack of control inherent in all partnership arrangements are likely to be surfaced. Rover/Honda should be examined in relation to the lessons emerging from the discussion to assess how well they conform to these lessons.

After this initial discussion, a number of the students might be asked to present their analyses on the two questions posed prior to the session (see section 5 above).

Rover's and Honda's contrasting cultures and styles of management could be addressed at this point. The issue could be discussed or whether the culture difference is an irritant. Perhaps it is an advantage, on the argument that you do not learn much from restricting close contact to those most like yourself.

6.4 Alliance evolution

Given the picture that will be developing, the issue needs to be addressed of what were the advantages and possible vulnerabilities resulting from an alliance between the two companies? Here Honda's dramatic growth, and Rover's consolidation into a segment player still with fragile finances, needs to be discussed. A view could then be taken on how the alliance had developed.

- What were the respective positions of the two partners in the world automobile market, more than a decade after the alliance was formed?

- Had their respective power positions changed in relation to their key competitors, and in relation to each other? It may become apparent that Honda was the stronger partner, and although the alliance had probably saved Rover from liquidation or break-up, Rover was still fragile. This factor may influence the prognosis.

Students may well focus on BAe's sale of Rover to BMW and suggest that the alliance has ended. Tutors can point out that the alliance is a legally binding agreement between Rover and Honda which will remain operative into the next century, what has ended is any new collaboration.

The alliance did not 'end' because it was flawed but because BAe made a decision to sell Rover. However, great the mutual trust and understanding between Rover and Honda was BAe had the final say as far as Rover was concerned, this is perhaps a fact that was overlooked by Honda.

At this juncture it is possible, if time allows, to introduce *The BMW acquisition of the Rover Group* case study by N. Potter (see separate teaching note in this manual).

To conclude the session, the lecturer might give a short summary drawing together the issues discussed, with some explanations and propositions related to the issues. Amongst the areas to be covered might be:

- The identification of some of the key *success factors* for alliances, namely mutual trust and commitment, success in achieving agreed objectives, a genuine win-win deal between the partners with realisable synergies, and a determination to achieve cultural understanding.

- The importance of organisational *learning* in the partner companies as a major benefit of alliance formation.

- The key proposition that if alliances do not evolve during their history and take on new projects, they tend to decay, and that therefore alliance *evolution is* a key to alliance success.

TEACHING NOTES

The BMW Acquisition of the Rover Group
Nick Potter

1. INTRODUCTION

The case covers the BMW acquisition of Rover Group and includes the rationale and events leading to the purchase. It is primarily intended for use in conjunction with the 1992 case study, *The Rover/Honda Alliance,* written by David Faulkner [1].

This particular alliance is still one of the best teaching examples of the benefits, issues and problems faced by two companies involved in very close collaboration. By acknowledging the BMW takeover, students can be encouraged to focus on an even wider range of strategic issues, without losing the benefits of discussing the original relationship between Rover and Honda.

The case includes coverage which can be used to concentrate students' attention on issues such as the scale and resources required to compete effectively in the future. It can therefore be used in relation to both corporate and business level strategies.

2. POSITION OF THE CASE

There are several themes running through the case, which makes it suitable for use at various points during the delivery of a strategic management course. It can be used in conjunction with the Rover/Honda case when teaching strategic alliances and the concept of competing through collaboration. It also provides an ideal background for a discussion on stakeholder issues, as well as a range of business strategy alternatives.

3. LEARNING OBJECTIVES

A complete understanding of the external environment and the strategic capability of an organisation, is required prior to the assessment of strategy alternatives. The case will help students to achieve this by focusing their attention on the following:

- The overall position and options for BMW in 1993.

- The position of both Rover and Honda before and since the takeover.

- Wide-ranging stakeholder issues raised by the sale.

- Business strategies of the combined BMW/Rover group.

- The future of vertical and horizontal collaboration in the car industry.

- The questions still facing BMW, even after acquiring Rover Group.

4. TEACHING PROCESS

The case can be used in a variety of ways. Typically, the tutor will lead a class discussion based on the questions below. Alternatively, groups can be asked to focus on particular issues and give a short presentation. Stakeholder issues can be tackled by giving each group a particular role.

Students can be directed to complete the three blank matrices prior to the session, by placing a number of manufacturers within appropriate segments. This provides a foundation for an interesting and useful debate.

5. QUESTIONS FOR DISCUSSION

These will vary, depending on the time available and the part of the course currently being taught. A broad introductory question could be as follows:

How would you describe the car industry in 1993?

Discussion around this topic will help students to develop their understanding of the continuing evolution of the industry, into one which is global, concentrating and collaborative in nature. More specific questions can then be used to focus discussion onto particular areas of interest Some suggestions are given below.

What was BMW's true position in this environment in 1993?

How has the purchase of Rover Group changed this situation?

Who were the main stakeholders in relation to the sale of Rover Group and what were their positions?

*What are the options facing BMW, in terms of integrating the model
ranges and their future management of the brands?*

Some students will conclude that even with the acquisition, BMW remains suboptimal in terms of scale. If time allows, discussion can move onto the possibility of a continuing relationship with Honda.

6. CASE ANALYSIS

The session can begin with a discussion about the car industry in 1993, which can be summarised as follows:

- Maturing in life cycle terms.

- Becoming global.

- Uncertain short-term growth prospects.

- Increased cost of technological innovation.

- Ever-increasing economies of scale.

- Quality improvement a necessity for survival.

- Structural change in the US and EU auto sectors as a result of Japanese and Korean activity.

- Reconfigured value chain, as assemblers try to get closer to customers.

- Brands associated with lifestyles.

Discussion can then move onto the students assessment of BMW's position in this environment in 1993.

A simple segmentation matrix can be drawn using price and volume as criteria Placing all major manufacturers onto that matrix will demonstrate the degree to which BMW was falling behind in terms of volume.

Although BMW clearly competes on a generic strategy based on differentiation focus, the company equally cannot ignore the economies of scale building up in certain parts of this maturing industry.

Toyota has also successfully entered the luxury car segment occupied by BMW, through its Lexus brand. Development and promotional expenditure necessary to compete on a global basis, has reached the point where even the largest players are collaborating.

Three other matrices can also be used to develop understanding of strategic mapping. The tutor can either put up the blank copies and ask for comments, or use the completed versions if there are time constraints.

OHP 1 – Stage One Geographical Spread/Product Range

Clearly this groups together some strange combinations of manufacturers, but it only represents the first stage in mapping the industry.

OHP 2 – Stage Two Brand Perception/Product Positioning

Now a clearer picture is forming, of which companies are jockeying for position relevant to others. It can be seen that concentration is particularly high in and around segments 2, 3 and 5. Segments 2 and 5 contain the ten top volume producers in the world with a concentration (CR 5) ratio of 70 per cent.

OHP 3 – Stage Three Competitive advantage/growth method

This demonstrates the degree to which certain companies were becoming isolated in 1993. Peugeot, Mercedes and BMW lacked economies of scale and had few collaborative links, Nissan and Toyota alone, have economies of scale without strategic alliances.

Other factors were also relevant:

- The build quality of BMW cars was not in fact as high as generally perceived.

- Range extension into the compact market risked compromising brand exclusivity.

- Despite this, the company needed greater volume and improved production methods.

- BMW lacked a four wheel drive and/or people carrier product range.

- BMW was suboptimal in terms of scale and this would continue to weaken its competitive position.

Options facing BMW in 1993 were:

- Product line filling and market development by organic means.

- Sale of BMW to one of the top five global players.

- Acquisition by BMW of a company with real strategic fit to its' assets and skills.

Discussion can include reference to Rover and Honda immediately prior to and since the BMW takeover.

ROVER – has used the period of the alliance to consolidate and competes as a fragile segment player.

HONDA – as experienced dramatic growth and European market penetration due partly to the styling influence of Rover – it is still the stronger of the two companies.

The class can asked to consider at this point, whether either company is in a position to compete effectively without the continued benefits of the alliance. This will help them understand that strategic action by almost every other player in the industry, means that collaboration is now virtually essential to even survive. This can be emphasised using OHP 4 – Global Car Industry – Major Collaborative and Ownership Links 1996.

Stakeholder analysis

Students can be asked to list all stakeholders, both to the original sale of Rover and the future of all three companies, these are as follows:

Rover
Honda
BMW
British Government
British Aerospace
Employees/Unions
Various shareholders
Customers
Suppliers
Competitors

They can then go on to discuss the ethics of the BAe decision to sell Rover.

They can be reminded that successful joint ventures are based on:

- Mutual trust.

- Commitment to shared ideals.

- Agreement and achievement of joint objectives.

- Cultural understanding.

They must also be made to realise that the decision to sell rested with the managers of British Aerospace who were not a party to the alliance and who would not therefore have felt bound by the same level of commitment as Rover's managers. It may be interesting to ask students whether they think that the Honda management were fully aware of this subtle distinction.

Future strategies for BMW/Rover

The class could then move onto consider the repositioning and integration of the combined model range.

It will be useful to show on the board how the model range complements but also overlaps in price terms. Mini and smaller Rover cars span the price range from around £5,500 to £15,000 and do not really compete with any BMW products.

The four-wheel drive brands are simply complementary and BMW's 7 and 8 series are effectively in a different segment to any Rover product. The two problem models are the 600, competing with the lower part of the BMW 3 series market up to around £22,000, and the 800 series which almost entirely overlaps the BMW 5 series price range, from £17,500 up to over £30,000.

Students can be reminded that Bernd Pischetsreider intends sales outlets to remain separate and also that his stated intention is to transform Rover into a brand, 'as strong and exclusive as BMW'.

They must be asked to discuss the implications of Rover withdrawing from the executive segment. Clearly BMW would not expect to gain more than a share of sales resulting from that move, as the rest would divide between other marques. Against all that, they can be asked to comment on the issues of continuing to fund development, production and promotion of two partly competing product ranges. BMW is investing £500 million per year until 2000, with no prospect of a profit from Rover until then.

Meanwhile the luxury car segment is increasingly being targeted by credible alternatives from Toyota, Honda and Volvo. Cost control is crucial, in order to fund R&D aimed at producing technologically advanced product features for the early part of the twenty-first century.

Students must be made to confront the issues facing BMW senior management. Few will question the logic of the acquisition or possibly even the investment in Rover. However, they should understand the dangers involved, as BMW spreads its resources and increasingly opens itself up to competition in the volume segment.

It is clear, that while Pischetsrieder intends to exploit the separate Rover brands, he is also determined to absorb Rover completely into the BMW management structure.

Students could be asked to list the sources of BMW's competitive advantage. The discussion can then centre on which of these will be sustainable in the future and therefore continue to act as mobility barriers. They must be made to realise, that several, including quality and customer loyalty are under threat from a range of increasingly credible alternatives.

The session could end with a class discussion based on their own views about the future of collaboration in the car industry. This can include the likely attitude of both BMW and Honda management to any continuation of collaboration beyond 2006 when the current agreements expire. The original industry matrix can be used again to pinpoint companies which are becoming isolated, such as Mercedes and Peugeot and to ask how long they can continue to compete on their own.

REFERENCE

1. G. Johnson and K. Scholes, *Exploring Corporate Strategy*, 5th Edition, Prentice Hall, 1999.

FURTHER READING

J. Burton, 'Partnering with the Japanese: Threat or Opportunity for European Businesses', *European Management Journal*, Vol. 13, No. 3, September 1995.

J.P. Womack et al., *The Machine that Changed the World*, New York, Rawson, 1990.

J.C. Jarillo and H.H. Stevenson, 'Co-operative Strategies: The Pay-Offs and the Pitfalls', *Long Range Planning*, Vol. 24, No. 1, 1991, pp. 64-70.

J. Burton, 'Composite Strategy: The Combination of Collaboration and Competition'. *Journal of General Management*, forthcoming.

A. Grundy, *Breakthrough Strategies for Growth: Delivering Sustainable Corporate Expansion*, FT – Pitman Publishing, Ch 8, 'International Strategies for Growth – The BMW and Rover Case'.

OHP 1

Strategic Groups within the Car Industry – Stage One

	Niche	Narrow	Broad
Global	1 (Lexus)	2	3 Toyota Nissan Honda
International	4 Rolls Royce Porsche Lotus Aston Martin TVR	5 Mercedes BMW ' Mazda Jaguar Mitsubishi Saab Fiat	6 GM & Ford VW - Audi Renault - Volvo Chrysler Rover Peugeot/Citroën
Domestic (some exports)	7 Ssanyong Metrocabs	8 Lada, Seat & Skoda Proton Hyundai Kia Daewoo Dacia Zastava Mahindra	9

PRODUCT RANGE

OHP 1a

Strategic Groups within the Car Industry – Stage One (blank)

	Niche	Narrow	Broad
Global	1	2	3
International	4	5	6
Domestic (some exports)	7	8	9

PRODUCT RANGE

OHP2

Strategic Groups within the Car Industry – Stage Two

BRAND PERCEPTION		Functional	Medium	Luxury

High		**1**	**2**
			
			Toyota
			VW
			Honda
				3 Rolls Royce
				
				Mercedes
				BMW
				   Jaguar
				     (Lexus)
				   Audi
				Volvo
				Saab

Medium		**4** Proton Daewoo	**5** Nissan Mazda Mitsubishi GM&Ford Rover Renault Peugeot/Citroën Chrysler	**6**
Low		**7** Hyundai Seat Lada Skoda	**8** Fiat	**9**

PRODUCT RANGE

OHP3

Strategic Groups within the Car Industry – Stage Three

MAIN SOURCE OF COMPETITIVE ADVANTAGE	Little collaboration	Strategic alliance	Acquisition
High Added Value +	1 Rolls Royce / Mercedes / Saab	2	3 BMW / Jaguar / Lexus / Audi
Some Differenti-ation +	4 Peugeot/Citroën	5 Honda / Renault - Volvo / Mitsubishi / Rover	6
Cost −	7 Lada Hyundai Proton Daewoo / Nissan / Toyota	8 Fiat / Mazda Chrysler GM / Ford / VW	9 Skoda / Ford / VW

GROWTH METHOD

OHP 4 GLOBAL CAR INDUSTRY - MAJOR COLLABORATIVE AND OWNERSHIP LINKS (1996)

TEACHING NOTES

Barclaycard
Kevan Scholes

1. INTRODUCTION

The case study is concerned with how a long-standing market leader maintains leadership and develops its business in a fast-moving industry undergoing significant change. There are many different strategic options open to Barclaycard, but which will be most suitable for them? Will all the options be acceptable in terms of the likely risk and returns and to the major stakeholders? Will they be feasible? The case invites readers to evaluate a range of strategic options against each other and choose the best way forward for Barclaycard.

2. POSITION OF THE CASE

The case is specifically written to illustrate the identification and evaluation of strategic options (in terms of the *development direction*) – at least through to an initial assessment of the options against the evaluation criteria of suitability, acceptability and feasibility. It supports the discussion of these issues in chapters 7 and 8 of *Exploring Corporate Strategy*.

3. LEARNING OBJECTIVES

a) Identification of development direction (for example by using exhibit 7.1 of *Exploring Corporate Strategy*).

b) Using the evaluation criteria of suitability, acceptability and feasibility to make an initial evaluation of strategic options.

c) Ranking options against each other.

4. TEACHING SCHEME

Although the case study is relatively short, it contains a lot of data – particularly about Barclaycard's market position in the late 1990s. It is important that students are familiar with this before class discussion in order to ensure that the debate about future options is specifically related to the market position that Barclaycard had established by 1997. It must be a debate specifically about Barclaycard and not about credit card issuers in general. This pre-preparation could be done either individually (prior to the session) or in smaller groups prior to plenary discussion. It is also possible to ask some of the smaller groups to develop strategies for Barclaycard's competitors – with the purpose of gaining UK market share at their expense (question d) below).

5. QUESTIONS FOR DISCUSSION

1. What alternative *strategic directions* are 'available' to Barclaycard in their future development?

2. Undertake an initial evaluation of each of these alternatives by using the evaluation criteria of suitability, acceptability and feasibility.

3. Which alternative(s) would you recommend? Why?

4. How might competitors erode Barclaycard's strong market position in the UK?

6. CASE ANALYSIS

6.1 Alternative strategic directions

Using exhibit 7.1 in *Exploring Corporate Strategy* as a checklist of general categories students should be able to produce a *specific* list of options. Examples of these are shown in appendix 1.

6.2 Evaluation against criteria

Appendix 1 also shows how these particular directions could be evaluated against the evaluation criteria of suitability, acceptability and feasibility.

6.3 Choosing options

Student groups will probably give different weight to specific options. The purpose of the plenary session is to see if they can justify their choice. It is likely that a *combination* of options will be needed to create a coherent strategy.

Although the case is primarily concerned with development directions, a coherent strategy must also address the other two 'strands' shown in exhibit 6.2 of *Exploring Corporate Strategy*.

- The positioning – the *basis* of the strategy. The case study clearly describes Barclaycard's current positioning as one of Differentiation (position 4 on the strategy clock). Students must be clear whether or not their options are concerned with maintaining this positioning.

- The development method(s) (internal, acquisition, alliances).

6.4 Competitor analysis

This question is included as a means of assessing how robust was Barclaycard's strategy. Try to ensure that the discussion identifies and 'assesses' a wide range of competitor strategies. For example:

- Further low price competition.

- Imitation of the Barclaycard differentiation strategy (additional services, etc.).

- Erosion of this basis of differentiation by new concepts of differentiation.

- Further segmentation of the market by niche players, loyalty cards, etc.

- More international entrants into the UK.

Appendix 1
Analysis of Strategic Options

Option	Suitability	Acceptability	Feasibility
A Maintain current strategy	Exploits core competences Improves value for money Fits with life cycle of the product	Should maintain and build on financial performance Low risk Unlikely to be contentious with shareholders	Required financial resources available internally Required competences already present within organisation
B Compete on price (APR)	Defends market share Will result in poorer financial performance Does not fit the stage they are in	Will significantly reduce returns to shareholders Low risk Likely to result in adverse shareholder reaction	Required resources are available to proceed Required competences are available
C Introduce multi-purpose card or electronic purpose	Differentiates product Improves value Exploits core competences Should improve financial performance	Should improve returns to shareholders Low/medium risk Should gain shareholder approval	Financial resources available for development costs Required competences available internally
D Grow market share (by acquisition)	Does not improve value for money Limited improvement in financial performance through economies of scale Large investment for Cash Cow business	Limited benefits to shareholders Medium/high risk Likely to result in adverse shareholder reaction	Internal financial resources unlikely to be sufficient for large-scale acquisition Will require heavy commitment of internal resources in short term

E Extend company branded cards	Improves value for money Will improve financial performance Strengthens balance of activities Exploits core competences Fits life cycle stage we are in	Will improve returns to shareholders Low/medium risk Unlikely to receive adverse shareholder reaction	Financial resources available for development costs Required competences available internally
F Expand overseas	Exploits core competences Fits with life cycle of product and strengthens balance of activities Potential to improve financial performance Markets under-developed	Should improve returns to shareholders Medium/high risk Unlikely to gain adverse shareholder reaction	Requires market research Requires new competences for working in foreign markets
G Increase market participation	46% don't yet use cards Exploits core competences	Market resistance Lower returns More bad debts?	Needs new product More market research

TEACHING NOTES

Coopers Creek and the New Zealand Wine Industry
Heather Wilson and Maureen Benson-Rea[1]

1. INTRODUCTION

The case enables students to examine the international growth of a new, small winery Coopers Creek. The case highlights the international strategies employed by Coopers Creek and the future aspirations of Andrew Hendry, its managing director. This is set against the background of a small, rapidly internationalising economy within a global market environment and the effect upon the New Zealand wine industry. It is against this scenario that students are encouraged to consider the future options for Andrew Hendry and Coopers Creek. The case is organised in three main sections.

Section 1 describes the company's formation and development, and the role of its founding entrepreneur, in the context of a rapidly changing environment. Andrew Hendry's early decisions about relationship building and export development are positioned against the effects of a rapidly deregulating economy.

Section 2 describes the New Zealand wine industry and its response to the withdrawal of government trade protection and subsidies. This response involved focusing on quality at all stages of the value chain and developing a strong export focus, primarily in the UK. This section also highlights the structure of the New Zealand wine industry, detailing the role of the Wine Institute, the Wine Guild, and the strong industry participation of Andrew Hendry.

Section 3 brings the reader up to date on the relationships developed by Coopers Creek and its export performance. Two network relationships are highlighted as being influential in the company's export strategy: the Wine Institute information and trade fair support for entry into the Australian and UK markets; and, the UK Wine Guild support in the form of shared transportation and promotional efforts with fifteen other wineries. In addition, the Country Action Groups for Canada and the US were highlighted as nascent but beneficial. Alongside this, Coopers Creek was exploiting a number of exports markets on its own, Holland, Belgium, Ireland, Hong Kong, Singapore and Switzerland, amongst others. In the domestic market, one network of four wineries and Coopers Creek is described which highlights the shared information, resources and costs. At the time of writing, Andrew Hendry's evaluation of the relationship with the Wine Institute was reserved, mainly because of concerns about relationships being based on compulsion. His enthusiasm for the other two networks in which he was involved is positioned against this. Section 3 concludes with a description of the organisational structure and capabilities of Coopers Creek as at 1996, and the future for Coopers Creek as seen by Andrew Hendry.

---

[1] © H. I. M. Wilson and M. Benson-Rea.

2. POSITION

This case can be used to explore internationalisation strategy and strategic management issues relating to a small business. Specifically, it can be used to assess *strategic capability*, and how this relates to the environment, resources, network activities and strategic choice of Coopers Creek over time. Two approaches can be taken with this case: to explore the strategic options available to Coopers Creek and assess whether its strategic capability will be appropriate for the future; and, to position the internationalisation strategy of Coopers Creek against the hypothetical outcomes of a born international strategy (that is, compare the staged approach to internationalisation with the likely consequences of internationalising at start-up).

These issues are examined in *Exploring Corporate Strategy,* chapters 4, 6, 7 and 9. In addition, the reader might want to consult the articles by Oviatt, McDougall and Shane [1].

This case has been used for class discussion with final year undergraduate students studying strategy and international business, as well as with MBA students. It is also appropriate for diploma-level students. The case can be used to explore specifically the strategic capability of Coopers Creek, or may be used as a small business-based integrative case for examination purposes.

3. LEARNING OBJECTIVES

The key to the case lies in first understanding why Coopers Creek has been successful internationally within the context of the New Zealand environment, this then sets the framework against which future strategic options can be considered. This can be achieved by analysing the strategic capability of Coopers Creek over time in terms of unique resources, core competences and the management of linkages.

Value chain analysis will help to visualise the key inter- and intra-organisational linkages. In addition, comparing actual strategy with the born international strategic option enables the exploration of the importance of domestic experience and networks. Core competence analysis is also required to identify inimitable competences and how they are used for cost reduction or adding value. The frameworks for directions and methods of strategy development can then be employed to consider the future strategic options available to the firm and the appropriateness of each.

4. TEACHING PROCESS

Because of the range of issues relevant to this case, it is suggested that the tutor require the class to prepare an environment and, perhaps, the organisation analyses prior to actual class discussion of the case. These could be useful background for the more specific questions which follow (section 5 below). This may be achieved by assigning different analyses to sub-groups within the class; for example, one group perform the PEST, another five forces, one construct the SWOT and consider the resulting implications for Coopers Creek, and so on. This might ensure more detailed information than if each student performed the range of analyses on their own. Each group could then report to the class and, together, determine the appropriate strategy and framework for the future.

It may also be useful to position this case against the Laura Ashley Holdings PLC case in *Exploring Corporate Strategy*. This would enable the comparison of the outcomes of two different internationalisation strategies, the systems view of Laura Ashley versus the network view of Coopers Creek, employed by the two family-based companies.

5. QUESTIONS FOR DISCUSSION

The following suggestions should be guided by time available for discussion, and the teaching objectives of the session. The following general questions are useful to initiate discussion:

Why has Coopers Creek been successful to date?

What key success factors contributed to this success?

More specific questions can be employed to explore, in detail, some of the issues arising from the discussion of the general question. They will also be useful in encouraging students to progress their thinking from analysis to strategy development. More specific questions include the following:

How has the current growth/development been achieved?

Will this stand by them in the future?

How would the strategic capability of Coopers Creek by 1996 be different if it had followed a 'born international' strategy?

Finally, providing the students have already considered the Laura Ashley Holdings PLC case, a broader discussion can result from asking the students to:

Compare and contrast the internationalisation strategies of Coopers Creek and Laura Ashley Holdings, PLC.

6. CASE ANALYSIS

This section offers a number of suggestions for discussing the above questions and exploring related issues.

Relevant sections in *Exploring Corporate Strategy* are indicated in brackets.

6.1 Key success factors to date

Coopers Creek was a typical entrepreneurial venture in that its development and growth were driven by the founding entrepreneur, Andrew Hendry. Andrew had prior experience in a number of areas on which the new venture was able to draw – his accountancy training and experience, working knowledge of the wine industry in the UK, and previous small ventures where he exploited his trading skills.

It could be argued that a critical factor in the success of Coopers Creek was Andrew Hendry's ability to manage linkages and activities within the context of an innovative and flexible approach. He demonstrated industry foresight, being in networks at inception or being instrumental in their development, and was able to use relationships to leverage resources to pursue growth.

Even in the early days of Coopers Creek, we saw Andrew's networking skills in action. For example, he financed the new venture by drawing on his suppliers' resources (finance and grape supplies in return for shareholdings) and also the resources of former colleagues at Coopers and Lybrand (finance and general business advice). This network has since dissolved, but it served him well in the early days.

The international development of Coopers Creek, its entry into new markets, and the development of domestic operations, were heavily dependent on the learning, the combined marketing efforts and the resources shared with other New Zealand wineries. Of particular importance was the combined effort to build the generic New Zealand wine label ahead of individual company labels. In addition, Andrew Hendry was 'a good industry player', in that he was a committee member of both the Wine Institute and the Wine Guild. He also initiated local networking efforts and enjoyed visiting existing and potential customers personally. No doubt his personal style, community perspective and industry knowledge have been major contributors to his adoption of network-based strategies.

6.2 How has the current growth/development been achieved?

(a) Unique resources (4.2)

In the early days of the company, Andrew Hendry's relationship with growers offered the company some advantages within the industry. The growers' financial stake in Coopers Creek meant that they had an incentive to ensure the survival and success of the company. However, the grape growers' concerns about pricing led to their withdrawal as shareholders and their relationship with Coopers reverted to one which was more commercially-based.

The audit of the company's resources reveals that Andrew Hendry (see subsection d) and the winemaker were the only resources which could be classified as unique (exhibit 4.2 in *Exploring Corporate Strategy*). Indeed, it might be claimed by all wineries that their winemaker represents a unique resource because the choosing and blending of the grape varieties is a critical skill on which their reputation is based. However, as has been pointed out in the case, export markets were not expected to figure the same brand loyalty as the domestic market because of the lack of local knowledge and insight. Export markets were expected to be more price sensitive and, therefore, those resources which contributed to cost reduction may have been the more critical in these particular markets.

In terms of Coopers Creek, it is hard to identify particular resources which directly contributed to cost reduction beyond the resource-sharing aspects of the networks in which the company was involved. Although Andrew Hendry had invested in land and plant, for the foreseeable future this would be operating below capacity and, therefore, contributing to increased fixed costs. In addition, the recruitment of the marketing director, although overdue, was expected to increase costs in the short term.

(b) Competences in specific networks (4.3)

The strategic networks of Coopers Creek can be analysed in terms of vertical and horizontal linkages.

Coopers Creek's historical vertical relationship with grape suppliers ensured both quantity and quality of supplies (see subsection c) in the early development of the company. This proved an effective strategy since, typically, the demand for grapes outstripped supply until 1996. Therefore, the ability to negotiate access at a reasonable cost represented a critical competence. It may be argued that Coopers Creek lost the ability to maintain this advantage when suppliers decided to relinquish their roles as shareholders. None the less, the previously successful partnerships with the grape growers must mean that Coopers Creek occupied a position of trust and good reputation which could be brought to bear when securing supplies, even though these relationships had become more arm's-length, transaction-based in nature.

The other vertical linkages of note were those with foreign distributors. Although Coopers Creek did not collaborate on-shore with its distributors, the arrangements were exclusive and long term, implying that relationship building and maintenance were important. One exception was the more collaborative relationship with the UK supermarket Tesco's, where there was direct input to the development of wine styles thereby helping to ensure a match with customer tastes in the UK.

Interestingly, the majority of the networks in which Coopers Creek was involved were horizontal or competitor-based (7.3.3 and 9.2.7). The most fluid of them was the local network in which a community or neighbourly perspective was dominant. Indeed, this network was most closely related to what might be termed a 'cooperative', and this is not inconsistent with traditional agricultural/horticultural industries in general. It should be stressed that the individual wineries did not subsume their identities to the collective. It is hard to gauge what competences this specific network afforded Coopers Creek other than the ability to 'act bigger' than actual size, and some planning and resource flexibility. The arrangement made sound operational sense even though the participants clearly maintained a focus on competition at the level of the individual winery label. There was certainly the potential for the level of competition in the domestic market to shift from individual wineries to groups of wineries, however, two forces mitigated against this: strong national anti-competitive legislation, not unlike arrangements in the EU and the US, and the controlling orientation of Andrew Hendry. As with the shareholding arrangements with the grape growers, Andrew Hendry was instrumental in the development of the local network.

The other horizontal network of note was the UK Wine Guild, the formation of which was influenced by government policy. This network adopted a more instrumental approach to collaboration than the local network. Clearly, the competence of most relevance here was the ability to enter a major export market without consideration to the constraints of size. This was not the first export market in which Coopers Creek was involved, so it is hard to claim that knowledge of the internationalisation process was a direct result of the company's involvement (although the company undoubtedly reamed something from this specific export venture (see subsection c)). However, in 1996, the UK was the biggest international market for Coopers Creek and representation there could be deemed strategically important for additional forays into other EU countries.

Coopers Creek was not unique in the New Zealand wine industry context for the use of network strategies to achieve competitive ends, especially in international markets. This industry-based strategy offered the potential for individual companies to shift the perceived level of competition in international markets from individual wineries to the industry level (evident in the promotion of the generic New Zealand label ahead of individual winery labels). However, the local network also serves to illustrate how Andrew Hendry strongly favoured the network-based approach at a more fundamental level. It may be that the company benefited from the critical mass afforded by the collaborative approach across multiple functions of the organisation.

(c) Managing linkages to gain leverage (4.3.5)

Coopers Creek was able to leverage critical resources and competences through the employment of network-based strategies.

The reputation of any winery rests on the quantity and quality of the grape supply. Quantity has proved to be an issue within the New Zealand wine industry, with climate and natural disasters (volcanic eruptions) contributing to a prevailing undersupply situation. Thus, the cyclical nature of access to grapes made managing the supply critical. 1996 proved to be an exceptional year in terms of the quantity of grapes available, however, only time will tell if this is a long-term trend. The emphasis on grape quality was promoted by the New Zealand wine industry to encourage participants to focus on the value added nature of international offerings. This strategy is in line with the nation's policy of moving away from commodity based products in international markets. Clearly, then, Coopers Creek was able to leverage critical supplies at the crucial establishment phase of the winery by encouraging growers to accept a stake in the profitability of the company.

Although the relationship with grape growers became more commercial over time, Coopers Creek was able to balance supplies of different grape varieties by negotiating and sharing with wineries in the local network. The management of linkages in the local network also enabled Coopers Creek to achieve greater efficiencies per dollar spent on advertising and promotion. Indeed, all the participating wineries avoided what might be termed wasteful duplication of effort and spending, not only in terms of advertising and promotion, but also in terms of production machinery and processing capacity. It should be noted that these shared efforts were not permanent; the supply and production collaboration occurred on a seasonal basis, and the promotional collaboration related to local holidays and trade tastings. Nevertheless, they had become part of the culture of the network and could be relied upon for planning purposes. At the time of writing, negotiations were taking place between the wineries to negotiate discounts with bottle makers which, if successful, would generate greater efficiencies.

Again, the UK Wine Guild offered Coopers Creek the opportunity to share costs with a number of other wineries, namely shipping and transportation expenses. Unlike the local network, this collaboration did not eliminate duplication between members since costs were incurred in relation to export quantity. However, it did offer the opportunity for some wineries to become involved in an export market which was beyond their individual capabilities. Although there was evidence that Coopers Creek had the capability to individually address export markets, the resources of the company would undoubtedly be spread thin without some collaboration in the international marketplace. It should also be borne in mind

246 **Exploring Corporate Strategy**

that indirect benefits from the Wine Guild meetings could have accrued to Coopers Creek. For example, the experiences of those members already in the UK marketplace would have been shared with the Guild subsequent to its formation. Similarly, Coopers Creek would be able to share knowledge and learning with the Canadian Country Action Group based on exporting experiences to date (4.3.1, 4.3.4).

(d) Core competences and inimitability (4.3.2)

As highlighted in subsection a, Andrew Hendry represented a unique resource of the Coopers Creek winery, and he actively managed the company's involvement in each individual network. He instigated the local network and was a strong industry player in terms of the management of both the UK Wine Guild and the Wine Institute. His community involvement enabled him to become known to other winery owners, and also helped to enhance his reputation. Both are essential in building the trust on which collaborative networks are based. The combination of Andrew Hendry's personal style, approach and business philosophy was probably the only inimitable, but not inconsiderable, competence of the company.

6.3 Will this stand by them in the future?

(a) What are the options?

Having taught this case with a number of MBA students, it is interesting how strongly they focus on the need for Coopers Creek to pursue a strategy of growth. In this section, we take both an organisational and individual perspective to illustrate how the personal aspirations of the – founder/owner potentially impact on the strategic directions considered (7.2).

The dominant strategy of Coopers Creek, in common with the New Zealand wine industry as a whole, has been one of focused differentiation. (6.3) To a certain extent, the focused approach has been forced on the industry because of the prevailing grape undersupply situation. Ironically, however, the 1996 grape surplus was causing concern within the industry that lower priced wines would impact on existing export markets. It is unlikely that Coopers Creek, and the majority of existing New Zealand wineries, would go down this route, having taken pains and time to develop the quality of their labels. The grape growers, on the other hand, rather than dump excess stock, could forward integrate to establish a collective to produce low-cost wine. With this scenario, Coopers Creek should perhaps focus on their existing export markets in order to raise consumer awareness of the winery's label. This would be a strategy that could be combined with other New Zealand wineries, however, maintaining share or increasing penetration would require considerable individual efforts as well. (7.2.1) Nevertheless, it should be born in mind that the grape oversupply situation might be temporary and Coopers Creek could miss out on valuable market development opportunities in the meantime.

Alternatively, we should consider whether the industry fears are unfounded and whether, indeed, low cost New Zealand offerings in export markets would damage consumer perception of the New Zealand brand. It is arguable that cheaper alternatives would compete with low cost wines already established in the export markets, for example, those wines produced by Spain, Italy, or Eastern European and South American countries.

If Coopers Creek goes down the market development route (7.2.3) it will be faced with the decision of whether to 'go-it-alone' or enter new markets in collaboration with other New

Zealand wineries. Certainly, there is evidence that the company has been successful with both approaches in the past, however, Andrew Hendry's personal philosophy and approach favoured the development of networks. This was probably driven by his desire to stay small in terms of infrastructure and it is not unlikely that the company would favour a collaborative approach to the exploitation of new market opportunities in future. However, the existing UK international collaboration was under threat because of concerns over relative contributions by members to the costs of operating the network. If this network dissolved, this would affect perceptions of future collaborative efforts between wine industry members.

Andrew Hendry's involvement in networks has undoubtedly contributed to the growth of the company, and there was the feeling that this growth was somewhat out of his control. This might prompt a more independently-focused approach to future market development. Certainly, the appointment of a marketing director was intended to enable greater concentration on international marketing efforts at the level of the company. However, if successful, this strategy could inevitably lead to the need to develop a more corporate approach to infrastructural and human resource capabilities, contradicting Andrew Hendry's stated aim of staying small and maintaining the one million New Zealand dollar turnover level. On the other hand, this would be a highly effective strategy if Andrew Hendry was thinking about selling the company to another buyer.

On the exit option, the case provides a useful example of choices facing the founder of a growing company. The literature is replete with examples of entrepreneurs striving to achieve a balance between growth, delegation, and bureaucracy. It was clear that Andrew Hendry's lifestyle aspirations, perhaps combined with his entrepreneurial desires to pursue alternative new opportunities, were coming into conflict with strategic decisions relating to further market penetration and development (7.2.1).

(b) Have they the capability to succeed?

Having established a foothold in existing export markets, Coopers Creek should be able to maintain and, perhaps, increase their market share (7.2.1). Even if low price New Zealand wine established a presence in these markets, the company has the capability to promote its label, and develop and maintain brand loyalty due to the increased emphasis on marketing with the appointment of the new marketing director. Should competition between New Zealand wineries become more fierce in international markets, perhaps developing the same level of intensity prevalent in the domestic market, then a closer relationship with distributors and agents may be indicated. Rather than maintain arm's length interactions with overseas agents, Coopers Creek may need to put more effort into retaining their loyalty and commitment. Again, Andrew Hendry's networking skills could be critical in this regard.

The threat of the introduction of a low-cost alternative is more serious for the development of new markets. Consumers, faced with the uncertainties surrounding new product trial, are likely to choose a low-cost alternative because of perceived lower associated risks. It is doubtful whether Coopers Creek has the capability to both enter a new market and instigate an intensive consumer education programme at the same time, especially when the company itself may be uncertain about the market response. This would imply that a collaborative proactive strategy is the best approach to new market development in the event of low-cost competition. Again, Coopers Creek has demonstrated considerable capability in instigating and managing network relationships, and may be able to maintain this approach even in the event of the demise of the UK Wine Guild (6.3).

Building the company to sell would appear to be within the capability of Coopers Creek. If the company can generate additional overseas orders and-if there are sufficient quality grape supplies, then the winery certainly has spare capacity to scale up operations. Additional investment in resources will probably be required since a network approach to leverage and growth may not enable the company to generate a sufficient asset base to attract a buyer. Indeed, for long-term viability following the sale, the ability to act independently may be critical as the new buyer may not be able to sustain and manage existing network linkages. This is because the social nature of network exchange and the associated requirements of trust and reputation take time to build between network partners.

(c) Will they build on current core competences?

The effect of the- involvement in networks on Coopers Creek should not be underestimated. Andrew Hendry has successfully managed a number of networks to see the company through the uncertain start-up phase of the company, to grow the company quickly and inexpensively, and to develop international earnings. It is likely that the particular linkages in existence for Coopers Creek at the time of writing will not stand by them in the future since, as was illustrated with the relationship with growers, network linkages are very fluid and change over time. However, the social skills and community knowledge of the founder, Andrew Hendry, will always be useful to future network development as long as he remains with the company and wants to pursue this approach.

Undoubtedly, the nature of the company would change if it entered a phase of self-generated growth and the base, on which the networks have been built, would have to change accordingly (see the hypothetical example in section 4). For the moment there is no clear indication that the company intends to go down this route, however, exit may be one possible option for Andrew Hendry.

6.4 How would the strategic capability of Coopers Creek by 1996 be different if it had followed a born international strategy?

The traditional approach to internationalisation rests on incremental learning in stages. Coopers Creek began, albeit hesitantly, with a foray into its closest geographical market, Australia. This was followed by entry into a market remote geographically but close in terms of psychic distance, the UK. The development of international markets by Coopers Creek proceeded from a firmly established domestic base.

An alternative internationalisation strategy might be the born international approach in which the firm develops competitive advantage by leveraging or acquiring resources and selling goods or services in multiple countries from start-up. This approach presupposes previous knowledge or experience and established networks of contacts. Andrew Hendry possessed knowledge of the UK wine market from his work with Sotheby and Christie and would have developed contacts in the process. In addition, he clearly demonstrated that building networks was a particular strength. The critical issue, however, is that Coopers Creek sought to leverage off the New Zealand brand, and this would have been impossible without the New Zealand-based networks already in place to support a born international strategy. It took time to build these networks, and it is no surprise that Andrew Hendry was instrumental in their development and management.

6.5 Compare and contrast the internationalisation strategies of Coopers Creek and Laura Ashley Holdings, plc

While there are a few similarities, for example strong entrepreneurial leadership in the early years and the production of fast moving consumer goods, the companies figureed fundamental differences in terms of their strategic choices.

Laura Ashley's approach was internalised growth through foreign direct investment in new markets. The international strategy of Coopers Creek was solely export-based. Laura Ashley's strategy was based on ownership and control of a vertically integrated value system, whereas Coopers Creek operated in one part the value system while developing and managing linkages with other parts of the system (4.3.1). Laura Ashley built the brand itself, while the UK Wine Guild and Country Action Groups developed the New Zealand brand and Coopers Creek leveraged off its perception and reputation. Laura Ashley's view of networks was a new phase in the management of corporate affairs and key stakeholder groups. On the other hand, the fundamental strategy of Coopers Creek has been a socially-based approach to leveraging critical external resources.

These fundamental differences in approach could prompt further discussion of new versus old business paradigms [2].

REFERENCES

1. See, for example:

Oviatt, B.M. & McDougall, P.P. 1993. 'Toward a theory of international new ventures'. *Journal of International Business Studies. 1:* 45-63.

McDougall, P.P., Shane, S. & Oviatt, B.M. 1994. 'Explaining the formation of international new ventures: the [units of theories from international business research'. *Journal of Business Venturing. 9:* 469-487.

Oviatt, B.M. & McDougall, P.P. 1995. Global start-ups: entrepreneurs on a worldwide stage'. *Academy of Management Executive. 2:* 3044.

McDougall, P.P. & Oviatt, B.M. 1996. 'New venture internationalization, strategic change, and performance: a follow up study'. *Journal of Business Venturing.* 11: 2340.

2. See for example:

Ray, M. & Rinzler, A. (eds.) 1993. *The New Paradigm in Business: Emerging Strategies for Leadership and Organizational Change.* New York: Jeremy P. Tarcher/Perigee.

TEACHING NOTES

Dutch PTT Telecom
Jan Eppink

1. INTRODUCTION

PTT Telecom was for a very long time a monopolist in its small home market. In anticipation of a more liberal telecom market the company decided it had to find new opportunities for growth abroad. It was expected that increasing competition would lead to a fall in profits. This was important in making the company an attractive investment for buyers of the shares when quoted on the Amsterdam Stock Exchange in the early 1990s.

The case describes what actions had been taken from the early 1990s until the end of 1997. At the end of 1997 the new managing director responsible for international activities had been with the company for nine months and wanted to decide the changes he thought were necessary to secure the future of PTT Telecom in a globalising industry.

2. POSITION OF THE CASE

This case lends itself to an examination of the issues related to the internationalisation of a one-time monopolist in its market, which was facing entry to its home market by new and often larger competitors.

One issue was the choice of which foreign markets to enter; another was the alternative methods that could be used for internationalisation.

Both these issues are discussed in chapter 7 of *Exploring Corporate Strategy*.

3. LEARNING OBJECTIVES

The case can help illustrate such issues as:

- assessing attractiveness of new markets;

- assessing synergy between new markets;

- choosing between internal development, acquisitions and alliances;

- risk and potential of alliances;

- implementing a chosen strategy.

4. TEACHING SCHEME

This is an introductory case which combines issues related to internationalisation and alternative methods of strategy development as discussed in chapter 7 of *Exploring Corporate Strategy*. It can be used in a plenary discussion to illustrate and discuss the main issues.

5. QUESTIONS FOR DISCUSSION

1. What are the opportunities and threats to PTT from the progressive deregulation of telecom markets worldwide?

2. How does a relatively small player like PTT position itself in a globalising industry?

3. Compare the methods of strategy development (internal, acquisition, alliances) in terms of their appropriateness to PTT's new developments

4. What are the risks and limitations of the strategy PTT had implemented so far?

5. What changes could be made to this strategy or in the way it was implemented?

6. CASE ANALYSIS

6.1 Opportunities and threats of deregulation

The main opportunity of deregulation is that in principle PTT Telecom can enter foreign markets. In this respect there are still considerable barriers to entry, even though the regulatory ones are diminishing. Think of the large investments involved and the scarcity of specialists required to set up business in new countries.

Another opportunity is that in the home market a telecom company may have more freedom to act than in the situation when it was a monopolist. For example, differentiated pricing policies that were very difficult to implement in a monopoly situation.

The big threat was the entry of new competitors into the home market – particularly because, from an early stage, the Dutch government had encouraged free competition and entry. It was felt that this would give PTT Telecom a strong position against those competitors who still hoped their governments would protect them for an extended period. Also because some of the new competitors had such deep pockets the only way to beat them was by being a stronger and more aggressive competitor.

The data in Exhibit A of the case study show that, although net profit after tax was increasing in absolute terms, as a percentage of turnover it was slightly decreasing (13.97 per cent in 1989; 10.95 per cent in 1994; 12.42 per cent in 1996).

This drop is particularly noticeable in international calls: turnover is dropping (DFL 2,704m in 1992 to DFL 2,188m in 1996), whereas the number of calls increased from 334 million in 1992 to 492 million in 1996. The pressure on prices in international telecom was considerable.

6.2 Positioning in a globalising market

From the case it can be seen that the countries that PTT Telecom had chosen to enter were very diverse. They ranged from developed countries in Europe (Ireland), to developing countries in Central and Eastern Europe (Czech Republic, Hungary, Ukraine), to developing countries in Asia (Indonesia). The economic systems of the various countries also were quite different, as was the political stability.

Also the type of services offered were diverse, from fixed telephony to mobile telephony and data traffic. This also shows that in different countries the customer groups were not always the same. An issue for discussion could be what seemed to be the concept behind the internationalisation. It may look like a scattered approach, with little synergy between the various positions. An alternative view could be to build up positions where one can, and in a later stages of market development try to reach more concentrated positions in a region or a country.

In the early stages of deregulation, governments in different countries had different views about co-operation with western companies. Being able to participate in a joint venture or buy a minority share in a local company required a different approach in each individual country. In many cases it would take considerable time from company managers, government officials and advisers before the contract could be signed.

6.3 Methods of strategy development

In the early stages of deregulation the only players were former monopolists in their own country. Often governments were not too happy to let new competitors enter the home market. This was especially true for countries that had only opened their markets as late as was legally possible. One can think of, for instance, France and Germany in this respect. In later stages of deregulation, local companies had to give access to new entrants to their own networks (so-called connectivity). Because of this it became possible to enter markets in a different way. Knowing the ins and outs of the various regulations and changes was of extreme importance in this industry.

Given the size of these countries, the required critical mass and the available human resources, one can conclude that the only way to enter the international arena on a larger scale is through co-operation with other telecom operators. In order to offer the customers, especially internationally operating businesses, one had to have access to a large international network infrastructure *and* local positions in individual countries. The large infrastructure was realised through the strategic alliances with Swedish Telecom in Unisource and the links with ATT and the other partners in World Partners.

The positions in individual countries were often built up by means of equity stakes.

The developments with Telefonica (Spain) showed that strategic alliances can be unstable ventures. The withdrawal from Unisource by Telefonica had a similar effect on the other partners as the sales of shares in the Rover Group to BMW.

It could be argued that it would have been advantageous for PTT Telecom to have had more influence in the ventures in which they were involved. Weren't they spreading their efforts too thinly? But if they had chosen a much smaller number of ventures with more influence in each, it might not have had the same impact in the market and the alliances as a whole.

6.4 Risk and limitations of PTT's strategy

There were a number of risks and limitations linked to the chosen strategy:

- that the companies in which PTT had a stake in did not develop well enough because of poor management;

- that economic growth in an area is slower than expected (Asia, 1997–98);

- that the interests of the partners diverge;

- political risks in some areas (e.g. Indonesia);

- limits of the financing possibilities of other operators by PTT-Telecom;

- the staff-like approach to internationalisation (orchestrator role of BD);

- insufficient influence in management and supervisory boards of partner organisations;

- availability of specialists with international ambitions.

6.5 Possible changes

Changes that might be suggested are:

- take a more managerial approach to internationalisation, rather than to continue the orchestrator role. This means more individual responsibility for reaching targets and more confronting of issues in case targets were not met;

- make more explicit what was the concept of internationalisation. What were the criteria for choosing markcts and products;

- investigate what new market approaches were possible under the coming regulations;

- build a large European infrastructure, in a way similar to what Worldcom was doing, by linking European capitals with its own backbone and gaining access to local operators.

TEACHING NOTES

The News Corporation
Julie E. Norton and Leslie P. Willcocks

1. INTRODUCTION

This case examines the applicability of traditional views of corporate strategy to the particular business of The News Corporation (TNC). In particular the case examines how the financial and business logic of an organisation's strategic development may be reinterpreted through the attitudes, values and resulting strategies of the key management officers of the business.

2. POSITION OF THE CASE

The case may be used to cover a number of issues in *Exploring Corporate Strategy*. Three major uses are recommended. First, to illustrate the importance of analysing the financial basis of an organisation's strategies. Second, to consider, in detail, the development of a diversified group – in terms of business and financial logic. Third, to show how the values, aspirations and style of a dominant personality influenced this development. These are core issues in chapters 4, 6, 7 and 5 respectively.

3. LEARNING OBJECTIVES

The case can be used to illustrate the following issues from the text:

(a) The need to understand the financial basis of an organisation's strategies (section 4.4.4 and section 6.4.2)

(b) Diversification as a direction for strategic development (section 7.2.5).

(c) Acquisition and joint ventures as methods of strategy development (sections 7.3.2. and 7.3.3)

(d) The cultural context within which strategy is developed (section 5.5).

4. TEACHING SCHEME

A number of the questions below require students to undertake an analysis of the financial situation of TNC from the details of appendix 1. It is recommended that students undertake this analysis prior to any discussion or written assignment in order that figures can be checked and amended and that subsequent analysis starts from the same, correct figures. An analysis of the financial data is provided at the end of these notes.

The suggested questions may be discussed in plenary sessions, with or without prior small group working, or used for group presentation purposes, with or without assessment, or as written assignments.

5. QUESTIONS FOR DISCUSSION

1. a) By comparing results for the mid-1980s with those at the end of the case, comment on changes in revenues and profit, and product and geographic profit margins; b)What financing strategies were adopted by TNC during the 1980s? Why were these particular strategies adopted?

2. a) By reviewing the development and progress of TNC up to 1990, identify the company's corporate objectives and detail the strategies and policies adopted to attain these. b) Comment on the business logic of these strategies, and how they relate to the cultural context within TNC.

3. What business and financial details assist in explaining the timing, nature and conduct of the Wapping dispute?

4. a) In 1990 TNC found itself in a 'turnaround' situation. How did this situation arise and how is it reflected in the company's financial results? b) What strategies were adopted to turn the company around? Do the financial results suggest this has been successful?

5. To what extent do the business and financing strategies followed by TNC in the 1990s suggest a continuation of old policies or the development of new ones?

6. What are the competitive forces behind the strategic alliances made by TNC in the 1990s?

6. CASE ANALYSIS

6.1 Financial analysis

Using the financial statements to consider the income and profitability of the group highlights key points for analysis, particularly in assessing the strength of the portfolio of businesses as discussed in *Exploring Corporate Strategy,* sections 3.5.4 and 4.5.

6.1.1 Sources of revenue and profit, and profit margin ratios are detailed in the table at the end of these notes. The following points can be made:

(i) In the 1980s revenues and profits were dominated by newspapers. In the 1990s an increasing share came from film and television. Furthermore by the 1990s revenues and profits were dominated by the US at the expense of both the UK and Australia. This represents, in financial terms, the product and geographic shift that began in the mid-1980s.

(ii) Profit margins doubled during the period of the case. Newspaper margins increased dramatically (as a result of increased circulation, the move to Wapping and capital investment). This product was the company's cash cow. Constantly high margins were also achieved from magazines. The potential of television is suggested by the margins for 1992–95.

6.1.2 Companies obtain funds from three main sources – retained earnings, borrowings (with various terms and marketability) and share capital issues. The Source and Applications of Funds Statement, the Cash Flow Statement and the Balance Sheet provide information on the choice of funding made by TNC. What must also be considered is the organisational context of these choices. Of importance for TNC were Rupert Murdoch's business objectives of growth and personal objectives of maintaining ownership and managerial control. These two constraints produced specific funding strategies:

(i) *Maximisation of retained earnings,* supported by policies of cost control, and low tax and dividend payments. The latter was made possible by the Murdoch family's controlling interest, low tax payments were due to a very active tax management strategy.

The News Corporation's growth strategy, however, demanded financing over and above that provided by internal sources. The issue of ordinary shares played a limited role due to their dilution of Murdoch family control should the family not be able to afford to subscribe to the rights issues (this was overcome in part by the issue of convertible shares and/or preference shares, attractive due to their classification as equity but, carrying limited or no voting rights). This resulted in:

(ii) *The importance of debt financing.* This can be highlighted by the company's debt:equity ratios which detail the extent to which TNC permanently came close to its debt limits (set at 110 per cent of equity by the multinational's major bankers).

Students can be directed to consider the traditional implications of high gearing and returns to shareholders, emphasising how debt financing provides the opportunity for decreasing the tax burden and increasing returns, which in this case are retained within the business.

Students can also consider the 'tactics' employed by TNC to stay within the debt/equity limits imposed by its bankers. Particularly this relates to the group's triennial revaluation of its publishing rights and titles. The percentage of shareholders' funds comprised by these intangible assets, and debt:equity ratios excluding such assets, highlight the importance of this accounting strategy and the group's ability to live within its bankers' conditions if the tactic were not available. These calculations also highlight how the ratios 'improved' in the years of revaluation (1984, 1987 and 1990).

Another accounting ploy adopted by the company involved off balance sheet financing. The HarperCollins joint venture resulted in TNC owning only 50 per cent of that company on which basis the investment could be equity accounted. Equity accounting requires only the net assets of the investment to be included in the consolidated balance sheet, thus full disclosure of the debt attached to this company was excluded from TNC's consolidated balance sheet. It is worth bearing in mind that the debt levels detailed in TNC's financial statements may not be the full amounts on which it is committed to meeting repayments.

Accounting regulators have also queried the 'equity' nature of convertible notes and preference shares. The former, until conversion, have all the qualities of debt (no voting rights and a guaranteed return) and in the US and the UK would be classified as debt. Preference shares also have the qualities of debt but for legal reasons are classified as equity.

The growth of TNC over this period coupled with the constraints of ownership and debt limits forced the group to be increasingly ingenious when considering the financing of its operations. What must be stressed is that these were self-imposed. The commercial and financial decisions taken by Rupert Murdoch led to the necessity of such techniques.

6.2 Corporate objectives and strategy

Discussion of this question is structured around exhibits 6.2 and 7.1 of the text.

The News Corporation's objective in the words of Rupert Murdoch, was to create 'a multi-national, multi-media company'. As a result the dominant strategy was a growth strategy. During the 1980s this was both externally, environment-led (extensive environment opportunities for growth existed) and internally, culture-led (the key corporate decision-maker, Rupert Murdoch, originating the strategy).

6.2.1 Development directions

Growth from an Australian newspaper base was achieved by the repeated application of a number of directional strategies:

1. *Related Diversification* into new market areas with newspaper acquisitions in the UK and US in the 1970s and 1980s (exhibit 7.1, Box D) and, in the 1980s and 1990s into the new product market areas of film and television in the US and the UK.

2. *Market and Product Development.* For example, the development of newspaper interests in the UK, US and Australia.

Market Penetration. Examples of this are given in the case with the increasing sales of newspapers in the News International stable during the 1980s and in the penetration of television in the US and the UK.

6.2.2 Development methods

The methods adopted to implement these strategies included:

1 Acquisition, particularly of 'turnaround' companies, for example, Times Newspapers and Twentieth Century Fox, but also of 'developmental' companies, for example, Metromedia. In most cases the initial cost of these companies was quite low.

However, perhaps in contrast to the impression given by a number of quotes from Rupert Murdoch, TNC also acquired highly profitable companies. These included, for example, Ziff Davis publications, *The Herald & Weekly Times,* and Triangle publications. The company was required to pay significant amounts for their acquisition, but they were also immediate 'cash cows' for the company.

In this respect debt financing may not only have been fundamental in maintaining Murdoch's personal control, it may also have been fundamental to the implementation of this expansionary business strategy as it may have provided TNC with a competitive advantage in the market for corporate control. This advantage accrued as a result of competitors having made greater use of equity financing, and in the context of functionally-fixated markets with perceived short-term horizons, being vulnerable to shareholder pressure to produce short-term results at the expense of longer term strategy. Murdoch's debt-financing strategy may have ensured that short-term equity market pressures were never a problem.

As a result it may be that Murdoch could adopt a different perspective on the value of potential acquisitions which enabled him to outbid competing acquirers (there is an example given in the case). It would also have similar implications for internally developed projects. Paying higher prices and possibly delaying the return on an investment did not risk shareholder discontent or exposure to a predator.

2 Internal development not only of 'turnaround' and 'developmental' acquisitions but also of original start-ups, such as Sky TV. Here, besides the financial muscle of the multinational other management practices were particularly important, for example, the introduction of new management, cost cutting and control. The case provides some details of this in describing the management of Times Newspapers.

6.2.3 Generic strategies

The generic strategies that the multinational adopted may not be clearly identifiable.

The choice of generic strategy may be broadly related to the stage of the product's life cycle of each SBU and its position within the company's portfolio. For example, with newspapers, the market was large but in slow decline and characterised by entrenched competition. However, TNC's large market share in the UK and Australia in the 1980s made this product the company's 'cash flow'. Capital investment for cost leadership purposes supported aggressive competitive strategies (particularly price wars) designed to erode the financial ability of competitors to survive and to ensure that TNC maintained its cash flows and increased its market share.

With television, where the market was growing strongly and where older (terrestrial-based) competitors were entrenched, but newer (cable- and satellite-based) competitors had yet to fully develop, TNC needed to adopt strategies that would turn 'question marks' into 'stars'. This was achieved by investment in a differentiation strategy with the multinational aiming to maintain/gain market share as the market grew by offering a product range of significantly better 'quality' than its competitors (for example with the acquisition of sporting events), which formed a barrier to entry for others.

The News Corporation was able to draw on several key competences in support of its objectives and strategies. For example, the skills and abilities learnt from years of creating and packaging news and entertainment items (initially in newspaper and magazine publishing), the company's financial muscle and its management control systems, and Murdoch's own 'eye' for the business and fast moving ambition.

6.2.4 Strategy development processes

However, for TNC this strategic development was largely 'opportunistic'. Any 'logic' that there was centred around Murdoch's vision of the company as a global media organisation and emerged only over time as the various elements fell into place. Students could usefully be asked to draw up their own profiles of strategy development for the company (exhibit 2.9). These would emphasise the limited role of planning and the importance of the visionary, political and cultural views of strategy development.

It is also important to highlight that what supported these strategies through the 1980s was a judicious conjunction of three elements of strategic management – the values and objectives of Rupert Murdoch demanded swift growth and expansion, the environment in which TNC operated offered the political and commercial opportunities for this, and the profitability of these opportunities during the 1980s and the support of the banking community at the time provided the resources to secure such activities.

In purely economic terms, however, the question to consider is whether these strategies were supported by any business logic in the traditional sense of adding value and providing increasing returns to shareholders. For example, finance theory suggests that diversification as a strategy is something that shareholders themselves may be more efficient at doing through their portfolio of shareholdings, than management may be through diversification. What was clearly of vital importance here were the attitudes, values and decisions of the chief executive, Rupert Murdoch. The case highlights the dominance (of ownership and management) that he had within the multinational and outlines the kind of man that he was – expansion-minded, fast-moving, visionary. The multinational in the 1980s followed that same track.

6.3 The Wapping dispute

The major US purchases of the 1980s required time and investment before generating acceptable profits. There was, therefore, strong pressure on the rest of the group to generate cash in the short term to support these purchases. The position of the UK was vital here. By the mid-1980s the multinational had in place, for all its UK newspapers, a business strategy that would provide for large increases in cash flow and profitability not to be found elsewhere. What these strategies faced was union intransigence and hostility at the implementation stage. The unions at News International, therefore, were not just a block on success within the UK but a possible block to the success of the group as a whole.

In terms of business strategy and multinational position it could be argued that the Wapping initiative, or something very like it was likely to occur. It was the need to maintain competitive position and maximise cash flow as well as perhaps a need to demonstrate to investors managerial capability that underlay the 'Wapping dispute'.

It is interesting that in the case of Wapping the financial logic of increasing profitability coincided with the demands of the group's commercial strategies, and very possibly with Rupert Murdoch's own personal attitudes and values regarding the role of unions within his businesses. However, we must be careful in attaching too much rationality and logic into business actions. One News International Executive has suggested that the Wapping initiative was more a function of Rupert Murdoch's restlessness and search for 'action' in his business, than any major necessity for increased profitability from the UK operations.

6.4 The 'turnaround' situation

Towards the end of the 1980s the actions and results of TNC suggest that its activities were becoming increasingly constrained. For example, the 1989 Media Partners initiative reflected a desire by Murdoch to continue his expansionary activities, yet highlighted that the financial structure of TNC was unable to allow him to do so. The placing of HarperCollins in an off balance sheet arrangement also reflected the strains surrounding the company's balance sheet, and the merger of Sky and BSB was a response to TNC's lack of resources to eliminate the competition. Even the necessity to issue convertible notes to fund the acquisition of HWT in 1987 may be seen as an early sign of this strain. The case details how, in connection with a changed environment, these constraints developed into a severe liquidity crisis requiring major financial restructuring. Analysis of the situation faced by TNC can usefully focus around the model of corporate crisis and turnaround used by Slatter (1984).

6.4.1 Symptoms of decline

For TNC the symptoms of decline were to be found particularly in falling profitability, increased debt (both in absolute terms and in relation to equity, even after a revaluation of intangible assets) and decreased liquidity.

The company's accounting practices have already been discussed. However, most of these were adopted a number of years prior to the 1990 crisis (save for the off-balance sheet example of HarperCollins, and even here such a tactic was probably adopted in earlier years). This could suggest that the symptoms of the company's decline were evident much earlier, or that any crisis, when it did occur, would be more severe.

The lack of detailed strategic thinking at TNC was also a long-standing factor. In fact Rupert Murdoch prided himself on the lack of strategic thinking in the company and the success achieved with the 'seat-of-the-pants' approach that he preferred. This suggests that some symptoms of decline may, in different circumstances have actually been particular strengths for the company. In the changed situation of 1990, however, it became a major weakness.

6.4.2 Causes of decline

The causes of the TNC's decline centre on the following:

1 Poor Management. The News Corporation was characterised by one-man rule. Rupert Murdoch was a dominant, autocratic chief executive who made all the major (if not also many of the minor) decisions. One-man rule is risky, but as the history of TNC during the majority of the 1980s shows, not always bad.

Indeed, Rupert Murdoch was both a strength and a weakness to the business. A strength in the expansionary, opportunistic 1980s, but a possible weakness in the changed conditions of 1990. This weakness stemmed from his inability to interpret changing economic and business conditions and respond in a timely and appropriate way. He remained attached to ill-suited strategies.

It is also possible that the development of TNC's US and television interests took up more senior management time, with the result that management and control of core, cash generating businesses, was neglected.

2 Inadequate Financial Control. The News Corporation had a sophisticated financial control system but it did ultimately depend on the attention paid to it by one man, Rupert Murdoch, who admitted he allowed his financial control to slip. It is worth noting that in 1980 TNC consisted of 60 separate companies. By 1995 this had grown to nearly 600.

3   Changes in Market Demand. The News Corporation was particularly affected by the downturn in the UK business cycle at the end of the 1980s. The important UK newspaper revenues were affected by declining advertising revenue. However, changes in the nature of the product in the 1980s exacerbated this.

Traditionally, the profitability of papers such as *The Sun* and the *News of the World* came from their high circulation levels. However, during the 1980s, the addition of weekend magazines and the ability to produce larger editions from the investment at Wapping meant that advertising revenue came to play an increasing role in profitability. The quality papers, *The Times* and *Sunday Times* had always usually only been profitable on the basis of their advertising revenues, which had been boosted by the possibility of producing larger editions and printing in colour. Magazines also saw most of their profits accruing from advertising rather than circulation.

Recession alone may not put a company into a turnaround situation but, coupled with other factors of often longer standing, it will significantly expose other weaknesses.

4   Big Projects. These included capital investment in new printing equipment in the UK and Australia and support for the investment in, and losses of, Sky Television and Fox. The former was not necessarily the wrong strategy, but became wrongly timed given the restriction in funds available to the multinational.

There was also significant underestimation of the market entry costs involved with the development of Sky TV (and Fox Television). Subscribers were less than expected, and, as a large enough target audience could not be guaranteed, advertising revenues were also lower than expected. The cost of the investment was also influenced by direct competition from BSB.

5   Acquisitions. While TNC generally showed itself successful in the choice and management of acquisitions during the 1980s, Murdoch himself admitted to having paid too high a price for Triangle Publications. This reflected both his inability to interpret changing business and economic conditions, as well as his own relentless desire for expansion, acquisition and action.

6   Financial Policy. While for many companies a high debt:equity ratio is a result rather than a cause of decline, in the case of TNC the aggressive use of debt financing was a conscious, voluntary (necessary) decision given Murdoch's business and personal objectives, and, therefore, a causal factor of its decline when linked with a changing economic and financial environment. Furthermore, the use of short-term debt, while cheaper, did mean that the effects of a tightened international debt market affected the company quickly, leaving a short time horizon within which to respond (even had the problem been identified at an early stage).

In conclusion, TNC found itself facing a pincer movement that left it with little flexibility of operation. From one side, elements of the multinational were making increased demands for cash, while from the other, traditional cash generating areas had not performed as well as in the past. When juxtaposed with changes in international debt markets Rupert Murdoch saw an erosion of the judicious combination of elements that had underpinned his expansion of the 1980s. The restricted financial situation clashed dramatically with his own bold expansionary temperament.

What the end of the 1980s highlighted was that the potential conflict between the goals of a company's chief executive and those of the financial suppliers upon which he depended was inherent in TNC as in any other company. A chief executive cannot manage indefinitely without taking account of the demands of financial stakeholders. By 1990 Rupert Murdoch's objectives were incom-patible with the use of other people's money.

Given that TNC's crisis was fundamentally a liquidity one, and not a product/market one, the case identifies debt restructuring and asset reductions as the company's most significant short term responses. However, medium and longer term responses are also detailed, including further financial restructuring, cost reduction strategies coming online. Improvements in profit margins, current ratios, interest cover and debt:equity ratios indicate the success of these strategies against the background of an improving economic climate.

6.5 Strategy for the 1990s

Much of the detail of corporate activity for the period post 1992 appears to suggest that Rupert Murdoch was continuing with the objectives and strategies of the 1980s – investment in original start-up businesses and acquisitive led growth, both of which were still funded largely by debt finance. Some differences from the 1980s may, however, be discerned.

For example, debt finance was long-term public debt, rather than short-term bank debt. No significant repayments need to be made until after the year 2000. Strategic planning, previously dismissed by Murdoch, was given a key place in his agenda for the future.

The move into Asia with the acquisition of Star Television-could be seen as very different from previous expansionary moves. The News Corporation had grown to dominate much of the media activities of the English-speaking democratic world. Would the company as successfully understand the different cultures and regulatory regimes of this new area? The case provides details of the company's difficulties in Asia This will be a strong test of Murdoch's vision of globalisation. The company has also made more significant moves into the distribution sector of the industry than before.

Joint ventures and strategic stakes were also new. Were they a response to the above problems, a further example of a new approach to managing what was an extremely large organisation or a response to a changing competitive environment? Or, as with the Media Partners initiative, did they merely reflect- the fact that Murdoch's appetite for expansion was greater than his ability to obtain the necessary debt funding?

6.6 Strategic alliances

6.6.1 Converging technologies

The case highlights corporate strategies of convergence in the media and communications industries which, in the 1990s, made those industries extremely competitive. These strategies were driven by the belief that combining the production and distribution of films, music, television programming and interactive software would create a company greater than the sum of its parts. From the case it can be seen that Murdoch accepted the conventional strategic logic of the industry, and indeed, was at the forefront of its development.

Companies in the television section of this industry could be classified into three groups: the content creators (who supplied the original information and entertainment items), the content packagers (who assembled individual items into marketable channels) and the content distributors (who broadcast these channels to the consumer). Many companies straddled two, if not all three of these groups.

During the 1990s, companies combining content creation and packaging played a dominant role in the industry (packaging created value by reducing the hassle for consumers involved in searching information and entertainment, and as content could be packaged and re-packaged in a seemingly endless number of channels, numerous, often specialised market segments could be catered for). These companies achieved their dominant position as a result of acquisitions, mergers and joint ventures creating entities of such size as to ensure their greater bargaining power. They were able to set up as 'gatekeepers' with whom any independent content creator must negotiate to reach the consumer.

Furthermore, the 'buyers' of their products, the distributors, were much more fragmented. Distribution systems included telecommunications networks, cable networks, satellite and terrestrial land-based transmitters, each of which was in competition with the other to obtain the kind of programming that would ensure the dominance of their technology and the maintenance or growth of profitability. One of the key undecided issues within the industry related to which form of distribution system, if any, would dominate the supply of programming in the twenty-first century.

6.6.2 Strategic alliances

With television, TNC had developed competences in content creation and packaging initially built and exploited in its newspaper and magazine publishing businesses. Twentieth Century Fox was the company's content creator, BSkyB and Fox Broadcasting, the content packagers (packaging also other companies content creation). Historically, TNC had used the distribution technologies (the satellites and cables) of other companies.

Rupert Murdoch believed 'content is king' – that the prerequisite for an effective and profitable superhighway was programming that people would pay for. He was also an ardent believer in the benefits of globalism. Strategic moves in the 1990s reflected these impulses. However, as previously noted, the methods adopted to implement these strategies now included several joint ventures, with content creators, packagers and distributors. How can these be explained?

A major influence in joint ventures with other content creators and packagers, such as that covering Latin America (one of the last 'gaps' in Murdoch's global empire) was the defensive requirements, in an increasingly competitive industry, to access markets quickly in order to pre-empt competitors and establish barriers to entry. This was difficult for TNC to achieve in Latin America as a single investor.

The company's experience in Asia suggested that the television markets in newly developing areas were a much greater 'question mark' in the company's portfolio of investments than others. The financial demands from the Latin American area would be significant, and would be made at the same time as the company was investing in its other major 'question mark' of Asia. The joint venture in Latin America reflected the financial constraints under which TNC was operating in order to achieve a global business in advance of its competitors.

Establishing barriers to entry required programming that consumers would buy (so successfully demonstrated by BSkyB with sport television). The News Corporation's competences lay in the creation and packaging of English-language programmes for English-speaking audiences – the limitations of which had been exposed in the Asian market. Meeting the requirements of the Latin American market would more successfully, more quickly and, perhaps, more cheaply be met by working with companies experienced in the language and culture of that area.

The News Corporation's main strategic moves in the television sector – BSkyB, Star, the Latin American joint venture and the acquisition of the last satellite frequency slot in the US – emphasised Murdoch's belief that satellite would be the dominant (and therefore, most profitable) distribution system of the future. However, as this was not yet clear in the industry, increasing links with other distributors, such as Telstra in Australia and MCI in the US, allowed TNC a 'finger in the pie' of all systems should Murdoch's analysis be incorrect. Joint ventures ensured access to the necessary distribution competences in a cost effective way. The link with MCI, however, was more significant than a joint venture, given that company's investment in TNC equity. How can this strategic alliance be explained?

As the case details, MCI was the second largest US long-distance telecommunications operator and, like all such operators, was facing the emergence of new competitors in what had previously been a very stable environment. To reposition itself and develop new businesses the company followed the prevailing logic in the industry and looked for a media partner. Why should TNC be interested?

MCI was prepared to pay a significant amount to obtain a suitable alliance. Such funds placed TNC in a much stronger financial position in the implementation of its corporate strategies, yet the investment tied TNC to nothing concrete for the future, while the ability of MCI to influence TNC's activities was negligible. Perhaps, even more importantly, the arrival of a friendly shareholder – the largest outside shareholder – was a bulwark against the attentions of any hostile predator at a time when Murdoch had reduced his family holding to only 30 per cent.

The News Corporation
Financial Data Analysis

	1984	1985	1986	1987	1988	1989	1990	1991	1992	1993	1994	1995
Revenues (% of total)												
USA	28	35	49	54	42	48	56	60	64	68	69	70
UK	37	32	30	25	28	22	20	20	19	18	17	17
Australia	35	33	21	21	30	30	24	20	17	14	14	13
Newspapers	67	65	51	38	43	37	34	28	29	29	25	23
Magazines	12	14	13	11	10	15	16	19	16	15	14	14
Television	7	8	9	13	9	9	13	12	12	15	18	21
Films	-	-	14	26	20	15	14	20	24	25	27	26
Book publishing	-	-	-	-	-	-	-	14	14	14	14	12
Printing	6	5	4	3	4	6	6	-	-	-	-	-
Operating income (% of total)												
USA	18	16	55	47	40	42	59	66	55	57	68	70
UK	41	46	32	40	37	28	10	13	24	24	18	20
Australia	41	38	13	13	23	30	31	21	21	21	14	10
Newspapers	49	48	29	43	47	47	48	34	37	39	27	29
Magazines	26	34	18	12	10	19	24	27	24	24	21	21
Television	5	5	10	14	8	7	0	8	16	22	29	31
Films	-	-	14	20	12	8	8	14	8	3	9	9
Book publishing	-	-	-	-	-	-	-	13	13	12	13	11
Printing	4	4	3	2	2	3	4	-	-	-	-	-
Identifiable assets (% of total)												
USA	20	37	71	47	38	52	47	50	49	53	52	49
UK	26	25	12	16	15	15	24	21	23	20	19	19
Australia	35	22	10	17	23	16	16	17	14	15	17	16
Newspapers	46	38	17	25	27	26	31	31	33	31	27	25
Magazines	10	25	11	7	6	20	15	14	13	14	13	13
Television	13	7	36	24	20	18	19	17	16	18	22	22
Films	-	-	23	14	11	8	6	9	9	9	10	11
Book publishing	-	-	-	-	-	-	10	11	11	12	11	11
Printing	2	2	1	1	2	2	1	-	-	-	-	-

The News Corporation
Financial Data Analysis (continued)

	1982	1983	1984	1985	1986	1987	1988		1989	1990	1991	1992	1993	1994	1995
Profit margins (%):															
Total	5	9	8	7	13	15	16		18	15	14	15	16	14	14
USA	1	6	5	3	13	12	15		16	16	16	14	13	13	14
UK	2	10	9	10	15	25	22		24	8	9	19	21	21	15
Australia	11	8	10	8	8	10	14		18	20	15	19	22	22	11
Newspapers		6	6	5	8	17	19		24	22	17	20	22	15	17
Magazines		18	18	16	21	18	17		24	22	21	23	24	20	21
Television		6	6	5	15	17	15		13	0	9	21	23	22	20
Films					14	12	7		10	8	10	5	2	5	5
Printing					11	10	8		10	11	11				
Book publishing		6	6	5								14	13	13	12
Current ratio	1.28	1.07	0.9	1.2	1.07	0.86	0.81		0.97	0.57	0.84	0.91	1.2	1.0	1.4
Interest cover	1.26	2.3	1.45	2.2	2.3	2	1.7		1.5	1.3	1.3	1.6	2.1	2.4	2.8
Debt: Equity %[1]	90	84	47	88	70	79	95		98	93	110	88	80	55	51
(ex. revaluations)	90	84	118	136	81	102	122		116	151	196	135	115	74	66
IA: Equity %	24	23	69	96	90	87	85		110	118	128	110	104	91	84
Source of funds %:															
Operations	27	31	19	11	8	11	85	0	(1)	20	20	16	10	29	32
Shares	0	16	22	0	0	29	15	17	19	8	0	24	8	18	4
Asset sales	16	4	18	17	2	4	13	17	41	22	42	26	3	22	29
Debt	47	45	50	56	45	46	43	66	41	50	38	34	79	31	35
Application of funds (%)															
Asset investment	61	70	67	88	79	67	63	61	88	63	40	20	7	32	48
Redemption of shares			6			25	14	16	1	18	14		2		
Repayment of debt	n/a	n/a	n/a	n/a	n/a	n/a	n/a	20	9	18	34	68	87	67	25
External payments[2]	28	7	3	5	2	3	3	3	1	1	4	4	1	1	6

[1] Debt = Current borrowings + non-current borrowings. Equity = TSE.
[2] Tax and dividends.

TEACHING NOTES

The Nokia Group
Martin Lindell and Leif Melin

1. INTRODUCTION

The case describes the entry process of a large company into electronics and especially into consumer electronics. This resulted in a significant reorientation of the company.

The influences of an overall vision in the beginning of 1970s is described. The case then deals with the continuous internationalisation of the Nokia Group from a Finnish company, to a Nordic company, to a European company and finally to a global player in world markets. The case concentrates on the acquisitions of consumer electronics businesses.

The focus of the case is on the integration process and the problems arising especially after the acquisition of Standard Electric Lorenz from ITT. Different integration modes concerning the degree of centralisation are exemplified. The students gain insight into the integration difficulties of large international acquisitions. Management, culture, strategy (organisation, production, marketing) problems are covered.

2. POSITION OF THE CASE

The case can be used in sessions focusing on *acquisitions,* but also more generally in sessions on *growth processes, internationalisation, international strategy and the development of an international culture.* The case can also be used in sessions discussing *patterns of strategy development.* The planning view gets little support in the Nokia case. The visionary, the logical incremental and the political views dominate.

3. LEARNING OBJECTIVES

The main areas of student learning are:

- The logic of acquisitions.

- Problems of integrating acquisitions.

- Identification of different integration modes.

4. TEACHING PROCESS

4.1 Assessing the logic and process of the acquisitions

The initiation of the acquisitions of Oceanic and SEL were clearly different from that Salora-Luxor. Therefore three subgroups of students, one for each acquisition can be formed.

Analysis of the logic of each acquisition can then be made in subgroups followed by a common session comparing the different initiation processes.

4.2 Analysis of different integration modes

Two patterns of integration can be seen. A gradual decentralised, 'looser' integration over several years (Salora-Luxor) and a fast centralised tight integration (SEL).

The class can be divided into two or more subgroups. One subgroup can be asked to find arguments for slower and 'loose' integration, and another arguments for fast and tight integration. Both subgroups can then present their arguments.

Finally, there can be a discussion of the divestment decisions (divesture of Nokia Consumer Electronics) made in 1992 and 1996. Here the class is expected to discuss synergies, core competences and the divestment decision. This can also be done first in subgroups and/or in plenary discussion.

5. QUESTIONS FOR DISCUSSION

1. Why and how did Nokia enter the consumer electronics industry?

2. Which problems and weaknesses do you recognise in Nokia's integration of their acquisitions in consumer electronics?

3. Would you have managed the process of diversification and acquisition differently?

4. Did the Nokia Group made the right decision when divesting Consumer Electronics in 1996.

5. How would you describe the processes of strategic development of Nokia Consumer Electronics from mid-1970s to 1995?

6. CASE ANALYSIS

At the core of the vision for the Nokia Group from the beginning of 1970s were internationalisation and high-tech products. Due to limited resources the internationalisation process for a smaller company is usually a stepwise process. The first step for The Nokia Group in consumer electronics and its internationalisation was to be number one in the Nordic market. The second goal was to be a big player at the European market and build up market shares at that market. And finally to be a significant player at the global market (telecommunications).

6.1 Why and how did Nokia enter the consumer electronics industry?

Comparing the situation in the mid-1970s and the situation in 1995, no one would have predicted the steps Nokia took in its internationalisation and diversification. Few would have thought that Nokia should be in consumer electronics.

Why Nokia entered the Consumer Electronics is explained mainly by the CEO's *vision about internationalisation and high-tech products* which indicated a changed strategic direction. The motive presented by CEO Kari Kairamo was the limited and slow growth within the so-called basic industries. However, this vision did not result in any specific action plan. On the contrary the vision functioned as a means to retain what might be described as a directed flexibility.

The vision played an important role as a legitimator of different acquisition proposals from different managers (cf. acquisition of Salora-Luxor and Oceanic). A new vision informs which type of actions have high priorities and will be legitimised.

How Nokia entered consumer electronics might be characterised as *seizing emerging possibilities* on the basis of:

- financial resources

- random factors (SEL)

- personal contacts (Salora-Luxor, Oceanic)

- companies for sale and propensity to divest

- the acquiring company's propensity to acquire

- the strategic situation in the market (strategic changes in Europe 1986-87)

- internal ambitions (SEL)

The corporate management created a freedom of strategic action, but the initiative in each acquisition process was from managers at the next level (with the exception of the acquisition of SEL). The substantial input in the strategic process typically comes from such levels in the organisation.

The first stage of the realisation of the *emerging* strategy started rather unrelated to the internationalisation aspect of the vision. In 1975 a *co-operation agreement* concerning mobile phones was concluded with Salora. It was further expanded and in 1982 this *jointly-owned* business unit, Mobira became a *subsidiary* to Nokia because of problems in Salora's main business, consumer electronics. However, in order to get Mobira, Nokia had to acquire 18 per cent of shares in the whole Salora company with its TV business as the dominating business unit. One result of the Mobira acquisition was the development of *close relationships* between Nokia's and Salora's top management groups.

In 1983, when Salora had been reorganised and was profitable, the general market trend improved. Salora became short of capacity and wanted production co-operation with the Swedish company Luxor, but without success. The President of Salora then tried to acquire Luxor, but the Swedish state – owner of Luxor – wanted a larger and financially stronger company. The natural step for Salora's president was to turn to the minority owner, Nokia, with a surprising acquisition proposal: acquire the package of both Salora and Luxor. This proposal seemed attractive for Nokia with its ambitions to internationalise and provided an opportunity to move further into electronics. An acceptable solution for all parties was found and the two acquisitions were made in December 1983. It is interesting to observe that an external initiative (by the President of Salora) brought Nokia into the consumer electronics sector – a totally new area for Nokia. Nokia also acquired mass production knowledge and production capacity which it had lacked before, and was now established in the consumer side of electronics with possible synergies with the professional side in the future.

Available *financial resources* determine when new strategic actions are possible. A surplus of resources provides opportunities for concrete strategic projects, such as acquisitions. Despite the fact that it is a long-term process to reach organisational fit between two integrated firms, a financial slack may initiate another acquisition long before the first organisation process has been completed.

The situation in the TV-sets market resulted in the acquisition of Oceanic and SEL. There were few possibilities for Nokia to grow in consumer electronics in the Nordic markets with a market share over 40 per cent. A *growth barrier existed*. The idea was to acquire European brands. As Nokia had very good results especially in 1987, resources were available for a further step towards growth and internationalisation. At the same time, one internal opinion was that Nokia had not reached the critical size it needed such that economies of scales could be utilised. A common belief was that Nokia had to be bigger in order to get consumer electronics components in the future and to become part of the HDTV-technology development. The acquisition of Oceanic was connected with the desire to get inside EEC markets. Another strong motive for further acquisitions was that the largest European competitors were acquiring companies in USA and Europe. Furthermore the internal competition (especially in connection with the acquisition of SEL) between managers in Nokia to expand their business units and to advance to the top also promoted big acquisitions. Together with the overall vision of the CEO to transform Nokia into a European company, these factors resulted in the very large acquisition of SEL from ITT. This acquisition doubled the production capacity of TV sets and gave new brand names and distribution channels, all important factor for further growth in Europe.

In the case of Salora-Luxor it was an external proposal which initiated the acquisition. For Oceanic it was an active search process (based on a strategic decision within the group) plus personal contacts which identified the candidate. In SEL personal ambitions had a significant role. All in all you can say that interactions and ambitions at different levels in the organisation and interaction with the external business environment generate acquisition candidates.

6.2 Which problems and weaknesses do you recognise in Nokia's integration of the acquisitions in the consumer electronics sector?

Problems

The integration process after the acquisitions of SEL and Oceanic was very difficult. There are several reasons for this. (1) the Nokia was not experienced in making international acquisitions. (2) there was no, or very little, preparation for the integration of SEL. (3) most of the German top managers had left SEL after the acquisition, and Nokia also changed most of the managers in consumer electronics. A whole new experience base had to be built up. (4) the TV business is a mature business with low profitability.

Two different patterns of integration can be recognised:

1. a quite loose, decentralised integration in the Salora-Luxor; and

2. an attempted total renewal of the organisation structure towards a strong centralised organisation and building up of a new culture after acquirement of SEL.

Of the two strategies the first one was more successful. A looser integration in the beginning might be preferable because the firm can get acquainted with the new business area and learn about it before integrating. Another reason to integrate gradually is that the European markets are fragmental which might make tight integration very difficult.

An example of quite a successful integration was the integration of the mobile phones business into Nokia (cf. the acquisition of Salora-Luxor), first by co-operation, then by joint venture and finally as a subsidiary. Acquisition as the final stage in a *collaborative process* might help overcome cultural barriers, governance and legitimacy problems.

However, when the business grows and acquisitions are larger, the gradual strategy might not be possible. Instead a *balance between control and autonomy is critical*. Problems increase in proportion to *the size and cultural differences* of acquired firms. A small acquisition can be incorporated into existing strategies of the acquiring companies, while larger acquisitions may require reformulation of prevailing strategies. Nokia's huge acquisition of SEL illustrates this problem.

When operations grow through new acquisitions, a movement towards managing an integrated network of operations is needed in order to *exploit possible scale advantages*. In Nokia this happened after the acquisition of SEL when control was increased. The number of chassis was reduced from twenty-five to three or four. There was a need for rationalisation.

The cultural integration of different companies cannot be achieved without an understanding and respect for the acquired companies' cultural characteristics. Inherent in an organisation's culture is a defence mechanism against rapid and radical change. A long-range process with a high degree of involvement from employees at all levels seems to be the least risky way. In order to meet this problem, Dahlgren and Witt (1988) note the need for closeness to the acquisition candidate. When cultural differences are evident such as between SEL, Oceanic and Salora-Luxor, acculturation is critical. Instead of reaching a stage of integration or assimilation, the result may be separation between the cultures to integrate or even a total deculturation of the acquired unit (Nahavandi and Malekzadeh, 1988).

European TV markets are fragmented with strong national culture and national differences, suggesting the avoidance of a uniform global strategy for firms. Nokia combined a universal brand, ITT Nokia, with one local brand name in each market. Three distribution channels were utilised, the specialised independent retailer, the large specialised channels selling only electronics and the supermarkets. They all use a different selling style. The strategy should simultaneously give possibilities to exploit system-wide economies and to exploit learning and facilitate renewal without losing the units' original ability to adapt to local requirements (Haspeslagh and Jemison, 1991, p. 264). The integration of a number of acquisitions involved a large amount of change, especially regarding the behaviour of staff as well as virtually all the systems in the organisation.

What to integrate and what to decentralise? Referring to Porter's value chain, Scale advantages can be reached in the beginning of the chain, in component developments, purchase strategies and in productions. But even in the production phase flexibility was needed. The change from one chassis to another, from one standard to another had to be fast. Greatest flexibility was However, needed in the marketing phase concerning brand, price, product mix and distribution channels.

Logistics and distribution became the most critical factors especially when not *technically* ahead of competitors. In the early 1980s The Nokia Group had a competence in professional electronics and short series production of high quality products (cf. computer-systems). What became necessary in consumer-electronics was competence in mass production and marketing.

Summarising, there is no one right way to integrate but entering a new industry through acquisition seems to be more successful in a decentralised way. However, when there are many acquisitions to integrate the complexity increases exponentially, especially in fragmentary markets such as TVs. In some aspects it is necessary to utilise scale effects (components, production); on the other hand it is necessary to adapt to the local conditions.

Peculiar *weaknesses* in the Consumer Electronics group expressed, among others, by the manager in charge of the home entertainment products in Geneva were:

1. Replacement of top management in the German SEL units and the disbanding of the original integration group to be replaced with managers with experience in consumer electronics. The consequences of these actions were that the integration process stopped totally in the summer 1988 and did not recommence for one year. The most natural solution for many of the managers in consumer electronics had been to continue with the original integration group. It was chaos in the organisation at the end of 1988 and motivation was low.

2. Too many managers changed at the same time. Changes ought to be more of a continuous process. Changes of cultures and concepts need time.

3. All top managers were located in Geneva without any connection to a large market or factory.

4. As a consequence of the choice of Geneva there was no 'management by walking around'. The drive in the organisation was not the same as before.

5. The existing competences in the company were not employed. In autumn 1988 everything was started again from scratch.

6. Strategies were formulated but not until 1-2 years after the acquisitions.

6.3 Would you have managed diversification and acquisitions differently?

When diversifying into a business three different methods can usually be used, internal development, alliances or acquisitions. Acquisition is a fast method to diversify but also difficult to manage. Large acquisitions might also contain products and markets of less interest to the acquirer. As can be recognised in the Nokia case, in retrospect it would have been much better to follow the original strategy to only buy new brands in Europe and not, or a least much less of, the production capacity. Another possible strategy would have been to form one or more alliances in order to minimise the risks. This method of growth had successfully been used in the mobile phones business.

Integration of SEL was managed badly. The Nokia Group had no master plan of how to co-ordinate and integrate the division when acquiring SEL. The work with the master plan started after the acquisition. As iterated above many strategic decisions had to be made in a short time after the acquisition of SEL. Some discussion issues are:

- The wisdom of disbanding the original integration group.

- The wisdom of locating the head office of Nokia Consumer Electronics in Geneva.

- The strengths and weaknesses of creating a centralised divisional organisation (especially concerning R&D and marketing decisions) in Geneva. A strength is that decision making became faster and perhaps more co-ordinated. On the other hand the local responsiveness became weaker and implementation more difficult.

- Purchase strategy (what to buy and what to produce by the group itself). The policy was to buy in more and more components and be an assembler of components, not a developer of components. The Nokia Group was only ninth in terms of TV production in the world.

- The choice and reduction of brands. The wisdom of introducing ITT-Nokia as universal middle range band. The wisdom of using the company name as a brand name. In France the effort to replace Oceanic with ITT-Nokia failed. After a six months period Nokia Consumer Electronics gave up its attempt to use ITT-Nokia and went back to using Oceanic in France.

6.4 Did the Nokia Group make the right decision when divesting Consumer Electronics in 1996? Was there a possibility for the Nokia Group to stay in consumer electronics? Which measures would you then have taken?

The result of the division has not been satisfactory. In only two years during the 1990s have there profits, 1990 when East Germany was built up again and in 1994 when Nokia had the best range of products. According to the present president of Nokia Consumer Electronics, Tapio Hintikka, volumes in Europe have decreased 4–5 per cent annually during the 1990s and prices by 5–10 per cent. More capacity has been built up in England where 4–5 million TV sets are produced per year. Also in China the production capacity has been expanded to such an extent that sets have to be exported somewhere. And that mean problems.

TV production is a difficult business. The markets in Europe and in the world are mature. You have to fight for market share and be amongst the strongest in the world. The Nokia group was quite a small player in the world (ninth, and third in Europe.) Nokia had too many businesses in a 'global' phase in order to work efficiently with all selectivity and focus was needed.

In order to stay in business Nokia Consumer Electronics seems to have at least two alternatives. First to choose between being a *smaller local producer* with some exports (go back to the Salora-Luxor situation) or second to grow to a *major global player* in the world. To be a global player (like Philips) would need substantial further investments. Nokia was number nine in the world. Some sort of *co-operation* seems to be necessary, with a European or a Japanese company. The most probable co-operator in Europe is the French Thompson and among the Japanese firms the company Fujitsu, the owner of ICL which acquired the Nokia Data.

6.5 How would you describe the processes of strategy development from the mid-1970s to 1992 in Nokia's consumer electronics sector?

The strategic path of Nokia was not straight forward. The first phase was the formulation of the vision. Later on the main pattern was a reaction to possibilities and internal power games; it could be said that an *incremental and emergent model* was dominating. Some trait of the *rationalistic or planning model* could found in the years 1986-87, when there was decisions about whether to expand to Europe or divest the consumer electronics. The realisation of the vision can be seen as a series of actions made in response to emergent problems and possibilities – often as part of internal power games – with a relatively weak overall interpretation (cf. Lindgren, 1982). The original vision gives a general direction usually without any precisely defined actions. The realised vision is more detailed, often modified and sometimes reformulated as a result of the strategic process.

REFERENCES

Dahlgren, G. and Witt, P. (1988). *Ledning av fusionsförlopp. En analys av bildandet av Ericsson Information systems AB*. Stockholm: Handelshögskolan i Stockholm, ekonomiska forskningsinstitutet.

Haspeslagh, P.C. and Jemison, D. B. (1991). *Managing Acquisitions. Creating value through corporate renewal*. New York: The Free Press.

Nahavandi, A. and Malekzadeh (1988): Acculturation in mergers and acquisitions. *Academy of Management Review, 13:* pp. 79-90.

TEACHING NOTES

Bord Gais Eireann
Eleanor Doyle & Frederic Adam

1. INTRODUCTION

The case presents an organisation that underwent strategic changes in its operations due to changes in the regulation of its market. Top management at BGE recognised that the only guarantee for continued success lay in their ability to become more customer-oriented, which represented a significant reorientation from their technology and engineering driven history. This case study focuses specifically on the implications of the new strategy and the role of the information technology (IT) department of BGE in implementing the new strategy. BGE's new customer-oriented strategy required major changes across all functional areas. The Information Technology department was one area forced to radically redevelop its role within the overall structure and had to pro-actively plan for the systems and services required to successfully contend with the new strategy.

The strategic changes in BGE included and required the restructuring of the organisation. The explicit aim of the restructuring was to enable the successful implementation of the new strategy. This involved efforts to alter significantly the role and duties of the information department at BGE. Top management realised the vital contribution of the information technology department to the long-term strategy and the IS department was called on to proactively develop and implement the systems required to support and accomplish BGE's metamorphosis.

2. POSITION OF THE CASE

The case can be used to explore the role of information in supporting and aiding a significant strategic reorientation. The case deals specifically with a large utility company that faced deregulation in its market when its status as a monopoly was altered as EU directives were applied to the Irish market for gas provision. BGE's strategic position – that of a monopoly - in the Irish market was changed, thus altering its entire competitive position and environment. The reorientation in BGE's status from a largely protected state-owned organisation to a company faced with competition in almost 80% of its market presented the company with a change imperative in an attempt to ensure its strong performance.

3. LEARNING OBJECTIVES

A range of learning objectives can be successfully attained through analysis of this case. They include:

- the important role of the information resource in managing an organisation and particularly as a support for and a critical success factor in strategic change

- the changing configuration of organisational structure & resources to support strategic change: business process engineering and re-engineering

- the allocation of resources necessary for success (resource creation and development): i.e. matching internal resources and competences to opportunities in the organisation's external environment

- the connection between resource allocation, and control of performance for successful strategy implementation.

4. THE TEACHING PROCESS

It is useful for students to appreciate the context of BGE's changing strategy. As a 100% state-owned company operating in the commercial sector with a monopoly in its market it did not have to deal with direct competition. However, the recent changes in EU policy heralded dramatic changes in how BGE perceived itself and its role in the gas-provision market.

Many issues relevant to BGE are dealt with in Chapters 9 and 10 of Exploring Corporate Strategy. In addition, readers might wish to consult the following prior to class discussion of the case if specific material on information technology is required:

- Earl, M.J. (1989) *Management Strategies for Information Technology*, Business Information Technology Series, Prentice Hall.

- Ward, J., Griffiths, P. and Whitmore, P. (1990) *Strategic Planning for Information Systems*, Wiley Information Systems Series, Wiley and Son.

- Robson, W. (1994). *Strategic Management and Information Systems*, Pitman Publishing.

5. QUESTIONS FOR DISCUSSION

The questions for discussion centre on an assessment of the implications of the new strategy for organistional structure, resource allocation and control systems at BGE. The questions below are ordered to relate to the overall company structure, management control, the importance of the role of information for the organisation and the management of IT development. Depending on the time available, these questions could be posed to students in sub-groups allowing them to focus on a particular issue in depth. Each subgroup's presentation of answers to a set of questions would provide for a sharing in the overall analysis of the case.

5.1 Overall Structure

- Why did BGE decide to restructure the company and why did they choose a move from a functional to a process structure?

- Could the changes in BGE's structure give rise to any difficulties for the company? (Consider both the changes required in the headquarters and in the regional offices).

5.2 Management Control

- Given the new organisational structure at BGE, what are the main centres of responsibility within the organisation? Do you think the control mechanisms are optimal (see section 10.4 in the main text of *Exploring Corporate Strategy* for comparisons)?

- Comment on the performance management culture at BGE. Focus particularly on the performance measurement systems implemented by the IS department.

5.3 The Importance of the Role of Information

- Based on figure 10.1 in the main text of *Exploring Corporate Strategy*, map out the main resource allocation and control process changes required in implementing the strategy of improving customer focus.

- Why, in the context of its reorientation to a customer-focus strategy, was information particularly important for BGE?

5.4 Management of IT Development

- What changes were implemented in BGE's IS department? In what way were the changes in line with the company's new strategy?

- How can the IS department ensure continued interest at all staff levels and increased funding for IT at management committee level?

6. CASE ANALYSIS

6.1 Overall Organisational Structure

The main stimulus to BGE's restructuring came from external sources in the form of Third Party Access which would change the face of BGE's market position by allowing competition in the Irish gas market for the first time. This forced management to conduct an analysis of BGE's efficiency, staffing and profitability levels in the context of its future development. Management at BGE realised that it was vital to create a sense of customer loyalty before competition established itself in the market – otherwise they faced the prospect of equipping their competitors with not only BGE's infrastructure but with its customer base also.

In BGE's initial attempts to begin the process of formulating a new competitive strategy it was decided to standardise procedures across all BGE's regional offices so that BGE was providing the same services to all its customers. As a result of its initial structure, BGE essentially found itself providing similar services from each regional office, causing a considerable and unnecessary duplication of work. As a direct result of its history where separate local companies had been acquired over time, and the absence of a set of company-wide procedures and practices, each office operated in effect in a separate capacity from other offices. The organisation operated less like a group of separate business units, among which relevant information and skills would be shared, but more like a group of individual businesses with reporting rather than operational linkages between them.

The decision to create a structure based on process rather than functional areas was in response to decisions to adopt a more customer-focused strategy. Each customer would deal with one member of BGE – a process manager – who would in turn ensure that tasks required to satisfy the customer's query were distributed to the relevant staff members. This would facilitate relatively effortless communication from the customer's perspective. Furthermore, once procedures were standardised across offices, BGE could be assured that all its customers received the same level of service regardless of their geographical location.

To support the functioning of the organisation's customer-oriented strategy required the internal restructuring of some staff as well as a change in the use of information within the organisation. Information had to be at hand for all relevant staff required to deal with a particular customer's query, hence, the need for the development of organisation wide computer applications, as functions were not replicated across each regional office.

Staff restructuring is always a difficult development within any organisation as are any efforts towards significant change. Resistance from staff and management was expected in BGE as job specifications were modified and procedures were standardised. For example, the focus of importance on 'key users' represented a potential change in the balance of power within the organisation, if used correctly by managers. The successful management of the key users would require a significant culture change in BGE but would ultimately allow for constructive co-operative developments in the IS area in BGE.

Resistance by middle management could be expected also as much local 'power' was effectively eroded by the increased visibility afforded to top management in headquarters by the organisation-wide communication and information systems. In addition, many middle managers whose roles involved the preparation of information were no longer required as reports previously prepared by them were prepared centrally.

6.2 Management Control

The main centres of responsibility within the organisation were the separate departments within BGE (see figure 1 of the case study), i.e. the Heads of Distribution, Engineering/ Transmission, Finance, Strategic Development, Gas Trading & Marketing, and the Chief Information Officer. The management committee, which included the function heads, the CEO and the company secretary, constituted the main decision-making and performance-monitoring groups in BGE. Each functional area essentially acted dependently in that each was accountable for its own budget, was in charge of its costs and monitored its own variances. Finance tended to act as arbitrator between different departments to indicate if budgets were being surpassed or if expected returns did not arise.

The control mechanisms operated on the basis of performance targets where on a monthly basis (at management committee meetings) each function head explained performance using accounting statements measured against budget targets and previous performance. The development of standardised reporting of regional offices also allowed the managers to get a clearer picture of the relative performance across each office.

Given the set of agreed performance indicators that had developed within BGE over the years, this type of performance target control system suited the company well and was consistently used by the main managerial committee. Reliance on a broad number of indicators as well as monthly accounting statements meant that an overall view of the organisation's performance was considered by the management committee and function heads rather than individual indicators that present only a partial picture of the organisation. The performance indicators were reviewed together by all members of the management committee, which provides an indication of the centralisation of decision making and performance review processes at BGE. It also reveals the interdependent nature of BGE's business in terms of the relationship between the extension of the pipeline and the ability to increase customer numbers – 'no pipes, no sales'.

The performance management culture was supported increasingly by information systems over time as the focus was on reports generated by computer applications that were standardised across all regional offices. Management's decision to deal firstly with information technology as part of its new strategic orientation shows the importance afforded to this function in terms of its supportive role for all other functional areas. Staff were aware of the basis on which assessment of performance was carried out, and over time such assessments became increasingly important as the intention was to develop an organisation in which targets and critical success factors were more transparent for individuals and departments alike.

6.3 The Importance of the Role of Information

The main resource allocation and control process changes required to implement BGE's customer-focus strategy centred on the changing role allocated to the IT department. Before the restructuring, information issues had been decided under the umbrella of the Finance department. Following the restructuring, IT became a separate department in its own right charged with dealing with both operational and strategic information management issues. The Manager/IT committee (see figure 2 of the case study) was in charge of resource prioritisation and allocation. Given the emphasis on the committee structure, IT decisions were not the sole responsibility of the IT department but rather emerged from requests and discussions throughout the various functional areas of the organisation. Through the committee structure IT requests and proposals were specified and their relative merits assessed.

Figure A below illustrates the role of resource planning and control in determining the success of BGE's strategy and its foundation on information.

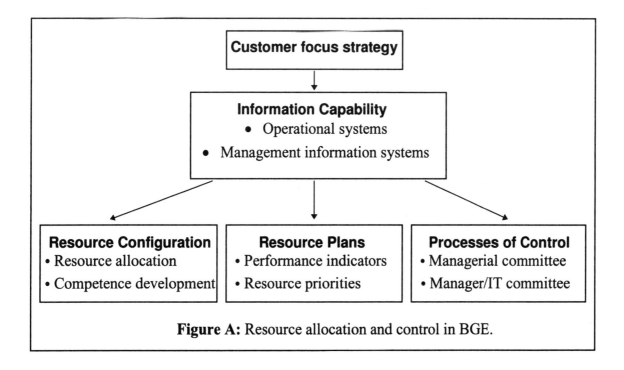

Figure A: Resource allocation and control in BGE.

BGE focused on information as providing the fundamental foundation on which to base its customer focus strategy. This had implications at both the operational and management levels in the organisation.

At the operational level it required the provision of excellent operational systems that could support the services provided for BGE's customers. A particularly important example of this is the changed invoicing system introduced at BGE which provided greater flexibility for customers who could opt for differential contractual arrangements. This flexibility had always been available for commercial and industrial customers but BGE decided to introduce and extend it to households customers also. This was one mechanism in BGE's attempt to build its loyal customer base. Further examples were the development of the nation-wide integrated telephone network to deal with customer requests and complaints and the gas-card metering system allowing customers the option of purchasing their fuel on a weekly basis. In addition to providing increased options for customers, the gas-card system provided a considerable boost to BGE's cash-flow system by reversing the usual process of consumption followed by payment. As a means of monitoring and estimating progress and success of BGE's chosen strategy, the implementation of data collection mechanisms to measure customer satisfaction ratings was vital. This allowed BGE to proactively develop relations with its customers that could encourage their loyalty in the face of future competition in the market.

The use of information in BGE's transaction processing systems had to resonate all the way up through the organisation in the form of executive systems to support the development and implementation of the performance management culture. The implementation of an organisation-wide network of computers was central in developing more reliable two-way communication links between headquarters and regional offices. This allowed top management the facility to disseminate the new strategy through dependable information channels as well as to monitor the company's developments across each of its functional areas. Furthermore, feedback from the market could be acquired by the managers for their own use and for further dissemination to management at local levels.

Organisational performance would be enhanced via successful key-user activities. Through the work of the key users, it was envisaged that the procedures in BGE would adapt over time to strike a balance between conflict and co-operation. Conflict is a potentially significant problem between managers who must consult their subordinates, in their function as key users, regarding IT requests and proposals. If the manager/IT committee structure (figure 2 of the case study) can operate effectively, it is possible that it can be used to lobby for increased resources for IT projects, which is necessary to ensure successful implementation of BGE's strategy.

6.4 Management of IT Development

The most important and significant change was the development of IT as an independent responsible area which was outside the direct control of Finance. In particular, the creation of the post of the Chief Information Officer, who reported directly to the CEO, was a crucial development. Under the previous structure the IS manager reported to the Head of Finance and the amount of time devoted to IT matters had been relatively small as the information function had not been identified as a priority area in the organisation. It is possible that sound financial performance could have obscured the development of IT had the structure not changed.

The technical systems managers and support managers were in charge of ensuring the excellence of the transaction processing systems so that operational issues were directed at them. The project manager dealt with all new developments whether they involved entirely new systems or the upgrading of old systems.

This division of tasks allowed the CIO to deal with the strategic aspects of developing the role of IT within BGE. Under the committee structure (figure 2 of the case study) the CIO carried out his functions in collaboration with other departments. Ideas for the development of IT were, therefore, to arise from the other functional areas since they had the expertise in their own areas and knew best what would aid them in their efforts to both implement their strategy and to achieve their performance targets.

BGE's committee structure is one where people get involved, and are expected to do so. If the key users manage to function as is currently envisaged they will open new avenues of cooperation and development. Managers in functional areas will be willing to participate constructively in the development of information support and provision, suitable for their needs. Staff generally will be interested and committed because of the benefits of getting involved and the incentives to do so, i.e., the development of systems that support the tasks that must be performed by them and aid in delivering better performance for their units.

The key is to ensure that staff develop a sense of achievement from the new structures operating in BGE. This can be achieved by:

- Managing expectations – the role of the CIO and project leaders have to be set in realistic terms regarding their promised benefits to users of the information systems. Promising more than the systems can provide may lead to dissatisfaction and frustration for users.

- Management of projects – a balance must be struck between the management of projects that will potentially lead to great benefits but take time to deliver and implement and the management of other projects – 'quick fixes' – that deliver relatively small benefits extremely quickly (known as early successes).

- Not all work & no play – organisational communication systems should normally be attractive to people as they make life much easier through connecting people and facilitating easier and potentially greater communication between them. Interdepartmental communication becomes seamless and is less likely to slow down decision making which benefits the organisation at all levels.

If these three factors can be achieved, successful information systems can be developed and implemented, thus supporting the organisational strategy. Furthermore, as staff become satisfied with the systems provided for them and use them to achieve their performance targets, funds are more likely to be allocated for future developments in the information area.

TEACHING NOTES

Doman Synthetic Fibres plc
Peter Jones

1. INTRODUCTION

The case study, whilst bearing a fictitious name, is based on a real organisation, who experienced this problem some years ago. The study describes a company which has drifted strategically letting an established and profitable product move into being marginally profitable. The product is at the interface of the chemical and synthetic textile market. It has a niche market which is not subject to the full international pressures experienced by textile producers, due to high transport costs of a bulky product. The company has developed a possible replacement product, and the case asks questions about if and how this potential replacement should be handled.

2. POSITION OF THE CASE

The case study can be used to explore the generation and evaluation of options, and the resource planning implications of change. At the end of the case three options are advocated by employees of the company. The student is invited to analyse these options in terms of the evaluation criteria in chapter 8, section 8.1 of the text. This will undoubtedly push the student back into the analysis phase of chapters 3 and 4 as the options make implicit assumptions about resource planning, company culture, market share, size, etc. The nature of these assumptions and their sense (or nonsense!) is a focal issue in the evaluation phase. Students will also be required to develop a detailed resource plan to implement their chosen strategy. Here they will need to relate to chapter 10 of the text (especially sections 10.2 and 10.3).

3. LEARNING OBJECTIVES

It is tempting for students to believe there is one optimal strategy in any situation. The case requires them to realise that there are multiple objectives, criteria, and constraints against which to assess any option. A key process is to identify the trade-offs being made.

Additionally no strategy is made with perfect foresight. There are risks in selecting any strategy, assumptions will not be exactly right. Students should be encouraged to define the nature of those risks and assumptions, to define the variables they would monitor to check those risks, and to create fall back positions.

4. TEACHING SCHEME AND QUESTIONS

This depends on time available. Possible approaches are:

4.1 Use case for class discussion. As time is available one can go progressively down the following list:

(i)   What criteria would you use for assessing the options?

(ii) Assess the pros and cons of the three alternative options advocated in the case using the criteria of (i).

(iii) Select your preferred option – argue the case in class.

(iv) Discuss the major risks in each option. What can be done to protect against those risks?

(v)   What data would you seek to alert you to each of those risks?

(vi) Create further options, and redo (ii)–(v).

(vii) Prepare a detailed resource plan to implement your preferred option.

The case is best handled as class discussion; it does not readily lend itself to role play. Beware of the danger that a strong student could persuade the class (as in (iii) above) that their preferred option is ideal.

4.2 Alternatively, the students could be asked to prepare and then make a (formal or informal) presentation to Board of DSF advocating their plans. Such a presentation task could have the following brief:

(i)   Outline the broad direction of your strategy in terms of:

   – product/market considerations
   – provision of capacity
   – internal changes to culture/employee relations
   – financing requirements

(ii) Upon what assumptions are these directions based?

(iii) What key indicators/data will you monitor to test these assumptions?

(iv) What tactical changes can you bring on-line if circumstances are different from expected?

5. CASE ANALYSIS

Relating the case situation to the text the following observations could be made.

5.1 Analysing the environment – chapter 3

- DSF have operated for a few years in a relatively simple and static environment for their product. Appendix 4 illustrates a market of some 32 +/− 2 m lbs in which they are the dominant supplier. Inferior Teklatite products have made up the difference between their supply of 25 m lbs and the market demand. They are in a small specialised segment of the textile industry as a whole; the movements in this larger industry market (Appendix 5) are a red herring (largely).

- The danger for DSF is that the removal of patent protection will move them to a dynamic environment in which their conservatism and caution could leave them unprepared for harsher competition.

- Paradoxically any attempt over the next two years to move Britlene to a more profitable position will only encourage competition once patent protection ceases.

- Considering Porter's 5-Forces analysis (exhibit 3.4 of text), the main threat is of potential entrants. Substitutes are always possible but the case does not hint at these (therefore nothing can be said). The capital cost of entry is not high – a new Britlene plant costs about £1.6m and can be built in 6 months. Also there might well be economies of scale in new capacity.

5.2 Resources and competences – Chapter 4

- DSF have a strong research tradition and department, but their development of ideas is weaker. Note how we often link together R&D but they do not necessarily go together.)

- The company have a dominant market share, and thus market power but seem reluctant to use it; inhibited perhaps by innate conservatism and caution, or confusing difficult general textile industry conditions with those in their more specialised segment.

- Their capital is ageing.

- Their financial resources are good. They have some £4m in Trade investments (virtually a liquid asset). They have no long-term loans. Thus there is considerable potential for acquiring long term cash for any Britlon expansion. Handled properly they could probably secure £5m in share capital and £10m in loans. Thus in the print outs in Appendix II of the case any strategy with cash needs not exceeding £15m would be feasible; i.e. all except C1.

- BCG analysis suggests that Britlene should be a Cash Cow, but DSF have let it become a Dog due to reluctance to match cost inflation with increases in price.

- Whilst no direct references are made, it can be inferred that DSF has a fairly paternalistic culture, in which the pursuit of efficiency and profit is not a high priority currently. One might be tempted to say they are relying on historical reserves and past glories – e.g. they have paid the latest dividend, not wholly out of profit but partly from reserves.

5.3 Strategic options and their evaluation – chapters 6, 7 and 8

The case identifies three possible options. Relating them to section 7.2 of the text they are:

- **Option A** advocated by Les Hall – this is 'Do Nothing'/consolidation.

- **Option B** advocated by Chris Henson – is some consolidation and some product development.

- **Option C** advocated by Trevor Bryant – is both market and product development.

Table I Comments on the criteria of chapter 8 for each option

Name	Option A Consolidate	Option B Two Horse	Option C Go for it
Suitability	A protracted decline Nowhere to go	OK	OK
Feasibility	Risk from aggressive competitor Would need to have shakeout to compete	Can be funded Why would customers want competing products? (This questions strategic logic.)	High capital needs Little/no margin for errors in terms of cash needs if anything goes wrong Risk of over-committing capital before market is established Needs more aggressive overall management
Acceptability	Dubious	OK Possibility of development being 'too little, too late'	Yes, if achieved Changes to R&D; more D less R Needs aggressive marketing in new areas (non-textiles) Needs loans; changes capital structure and possibly control

The above probably leads to a decision to invest in Britlon, but maybe not at the rapid pace and high ultimate level advocated in Option C.

The difficult period for any strategy which introduces Britlon is in 1998–2000, when the high revenue costs of introducing Britlon (costs of training and promotion) together with the high capital costs will severely test the ability to finance the strategy. The more bullish the strategy the bigger the risks of not being able to negotiate those tricky years.

Overall in BCG terms the case shows the difficulty of funding a Question Mark or Star (Britlon) from a Dog (Britlene post-1998). It re-enforces the message that a company needs a balance of Cash Cows (Britlene pre-1998), Stars and Question Marks.

5.4 Resource planning

The Doman case study is ideal for illustrating the links which exist between the issues and criteria of evaluation (above) and the practicalities of resource planning.

Students should be encouraged to compare the three strategies in the case study in resource planning terms as follows:

- against resource planning criteria outlined in exhibit 10.2 of the text.

- against the critical success factors of illustration 10.4.

Ideally students will wish to develop a strategy which bridges two or more of the alternatives outlined. Exhibit 9.3 can be used to check that the resource planning would work as a whole.

Teachers should note that there is a simple computer planning model available to accompany the case study which would allow students to develop and test out a range of options in the way described in the case study. For further details contact Peter Jones at Sheffield Business School (0114) 253 2833. This is a very powerful addition to the case study where resource planning is the key learning focus.

TEACHING NOTES

The Royal Alexandra Hospital
Sandra Hill

1. INTRODUCTION

This case study examines the changes faced by a general hospital, the RAH, from the time it became a National Health Service (NHS) Trust in April 1993 (in shadow form from January 1993) until January 1998. It covers a period when the management of the health service was undergoing many changes in response to the Conservative Government's policies in the shape of Working for Patients. Clinical and managerial staff were struggling to come to terms with the notion of increased accountability, tighter control on the use of resources, the drive to involve clinicians in management and greater consumer awareness. These factors, coupled with the introduction of trust Boards and the appointment of non-executive chairmen and directors, instigated an unprecedented period of change for the NHS.

2. POSITION OF THE CASE

The central theme of this case study is managing strategic change in a complex organisation where stakeholder interests are wide and varied, professional groups carry considerable power and influence, and political values and priorities shape the strategic agenda. It illustrates various barriers to change and is an example of how various cultures within one organisation behave differently.

3. LEARNING OBJECTIVES

The case is concerned with the process of managing change in an environment where a governmental reform of the sector resulted in a need for individual organisations within it to change their behaviour and, in particular, illustrates the need for the NHS to adopt a greater customer focus in the delivery of its services. Continuing financial pressures and increasing demands from purchasers, i.e. health boards and GP fundholders, and from the public, led to a much more focused view of the efficiency and appropriateness of the services offered by the RAH.

There is a crucial role for the leaders within the RAH, both managerial and clinical, to ensure that strategic change is inexorably linked with changing behaviour related to the delivery of operational objectives.

Specifically the case illustrates:

a) Understanding and analysing the environment – externally and internally.

b) Understanding the organisational culture – particularly power control and rituals and routines.

c) Analysing strategic change needs.

d) Identifying triggers for change.

e) Understanding cultural barriers to change.

f) Managing the strategic change process.

4. TEACHING SCHEME

It is important that students understand the context in which the changes at the RAH are taking place. Some initial discussion about the NHS is a useful way to introduce the case. The students' understanding of government policy and the expectations and perception about the service will be a useful scene-setting exercise

Depending on the background and experience of the students it may be useful to start the session by asking students to examine the cultural web and the shifts in culture as a result of trust status.

Another useful activity might be to explore the stakeholder expectations and their power and influence over the service. Students could be asked to examine various stakeholder reactions to the strategic change issues in the case study and the positions they are likely to adopt in response to the various strategic changes which have taken place, i.e. creating an autonomous organisation through the introduction of trust status, methods used to increase efficiency and the RAH's response to the demands of purchasers and patients. They may also be asked to discuss how successful the hospital was in responding to these needs and to what extent, if any, stakeholders' needs are compatible.

5. QUESTIONS FOR DISCUSSION

- What shifts in power between stakeholders are evident and how has this affected the culture of the organisation?

- Using the cultural web, identify blockages and facilitators of change in the RAH.

- Given the agenda facing the hospital, what cultural change should the Trust be aiming for in delivering its strategy?

- What internal and external triggers signalled change for the hospital?

- How effective was the Trust board at managing change?

- How would you have encouraged the involvement of staff in the strategic management decision-making process?

- What are the key strategic change issues facing the RAH under the Labour Government?

6. CASE ANALYSIS

6.1 Environmental issues

The introduction of control of the use of resources through market mechanisms in health care introduced by the Working for Patients legislation, changed not only the traditional management of the service but also the way in which it was delivered. The 'internal market' necessitated very different relationships developing between purchasers, i.e. Health Boards and GP fundholders, and providers of health care, i.e. Trusts. In order to successfully participate and ensure its long-term survival, the RAH had to develop management skills to address the key challenges facing all providers of health care. These included anticipating the needs of purchasers, negotiating contracts and services agreements and designing services to meet the agreed contracts alongside attempting to influencing Health Boards and GP Fundholders in their purchasing decisions.

The key changes in the environment as a result of the move to Trust status were:

- the separation of the purchaser of health care from the provider and the resulting contractual relationship which was to be developed

- greater accountability of not only managers of the service but individual accountability of all staff

- the formation of a Trust Board which included a Chairman and Non-Executive members and the strengthening of managerial roles

- the introduction of competition for contracts in an increasingly tight financial regime of public spending

- increasing interests in the RAH from community groups and the local media.

Communication within the Trust also had to be improved to ensure that key clinical staff, particularly clinical directors, were in a position to influence not only what happened within their directorates but were also able to participate more fully in shaping the strategic direction of the Trust which would be largely influenced by purchasers' decision-making.

The above brought about challenges for management, particularly for the newly appointed Chief Executive who had to demonstrate the value of his new post and justify the benefits of moving to Trust status to a workforce, many of whom opposed, in principle, the governments reform of the NHS, and were not wholly supportive of the RAM's move to Trust. Many staff had very real concerns regarding the effect Trust status would have on their terms and conditions of service and working environment. It was inevitable that such significant changes would require a culture shift if the new organisation, in the shape of the RAH Trust, was to be successful in the internal market.

6.2 Creating an Autonomous Organisation

The creation of the Trust board brought new responsibilities in terms of accountability to both the Management Executive (ME) and the public. The hospital had separated in management responsibility and accountability from the health board and had acquired new local responsibilities for staff, the delivery of services and satisfying the purchasers demands. Whilst responsibility for delivering the agreed contracts for services was still to the local purchasers, managerial accountability of the Chief Executive, through the Chairman, was now direct to the Secretary of State via the ME. The appointment of non executive directors was seen to be the key vehicle in the delivery of local accountability. The establishment of new information systems and effective communication channels were vitally important if the RAH was to be viewed as successful in the eyes of its stakeholders.

Stakeholder Power

Sources of Power	Indicators of Power	
Internal	**Internal**	
• Influence of medical profession • Specialist knowledge of doctors • Trust board's control over strategic resources, shaping strategic direction of the trust • Managers positions within new structures	• Status given to doctors Doctors as main users of NHS resources • Representation on influential committees • New offices, changes to job titles	
External	**External**	
• Government as policy makers, • Health Board and GPs as purchasers • Patients exercising their rights under the Patients' Charter • Trade Unions and professional bodies concerns over terms and conditions of staff	• Status • RAH's dependence for resource allocation • More explicit complaints procedures • Negotiating arrangements	

6.3 The change agenda

6.3.1 Triggers and Barriers to change

The case throughout illustrates the transformational change which faced the Trust. Students may be asked to do a Force Field Analysis of the driving and resisting forces for change.

Driving Forces		Resisting Forces	
• Government Policy		• Lack of support for Government Policy	
• Influence of purchasers		• Fear of professional standing and influence of professional groups	
• Increased availability of information		• Fear of increasing power of managers	
• Push to involve clinicians in the management of resources		• Concerns that efficiency drives would lead to a fall in standards of care	
• Financial restraints - the need for organisations to be 'leaner and fitter'		• Structural changes leading being to doctors being more accountable in the use of resources and clinical freedom potentially being restricted	
• New technology and treatments changing the pattern of health care delivery e.g. day surgery and reduced lengths of stay			
• Greater public awareness of services and Patients Rights			
• Increased public accountability , locally and nationally			

One of the main barriers to change was the traditionally medically dominated culture which existed within the NHS. The autonomous position of the consultant body was , and still is, the dominant power with the sector. However, external pressures for change were such that the hospital had to become more responsive to its customers in order to retain existing contracts and bring new business and development to the Trust. Martin Hill had a significant task to improve channels of communication, gain then trust of the doctors and persuade them and other staff that changes in behaviour were required if the RAH was to be a successful Trust in the eyes of the stakeholders.

6.3.2 Cultural Changes

What does the cultural web signify pre Trust status? To what extent have changes in the culture occurred as a result of Trust status?

- Paradigm
  The assumption that the NHS is underfunded has not changed to any extent. However, within the RAH, as in many other Trusts, there is a shift towards a more efficient service with measurable outcomes and a greater concern over patient rather than professionally centred care.

- Power Structures
  There has been a long standing assumption by the public and staff that doctors were the most powerful group and that 'doctor knows best'. The control over priorities, developments and activities through contracts plus increased power of senior managers started to challenge, albeit to a limited extent that whist doctors would retain considerable power, others would be influential in the allocation of resources.

- Controls
  A business environment was not seen as relevant to the NHS as the treatment of patients took priority over financial considerations. Clearly financial restrictions had always been imposed upon the service but Working for Patients and the introduction of the internal market made explicit, for the first time, financial controls and mechanisms which organisation would have to work under.

  The power given to the managers to implement these financial controls were to create concerns amongst the clinical body many of whom believed them to be interfering in clinical matters rather that attempting to improve the efficiency and effectiveness of the hospital as a whole. Much of the resistance to change by clinical staff could be as a result of fear of loosing control and, for some, fear that managers would attempt to control activity and professional development and thereby interfere with clinical freedom. Nurses on the other hand saw their traditional hierarchical structures flattening resulting in loss of professional power.

- Organisational Structures
  The introduction of new structures are significant in the case as it illustrates how the trust board attempted to continue its efforts to devolve responsibility and accountability closer to the delivery of patient care. The new Trust Board also added a new dimension to the organisation as it took on its role of looking after the interests of the community it served and implementing government policy.

- Ritual and routines
Devolved responsibility and accountability resulted in the need for managers and clinical staff to work closer together to determine and achieve closer multi disciplinary working practices. The development of breast cancer services and Care Net are clear examples of the increased awareness within the Trust of patients needs and expectations and indeed greater demands of GPs resulting in much more open channels of communication and sharing of information.

- Symbols
The 'business' of health was to raise concerns for both staff and public. This was particularly the case for the RAH which is located in an area which is heavily dominated by Labour both locally and nationally. Grey suits replacing white coats and more managers with little or no direct contact with patients were viewed by many as directing resources away from patient care. Photographs of staff in the hospital foyer, the distribution of the annual report to every household and opening board meetings to the public was an attempt to involve the public more in its local hospital. Many were to question the value of these activities.

- Stories
The media has always shown an interest in the NHS. The RAH is no exception to this. Under the reform of the service, it rose significantly. Stories relating to increased numbers of managers and their 'fat cat' remuneration packages were commonplace, adding to much of the public's concern that privatisation of the health service was inevitable

6.4 The Future

The publication of the Labour Government's reform of the NHS 'Designed to Care' in December 1997 will mean that the RAH will no longer exist by the end of 1998. A consultative document is currently being considered. The proposal is that the RAH joins with the two other acute trusts in the health board area and becomes a Renfrewshire Acute Trust. The Trust Board will be disbanded and executive directors will compete for posts with the newly formed trusts throughout Scotland which sees a reduction in numbers of trusts from 47 to around 25. Students could be asked to analyse the impact that this merger is likely to have on the core business of the RAH and to what extent downsizing and rationalisation of services will take place. They could also be asked to draw up a competency profile for the incoming chief executive and chairman. Finally they may be asked to devise the change agenda to take the new trust into the next millennium.

TEACHING NOTE

The Burton Group A, B and C
Gerry Johnson and Jacqui Gush

1. INTRODUCTION

The activities of change agents need to be seen in context. These case studies cover the period 1970–97 during which the context, strategy and performance of the Burton Group changed dramatically. Before 1970 Burtons was essentially a made-to-measure tailor with massive manufacturing facilities, distributing suits through an extensive high street presence. The attempts to change and diversify in the early 1970s failed. However, by 1984 Burtons was a highly successful, multi-focused, differentiated fashion retailer, and in that year it also decided to acquire the Debenhams departmental chain. By 1990 the company was in trouble again, but 1990-97 saw a turnaround and the return to success.The three cases cover the whole of this period. Case A concentrates on the attempted turnaround in the early 1970s by Ladislas Rice; case B on the successful turnaround of the late 1970s and 1980s, by Ralph Halpern, on the acquisition of Debenhams and the decline in the late 1980s; and case C on the turnaround in the 1990s led by John Hoerner.

The series therefore provides the basis for a discussion of the relationship between the context of the organisation, the role of the change agent and organisational strategy.

2. POSITION IN THE COURSE

This case series is best used in relation to issues of strategic change and therefore towards the end of a strategy course.

3. LEARNING OBJECTIVES

The main purpose of this series of cases is to allow students to consider the reasons for the effectiveness in strategy development and strategic change of the different change agents (Rice, Halpern and Hoerner). With this in mind the overall objective should be to ensure that students see successful change agency as dependent on a number of interrelated factors rather than any one factor (such as the personality of the chief executive). These interrelated factors may be described as follows:

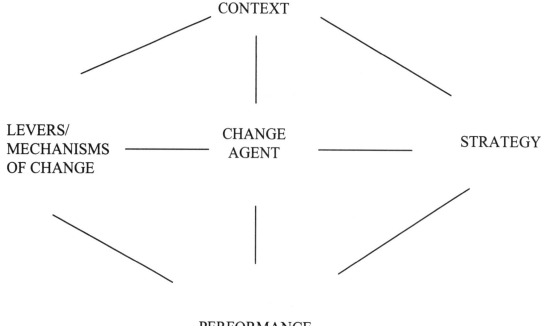

The case may also be used as a vehicle by which to evaluate the different strategies being followed by Burton at different times.

4. TEACHING SCHEME

The following teaching scheme assumes that the case is to be used primarily to examine the role of the change agents.

- *Opening plenary session.* This session might deal with:

a) A discussion of the framework above; ie the extent to which effective change agency is dependent on multiple factors and influences. Section 11.5.1 in the text also provides a useful background to such a teaching session.

- *Small Group Work:* The class can then be split into three groups (or multiples of three), each responsible for considering the effectiveness of one of the chief executives as change agent in the context of the discussion in the plenary session (and the model above). They might be asked to report back, therefore, on interrelatedness of the various factors contributing to effective change agency.

- *Closing plenary session:* the closing plenary session can consist of presentations made by groups on each case study (or on the issues they have considered). There can then be a tutor led discussion which examines the factors explaining the varying success of each CEO.

5. QUESTIONS FOR DISCUSSION

The questions below can be given to each group for each case:

1. What were the key strategic issues facing Rice/Halpern/Hoerner?

2. What were the strategies he followed?

3. Did these strategies make sense?

4. How did he seek to implement strategic change?

5. How effective was the programme of strategic change which was followed? Why?

6. CASE ANALYSIS

The following notes are not meant to be exhaustive of the issues raised by the cases. However they do give an indication of the range of issues and some of the points that can be made in the discussion.

Case A: Ladislas Rice

Ladislas Rice took over Burtons at a time of major upheaval in their trading environment and tried to implement strategic change. Rice's strategies can be summarised as follows:

*   An overarching strategy of switching from made-to-measure manufacturing to retailing.

*   A strategy of diversification within retailing.

*   In menswear retailing, a switch from made-to-measure to ready-to-wear and casual wear.

*   The utilisation of property assets by the setting up of a property company, the revaluation of those assets against which increased borrowing could be raised for the purposes of acquisition.

There are then implementation measures including:

*   The setting up of a divisional structure and the expectation that each of these would operate as profit centres.

*   The recruitment of new senior management to head their divisions.

*   The establishment of corporate planning and MBO systems.

*   The setting up of training systems.

*   The setting up of reward systems linked to performance.

Did this make sense? Arguably much of it, and particularly the implementation measures, can be defended. Indeed if they are placed in the context of the 1960s they were virtually 'text book'. One way of handling the case is for the tutor to defend some of the core strategies so as to demand that students analyse the problems in depth, and discuss issues of implementation. The case raises the following:

- The basic issue of what business Burtons was in. Students may say that the fundamental mistake made by Rice was that he did not 'stick to his knitting', that Rice should have stayed closer to the core business of menswear retailing. However was this the core business of Burtons? For fifty years it had been a manufacturer of made-to-measure suits with distribution points in the high street. The business had no skills in modern retailing or in the growing area of fashion retailing. There was no experience in merchandising, stock control, measurement of retail sales, shop layout, etc. In short a concentration on menswear retailing would have entailed a move away from the traditional core business in any case.

- The case also allows the exploration of the problems of forecasting market and economic trends. There was an exponential rate of change in menswear fashion which could not have been foreseen in 1970. There was also the 1973 oil price increase which raised unemployment and lowered disposable income, thus affecting employment agencies and electrical goods sales; and there was the collapse of the office building boom of the 1960s which harmed office furniture sales.

- Students usually say the strategy of diversification does not make sense. But it can be defended. The core business was in decline and under threat but could yield assets which could be used to grow other businesses. All the businesses which Rice moved in to in 1970/71 had high growth potential and needed cash or properties. He had both. In effect Rice was choosing to operate a portfolio system of management: you can use the BCG matrix here to argue that Rice might have seen himself as raising funds from the cash cow of menswear or property to fund growth businesses. The problem was more to do with managing diversification than it is with the strategic logic of diversification.

- This could lead to a discussion of the problems of managing a portfolio of businesses. Rice saw potential synergistic benefits from an asset point of view. But he failed to understand the difficulties of managing a diversified set of businesses. He set up an organisational structure designed to allow the corporate centre to manage the diversity, whilst passing the responsibility of the implementation of business unit strategy to the boards of businesses. However as performance slipped, where should the concentrations of effort have gone? This was not a matter for business unit decision, but for corporate decision, yet the organisation seemed too complex, and the past recipes (particularly on the menswear side) too entrenched, for fast action to be taken.

- So the case raises the issues of structure and control. In true 1960s style Rice went for a formalised divisionalised structure. He saw implementation in terms of systems of control (planning, MBO, fairly tight job descriptions, and so on). The whole thing sounds very mechanistic. Was this a suitable approach to managing the degree of change that the business faced?

- This then raises issues of organisational culture. Students might think about what they mean by organisational culture in the context of a business that had been working the same way for about fifty years by drawing up a culture web for Burtons menswear in the 1960s.

Appendix 1 gives some indications of the sorts of points which might emerge. The manufacturing side was very powerful; Hudson Mills was a symbol of the traditions of the company, the family a powerful symbol of those traditions too, no doubt preserved in stories and myths to do with that family; the everyday rituals and routines would no doubt have been to do with manufacturing and distribution of made to measure suits, as would the control systems in the organisation. And the organisation structure of the 1960s was essentially functional in nature with little expertise in general management. The paradigm was all about being the biggest tailor in the world and, no doubt, the employees felt that the business was safe and dominant in its market; and, of course, the family would look after them. To what extent Rice did do anything to get to terms with changing the paradigm and the culture? Arguably, he did little more than to package it into one or two of his divisions and rely on newcomers to the business to change it. Compare this with the approach taken by Halpern, who clearly, regarded changing the culture as centrally important and his responsibility.

The tutor can therefore get the class to consider if it was the content of the strategy, the difficult market conditions or the inability to change the organisation's paradigm that explains why the strategy introduced by Rice ran into difficulties. Hopefully, the class will conclude that these factors are related and all account for the problems that occurred.

Case B: Ralph Halpern

After 1976 the Spencer and Halpern team took over; and Halpern played an increasingly central role. He was a very different individual from Rice and in its most successful era ran the business quite differently. The issues which are raised include:

First, the new team divested the business of what they saw as peripheral retail activities and opted for a focus on fashion retailing. However, it is the nature of the strategy introduced for the fashion business that is particularly important. This is one of *multi-focused differentiation* or in terms of the Strategy Clock, the pursuit of *route 5*. Burton's managers talked about *life style retailing* by which they meant the development of specialist fashions shops to meet the aspirations and behaviour of a clearly identified market segment. The retail businesses were not differentiated just in terms of their products, but throughout the different operations which are described by the value chain. The sort of people who served in the shop, the music played, the layout of the shop, the width of the aisles were all designed to meet the expectations of the market segment. But it went further: the buying team was dedicated to that market segment; so were the type of service provided; the lead times for buying and the rate at which shop layouts changed (Top Shop was changed every three years whether or not performance was declining). In short the value chain was designed specifically for that market segment. It is a good example of multi-focused differentiation.

- This leads into organisational *structure and control systems*. Get the students to map out the management systems and organisational structure of Burtons under Halpern. It is an interesting exercise. Ralph Halpern was Chief Executive with a functional main board. Each of the businesses – and there were thirteen of these towards the end of the 1970s – then had a main board with similar functional directors on it. There were no chief executives of these businesses, but rather each functional director of a business reported to a functional managing director on the main board. It is a most unusual structure which Ralph Halpern claimed had a number of benefits; information – particularly problems –

got to the top quickly since there were few blockages in the system; resources could be moved around the organisation by the main board very fast; and each business, whilst required to follow its own business strategy, was subjected to the corporate decisions of the centre. It was also a business built on change; if the students put themselves in the situation of trying to operate within such a business they will find that the only way they could handle difficult problems was either to abrogate responsibility and pass it up the line or fight out their views with their colleagues. It had been argued that it was a management structure built on conflict, but equally it could be said to be built on challenge of the taken-for-granted and therefore a means of galvanising change.

- Halpern was more successful at *managing strategic change*. But what does this mean? Students might argue that he was in a more fortunate position than Ladislas Rice: the business was in crisis and more ready to accept radical change. They are also likely to identify the changes in reward and control systems as important: they may also suggest that he and Spencer were able to reduce the conservative influence of the family (though they may overlook that the changes in share holding did not take place till later in the 1970s: and they may be unclear as to how else this might have occurred).

- It is worthwhile plotting out some of the ways in which Halpern signalled the need for and content of change in ways significant to those in the organisation. Here students need to take not so much a 'rational' view of change as a behavioural, political and even symbolic view (perhaps a re-read of Chapter 11 might be useful). Take the *culture web* that was generated for Case A and look at what Halpern did to it. He dramatically reduced the manufacturing capacity at Hudson Mills, a major symbol of the past, and a move which signalled management rather than family control – further emphasised by the sale of shops. He demonstrated, not through words but through action, that the business was now in retailing, by spending large amounts on refurbishing shops fast. He changed the organisational structure to that described above, and the control systems to emphasise rapid feedback of key retail performance measures and rapid change (e.g. seven-year depreciation rates cut to three years). Halpern himself became a symbol of the change process, of the energy expected in running the business; and stories certainly spread around the business about both him and the success of the operation. At the centre of all this he had a very simple message: Burtons was about *life style retailing and the management of strategic change* – what Peters and Waterman would regard as a clear corporate mission capable of communication through the business at all levels.

- Throughout all this the class might insist that what really made the difference was the *leadership* and vision of Halpern. This begs the question of what is meant by *leadership* and *vision*. Perhaps the effective leader is one who can bridge the logic of formulation of strategy with an understanding of (essentially cultural) means of implementing strategic change.

So why did it all seem to go wrong by the late 1980s? Students may suggest the following, which can be discussed:

- One of the interesting features of the Burton B case is the extent to which, arguably, it comes full circle. The Burton A case deals with the ill fated attempts of Ladislas Rice to diversify the Burton business. Some twenty years later Burtons again suffered from the diversification of its interests into areas unrelated to its core skills and capabilities. In the late 1970s and first half of the 1980s Burton benefited from a focused strategy in which the capabilities of the various businesses were developed around meeting the needs of identified customer groups. It was run as a linked set of retailers and emphasised retail skills at the business level. By the end of the 1980s, the strategy moves much more towards corporate level diversification into property, financial services, etc. To what extent did Burtons really have such skills: and to what extent did moving to these ventures have the effect of 'taking their eye off the retail ball'?

- The tight retail positioning of the early 1980s was replaced by a proliferation of retail *brands* in which *identity* of any one was unclear.

- Some commentators have suggested that the decline was inextricably linked with Halpern himself. Reasons here have varied from him becoming bored with just running retail businesses; his concern to grow the business whether for shareholder, director or employee value; his personal ego and ambition; and so on. No doubt the class will wish to debate this. Whilst this is interesting conjecture, the discussion can end up as little more than this. It might, therefore, be wise to direct such a discussion around the question of how, if such personal influences prevailed, the structure and control of organisations might handle it? If the students feel that the power and influence of an individual eventually had a damaging effect, how would they recommend this should be prevented? Moreover, they may well have argued that the very same man had a positive effect. Even if they had suggestions about how negative effects can be limited, when would these have been introduced; and by whom? This could lead to an interesting discussion about internal structure and control the power of boards of directors to control, and the power of the financial markets and shareholders to controls – which of course eventually they did.

- It is arguable that a contributory factor to Burton's strategy problems was the combination of a high risk financial strategy with a changing business and competitive strategy. This is illustrated by the use of principally debt financing during a period of rapid growth in that no significant equity issues were made after 1985. Another illustration of this was the use of a low coupon convertible loan stock with an earlier redemption option on the part of the bondholders (i.e. making them lenders rather than permanent shareholders). It was also suggested in the press that the earnings per share growth bonus scheme initiated for the top executives of the group during the 1980s exacerbated this problem. This bonus scheme created a significant emphasis on the short-term accounting performance of the company as represented by earnings per share in the current year over the previous year. In order to improve this measure any reductions in financing costs or avoiding the issue of new equity could result in significant bonus payments to the senior executives irrespective of the impact in the longer term on both the share price and the sustainable competitive performance of the company.

- External factors: Burtons problems coincided with the recession of the late 1980s. It should be borne in mind that the retail strategies of the 1980s had moved the business much more away from 'standard' clothing into fashion (e.g. with Principles). Arguably some of these moves took the businesses into areas which suffered most from a slow down in discretionary spending. Moreover, the really profitable businesses of Burtons had always been Dorothy Perkins, Evans and Top Shop. The higher fashion end was never that profitable.

- To what extent did any one of the big ventures such as the acquisition of Debenhams, or the move into property and finance, in itself, damage the business. It is difficult to suggest that Debenhams did. By the late 1980s the much criticised takeover of Debenhams was proving to be successful. Debenhams was trading profitably; and after the demise of Halpern himself, it was the Debenhams chief executive who eventually took over the running of the group. However, it is more arguable that other ventures into property and finance were very damaging; and this takes us back into the financial strategy and its limitations. Perhaps rather more than debating whether any one individual major venture had a damaging effect, it might be better to direct the attention of the class to a discussion of diversification itself into areas in which the company did not have core capabilities.

Again, then, the class should conclude that accounting for the success (and lack of success) of a change agent is not easily attributed to any one factor.

Case C: John Hoerner

A good starting point is to ask the students to describe the strategy adopted by Hoerner. They are likely to describe it in quite similar terms to that introduced in the 1980s by Halpern. So where is the difference? Students may arrive at the view that the overall strategy is not so different; but Hoerner has got back to the basics of multi-focused differentiation, done away with the peripheral activities that clouded clear focus and concentrated on implementation and control. (An interesting excursion for discussion on strategy is the apparently cyclical pattern in Burton. Diversification followed by focus, followed by diversification, followed by focus.) Moreover like Halpern, Hoerner was able to move quickly because of the problems Burton faced. The Group was under pressure to perform; so time was short to make changes. Hoerner himself probably recognised that his own tenure as CEO depended on making an impact fast. And this had to happen despite an economic recession at the time.

There are also important aspects of Hoerner's style and tactics to consider.

- The case makes clear the characteristics of John Hoerner. He was a dispassionate, determined and strong-willed person who knew exactly what he wanted to achieve and went out to get it with a clarity of vision and focus, stream rolling anyone who got in his way. He was well respected, indeed held in awe by many, did not suffer fools gladly, would not tolerate resistance, and endeavoured to surround himself with colleagues with whom he could work and who shared his vision. Students might discuss the extent to which these tend to be common characteristics of change agents. Evidence points to strategy-making as top-down but incremental working closely with a small number of key executives in decision-making. He was obviously very controlling, and this included external stake-holders as much as internal, e.g. media and presentation of a public face.

- An interesting area for discussion is to look at the extent to which this style is a product of the environment, and to what extent the environment in the 1990s and the state of the company in the early years of the 1990s produced the need for Hoerner's style of leadership. The students could do a compare and contrast exercise of Halpern/Hoerner in the contexts of the environments they were facing at the times. To what extent did the constraints of the environment dictate the strategy with the CEO's scope for influence limited. And what of the constraints imposed by the state of the organisation at the time.

Would the strategies of the different times have been the same under different leaders. Was Hoerner's leadership style appropriate to the needs of the business and its environment? Was style the cause of or effect of change?

- Given the information we have on Hoerner, is Burtons overmanaged and underled? This raises a discussion on the difference between management and leadership which could help to inform further analysis of the case. It might also be worth reminding students that Hoerner is an American. To what extent does he characterise an American business culture and philosophy and to what extent does this differ from the Burton's culture he inherited?

- Hoerner's strategy may not have been substantially different to Halpern's in the 1980s? (Lifestyle retailing and the management of strategic change.) However the way it was implemented was different and this has a big implication for structure. Hoerner dramatically changed the structure and laid strong emphasis on getting systems and controls in place. He seemed to take a technical or 'mechanistic' view of change. This presumably assumes a change in the process of strategy making and the mind set of the company. However in practice, to what extent was the culture which built up under Halpern changed? Students may argue that from the evidence to date in 1997 the management of culture change was not wholly successful. If the main job of a leader is to manage the values of the organisation, to what extent has Hoerner been successful in doing this? Or has he concentrated on structure and control to the exclusion of culture change?

- It could be argued that unless the cultural processes of the organisation are addressed and brought into line with the changes in structure/strategy the company will not maximise its potential. There is evidence that the culture of Debenhams is far more cohesive and coherent and it is interesting to note Debenhams continuing superior performance. This was a major factor in the decision to demerge the 2 companies, as Hoerner could not focus on developing the same coherence with the multiples while Debenhams had to be managed along side the other Divisions.

- There appear to be contradictory reports of behaviour in the organisation. Is this linked to Hoerner's style and the cultural legacy? One could argue that the existing culture of competitiveness, fear of failure and highly geared reward systems, when harnessed to Hoerner's forceful style will be a potent mixture to fire performance. It worked well for Halpern and hasn't changed significantly since. Yet Hoerner is determined to engender a sense of co-operation and sharing if only to create synergy in terms of cost savings and the generation and circulation of information and best practice. Is he going about this in the right way, will it be possible? Are apparent contradictions inevitable? Can a less than participative, yet espoused empowering, team based culture sustain performance in the long term at the end of the 1990s?

It might also be worth pointing out that there has been a consistent high turnover of senior management in the organisation which has persisted across the years and different leaders. What is this a function of and how damaging is it?

APPENDIX 1

A Cultural Web for Burtons in the 1960's

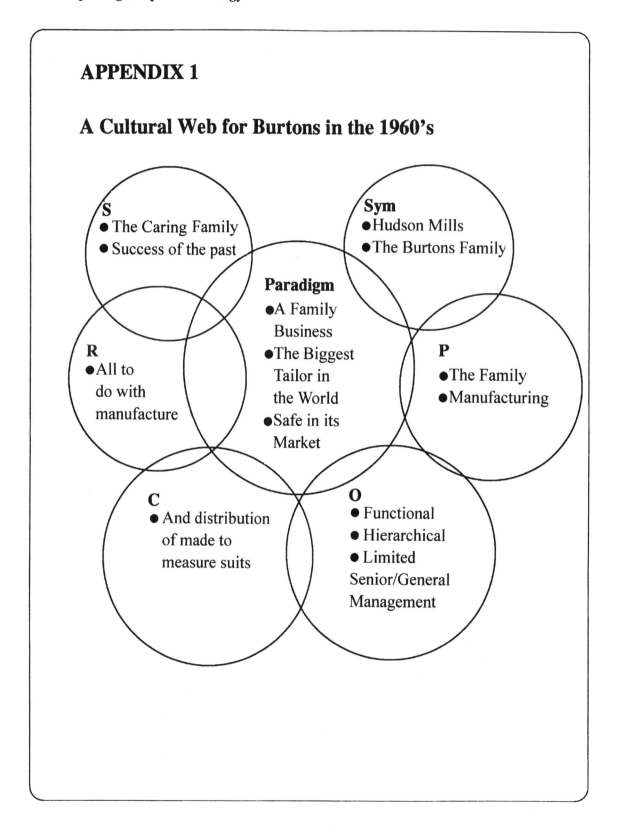

S
● The Caring Family
● Success of the past

Sym
● Hudson Mills
● The Burtons Family

Paradigm
● A Family Business
● The Biggest Tailor in the World
● Safe in its Market

R
● All to do with manufacture

P
● The Family
● Manufacturing

C
● And distribution of made to measure suits

O
● Functional
● Hierarchical
● Limited Senior/General Management

TEACHING NOTES

KPMG (B): Managing Strategic Change
Gerry Johnson

1. INTRODUCTION

This case study builds on the case example (KPMG: A) at the end of chapter 2 and chronicles the processes of change that took place between 1992 and 1996. It includes verbatim explanations of the problems they faced in managing the changes and the means adopted to achieve them. The case is largely based on speeches and interviews with Colin Sharman, the senior partner of KPMG in the UK, and other senior partners in the firm.

2. POSITION OF THE CASE

The case can be used primarily to consider the role and effectiveness of different strategic change processes and is therefore most useful at the end of the course on strategic management. However, change processes cannot be considered outside the context of the organisation and its strategy. KPMG provides an interesting example of the extent to which organisational culture and stakeholder influence play an important part in developing strategies and in change processes. So the case study can also be used in relation to an exploration of issues covered in chapter 5.

3. LEARNING OBJECTIVES

This is a rich case study with many potential learning objectives. However, the primary learning objectives are concerned with the management of strategic change. In particular:

- Building on the background to KPMG in the case example at the end of chapter 2, the importance of understanding barriers to change in relation to organisational culture and stakeholder influence.

- The extent to which change can be managed; and therefore the links to models of and approaches to strategic change explained in chapter 11.

- The role of HR and control systems in managing strategic change.

- The importance of symbolic aspects of change management.

4. THE TEACHING PROCESS

It is important that students understand the context within which the changes in KPMG are taking place. If this has not already been done, using the case example at the end of chapter 2, then it is a good idea to do so. (See the teaching notes on *KPMG: Developing a Global Firm*.)

It may also be sensible to have a discussion in plenary about the strategy being adopted by KPMG. The workshops, with the support of Sharman, advocated a strategy of differentiation based on a clear understanding of client needs and service delivery. The importance of the implementation of this strategy as opposed to its distinctiveness might be discussed in relation to other professional services firms. In the case study Sharman says he accepts that there is nothing especially distinctive about the strategy; the firm that achieves competitive advantage will be the one that *implements* such a strategy effectively.

If required, some of the themes of chapter 2 relevant to managing strategic change (and thus to chapter 11) could also be revisited. Specifically:

- A recapitulation of the different accounts of strategy development and formulation in chapter 2; emphasising the links between the development of strategy, and political and social processes in organisations.

- An explanation of the cultural web as a means of showing links between organisational strategy and the taken for granted assumptions and routinised behaviour of organisations. The chapter 2 case study example provides material to all students to draw up a web and this is a useful input to class discussion on this case, not least because it can be used to identify blockages to and facilitators of change drawing on the web and using force field analysis.

Either in plenary (or if time permits in groups) students can then consider and evaluate the various ways in which the change programme in KPMG has been managed drawing on the discussions in chapters 9, 10 and particularly 11.

In the interview with Colin Sharman included on the video he gives his personal views on the success of the change programme. This can be used as part of the input to this plenary discussion.

At the end of the case study (and of the video) Colin Sharman suggests that the aim for the future should be to build a truly learning organisation. This can be used as a cue for students to discuss in class the concept and practicalities of the learning organisation.

5. QUESTIONS FOR DISCUSSION

In preparation for the class students might be posed the following questions.

1. What were the main strategic issues facing KPMG in 1992.

2. What were the main barriers to strategic change for KPMG at that time?

Assess the means of strategic change employed in the change programme.

6. ISSUES FOR DISCUSSION/CASE COMMENTARY

6.1 The strategic issues facing KPMG in 1992

The competitive environment
The main components of an analysis of the competitive environment might include:

The increasing *size* of the major competitors (not least because of merger activity in the late 1980s), all of whom provided somewhat similar services and were historically reliant on audit services. The result was a lack of differentiation between firms of roughly equivalent size – a recipe for high degrees of competitive rivalry.

- The market was becoming more *sophisticated*. Sharman suggests that partners needed to be better able to understand the wider expectations of clients; and be able to advise knowledgeably on a range of services.

- At the large corporate end of the market clients were becoming more global in their organisation, increasingly requiring *global delivery of services*.

- For some of the services provided by KPMG they were vulnerable *to competition by specialists* such as boutique operations (eg as in taxation); or by smaller scale specialists picking off major clients, for example in strategic consultancy.

Strategic options for KPMG
If time allows the strategic options for KPMG can be considered using the *strategy clock* outlined in chapter 6 – an activity undertakes by the partners in the workshops. In most of the areas KPMG is in a similar position to its rivals.

- Could KPMG have sought to reduce fees? Would other firms follow? If they did there could be a reduction in margins without increased share. Students might suggest, of course, that this could be done if the overheads of the firms were cut significantly, for example by reductions in manning levels. It is worth reminding them of the nature or partnerships, and asking them how feasible this would be?

- More likely, students might suggest *route 4* – a strategy of differentiation through added value. But what does this mean in terms of the provision of financial services? Arguably, this might be achieved through truly integrated service delivery. However, integration is difficult to achieve both because of the historic culture of the firm; but also because, by definition, integration requires the sort of linkages within the firm's value chain, and between its value chain and its customers, as discussed in chapters 4 and 6. This illustrates that whilst such integration would indeed be difficult, if achieved it could be difficult to imitate by other firms - the argument advanced by Colin Sharman in the case.

- Some might also suggest *route 5*: a more focused approach to the business might be necessary if real client centredness is to be achieved. Is it possible for partners and managers to understand each separate client business sufficiently in order to deliver integrated services unless they become more specialist in what they do?

6.2 Barriers to strategic change

Colin Sharman points out in the case study that one of the barriers to change is, paradoxically, the success of the firm. There was no evident *trigger* for change.

In addition the cultural heritage of the firm provides blockages which can be identified by drawing up a cultural web. See the teaching notes for the chapter end case example for chapter 2 for notes on the cultural web and possible blockages.

6.3 The strategic change programme

Given an understanding of the strategy, and of possible blockages to change, the class can turn its attention to assessing the change programme itself. This can be considered in terms of its various aspects:

A trigger for change
The problem of a *trigger* for change can be explored further. The firm is successful – albeit there are signs of a drop in performance from the highly successful 1980s. Could the appointment of Colin Sharman itself have been a trigger? Might poorer performance, which would be reflected in partner earnings, be a trigger? It might be interesting to debate with the class if they were managing the situation, if they could find, perhaps creates, a trigger. Colin Sharman himself, believed that the redundancies, particularly of partners, in the early 1990s signalled the seriousness of the situation and did act as a trigger.

The workshops
An important part of the change process was the *workshops*. These were attended by influential partners with a propensity for change; not necessarily those who held Colin Sharman's views; and not according to hierarchy. About a third of the partners in the South East region had taken part. A broadly similar pattern was followed in each workshop:

- First participants were asked to discuss the *key issues* each of them felt the firm faced. So agreements – and disagreements – were surfaced early on.

- Next they debated the market and *competitive forces* influencing the firm. As explained in the case, it emerged that there was very little in the way of competitive advantage between the main competitors.

- Competitive strategy was then discussed; and the critical question of how to achieve *competitive advantage* was posed. So participants discussed the sort of issues raised in the strategy clock in each workshop. As explained in the case, the outcome was that strategies of differentiation, and probably selective focus were necessary. It was recognised that this meant understanding and delivery against client need: and greater integration of services. The point that needs emphasis, therefore, was that the workshop participants themselves, were taking ownership of the strategic direction.

- The workshops moved onto map out a *cultural web*, examine past emergent strategies in this context, and identify blockages for change; indeed the type of exercise the class might have undertaken.

- They then worked to translate the strategic direction into action. This was done by identifying *critical success factors*, bearing in mind the strategic direction and the blockages.

- When critical success factors had been identified, workshops tried to identify the *detailed actions and symbolic changes* required to deliver against the critical success factors. This was probably the most difficult task of all. Participants were having to examine the detailed procedures and routines of the organisation and consider how these needed to be changed to achieve competitive advantage. (The evidence we have at Cranfield is that this is often the most difficult task of all because it challenges many of the taken for granted routines, and threatens many of the power bases of managers).

- Colin Sharman attended the debriefing of each workshop, hearing the recommendations of the workshop or syndicates within the workshops, answering questions and explaining where he stood. This was a strong signal of his personal commitment to the process.

- The workshops also had the effect of debating issues amongst an influential set of partners which were rarely discussed, except perhaps informally within the firm. In effect the partners entered zones of uncomfortable debate (ZOUD), for example to do with the culture of the firm, power relationships vested interest and so. Arguably this, too, was an important means of increasing commitment and signalling the need for change.

- After the formal workshops all partners (workshop participants and non-participants) were also debriefed on the main findings of all the workshops. However students might feel that the workshop process, valuable though it was, was not cascaded far enough down the organisation; it is one thing to gain commitment of 100 partners through such a process; but could it have been taken further to gain commitment more quickly 'down the line'?

Clarity of strategy

No change programme is likely to work unless there is a clarity of strategy for the organisation. In KPMG the partners in the workshop became convinced of a strategy of focused differentiation. This was communicated throughout the organisation in a variety of ways; through videos, written communication (often in glossy brochures), through the sort of conferences described in the case, by personal repetition by Colin Sharman and so on. All of this was done within '20:20 Vision' as a theme. It is however worth noting that, despite these endeavours of communication, it became clear that continual repetition of the intended strategy over a period of considerable time was necessary. The KPMG case illustrates that clarity of strategy is not likely to be achieved quickly but rather by persistence and repetition.

Later in the process the communication of the strategy was not only carried out through internal communication but became very public in the media (e.g. the financial press). Whilst this was, on the face of it, external communication of strategy, it also had the effect of a powerful confirmation of strategic intent within the firm.

Organisational structure

Chapter 9 makes the point that organisational structure should be suited to organisational strategy. The structure of KPMG was changed in 1992 to establish four industry groups with the intention that over time the traditional discipline based structure of the firm would change to become industry based. The issues that might be debated in class include:

- Initially the plans for introducing the industry groups were somewhat tentative with a long time frame. This was speeded up. In the case Colin Sharman expresses the view that the most success came from the industry groups rather than the residual discipline based areas of the firm. Could a more ambitious structural change have been undertaken more rapidly? Or would this have upset the change programme given the sensitive political situation within the partnership?

- This in itself raises the issue of what underpins power structures in organisations. The areas of the firm most resistant to structural changes were tax (initially) and consultancy (for some time). In the latter case this appears to have been because absorption into industry units was seen as a loss of identity for consultancy and therefore for senior consultants who had spent many years building up a consultancy practice within the firm.

- In 1996 the structure was changed again linked to the development of a more integrated and managed UK firm. The class is likely to applaud the greater integration across the UK and therefore see the necessity for the structure to be addressed. But class discussion might address:

  - The complexity of the matrix structure that was put in place. Does there come a point where the dimensions of a matrix structure means there is no effective structure at all?
  - The paradox that, despite the espousal of the need to tackle cultural issues, the visible emphasis is on structural changes and changes in the HR and control systems (see below). Are these the most appropriate emphases by which to address culture change?

HR and control systems
KPMG provides an example of how HR/control systems can help implement a strategy. The identification of competences for the delivery of strategy was a key part in its implementation. Such competences then formed the basis for appointment to partner, staff appraisal, staff development, appraisals, reward systems and eventually recruitment. Appendix 1 of this note summarises those competences in brief. Whilst they appear very general, students should see that they provide the basis for more specific characterisation of what is expected of the KPMG partner and thus provide a basis for strategy implementation through people.

However the class might debate the extent to which such an approach had the required impact. For example:

- There are different views within the case as to whether more time should have been spent refining the systems associated with the competences before they were put in to effect. David Westcott suggests this might have been appropriate; Colin Sharman believes it was important to move more quickly, if imperfectly.

- There are some signs that the formal systems were, at times, subordinated to traditional ways of doing things, especially when faced with a need to generate revenue. In principle it might be desirable to invest time in understanding the client better; but in difficult times fee-earning might override this.

- As explained below, changes in formal systems do not always ensure changes in day-to-day behaviour.

The management style of the change agent - Colin Sharman (see section 11.4.2 of chapter 11)
The role of Colin Sharman is obviously significant in this case. How he approached the task would be critical. A useful approach to the discussion might be to consider which of the *styles* of managing change he adopted. It certainly was not edict; nor was it persuasion – he had no neat package of solutions he was trying to persuade others to accept. There was participation, but it was guided participation. Arguably he was adopting tactic of *intervention*: getting influence formers involved, making clear where he stood, challenging others to decide where they stood and gradually evolving a set of solutions out of this.

This intervention style seems to have continued later as national senior partner in the way he, again, tried to involve others in the development of a more co-ordinated UK firm. For example the Leadership Project was headed by the senior partner of the Birmingham office.

Political action (see section 11.4.5 of chapter 11)
The programme for change could also be considered from a *political* perspective. Given the potential blockages of individual partners and traditional networks, how was this to be coped with? There are a number of points worth noting:

- The involvement of partners in the workshop, and their conclusion that the firm had to become much more integrated around client based problem solving, was crucial.

- Given that a major blockage to change, politically, was the long established network of partners, the fact that a number of partners were asked to leave the firm during the change programme was a major signal, not only of change, but of the extent to which traditional partner influence had been diminished.

- This, in turn, signalled a shift to a much more "managed" firm. Whilst partner influence remained strong it became clear that the senior partner had taken on more of a chief executive role.

- The more managed nature of the firm might, of course, have been further signalled by the move to a more integrated UK firm.

Change tactics (see section 11.4.7 of chapter 11)
A number of the other tactics outlined in chapter 11 are illustrated in the case and can be discussed. For example:

- Important issues of *timing* can be discussed. For example should the structure have changed more rapidly? Should the HR systems have been developed more fully before they were implemented? Should the problem of specialist consultancy units have been addressed more rapidly? Students often feel that programmes such as this can be carried out more rapidly but evidence suggest that they may take many years. This highlights the need for persistence and a continual repetition of the main messages of the strategy and its components. Overall, it may need to be recognised that change programmes take a long time to achieve success

- The importance of some of the departures and *job losses* that took place has already been made. They were signals of change both in terms of the competences required to deliver the strategy and the political fabric of the organisation.

- *Short term wins* were also important. These began with the workshops and the fact that a number of influential partners became committed to change. The early success of the first industry group became a significant signal of change. The later visible commitment of other influential partners to the strategy was also important.

Routines and symbolic activity (see sections 11.4.3 and 11.4.4 of chapter 11)
One of the most difficult tasks for KPMG was to identify the *routinised behaviour, systems and symbols* which needed to be changed in order to effect change. Some of the changes which were made fairly early on in these respects are touched on in the case study:

- Doing away with the exclusivity of different *dining rooms*;

- *Co-location* so that industry groups worked together;

- The expectation that partners would *work with clients* more in situe;

- Reducing *committees* and *meetings* (ie reducing the internal focus);

- Setting up *control* mechanisms to monitor client satisfaction;

- The open *questioning* of strategy eg at workshops and the strategy conference;

- Presenting the need for change in a *challenging* way (eg the pop art approach);

However, students might question if such changes tended to be less emphasised as the 1990s progressed and suggest others changes that might have been made to signal and help deliver an integrated, client centred strategy.

One of the major issues that needs to be dealt with in the class is that, despite all that was undertaken at KPMG, the most difficult aspect of change was to drive it down to the *point of delivery* of strategy. Students need to understand that strategies do not actually change until they are delivered differently to customers (or in this case clients); and that the delivery of strategy depends on those who interact most with such customers (in this case often junior managers and staff). If the day to day routines and symbols that surround such people have not changed, then strategic change is little more than intent. There is evidence in the case study that, certainly at the beginning of the change programme and even towards the end, the changes had not had sufficient impact at this level. The question, therefore, arises as to whether more could have been done in the managing of routines and symbols to signify such change. Though there is little in the way of specifics that can be drawn on from the case study students might flag up the importance of, for example:

- The importance of day to day behaviour of senior members of the firm for *role models* for more junior members;

- The visible support and reward of *behaviour* of junior staff when acting in line with the strategy;

Colin Sharman became well aware of the need for such changes and, though not discussed in the case, personally tried to ensure such as:

- Doing away with day to day aspects signalling partner primacy such as the different status of office furnishing.

- More lively, even exciting, partnership (and other) meetings with an emphasis much more on informality;

- The doing away of special privileges for partners;

- The transparency of partner earnings;

- Day to day behaviour (e.g. by telephonists) reflecting the importance of clients.

6.4 So has the change programme worked?

The class might conclude by considering:

- Has strategic change been achieved in KPMG? Students might conclude that a great deal has been achieved in terms of formal systems but there remain questions of the extent to which the change has been driven down to everyday behaviour. This seems to be a view shared by Colin Sharman and some of his colleagues.

- Was the balance on the emphasis in the 'change levers' employed appropriate? Arguably the emphasis was on structures and systems whilst espousing culture change.

- Colin Sharman argues that change needs time: that the change programme in KPMG should be seen over something like a ten-year period. Does this seem appropriate give the lack of a clear trigger for change?

- The challenge at the end of the case is from Colin Sharman himself who argues that the firm needs to build a truly learning organisation. This implies continual change owned throughout the organisation rather than managed from the top. In turn this emphasises the need for the ownership of strategy and client centredness throughout the firm. Is this a realistic ambition?

Appendix 1

The Competency Framework

The leadership competences were set out under the following six categories. Examples of specific competences within these categories are provided.

Client responsiveness
1. Relationship building – establishes rapport and builds long term relationships with key decision makers.
2. Professional judgement – knows who the 'real' client is at all times and uses this knowledge to operate effectively for KPMG.

Business skills

1. Commerciality – relates all aspects of KPMG's service to client's business perspective and commercial drivers.
2. Business development – is seen by existing clients to market effectively and appropriately.

Management

1. Task management skills – controls the process of delivery to the client.
2. Team skills – encourages openness and co-operative working.
3. People development – gives staff responsibility and autonomy appropriate to their level of competence.

Personal effectiveness

1. Drive and commitment to results – goes beyond client's expressed requirement and meets their real need.
2. Resilience – recovers crisis situations; is resourceful at times of pressure and stress.

Social skills

1. Communication skills – speaks clearly, and with impact.
2. Social confidence – is perceived to enjoy the company of a wide range of people.

Thinking skills

1. Analytical thinking – analyses large amounts of complex data, extracts essentials.
2. Proactive thinking – comes forward with ideas unprompted by clients.

TEACHING NOTES

KPMG (C): Developing a Global Firm
Gerry Johnson

1. INTRODUCTION

This case study not only updates the KPMG situation, but adds an additional dimension to it. In 1997 Colin Sharman was appointed as International Chairman of KPMG. His immediate task was to develop a global strategy for the organisation; and it is this that the case study deals with. It is particularly useful as a global case study because the heritage of KPMG is one of a federation of local firms – approximating to Bartlett and Ghoshal's locally responsive international subsidiaries. The question therefore, is what does global mean in the context of such an organisation?

2. POSITION IN THE COURSE

It is important in considering the issues raised in this case that the students have an understanding of KPMG. The case can therefore be used in sequence following the other two cases; or possibly as a free standing global case study in conjunction with the first case at the end of chapter 2, KPMG: Strategy Development in a Partnership.

3. LEARNING OBJECTIVES

1. To consider the drivers for globalisation for a professional services firm

2. To understand that international structures of organisations may take different forms and that each raises different management issues and problems.

3. To consider appropriate structures and control systems for the management of KPMG International.

4. To consider the role of the corporate centre given the choice of international structure?

4. THE TEACHING PROCESS

Assuming students understand the nature of KPMG as a professional partnership and in particular the historic emphasis on the local firm, then the case can be taught in terms of the series of broad issues posed above. Consideration of these and discussion around them can be facilitated by asking students to consider more specific questions within each issue. The teaching notes below are prepared in this way giving a suggested set of quite specific questions in the form of questionnaires and checklists that students can use. The teaching session might therefore consist of students preparing the questionnaires before the class, the tutor taking each of the broad issues in turn and exploring it with a brief lecture; and then the students debating their views on each theme based on the answers to the questions they have prepared.

5. QUESTIONS

The overall questions which might be used for class discussion are as follows:

1. What are the drivers for globalisation for KPMG?

2. What form of international operation is KPMG currently; and what form of international operation should it be? Specifically, should it be organised in terms of:

   - an international division
   - a global structure
   - international subsidiaries
   - a transnational?

3. What implications does this have for the way in which the firm should be managed and the role of the international centre of KPMG?

6. ISSUES FOR DISCUSSION

This section is laid out as a series of questionnaires together with comments as to how to interpret them. Although here they are specific to the KPMG case, each questionnaire is derived from books and papers in the public domain; so tutors can amend them as they wish. They might also be adapted for use with other case studies which raise issues of globalisation.

6.1 Drivers of Globalisation

George Yip's book *Total Global Strategy* is used in chapter 3 of the text to explore drivers of globalisation. Some of the issues raised are incorporated in the questionnaire in Exercise 1 to assess globalisation drivers for KPMG. Students should be able to see that there are a number of such drivers, notably:

- The similar needs of increasingly global customers

- Similarity of required services worldwide, particularly in management consultancy and to some extent audit. But what of e.g.tax?

- Increasingly global competitors.

- De-regulation and privatisation in areas of the world previously state controlled, leading to a growing demand for auditing, financial advice and consultancy in such areas.

- Increasingly uniform technical standards

- Some economies of scale and scope

• High development costs both to enter new geographic areas and to develop the technology for new services; therefore the need to recover such costs on a global basis.

(SEE EXERCISE 1)

6.2 The Time Frame for Global Development

If there are forces for globalisation acting on KPMG, how long does the firm have to change to a global operation? Based on their understanding of the time it takes to change a partnership (see KPMG: Managing Strategic Change), students may suggest it will take many years. Is this realistic given that competitors are moving much faster and some major clients are requiring global services already? Also, if the way in developing market opportunities such as Eastern Europe or China are already being entered by competition and requiring huge investment, can the firm afford to take its time?

At the time of the case study the view at the top of KPMG was that, given the above, and the window of opportunity afforded by the failure of merger discussion, the time frame was perhaps 2 years, not 5–10 years.

6.3 The Form of the Form

Exercise 2 has proved to be useful in exploring the type of global firm KPMG is at the time of the case; and the type students think it should be. (And here time frame needs to be agreed). The more the students see the firm to the left of the scales, the more it points to an international subsidiaries or multinational-type firm; and this is likely to be where students see KPMG as described at the time of the series of cases in the book. They will probably argue that in the future the firm needs to be more 'to the right' on the scales. But how far to the right and in what respects? It is interesting to debate what activities should be more or less global and whether this should vary by type of service (eg consultancy versus audit versus tax). An interesting discussion might also be the extent to which student views might coincide with, say Sharman's and with the senior partner in a successful national partnership of KPMG (say, Germany). Sharman's views might be to the right, but would the national senior partner's?

The conclusion from this discussion might be mapped onto Bartlett and Ghoshal dimensions shown in figure 1. It is likely that the students will recognize that the current situation is bottom left (international subsidiaries), that many of the indicators are for the need for *both* global co-ordination and local responsiveness (transnational) but that Sharman's leanings seem to be moving more towards a more centralized global firm.

(SEE EXERCISE 2 AND FIGURE 1)

6.4 Management and Control in an International Structure

The discussion can move on to consider how the firm might actually be managed given the conclusions from the proceeding exercise. This might be done, for example, using the sort of dimensions of control outlined by Gould and Campbell and in chapter 10 of the text. Exercise 3 is based on this, though it adds in a fourth form of control, that of 'Strategic Coach', which is more in line with the sort of means of co-ordination and control suggested by Bartlett and Ghoshal as suited to transnationals.

Again, students could use the listing as an exercise to consider what might be appropriate for KPMG if they were to try to put into effect a global or transnational approach. They will probably conclude that a 'Strategic Control' or 'Strategic Coach' approach is appropriate and that a 'Strategic Planning' approach would not be acceptable in the partnership. Does this suggest that the pace of change towards a globally co-ordinated firm will be too slow, or that the formation of a coherent global strategy will be compromised because of the difficulties of managing the global firm where local power and responsiveness is high. Might speed of change in fact suggest a more directive 'Strategic Planning' style?

(SEE EXERCISE 3)

6.5 The Role of the Global Centre

The next question that might be raised is just what the international centre of KPMG might do to develop a global firm. This raises the question of parenting in a global context. Figure 2 is a checklist of possible roles of such a centre. (It is similar to figure B in the appendix of the Burmah Castrol Chemicals case). Students might use the figure as a checklist to think about what the appropriate roles are for the international centre as distinct from, for example, the head office of one of the national partnerships within KPMG; and what should not be done at all.

Opinions may vary a good deal on this. Some will argue for a powerful centre attempting to add value in many ways. More perceptively, others will try to identify the key *added value* contributions the centre can make to develop a global operation – arguably such as transferring knowledge and best practice (and intervening to do so where necessary), strategic questioning and challenge, building a cadre of partners able to operate globally, developing the services which can provide some real advantage for the firm and providing support to develop new geographic regions.

(SEE EXERCISE 4)

6.6 Comparing KPMG with other Firms

This approach to teaching the case and the same sequence of exercises does, of course, provide the opportunity to use KPMG as a basis for comparison with other firms.

6.7 Integrating the Issues

Overall the issues which are surfaced by the use of the questionnaires and figures need to be pulled together and related to the students' understanding of a firm such as KPMG. The key question is how does a firm with a long history of dispersed power and propensity for a slow pace of change deal with a major strategic challenge such as globalisation? Indeed, can it?

Exercise 1:

INDUSTRY DRIVERS OF GLOBALISATION

Please rate how important the factors on the left seem to you
by circling one of the numbers in the right-hand column.
Number 1 is low importance and 5 is high importance.

MARKET FACTORS	LOW				HIGH
Common client needs	1	2	3	4	5
Global clients	1	2	3	4	5
Global competitors	1	2	3	4	5
Common services worldwide	1	2	3	4	5
Transferable marketing across countries	1	2	3	4	5
Other:	1	2	3	4	5
COST FACTORS	**LOW**				**HIGH**
Global economies of scale	1	2	3	4	5
Global economies of scope	1	2	3	4	5
Differences in country costs	1	2	3	4	5
High development costs	1	2	3	4	5
Fast changing technology	1	2	3	4	5
Other:	1	2	3	4	5
GOVERNMENT FACTORS	**LOW**				**HIGH**
Reduced barriers to trade	1	2	3	4	5
Reduced government buying from local suppliers	1	2	3	4	5
Uniform technical standards	1	2	3	4	5
Common marketing regulations	1	2	3	4	5
De-regulation and privatisation	1	2	3	4	5
Other:	1	2	3	4	5

Exercise 2:
THE FORM OF THE FIRM   1/2

Please indicate where you think KPMG is now with a C.
And please put an F where you think the firm needs to be in the future.

1. **How are national markets developed?**

For their local potential   As part of a global strategy
                                                             eg following key clients)?

L_____J

2. **How do KPMG compete for clients?**

On a country-by-country basis?   On a worldwide account basis?

L_____J

3. **How would you describe KPMG services?**

Locally distinct?   Standardised across national markets?

L_____J

4. **How would you describe KPMG brand image?**

Different locally   Consistent worldwide

L_____J

5. **How do KPMG gain significant competitive advantage in national markets?**

From local connections (eg political) local   From your global standing
relationships and locally specific   and infrastructure?
knowledge

L_____J

6. **How do national or local offices tend to operate?**

They are free to develop their own service   They are required to employ
offerings or modify corporate services or   corporate services
products

L_____J

7. **How much do activities in one country affect activities or outcomes in other markets?**

Little   Significantly

L_____J

THE FORM OF THE FIRM

Please indicate where you think KPMG is now with a C. And please put an F where you think the firm needs to be in five years.

8. Where do most new service ideas come from?

Locally   From the centre

```
 └──────────────────────────────────────────────────┘
```

9. How is information and knowledge communicated?

Within units only   Between units   Through the centre

```
 └──────────────────────────────────────────────────┘
```

10. If KPMG had a business unit in a significant European country and a global competitor started to make inroads into that unit's market, what would the international corporate centre do?

Leave it to the managers in the local market to decide what to do	Counsel or coach the managers in the local market as to what to do	Intervene directly

```
 └────────────────────────┴──────────────────────────┘
```

Exercise 3:

STRUCTURE AND CONTROL

What form of control is likely to be suited to KPMG's global strategy?

FORMS OF CONTROL	Key features	C/F?
FINANCIAL CONTROL	• 'Shareholder/banker'	
	• Financial targets	
	• Control of investment	
	• Bottom-up	
	• Independent international subsidiaries	
STRATEGIC PLANNING	• 'Masterplanner'	
	• Top-down approach	
	• Detailed controls	
	• Central direction of national organisations	
STRATEGIC CONTROL	• 'Strategic shaper'	
	• Strategic and financial targets	
	• Less detailed controls	
	• Negotiation of strategy between centre and units	
STRATEGIC COACH	• 'Vision creator'	
	• Disseminator of values and culture	
	• Local responsiveness within corporate values and standards.	
	• Coach and counsellor	

EXERCISE 4
PARENTING SKILLS AND COMPETENCES
Where should the following take place?

Parenting skill/Competences	Global centre	National	Not at all
INTERVENTION IN BUSINESS UNITS			
Acquisition and disposal			
Turnaround			
Change agency			
Skill injection			
PLANNING COACHING & CHALLENGE			
Questioning and challenging business units			
Strategy development/planning			
Setting goals and objectives for business units			
FINANCIAL			
"Banking"			
"Insurance"/Risk planning			
Treasury			
SPECIALIST EXPERTISE			
- Research and development			
- Legal			
- Global account management			
- Information systems			
EXTERNAL RELATIONS			
- With governments			
- With financial and other institutions			
- Encouraging alliances and networks with clients, suppliers etc			
LINKAGES (Within portfolio)			
- Transferring knowledge			
- Transferring skills and best practice			
- Encouraging cross-SBU working			
SHARING			
- Capabilities and competences			
- Resources (eg offices etc)			
LEVERAGING			
- Buying power			
- Marketing power			
- Developing/promoting the brand			
PEOPLE DEVELOPMENT			
- Recruitment			
- Partner selection			
- Management succession			
- Management development			
- Placement of people			
INTERNATIONALISATION			
- Geographic expansion			
- Understanding cultures			
- International structuring			
- Integrating activities across borders			

FIGURE 1

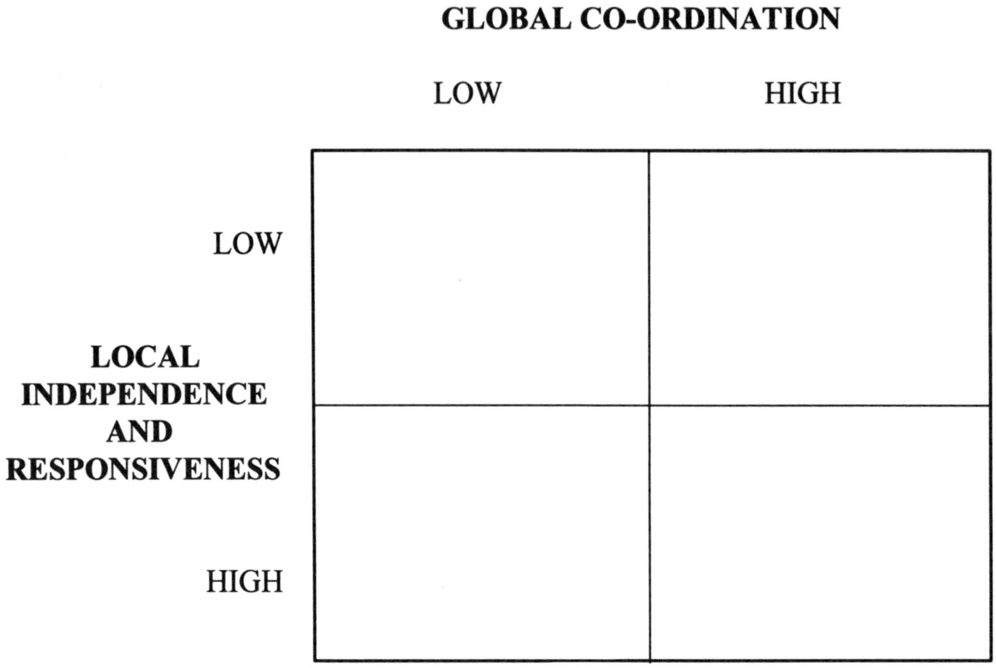

GLOBAL CO-ORDINATION

	LOW	HIGH
LOW		
HIGH		

LOCAL INDEPENDENCE AND RESPONSIVENESS

TEACHING NOTES

UNHCR – Achieving the Impossible
Ian Sayers and Gerry Johnson

1. INTRODUCTION

This case is about managing enforced change, in large, hierarchical and highly politicised organisations. It looks at the complex dynamics and interactions of 'going public' with change, what mechanisms can be used and what components need to be in place to provide some chance of success for the change agent. A major change process at The United Nations High Commissioner for Refugees is used to illustrate such issues; however, the experiences described in this case would also translate to any large multinational commercial Group or other public sector context and provides a useful comparison with such organisations. The case particularly highlights the type of difficulties that can be experienced during a protracted change programme.

UNHCR was arguably the first of the major UN Agencies to consider and embark on radical change. The change process was undertaken in the full glare of public scrutiny and whilst the Organisation was stretched to respond to some of the worst humanitarian disasters ever seen.

Additional background meterial is included in these teaching notes so that lecturers will be able to 'set the scene' for students and provide further insight into the political aspects of change in the public sector.

The case concludes by looking at the challenges and dangers for the Board of Directors, who, after inviting full staff participation in the change process had subsequently to live with the consequences of being the centre of attention.

2. POSITION

This case study is primarily about managing strategic change and, in particular, detailed processes associated with change. The case is probably therefore best taught towards the end of a strategic management course and, possibly, as a comparison with other strategic change contexts (e.g. using cases such as KPMG or the Royal Alexandra Hospital).

However strategic change cannot be considered in isolation and the case does raise many other issues such as structure and control, communication, stakeholder analysis, the role of the corporate centre and problems of managing a multinational organisation on a global scale.

3. LEARNING OBJECTIVES

The UNHCR case allows students to gain an understanding of the various influences and tensions within a complex organisation operating on a global scale when it comes to the development of a clear strategy and the management of change. Within UNHCR these tensions centre principally around the need for local responsiveness to conditions 'in the field' and global control of the organisation : it is therefore in many respects a transnational problem. In studying the case students are inevitably faced with the complex problem of understanding strategic change in context; and in this case a highly complex situation.

4. TEACHING PROCESS AND DISCUSSION TOPICS

Students should be familiar with material covered in Exploring Corporate Strategy relating to :

- Organisation structure and design, as discussed in chapter 9.

- Managing strategic change as discussed in chapter 11.

The class might be subdivided into groups, each taking a different viewpoint in terms of different stakeholders. For example, the questions below can be looked at usefully from the different perspectives of :

- Major donors, implementing partners, other UN agencies or governments;

- Field personnel in UNHCR;

- A notional management consultant or external change agent.

5. QUESTIONS FOR DISCUSSION

1. What is an appropriate organisational structure for UNHCR?

2. Bearing in mind the advantages and disadvatages of different types of change process, what was done well at UNHCR and what would you have done differently?

3. What would you advise the High Commissioner to do in 1997?

6. CASE ANALYSIS

6.1 Choosing an organisational structure for the future

Given the complex structure of UNHCR in 1992, at the beginning of the case study, it might be helpful to get students to rehearse the reasons for and against such a structure. For example:

Arguments for strong centralised control:

- Maintain consistency of delivery and equitable distribution of aid throughout all crises areas.

- Accountability and control afforded to the centre through Headquarters communications hub.

- Encourages stakeholder involvement and allows political influence (especially on the part of wealthy donor countries)

- Addresses the need for government/public bodies to appear to be answerable.

- Acts as a diplomatic and political buffer for brokering international agreements and provides a neutral forum for settling cross-border disputes.

- Remoteness from field problems avoids emotional entanglement when difficult decisions have to be made.

Arguments against centralised control and for devolution of control and responsibility to the field:

- High overhead cost of centralised administration in expensive city location and calls by pressure groups for increased cost effectiveness

- Lack of flexibility and responsiveness, inefficenticies and slow decision-making embodied in political processes

- Remoteness from field leads to 'second-guessing', lack of understanding and suspicion of motives.

- Local or regional coordination of implementing partners at the field officer level works with much less fuss because of the genuine will of front-line workers to sacrifice pride to help those in need above all else, particularly in regions of open conflict

Financial pressures mentioned in the case include: competition from within the UN family, a realisation that humanitarian aid organisations were competing for funds from donors, that donors were increasingly responding to home country pressure and earmarking funds for bilateral aid to specific projects or home country agencies and that inefficiencies were being picked-up by an increasingly perceptive media.

It is in this context the students need to address topic I. What would they have done? The answers might differ according to the perspective they take (e.g. donor country versus field operative). Mintzberg's organisational configurations and the structural options raised by Bartlett and Ghoshal both discussed in chapter 9 of *Exploring Corporate Strategy,* may be used to help facilitate student discussion of the various forces that pull organisations in different directions. Students might conclude that a *transnational solution* most clearly approximates to UNHCR's situation. It is also likely that most of the class will sympathise with the fieldworkers and argue for much more decentalisation in order to improve responsiveness. Given the diversity of UNHCR's staff, how then, will the issues of accountability and consistency of approach be resolved? And would they be resolved or compounded by a transnational type structure. The point is that donor interest and power exerts a pull to centralisation and local field needs to decentralisation.

6.2 Stimulating, managing and accomplishing major changes

The new environment in which UNHCR was operating during the mid-1990s meant that there was an urgent need to change the organisation's structure, and do so whilst taking into account the viewpoints of some powerful stakeholder groups. The problem was how to stimulate, accomplish and manage change on the scale of that to be undertaken at UNHCR, whilst achieving buy-in from these groups.

Students should consider what style of change programme would be most likely to achieve success in an organisation like UNHCR. The analysis and tabulation of the range of managerial approaches for change found in Exhibit 11.6 Styles of managing strategic change of chapter 11 of *Exploring Corporate Strategy* and section 11.4.2 covers 'change by edict' to 'full participation' and is a useful starting point. The various styles are context-specific and dependent on many variables.

The approach actually adopted was highly participative. It involved many staff. The danger, as here, is that such an approach might generate ideas and galvanise enthusiasm, but does it achieve change? Was there a prior need to ensure the commitment of key top management and key stakeholders? Who were they and were they committed to (what sort of) change?

Certainly in UNHCR there were difficulties that led to implementation taking longer than expected and some of these difficulties arose because of the use of a participative process. Difficulties included:

- The close attention of the world's media to every aspect of the organisation's field operations, invited global comparisons quicker than management could respond.

- Some individuals who wished to block progress held 'indefinite' contracts and could not be removed.

- Key sponsors and managers of the change process still had to abide by the principals of compulsory rotation and many were dispatched to the field in mid-project.

- The legacy of centralised control also gave its own problems when trying to orchestrate simultaneous change throughout the world by relying on staff participation. Until a critical point in the devolution of processes had been passed staff, were enthusiastic but wary about taking on additional responsibilities.

In answering the question about 'what was done well and what would students have done differently' the following issues might be raised:

- The style of change: as discussed above.

- Choosing and installing the change agent

The way an external change agent was introduced, in this case by secondment, is also critical to success. On the positive side a seconded change agent was perceived as non-aligned to any internal factions and could start work early. On the negative side many long-term Directors thought the arrangement was for a limited duration and therefore any difficult issues could be avoided by prevarication or by keeping their heads down.

- Communicating change and removing barriers to information flow

By identifying and championing best internal practice processes and applying them in a team matrix structure throughout UNHCR several 'blockers' had their power base swept away or effectively neutralised. Communications were a key lever for change in this process. Examples are: *Delphi News*, 'Lunchtime learning' and 'in the hot seat', changes in management style such as coffee meetings and office design such as new transparent walls. Horizontal direct communications avoided the possibility of messages becoming distorted in their delivery down the hierarchy and reinforced the idea of working with a 'flatter' organisational structure.

- The (lack of) use of outsiders

UNHCR went to great lengths to publicise the lack of involvement of any external consultants (see example in the *Additional Background Material* at the end of these notes *Report of the Third Meeting of the Standing Committee 1996* '... noting that the process has been an almost entirely in-house exercise...'). It might be argued that an external change agent might have been useful in dealing with some of the difficult issues such as reducing the number of staff in 1997) but would the level of enthusiasm generated for change be as high?

- Top team perceptions and priorities

In the closing paragraphs of the case it is clear that not all of the management team had put themselves in the place of their staff. What Directors saw as progress was considered by their staff to be inaction. 'Wins' as seen by staff and management may be entirely different. Some Directors tried to distance themselves from the Delphi process. Unfortunately in a highly visible Delphi programme there is no place for management to hide. These Directors became exposed because the staff had changed their behaviour and bought into the philosophy of the process whilst the Directors had not. Buy-in of senior management to the philosophy of a Delphi type programme is vital for success.

It also appears that some members of the management team had become immersed in the process of change and were no longer well focused on the objectives. Directors saw progress whereas their staff often saw inaction. For example changes in the budgeting process were seen as a major achievement by the SMC but had very little impact on the day-to-day work of the majority of staff. They were waiting for tangible structural changes that seemed not to get off the drawing board.

6.3 Recovering the situation after the change impetus has faltered

This question is intended to highlight difficulties in timing and in maintaining momentum during change programmes that take place over a number of years. Loss of morale or momentum or both are real problems that have beset a number of protracted change programmes. Students should be asked to come up with a range of options and 'next steps' that they would ask the High Commissioner to consider in 1998. The tutor can use discussion around the following broad options to prompt responses:

Identifying the problem: If the situation is judged to be the result of a communication problem, have the substantial benefits of the changes that had occurred been communicated to the staff sufficiently well? Would staff confidence be restored if benefits gained were highlighted?

- Turning the situation around – how could it be demonstrated to staff that management had recognised that a problem existed and intended to rectify the situation? What mechanisms could be used to help the SMC see how it was perceived by observers and how it was causing such a reaction from the staff?

- Removing difficult Directors – What could the High Commissioner do to bring the remaining 'doubters' and 'blockers' on the SMC into line given that in 1998 they were not due to be rotated or seconded elsewhere? How would staff interpret such moves?

- Stopping the change programme – Is it time to call a halt to Delphi and then start again under a different banner? Given the external pressures is this even a realistic option?

6.4 Reviewing the lessons learned

So what do we learn about managing change in UNHCR? Arguably the essential requirements for success identified in the case are a combination of the following:

- Solid commitment and support from the hierarchy above the change agent

- Strong, sensitive but charismatic change agent

- Control of IT and communications, Finance and/or budget and backing from the Human Resources Director

- A majority of staff in support for change from either the general staff, the Board or middle managers.

- Security for staff to say what they really think, criticise and challenge the established order without fear of recourse. This takes some courage on the part of management.

- Continued feedback to maintain the momentum, manage expectations and enthusiasm.

- Identification of the levers for change, 'blockers' and supporters at an early stage.

- Early establishment and control of programme scope.

- A thorough and robust advanced planning process for implementation.

- Well thought through succession planning for key individuals.

- Scenario plans covering the impact on the change programme of a number of possible changes to the external environment

- Buy-in of senior management to the philosophy of a participative type of programme.

7. ABOUT UNHCR

It may be helpful to start the case session by providing some additional background on UNHCR and it's immediate environment. Exhibit 1 illustrates UNHCR's position in relation to governments, the UN Secretariat, implementing partners, donors and recipients.

UNHCR is by definition in its operational mandate, and by the nature of its work, a global organisation. Through the reports of CNN and other television networks UNHCR and its sister Agency UNICEF have become household names. Yet the management has to balance transparency in the face of the media with diplomacy and political astuteness in dealing with its high level governmental stakeholders. The case attempts to give students a glimpse of the tensions that exist within the international humanitarian and diplomatic communities and of the challenges of implementing uniform policies equitably in 185 offices spread around the world – a truly 'transnational' problem. Although the Delphi process provides essentially demand led change the initial creation of the right ambiance for it to flourish had to come from the top - down through the hierarchy. In UNHCR's own terms first, it had to be acceptable to 'think the unthinkable', then staff had to feel secure and comfortable with 'speaking the unspeakable' and finally 'achieving the impossible'.

Additional background material can be found in the notes at the end of this teaching note, through UNHCR Centre for Documentation and at the UNHCR Internet site: *Refworld.* The notes include public statements on the change process made by both the High Commissioner and the Deputy High Commissioner.

EC/46/SC/CRP.42
22 August 1996
STANDING COMMITTEE
4th Meeting Original: ENGLISH
DRAFT REPORT OF THE THIRD MEETING OF THE STANDING COMMITTEE (25-27 June 1996

IX. MANAGEMENT AND ADMINISTRATIVE MATTERS

The Deputy High Commissioner introduced a progress report on Project Delphi (EC/46/SC/CRP.38), noting that the process has been an almost entirely in-house exercise focused on three broad areas of UNHCR's management processes – operations, people and money. Staff participation, key to the change management process, was reinforced with an extensive staff survey in March, which identified several key areas perceived as needing improvement. Consolidating output from the survey, the focus groups and more than 100 Delphi cells world-wide, the Change Management Group Report, submitted to the High Commissioner in May, presented a broad conceptual framework of the changes needed. Project Delphi then entered Phase Two, the aim of which is to transform the conceptual framework into a Plan of Action by the end of August. The High Commissioner had agreed to the creation of a Change Management Support and Co-ordination Unit to implement the Plan of Action. Existing posts in the Organisation and Methods Section will be re-deployed to staff this unit. The Plan of Action, once endorsed by the High Commissioner, would be forwarded to the Standing Committee for consideration at its September meeting.

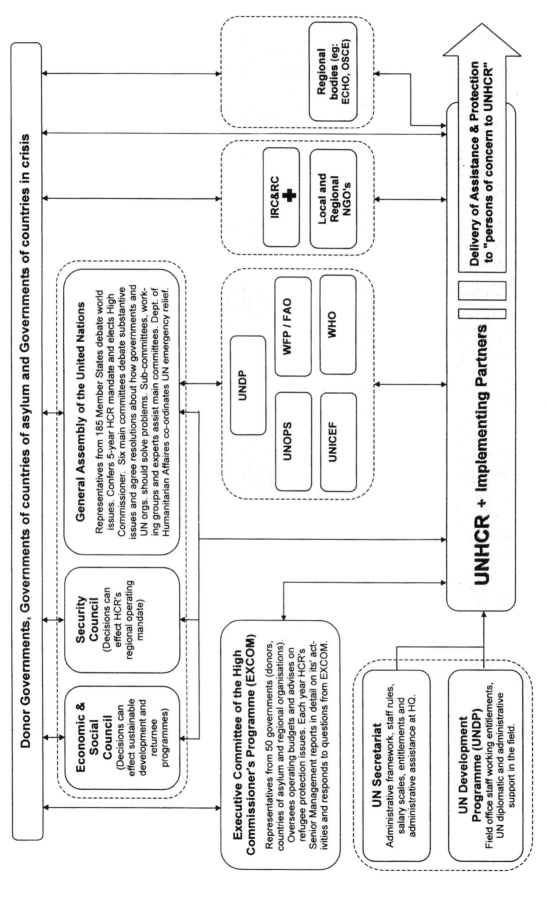

Figure 1. UNHCR's position within the United Nations and Humanitarian Assistance Communities

TEACHING NOTES

Burmah Castrol Chemicals Group
Gerry Johnson

1. INTRODUCTION

The Chemicals Group of Burmah Castrol grew throughout the 1980s and early 1990s largely by acquisition. This case study is based on the deliberations which followed Mike Dearden taking over as Chief Executive of the Chemicals Group in 1995.

On taking over as Chief Executive he had a series of related questions concerning the development of the Group.

- What is the strategic logic to the businesses in the Group?

- What should the 'corporate' aspirations and purpose of the Group be?

These in turn raised such questions as:

- What value can the Group add to the business units, if any?

- Based on what core competences and bases of competitive advantage of the business units.

- How should the Group be organised in terms of the control it exercises over its businesses; and also to deliver the international strategy expected of it by its parent, Burmah Castrol?

To resolve these questions he decided to begin by asking the businesses to identify their own competitive strategy and core competences; and to ask them to comment on their desired role of the centre.

This case describes the outcome of those deliberations in considerable detail. The information is in large measure that which was made available to the Executive of the Chemicals Group itself for their deliberations. It is, therefore, fairly detailed and not greatly interpreted. It therefore provides the students with the opportunity of considering complex input into an important set of strategic decisions.

2. POSITION

This case study is complex both because of the types of data it includes and also because of the multi-dimensionality of the questions posed by Mike Dearden. To deal with the case, students are required to have an understanding of:

- Aspects of corporate strategy (including organisational design and strategic control);

- Notions of competitive advantage and core competence;

- Portfolio management;

- Multinational/global/transnational management.

Given these requirements the Burmah Castrol case study should come at the end of a course in strategic management and can be regarded as integrating a number of the concepts covered in *Exploring Corporate Strategy*.

3. LEARNING OBJECTIVES

After using the case study students should be able to:

- See the importance of a clear corporate strategy in making decisions about the scope of businesses and organisational structure.

- The role of the centre in enhancing SBU strategy

- The implication for:
  Parenting skills
  Portfolio decisions
  Organisational structure and design

- Understand that decisions on such matters are dependent one on another.

4. TEACHING PROCESS

Given the complexity of the case study it can be taught at two different levels.

1. As a case study used by the tutor to illustrate the problems of developing corporate strategy and the linkages between the corporate centre and business units. Here the sequence might be as follows:

(i) Students should read the case study to familiarise themselves with the material but not to work on it extensively

(ii) The tutor would then use the notes below as a basis for a lecture on the above topics, referring students to the material in the case study.

2. However, the case can be used more extensively to require students to explore concepts and tools themselves. It is likely that this will require:

(i) extensive preparatory work by students working in groups either with tutorial guidance and/or with interim plenary feedback session;

(ii) An extensive (at least two hours) plenary session to compare and contrast the conclusions reached by different groups.

A good way of working is to split the students into three groups (or multiples of three groups) around the three different arguments and proposals made by members of the Executive in the case study. These different views resemble the three different control styles of financial control, strategic control and strategic planning explained in chapter 10. The three groups can then be asked to consider the logic of such views given the material provided in the case study and the implications of such views for the purpose of the Group, the portfolio of the Group and the structure of the Group (including its international dimensions). In this way a group basis of working can be used to explore the complexities of the case.

It may then be useful to draw together the discussion by using one of the approaches to structure a debate in plenary.

4.1 Use of video

If the video relating to Burmah Castrol is used, its first few minutes can be used to set the scene, in particular with regard to the nature of the different businesses and technologies involved in the Group. The interview on the video with Mike Dearden can then be used at the end of the session for two purposes:

1. To build his de-briefing of events into the plenary session.

2. As an additional input for class discussion: do the students agree with his views and the conclusions he has come to?

5. QUESTIONS FOR DISCUSSION

3. Is there a strategic logic to the businesses in the Chemicals Group?

4. What should be the corporate aspirations/purposes of the Chemicals Group?

5. What value can the Chemicals Group as a 'corporate parent' add to the business units?

6. What are the portfolio implications?

7. How should the Group be organised?

6. CASE COMMENTARY

Given the circularity of the issues in this case study, tutors could start from a number of different points. However, the following sequence reflects that adopted by the Chemicals Group itself (indeed the class might consider if this sequence was the most appropriate).

6.1 Competitive strategy, core competences of SBUs and the logic of the Group

This process began by representatives of SBUs addressing issues related to the strategic logic of the Group, starting at the SBU level. In each of the workshops on SBU strategy the format followed was as follows:

(i)   A review of bases of competitive strategy including the definition of competitive strategy and competitive position (in relation to competitors).

(ii) An attempt to identify bases of competitive advantage (actual or potential).

(iii) The identification of required and existing parenting skills.

(iv) A discussion of the linkages between SBUs.

The main conclusions arising from the workshops, summarised in the report to the Board, were that:

- Virtually all the SBUs recognised the need to follow a strategy of differentiation or focused differentiation. They also recognised that, in the past, bases of differentiation had not been well developed, there had been little clarity on core competences and there was a consequent dependence for many on price competition.

- In almost all cases, bases of differentiation were recognised to be more concerned with the services offered to clients than product or technology. In the main where these services were effective and had led to competitive success, they were based on establishing an intimate knowledge of customers' businesses and delivering this by cross-functional teams working on customers' problems.

- There were very few linkages between the businesses within the Group on the basis of markets or technologies.

- There was a feeling amongst almost all the SBUs that the centre needed to play an important role in developing the businesses. They saw this as particularly so in the development of competences concerned with service delivery, management development and movement of people on an international basis.

The above is not presented in summarised form in the case study. Students can be required to work through the extensive data provided on the outcomes of discussions in the workshops in order to discern the above.

6.2 The role of the corporate parent

Having received the report from the workshops the executive considered:

- The corporate purpose and aspirations of the Group;

- Portfolio issues;

- Structural implications within an international context;

- And the implications for corporate control.

If the student groups are set up to reflect the three different management styles (see section 4.2 above), then it is likely that differences will emerge for all of these issues from the different groups. Figure 1 shows how this might be the case.

The 'financial control group' is likely to see the centre as, primarily, concerned with maximising returns to the parent, exercising arms length control on key dimensions of performance with essentially autonomous operating units. There is no search for synergy or linkages in competences; and little concern about the centre trying to enhance value in such ways.

The 'strategic planning group' are likely to see the international aspirations of Burmah Castrol as centrally important; and that it is the purpose of the Chemicals Group centre to be pro-active in ensuring that these international aspirations are met in portfolio terms and in terms of the strategies followed by businesses. The Group centre needs to be directive in doing this.

The 'strategic control group' may take the view that there are, indeed, linkages between the businesses, not so much in terms of market and technologies but in terms of the service competences required in each of the businesses. However, this is not an obvious conclusion and may need the tutor to remind students of the nature of core competences (see below and sections 4.3, 6.4 and 10.5 of the text). The purpose of the centre is to develop a Group which is characterised by high margin businesses built on adding value. The role of the centre therefore becomes that of facilitating SBU competences to deliver such added value. This was, in fact, the view adopted by the Executive and is discussed more fully below.

There are a number of elements outlined above which are worthy of exploration either within groups or in plenary session. These are now discussed.

6.3 Generic Competences and Linkages

It is useful to consider the extent to which there are linkages across the SBUs because it encourages students to think about the nature of core competences. Arguably it is very unlikely that a core competence yielding competitive advantage will be based on simple technology. The view emerged in the Executive debate that there were 'generic competences across but not all' of the SBUs which could be summarised as follows:

- Managing customer interfaces, particularly where they are complex and require team deliver, usually involving sales and technical personnel;

- Applications rather than manufacturing know-how;

- Bringing new ideas to market based on customer need;

- A necessity to know customers businesses intimately in the generation of new ideas and in applications know-how;

- All this often focusing on small often localised market niches.

- And that all these required team collaboration in terms of marketing, technological and commercial skills and functions.

6.4 Corporate purpose

There are a number of dimensions to the issue of corporate purpose and aspirations which should come out in the group discussions. They include:

- The extent to which the Chemicals Group should, in itself, be directed by its major stakeholder, Burmah Castrol. What does Burmah Castrol expect of the Chemicals Group? This is not addressed explicitly in the case except that it is clear that Burmah Castrol expect the Chemicals Group to be more global than currently. A debate in class might, for example, address the extent to which it is important for a corporate body such as Burmah Castrol to be clear about its own purpose and aspirations in relation to a major part of its operations.

- An issue that is raised in the case and was the subject of a good deal of debate by the Executive was the extent to which 'Chemicals' was a true descriptor of the Group. What emerged in discussion in the Executive was that, whilst the businesses had chemicals as raw materials, a more accurate descriptor might be 'industrial consumables'; and profits were made, not so much out of providing chemical raw materials, as solutions to customer problems employing chemicals. In itself this had implications for core competences and competence development (see below). The Executives saw the purpose of the Group as identifying and developing businesses capable of achieving higher than industry average margins based on such solution development.

- In fact in the debate by the Executive they concluded their aspirations were to develop:

a) Businesses in growth formulated industrial consumable markets capable of generating high returns on the capital invested or employed and which offer investment opportunities with returns greater than the cost of capital.

b) Businesses which are either currently operating or capable of being developed internationally.

c) Market driven businesses generating above industry average margins through the creation of premium brands and the marketing of products (in its broadest sense – product, service, alliance) which improvise customer profitability.

They, therefore, saw the Chemicals Group's purpose and aspirations as informed as much by SBU competences as by Burmah's overall purpose. The class might debate if this is an appropriate way of establishing a purpose for the Chemicals Group.

6.5 Parenting skills

The parenting skills required according to the different control styles vary:

- If the role of the corporate centre is seen as one of financial control then, arguably, there are few parenting skills required. The centre sets targets and monitors performance. It may acquire and dispose of businesses but does not intervene in their working.

- If a strategic planning approach is taken then the role of the centre becomes much more directive. At the extreme it directs the strategy of the SBUs along specified lines, may require linkages and synergies to be built between businesses and the building of a portfolio with in line with its overall purpose. In these circumstances it is likely to focus on a smaller number of businesses in order to be able to adopt this 'hands on' approach.

- In fact the view taken by the Executive was that, since they aspired to developing high margin businesses based on the provision to solutions to customers, the role of the centre became one of enhancing business capabilities and competences to do this. They concluded that the key parenting skills required were those set out in figure 2.

The view was that there was a need to develop people much more around the competences that provided for success in the businesses. This required more attention to the definition of competence requirements for managers and their assessment to deliver against these. Since there was also a need for means to transfer competences across businesses, this meant identifying managers who had achieved skills and competences which could be transferred and proactively managing such transfers. The centre could also be more proactive in transferring best practice across businesses in other ways. Co-ordinators might take a group wide interest in common skills and competences and help transfer them. Information systems might be useful as might centres of excellence. The emphasis needed to move much more towards networking with the centre acting to facilitate that.

The centre was also seen to have a role in 'strategic challenge' which could be done in a number of ways. By explicitly challenging the strategy at business unit level; by making clear Chemicals Group corporate strategy to provide the businesses with overall direction and encouraging them to develop their own strategies within that overview-, and training should develop managers' capabilities in strategic thinking and analysis.

Internationalisation was also seen as a key role for the centre, not just by responsive encouragement but also by encouraging local management to help start up and settling in where other businesses wanted to enter a country; and by providing basic services such as check lists of best practice based on successful experience of internationalisation processes; and contact across the businesses to help transference of know-how.

6.6 The parenting matrix

The parenting matrix is a useful device to look at the portfolio implications of all this. Parenting matrices might take different forms. The one in chapter 6 of the book is based on the work of Gould, Campbell and Alexander. However, building on the executive debate, the matrix might be built up on the following dimensions:

(i) The extent to which the SBUs fit within the aspirations described above, in particular to build an international group of businesses built on high margins achieved through providing customer solutions; in turn depending on intimate knowledge of customers businesses.

The class can take a view on which of the SBUs best fit this description given the information at the beginning of the case. Arguably those that do most are:

Printing Inks (PI), Foundry (F), Steelmills (S), Aluminium (A), Fosbel (FO), Construction (C) and Mining (M)

Those that are less clearly so are:

Cable Products (CP), Investment Casting (IC), General Waxes (GW) and Timber Treatment (TT).

Adhesives (AD) does not seem to meet such criteria.

(ii) The extent to which the needs of the businesses can be enhanced by the parenting skills of the centre. One way of considering this is to examine the SBUs against the sort of parenting skills for competence development shown in Figure B of the case study: arguably these are people development, transferring best practice, internationalisation and strategic planning/coaching. Figures C and D in the case give the views of the SBU managers on their needs in these respects (marked * in figure 3); and figure 3 also shows what the executives' views of priority needs and opportunities were for the SBUs (though this information is not given in the case study). If these dimensions are used the resulting matrix is like that shown as figure 4.

Of course, the point needs to be made that the configuration of businesses within this matrix will differ according to views on the purpose and aspirations of the Group and the perceived parenting skills of the Group and the parenting needs of the SBUs.

Different parenting matrices could therefore be drawn up by varying one or both of the axes.

Issues for debate on the basis of such a parenting matrix exercise include:

- Should the Group try to operate a portfolio of all the businesses as they currently exist? Should the Group focus on those businesses which most meet its corporate aspirations and most benefit from the added value services of the centre?

- Should the Group attempt to manage all businesses in the same way? For example it could be that those businesses that most benefit from the parenting skills of the centre should be managed in a more 'strategic control' style whilst those that meet the aspirations well but do not need the parenting skills of the centre should be handled more through a 'financial control' style.

- Does the parenting matrix suggest that some businesses should be disposed of; for example those that neither meet the aspirations nor benefit from parenting skills?

- What are the implications for Group structure? For example, is the current divisional structure most appropriate? If there were less businesses would an intermediate divisional level, as at present, be needed?

6.7 The international dimension

Figure 2, 3, 4 and 5 in the case study provides a useful basis to discuss some of the issues concerning multinationals. Burmah Castrol operates on a multinational basis. Traditionally many of its businesses operated with international divisions of domestic companies or as international subsidiaries. Increasingly some have developed global strategies. In executive and SBU debates on international implications, it became clear that many of the businesses saw themselves as simultaneously requiring clear global strategies but high local responsiveness if they were to deliver competitive advantage based on the intimate knowledge of customers businesses. It is the problem' The sort of questions which emerged were:

- Should the emphasis be on global strategy or local responsiveness? Can they be reconciled?

- Evidently the simultaneous fulfilment of both requires more reliance on cooperation of people, the internalisation of strategic intent rather than on formal systems. How is such cooperation to be developed and encouraged?

- What is the role of the centre in ensuring an appropriate balance between global co-ordination and local responsiveness? It is unlikely that this can be achieved by formal systems of control; that the role of the centre needs to become one more of coaching than control as, identified in the parenting skills identified above; but what is entailed in doing this for a Group as diverse in products and geography as the Chemicals Group?

6.8 Structural implications

Throughout this commentary a series of implications relate to organisational structure have been raised. In summary:

- The Group structure will need to be different according to the control style adopted.

- It may be that the size of the portfolio will need to differ depending on the control style.

- Can different control styles be adopted for different parts of the portfolio?

- Given the parenting role adopted, the size of the portfolio and the needs of SBUs what is the required divisional structure? Is the current divisional structure appropriate? Should divisions be based on related technologies (which are few), competence linkages, parenting needs, control style adopted, or what?

Figure 1

	Financial Control	Strategic Planning	Strategic Control
Purpose/Aspiration	Establish expected return to parent and shareholders	A global chemicals busines	Developing high margin, service oriented industrial consumable businesses
	Portfolio management to achieve return		
Portfolio	Based on SBU ability to generate expected	Based on fit with global aspirations	Based on fit with: - group aspirations as above - extent to which group can add value
Structural and Control Implications	A (potentially) large and diverse group of SBUs operating relatively autonomously	A smaller group of global SBUs with centralised direction of strategy	A smaller number of SBUs which can benefit from the group's assistance in similar ways; perhaps with other SBUs not requiring such assistance operating more autonomously

Figure 2 Competence development

Competence development of PEOPLE requiring:
-     more thoughtful DEFINITION of competence requirements;
-     ASSESSING people's ability to deliver against these;

TRANSFER of competences between businesses involving:
-     Transfer of EXPERIENCED MANAGERS;
-     Transfer of BEST PRACTICE through NETWORKING by means of:
  co-ordinators,
  information systems,
  centres of excellence.

STRATEGIC CHALLENGE by:
-     Making EXPLICIT GROUP STRATEGY;
-     Explicit CHALLENGE of SBU STRATEGY;
-     TRAINING in STRATEGIC THINKING;
-     TRANSFER of PERSONNEL.

ENCOURAGING INTERNATIONALISATION by:
-     Encouraging existing LOCAL MANAGEMENT to help
-     Providing best practice CHECK LISTS for internationalisation
  Providing BUSINESS CONTACTS

Figure 3 Parenting opportunities/skills

Parenting skill	People development	Transferring best practice	International-isation	Strategic planning / coaching
Printing inks (PI)	✓	✓	✓*	✓
Timber treatments (TT)			*	
Investment casting wax (IC)			✓	
Foundry .(F)	✓	✓		✓*
Steel mills (S)	✓	✓		✓*
Aluminium (A)	✓*	✓	*	✓*
Construction (C)	✓*			*
Mining (M)				
Cable products (CP)			✓*	
General waxes (GW)			*	*
Adhesives (AD)	✓		✓*	✓*
Fosbel (FO)		✓		

* SBU views from Exhibit C
✓ Executive view of priority needs/opportunities

Figure 4 A parenting matrix

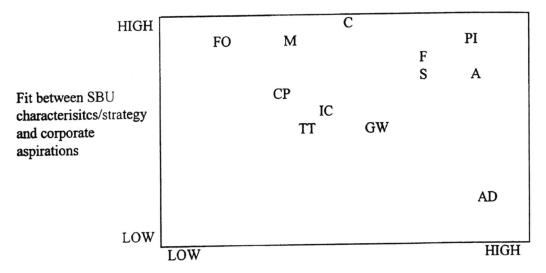

Fit between SBU parenting needs and corporate parenting
capabilites

(For codes for businesses, see figure 3.)